SELF-GUIDED
England
and Wales

SELF-GUIDED

England

and Wales

With 130 illustrations and photographs;
51 maps in color and black and white

LANGENSCHEIDT PUBLISHERS, NEW YORK

Publisher:	Langenscheidt Publishers, Inc.
Managing Editor:	Lisa Checchi Ross
U.S. Editorial Adaptation:	Stephen Brewer, Pamela Nelson, Ingrid Nelson
U.S. Editorial Staff:	Ellen Rosenbush, Dana Schwartz
Cartography:	Kurt Zimmerman and Ferdinand Helm; Adaptations by Polyglott-Redaktion
Illustrations:	Margit Rein
Cover Design:	Diane Wagner
Cover Photograph:	Image Bank, Munich, W. Germany
Text Design:	Irving Perkins Associates
Production:	Ripinsky & Company
Photographs:	No. 1, No. 2, No. 3, Christa Proelss; No. 4, Marituis, Mittenwald, W. Germany; No. 5, No. 6, No. 7, No. 8, No. 9, No. 10, No. 11, No. 12, Bavaria, Munich, W. Germany
Translation:	Translation Company of America
Original German Text:	Dr. Hans Lajta (author); Polyglott-Redaktion (editorial)
Thanks to:	The British Tourist Authority, New York
Letters:	We welcome your comments and suggestions. Our address: Langenscheidt Publishers, Inc., 46–35 54th Rd. Maspeth, N.Y. 11378.

Contents

General Trip Planning: Choosing When to Go 297; Average Temperature and Climate 297; Metric/U.S. Weight, Measure, Temperature Equivalent 298; National Holidays 299; Time Zones 299; Passport and Visa Requirements 299; Customs Entering Britain 299; Customs Returning Home from Britain 299; Embassies and Consulates in England and Wales 300; British Embassies and Consulates 300; Getting to Britain by Air 301; Getting to Britain by Boat 301; Hotels and Other Accommodations 301; Currency Regulations 303; Business Hours and Closings 304; Postage 304; Telephones 304; Travelling in Britain 305; Driving in Great Britain 306; The Tunnel Under the Channel 308; Ferry Service 308; Trains 308; Restaurants and Pubs 310; Shopping 310; Clothing Sizes 312; Sports 314; General Sources of Information 315

Foreword

Although the British are said to have invented modern tourism, Britain itself is as delightful a destination as any its inhabitants wandered off to visit. The beautiful and varied landscape, the antique charm of town and village, the cacophony of modern industrial England—each has its allure for today's traveller. North Americans in particular may feel a kinship with the "mother country," whose culture and language (more or less) we inherited.

Langenscheidt's *Self-Guided England* is written especially for seasoned travellers by writers who specialize in the areas they cover. This unique guide offers extensive detailed tours of London, Britain's other great cities, and the countryside of England and Wales. Travellers will find all the information they need to explore Britain at their own pace and follow their own interests.

Self-Guided Tours

The heart of this book is its self-guided tours. Walking tours of each major city describe all important sites and put them in historical perspective. Travel routes connect major cities and other areas of interest, covering many fascinating and beautiful areas of the countryside. Detailed maps outline every route.

Because most travellers begin in London, we begin our tours with a selective guide to London and short trips within a day's drive. Following London are a series of tours of England's other important cities from Cambridge to York. Then, 35 Travel Routes cover the most scenic and interesting areas in each major region: English Channel Ports, Southern England, the West Country, East Anglia, the Midlands, Northern England, and Wales. The final tour takes you to the Channel Islands.

Using This Guide

This travel guide helps you plan, organize, and enjoy your holiday in England and Wales. In "Getting Your Bearings," a brief rundown of England's different regions will help you choose the areas in which you'd like to spend the most time. It also offers insights into British culture. An historical chronology and essays on art, literature, and architecture provide helpful background and perspective on the sights you'll be seeing.

Langenscheidt's writers also offer a subjective guide to the most appealing sights. Our unique three-star system appears throughout the guide:

*** Worth a special trip—don't miss it!
**   The most important sights on the tour
*   Highlights

Other sights along the way are also worth seeing, but are not necessarily as important as the starred sights.

Total mileage is provided in kilometers and miles from the departure point of each tour. Major towns and sights appear in boldface for easy reference, while other notable places appear in italics. Numbers in parentheses correspond to locations on the maps.

The guide concludes with a Practical Information chapter divided into two parts. The first is General Trip Planning, to help you gather information you'll need before you depart for England. The second part is specific information—such as local tourist information offices and hotels—listed town by town.

Notes and Observation

Travel information, like fruit, is perishable. We've made every effort to double-check information in this guide. But hotels do close and museums do shut down for renovation, so check ahead wherever possible.

We welcome your comments and updates of our information. Please write us at:

Langenscheidt Publishers, Inc.
46–35 54th Road
Maspeth, N.Y. 11378

Getting Your Bearings

The pleasures England has to offer the traveller are as varied as a busy shopping day in London's West End, a walk across the Yorkshire moors, or a picnic in the ruins of a castle on the Welsh border. While just about all of England—even such areas as the industrial Midlands—is rich in history and scenery, most holiday travellers will choose to spend their time in London or in one of the following regions:

Yorkshire and the North: High mountains, the beautiful scenery of the Lake District, a wild seacoast, and romantic moors—these are the geographic attractions that give the north of England its distinctive character. There are many man-made treasures here, too, none more romantic than the Medieval city of York and its magnificent cathedral. Even Liverpool, the industrial port city on the Irish Sea, attracts millions of visitors each year, many of whom come to pay tribute to those famous native sons, the Beatles.

The Midlands: This region at the very center of the country is also its spiritual heart. Shakespeare was born here, in Stratford-upon-Avon, and nestled in the Cotswolds are stone villages that are so quintessentially British that it's hard to believe they weren't constructed just for show. Gloucester, Worcester, and Shrewsbury are magnificent cathedral towns, while Birmingham and Coventry are old industrial centers that remind us that it was here that the Industrial Revolution began.

East Anglia: All too often visitors to this region never venture farther than the university city of Cambridge. Beyond those graceful spires, however, stretch gentle river valleys, the mysterious landscape of the Fens, the watery expanses of the Broads, and, on the North Sea, lovely, unspoiled beaches.

The Southeast: This rural region lying between London and the sea is as rich in history as it is in places for recreation. Standing amid the orchards and fields of Kent are some of England's finest old estates, among them Knole and Penshurst. Canterbury, a famous destination for travellers since the Middle Ages, is here too, as is Winchester, another cathedral city that was also once capital of all of Britain. The North Sea and Channel coasts are lined with the towns of Broadstairs, where Charles Dickens summered, Folkestone, Dover, Southampton, and many other busy seaside resorts and ports.

The West Country: This is walking territory, from the dramatic cliffs that drop into the sea at Land's End in Cornwall to the farm lanes of Dorset. Two large national parks, Dartmoor and Exmoor, preserve the landscape much as it was when King Arthur roamed the region a thousand years ago.

Wales: Small as this nation that clings to the west of England is, it contains ten of the major national parks in the United Kingdom, has miles of deserted beaches, and is peppered with the remains of some of the best Medieval castles in Europe. One of the best ways to explore the brooding landscape of Wales is by scenic railway, including the one that climbs Mount Snowdon.

Size and Geographic Location

The United Kingdom of Great Britain and Northern Ireland is a constitutional monarchy located in the northeastern part of the Atlantic Ocean and covering an area of 244,111 square km. (93,598 square miles). England and Wales make up the southern part of the island of Great Britain. The Strait of Dover, barely 33 km. (20 miles) wide, separates England from France. In the east, England borders the North Sea; in the south, the English Channel; in the west, the Irish Sea; and in the north, Scotland.

The Isle of Man, located in the Irish Sea off Great Britain, is a self-governing dependency of the British Crown, as are the Channel Islands (Jersey, Guernsey, Alderney, Sark, and others), which lie off the French coast. The Isles of Scilly off the west coast of Cornwall and the Isle of Wight in the English Channel are considered part of Britain.

Topography

England is a hilly country—few stretches of land are flat and the north and southwest are mountainous. Throughout the country you will find rolling hills, brilliant green meadows, crystal blue streams, and dark loamy woods.

The Cheviot Hills separate England from Scotland. The Pennines, known as the "backbone of England," extend from the Scottish border more than 240 km. (150 miles) to Derbyshire and Staffordshire in central England. The highest peak, Cross Fell, is 892 meters (2,930 feet) high. The area south of the Pennines, known as the Peak District, has more than 700 mountains. To the east, they gently slope into the broad valley plain of York, an area filled with heather and moors.

To the west, the Pennines join the Cumbrian Mountains, whose Scafell Pike is 984 meters (3,210 feet) high. This is the Lake District, an area of spectacular lakes, lush meadows, and gentle valleys. Today the most popular tourist area in England, in the past the Lake District attracted a host of writers and poets, among them William Wordsworth, Robert Southey, and Samuel Taylor Coleridge.

Wales forms a wide peninsula on the west side of Great Britain, beneath the North Sea. It is a mountainous land—the Cambrian Mountains run throughout the country; their highest peak is Snowdon, 1,088 meters (3,560 feet) high.

The Bristol Channel separates Wales from the scenic west counties of Cornwall, Devon, and Somerset. Here you can explore the heather-covered mountains of Dartmoor, Exmoor, and the Cornish Heights.

The beautiful Cotswold Hills in the south of England overlook the fertile valley of Gloucester. They are covered with pleasant beech woods and verdant pastures. East of the Cotswolds, the chalk region begins. Deposits are particularly rich in the Salisbury Plain in south central England. It is there that the Chiltern Hills turn toward the northeast.

Rivers and Lakes

The Thames (323 km., 210 miles long) is the longest and most important river in England. It originates in the Cotswold Hills, flows through the center of London, then empties into the North Sea. The second longest river, the Severn (300 km., 180 miles), rises in central Wales, crosses into England near Shrewsbury, and empties into the Bristol Channel. Shakespeare's River Avon is among its tributaries.

England's best-known lakes lie, understandably, in the Lake District. The largest, Windermere, is 17 km. (10½ miles) long. Others in the area include Coniston Water, Derwentwater, Bassenthwaite, Buttermere, Ullswater, Grasmere, and Crummock Water.

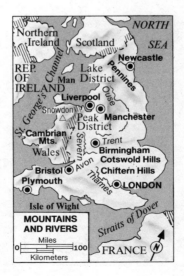

ADMINISTRATIVE DISTRICTS IN ENGLAND AND WALES

Miles
120
Kilometers

NORTH SEA

Hull

(39)

(31)

gham

Norwich

(18)

(19)

Cambridge

(17)

(21)

(20)

(11)

(13)

(12)

LONDON

(3)

(1)

Canterbury

mpton

(2)

Calais

FRANCE

English Channel

1) Kent
2) Sussex
3) Surrey
4) Hampshire
5) Berkshire
6) Wiltshire
7) Dorsetshire
8) Somersetshire
9) Devonshire
10) Cornwall
11) Essex
12) Greater London
13) Buckinghamshire
14) Oxfordshire
15) Gloucestershire
16) Avon
17) Suffolk
18) Norfolk
19) Cambridgeshire
20) Hertfordshire
21) Bedfordshire
22) West Midlands
23) Northamptonshire
24) Warwickshire
25) Hereford and Worcestershire
26) Salop
27) Staffordshire
28) Leicestershire
29) Greater Manchester
30) Lincolnshire
31) Nottinghamshire
32) Derbyshire
33) Cheshire
34) Lancashire
35) North Yorkshire
36) West Yorkshire
37) South Yorkshire
38) Humberside
39) Cumbria
40) Cleveland
41) Durham
42) Tyne and Wear
43) Northumberland
44) Merseyside
45) Powys
46) Clwyd
47) Gwynedd
48) Dyfed
49) West Glamorgan
50) Mid Glamorgan
51) South Glamorgan
52) Gwent

Constitution and Representation

The United Kingdom of Great Britain and Northern Ireland is a heredi-
tary, constitutional monarchy. Legislative power rests with the Parliament, which consists of the House of Commons and the House of
Lords. The 635 members of the House of Commons are elected by a
simple democratic majority. The House of Lords has about 1,000
eligible members, although far fewer choose to serve.

Executive power rests with the Government, headed by the Prime
Minister, who must be a member of the House of Commons.

The Queen is titular head of England and Wales, and many other
countries in the Commonwealth. She has, in fact, virtually no executive function, yet to the people the Queen and the Royal Family
represent Britain, its history, and its future.

Food and Drink

England's bad reputation when it comes to dining is not really
deserved, although you may have to search if you want truly wonderful
meals. It is especially difficult to understand why you encounter so
much average fare, given the bounty of the land.

Throughout the country you will find almost any type of seafood,
from plain smoked herring to the most exquisite oysters from Colchester. Shrimp, crab, crawfish, smoked shellfish, spicy bloaters, halibut,
turbot, cod, Dover sole, fresh salmon, and trout are all within easy
reach. Lobster flourishes along the entire English coast, and English
lobster is among the best in the world.

The most popular viand is beef, especially the traditional roast beef
accompanied by Yorkshire pudding. Other specialties include pork,
ham, duck, turkey, lamb, bacon, sausages, and fine game. And, of
course, steak and kidney pie is one of England's prides. Native cheeses
abound—Cheddar, Caerphilly, Cheshire, Stilton, and Wensleydale are
best known. Luscious fruit comes from Kent, the orchard of England,
and from Worcestershire.

In larger cities, young chefs are placing increasing emphasis on the
country's fine fresh food, and throughout the land you can find excellent
regional fare. Ethnic cuisine is ubiquitous in large metropolitan areas,
where you are likely to find a wide variety of Indian, Italian, Greek,
Thai, French, and even East African menus.

The traditional English breakfast is unbelievably filling and rich. It
begins with cereal, fruit juice, melon, or hot porridge served with milk
and sugar. Next comes fried eggs with ham, bacon, sausage, or tomatoes. Fish, usually kippers, also appears frequently on the traditional

breakfast table. Finishing touches include bread, rolls, or toast, served with butter and marmalade or jam, and accompanied by tea or coffee. Unfortunately (or fortunately, if you are concerned about cholesterol counts and the like) this fabled feast has recently given way to the modest continental breakfast.

Lunch is usually simple, taken in a fish-and-chip shop or in a pub serving standard fare, such as sandwiches and ale. The "ploughman's lunch"—bread, cheese, and salad—is common, inexpensive, and often much safer than such dishes as shepherd's pie, a soggy combination of mashed potatoes, peas, and ground beef, and toad in the hole, a greasy sausage in Yorkshire pudding.

Wine bars are becoming more and more common, and most serve simple, inexpensive lunches of salads, soups, cold fish or meat, and other light fare.

Tea is a British tradition, served from 3:30–5:30 (or 6:00) P.M. Don't feel that you have to order a full cream tea—a generous offering that may include tea, clotted cream, little sandwiches, bread and butter, sausages, cold meats, and cheeses. Many shops will gladly serve you a hot pot of tea and biscuits or pastry, or bread and butter.

Dinner can range from a quick snack to an elegant meal served in a sophisticated restaurant. If you are travelling in the countryside, make sure you know when meals are served, especially if there are only one or two restaurants about.

When it comes to drink, the heady ales and beers of England reign supreme. Favorites include bitter on tap. Stout is a strong, dark beer; porter is sweet. Most of these drinks are served at room temperature, so many visitors prefer lager, which is served cold.

In Great Britain, the best of spirits are at your fingertips—British gin and Scotch and Irish whiskey are well known. Increasingly popular are the magnificent single malt whiskies. Try taking them "neat," without ice.

Better restaurants offer a large selection of wines. Experiment a little: In addition to the usual French, German, and Italian wines, try those from South Africa and Australia, which can be outstanding.

Whatever you drink, enjoy it in a pub. You may get a strange look or two if you order something other than beer, because that is the standard pub drink. The real pleasure of pub life, though, has nothing to do with beverages. Rather, the true joy is to sit back (actually, you will probably have to stand) and watch the English at their friendliest and most loquacious. By law, pubs and other bars in Britain must close in the afternoon, usually from 3:00–5:30, and at 11:30 for the night—an annoyance for residents and travellers alike yearning for spirits on those cold, dark afternoons of a British winter. However, changes are afoot, and the afternoon closings may soon be lifted.

Customs and Manners

The English are known for their reserve and for their fiercely protected privacy, so much so that it has become something of a cliché. As you travel throughout England and Wales, you will discover that the people are, in fact, among the most tolerant in the world. You will see elderly white-haired women from sleepy country villages sitting in parks next to teenagers decked out in leather and metal, barristers with impeccably rolled umbrellas mixing with mechanics in the underground, and virtually every other combination of ages and types possible. Keep an open mind and you will be well on your way to discovering the real England and Wales.

There are certain traits that the British favor, chief among them punctuality, self-discipline, order, and appropriate behavior. Dress conservatively for formal occasions, such as evenings at the theater, be on time for appointments, and act with appropriate solemnity when you visit the country's churches and cathedrals.

Be forewarned about the important practice of queuing. Whenever three people stand waiting for a bus or a train, they immediately form a line, and each patiently awaits his or her turn. Barging into a queue is the worst possible behavior, and it *will* be frowned upon.

Should conversation turn to politics or soccer, proceed cautiously. Respect the widespread belief that in these two realms England leads the world. Note, too, that pets are adored throughout Great Britain. Dogs are particularly cherished and even given priority in traffic over pedestrians. Respect the animals that you encounter and treat them adoringly, at least in the presence of their owners.

No matter how awful the weather is, try to talk about the nice days in the offing. "Lovely day" is a figure of speech that you will hear constantly.

Americans are often surprised to see the respect that the English show to public servants—policemen, hotel porters, receptionists, waiters, bus conductors, and cashiers. If a bus conductor explains to those waiting at a stop in torrential rain that the bus is full, it is quite likely that no argument ensues, even if some believe that there is room for yet another dozen passengers inside the bus. In smaller eateries and in the countryside, meal hours in inns and restaurants are strictly observed. If the manager explains that no food is being served, cheerfully accept the fact and never plead or argue.

Finally, here are three pieces of advice that will stand you in good stead, whether you are travelling to Great Britain for the first time or the 21st. Praise people sparingly and avoid criticizing them. Never indicate that you find traditional customs and manners comical, odd, or antiquated. And, most important, never, *never* refer to the Scottish, Irish, or Welsh as "English," and don't use the term "England" when you mean Scotland, Ireland, or Wales.

Chronology

Prehistoric England

Flaked stone implements attest to the presence of primitive man in England during the Paleolithic period. Beginning around 5000 B.C., Neolithic peoples migrate to England. Today their landmarks remain throughout the English countryside, the most important being the mysterious circle of stones at Stonehenge (see page 149), which is thought to be 3500 years old.

c. 800 B.C. The Celts arrive in England.

England Under the Romans (55 B.C.–A.D. 412)

55 B.C. Julius Caesar crosses the Channel with two legions of troops. His attack is unsuccessful.

54 B.C. Julius Caesar again lands in England, this time on the coast of Kent, and crosses the Thames. He fails to establish a permanent settlement.

A.D. 43 The Romans successfully invade Britain.

122 The Romans begin to construct Hadrian's Wall, a gigantic structure built to protect their northern borders against warlike tribes.

Second–fourth centuries The Romans build roads and found London, York, Lincoln, and other cities. Trade flourishes and agriculture develops. Roman culture leaves most untouched. Christianity arrives in the third century. From the early fourth century on, Saxons begin to attack the coasts of England.

407–412 The Roman legions gradually leave the country to defend other parts of the Empire against the onslaught of Germanic tribes.

420–450 The Jutes, Angles, and Saxons arrive in England and found seven kingdoms (Kent, Sussex, Essex, Wessex, East Anglia, Mercia, and Northumbria).

Fifth–seventh centuries Germanic settlements are established. The Jutes settle in Kent, on the Isle of Wight, and in Hampshire. The Saxons and Frisians occupy the Thames basin, Sussex, and Essex. The Angles spread out over central and northern England. By the end of the sixth century, Christianity is the dominant religion.

Eighth century Vikings from Norway and Denmark attack England more and more frequently, plundering London and battling fiercely with the Anglo-Saxons.

England under the Anglo-Saxons

Saxon Kings (802–1017)

Egbert	802–839
Ethelwulf	839–858
Ethelbald	858–860
Ethelbert	860–866
St. Ethelred	866–871
Alfred	871–901
Edward the Elder	901–925
Athelstan	925–940
Edmund I	940–946
Edred	946–955
Edwy	955–959
Edgar	959–975
Edward	975–979
Ethelred II	979–1016
Edmund	1016–

Danish Kings (1016–1066)

Canute	1016–1035
Harold I	1035–1040
Hardicanute	1040–1042
Edward	1042–1066
Harold II	1066

827 Egbert, the Anglo-Saxon King of Wessex, subdues the smaller independent kingdoms and founds Anglia, a kingdom of all the Anglo-Saxons.

871–901 Alfred the Great defeats the Danes in several battles and agrees to a truce with them. He completes the Christianization of the country and through wise legislation succeeds in restoring law and order to the war-torn country.

959–975 Edgar, a great-grandson of Alfred, expands Anglo-Saxon rule to Norway and Ireland.

1002 Under Ethelred, the Danes begin to break their truce and fierce wars follow. Ethelred levies taxes to pay the tribute that the Danes demand.

1016–1035 The Danish King Canute the Great takes possession of the whole of England and of the Scandinavian empires. Under his rule peace returns to the country.

1042 Edward the Confessor becomes King of England. When he dies childless, Harold II is elected King.

The Norman Era (1066–1154)

William I	1066–1087
William II	1087–1100
Henry I	1100–1135
Stephen	1135–1154

1066 William the Conqueror, Duke of Normandy, claims the English throne and invades England. On October 14, in the Battle of Hastings, he defeats Harold II, who dies on the battlefield. William is crowned King of England on Christmas Day in Westminster Abbey.

1067–1074 After a bitter seven-year war, the Normans are victorious over the Anglo-Saxons.

1087–1100 William II (Rufus), third son of the Conqueror, suppresses a rebellion of Norman barons who oppose the separation of Normandy and England. He fights King Malcolm III of Scotland and forces him to give him homage. William dies (or is murdered) in a hunting accident in 1100.

1100 Henry I, the youngest brother of William II, takes the throne. He improves relations with his Anglo-Saxon subjects, increases the power of the King, and restores friendly relations with the clergy. After his son perishes in a shipwreck, Henry names his daughter, Matilda, heiress to the throne and arranges her marriage to the 16-year-old Count of Anjou, Geoffrey Plantagenet.

1135 Henry I dies. Stephen, a grandson of William the Conqueror, claims the English throne. His reign is marred by invasions, mismanagement, and unrest.

1150 Matilda's son, Henry, is made Duke of Normandy and unites it with Anjou, inherited from his father.

1153 Henry II invades England, claims the throne, but avoids a decisive battle. Stephen makes his peace with him and adopts him as son and heir to the kingdom. In return, Henry agrees that Stephen will rule until his death. When Stephen dies a year later, Henry becomes King and the House of Anjou (Plantagenet) rules England.

1154–1189 Henry II extends his reign over a large part of France and campaigns in Wales. After quarreling with Thomas à Becket, Archbishop of Canterbury, he has him exiled from 1164 to 1170. On December 29, 1170, Henry's followers murder Becket at Canterbury Cathedral.

The House of the Plantagenet (1154–1399)

Henry II	1154–1189
Richard I	1189–1199
John	1199–1216
Henry III	1216–1272
Edward I	1272–1307
Edward II	1307–1327
Edward III	1327–1377
Richard II	1377–1399

1189 Richard I (the Lion-Hearted) embarks on a crusade against the Moslems. His brother John takes the throne after rumors spread that Richard has died. Richard I is taken prisoner by Duke Leopold of Austria, and then sold to the Holy Roman Emperor Henry VI. After payment of a huge ransom, Richard is returned to England in 1194. Richard subjugates John, but dies of an arrow wound during a campaign he wages in France.

1206 King John refuses to accept Stephen Langton as Archbishop of Canterbury and is excommunicated in 1209.

1215 A rebellion by the aristocracy forces King John to sign the Magna Carta at Runnymede. This document becomes the cornerstone of English constitutional history.

1265 Henry III is summoned to the precursor of today's Parliament, a representational gathering of English citizens.

1282 The chief Welsh emperor, Llewelyn, falls in battle. His brother is executed in Shrewsbury, and Wales is brought again under the English Crown.

1301 Edward I declares his infant son (Edward II) the Prince of Wales, a title that has since belonged to the male heir to the British throne.

1338 Edward III claims the French throne and the Hundred Years' War begins.

1348–1350 The bubonic plague, or Black Death, sweeps through England, reducing its population by half.

1399 Richard II is forced to abdicate and soon dies (murdered). Henry Bolingbroke, a Lancastrian, ascends the throne as Henry IV.

The House of Lancaster (1399–1461)

Henry IV	1399–1413
Henry V	1413–1422
Henry VI	1422–1461

1400 Wales tries again to regain its national independence under the leadership of Owen Glendower. The Welsh forces stand undefeated for almost 10 years. Henry IV wages war for many years against rebellious leaders from Northumberland and York.

1415 Henry V lands in France and defeats the French at Agincourt.

1420 The Treaty of Troyes makes Henry heir to the French throne.

1422 At the age of nine months, Henry VI becomes King of England, then, two months later, King of France.

1455 The War of the Roses, fought between the Houses of York (white rose) and Lancaster (red rose), begins.

1461 Edward, Duke of York, defeats the Lancastrians. Henry VI is deposed and Edward IV takes the throne.

1470 Henry VI regains the throne, but is soon murdered.

The House of York (1461–1485)

Edward IV	1461–1483
Edward V	1483
Richard III	1483–1485

1483 Twelve-year-old Edward V is imprisoned and, along with his brother, allegedly murdered in the Tower of London by his uncle, who seizes the throne as Richard III.

1485 Henry Tudor, Count of Richmond, defeats and kills Richard III in the Battle of Bosworth.

The House of Tudor (1485–1603)

Henry VII	1485–1509
Henry VIII	1509–1547
Edward VI	1547–1553
Lady Jane Grey	1553
Mary I	1553–1558
Elizabeth I	1558–1603

1486 Henry VII, a Lancastrian, marries Elizabeth of York, bringing the War of the Roses to an end. During his reign the kingdom becomes peaceful and prosperous and order is gradually re-established. England joins the circle of leading European nations.

1509 Henry VIII ascends the throne. Five of his wives die or are executed or divorced by Henry. He breaks away from the Roman Catholic Church and becomes the head of the Church of England.

1536 The Act of Union unites Wales with England.

1547 At the age of nine, Edward VI ascends the throne.

1553 For nine days, Lady Jane Grey rules England, until the rightful heir, Mary I, daughter of Henry VIII and Katherine of Aragon, ascends the throne. A devout Catholic, and later wife of King Philip II of Spain, she has the Protestant Archbishop Cranmer and his bishops burned at the stake. She quickly earns the title Bloody Mary.

1558 Queen Elizabeth I, daughter of Henry VIII and Anne Boleyn and the last of the Tudors, reinstates the Protestant Church of England. Her reign brings security and power to England. It is the age of Shakespeare, Marlowe, Bacon, and Spencer.

1577–1580 Francis Drake circumnavigates the world.

1584 Walter Raleigh founds the first English colony in North America.

1587 Elizabeth I has Mary, Queen of Scots, executed.

1588 British ships win a glorious victory over the Spanish Armada. England rules the waves.

The House of Stuart (1603–1714)

James I	1603–1625
Charles I	1625–1649
Council of State	1649–1660
Charles II	1660–1685
James II	1685–1688
William III and Mary II	1689–1702
Anne	1702–1714

1603 James VI of Scotland, son of Mary, Queen of the Scots, ascends the English throne as James I. For the first time, one king reigns over both Scotland and England.

1605 Guy Fawkes, in the Gunpowder Plot, tries to blow up the Houses of Parliament to protest laws against Roman Catholicism.

1620 The *Mayflower* sets sail.

1625 Charles I becomes king, battles against Parliament, and dissolves the House of Commons. Beginning in 1629, he rules alone for 11 years.

1642 The King refuses to give up his supremacy to the newly instated Parliament. Civil War begins and lasts for four years.

1649 Charles I surrenders to the Scots, then is handed over to the English, who execute him. The House of Lords is dissolved, a State Council is installed, and the Commonwealth is proclaimed. The new Commonwealth is ruled with sovereign power by Parliament until 1653, then by the Puritan Oliver Cromwell as Lord Protector until 1658. Upon Cromwell's death, his son Richard takes on the position until he is forced to resign in 1659.

1660 Charles II is appointed King.

1665 The Great Plague sweeps through England.

1666 The Great Fire destroys much of London.

1679 Parliament passes the Habeas Corpus Act, which ensures one of the most fundamental of English rights by prohibiting the arbitrary and unlawful imprisonment of English citizens.

1685 James II ascends the throne and prosecution of the Protestants begins again.

1688 William of Orange is invited by Parliament to begin a revolution. He lands on the coast of Devonshire with a large army, and James II goes into exile in France.

1689 William of Orange and his wife Mary (daughter of James II) jointly rule England and Scotland as William III and Mary II. The monarchy is now constitutional. Freedom of the press is initiated and national prosperity grows. An Act of Parliament states that no Catholic, or spouse of a Catholic, can be King or Queen of England, putting to an end the ongoing battle between the Protestants and the Catholics. With French help, James II lands in Ireland.

1690 William III defeats James II in the Battle of Boyne, and James flees to France.

1702 War breaks out with Spain. With John Churchill, Earl of Marlborough, in command, England wins major victories.

1707 Under Queen Anne, the Act of Union is sealed between England and Scotland, making them one country, Great Britain.

1713 After the victory in the War of the Spanish Succession, England obtains Gibraltar, Minorca, and large portions of North America (Hudson Bay, New Scotland, and Newfoundland) under the Treaty of Utrecht.

The House of Hanover (1714–1901)

George I	1714–1727
George II	1727–1760
George III	1760–1820
George IV	1820–1830
William IV	1830–1837
Victoria	1837–1901

1714 Queen Anne dies. In accordance with the Protestant Act of Succession, the crown goes to the closest Protestant relative of the Stuarts, the Hanoverian George I.

1745 Prince Charles Edward, grandson of James II, lands in Scotland and tries to regain the crown for the Stuarts with the help of a Scottish army. After his defeat in 1746 near Culloden, he is smuggled away to the Western Isles. Later he moves to France, and dies years later in Italy.

1773 North American colonists express their anger at British taxation by staging the Boston Tea Party.

1776–1783 Colonists declare their independence from Britain, and war follows. The United States is victorious and England loses most of North America.

1789 The French Revolution begins.

1801 The Act of Union unites Ireland and England.

1803 Napoleon tries repeatedly to invade England.

1805 Admiral Nelson dies during the victorious battle over the French and Spanish fleets off Cape Trafalgar. The British Navy consolidates its power over the oceans.

1815 The Duke of Wellington and Marshall Blücher defeat Napoleon at Waterloo.

1832 Under King William IV, the Reform Act is passed, redistributing seats in Parliament.

1833 Slavery is abolished throughout the British Empire.

1837 Upon the death of William IV, the 18-year-old Princess Victoria, daughter of the Duke of Kent, ascends the throne.

1837–1901 During Queen Victoria's 63-year-long reign, the conservative Tories and the liberal Whigs alternately gain power. Political and social reforms are made. England wages numerous wars in Egypt, South Africa, and elsewhere, strengthening and enlarging the British Empire.

1851 The Crystal Palace Exhibition, planned by Victoria's husband Prince Albert, draws six million people to London. The proceeds of the exhibition are used to purchase land in Kensington on which museums, colleges, and halls devoted to science and the arts will be built.

1853–1856 The Crimean War is fought.

1876 Victoria is proclaimed Empress of India.

The House of Saxe-Coburg (1901–1910)

Edward VII	1901–1910

1901 Victoria's son Edward VII of the House of Saxe-Coburg ascends the throne.

1902 The Boer Wars end.

The House of Windsor (1910–   )

George V	1910–1936
Edward VIII	1936
George VI	1936–1952
Elizabeth II	1952–

1914–1918 World War I.

1918 Women are given the right to vote.

1920 The Government of Ireland Act partitions Ireland into religious zones.

1936 The crown passes to George's son, Edward VIII. He relinquishes his rights to the throne to marry a divorced American, Wallis Simpson. His brother, George VI, becomes king.

1939–1945 During World War II, England suffers heavy damage from German air attacks.

1945–1950 With a Labour government in power, the Bank of England, gas and electric companies, health services, and many industries become state owned, introducing what came to be known as the welfare state.

1947–1960 Large portions of the far-flung British Empire gain independence.

1952 Elizabeth II ascends the throne.

1961–1970 Attempts to join the European Economic Community (EEC) fail.

1969 Prince Charles is invested as Prince of Wales.

1971 British currency is converted to the decimal system.

1973 Great Britain becomes a member of the EEC.

1979 Margaret Thatcher becomes the first female Prime Minister of Britain.

1981 Prince Charles, heir to the throne, marries Lady Diana Spencer. The Social Democratic Party (SDP) is founded.

1982 In a war with Argentina, Great Britain defends its possession of the Falkland Islands.

The Arts in England

English Painting

Strong and vigorous manuscript illumination, with beautiful, intricate artistry its keynote, flourished in England and Ireland in the eighth century. An outstanding example of the work of Irish monks can be seen in the Lindisfarne Gospel (at the British Museum), done around A.D. 700. In it, you can see a spectacular combination of writhing, snakelike creatures and Christian motifs.

Painting lay fallow for hundreds of years after the flowering of manuscript illumination. When the art once again came to life, it was dominated by foreign-born artists, among them Hans Holbein (1497–1543), Peter Paul Rubens (1577–1640), and Anthony van Dyck (1599–1641). Holbein became Henry VIII's court painter in 1536, and his influence on English painting remained strong for decades.

One of the few early English artists who can be identified is Nicholas Hilliard (1547–1619), noted for his tiny, delicate, and detailed portraits on parchment.

The golden age of English painting was inaugurated by an Englishman, William Hogarth (1697–1764). In his work Hogarth captured snatches of everyday life, bathing them with moralistic commentary—young men succumbing to the temptations of drink, young women forgetting their virtue, and other social issues of his (and our) time.

Hogarth's contemporaries Thomas Gainsborough (1727–1788) and Joshua Reynolds (1723–1792) raised the art of portraiture to a new high. Other portraitists of note include George Romney (1734–1802), the Scottish Sir Henry Raeburn (1756–1823), and Sir Thomas Lawrence (1769–1830).

The sporting pictures of George Stubbs (1724–1806) begin a quintessentially English genre. He is especially noted for his portraits of race horses. In a more serious vein is the work of William Blake (1757–1827), who created visionary and fantastic images to illustrate his books of mystical poems.

It is perhaps landscape painting for which England is best known. (Gainsborough himself was a gifted landscape artist, not just a portrait painter.) The master of the art was John Constable (1776–1837) who captured in his work the serene beauty of the English countryside—not only the trees, fields, and rivers, but also the changing glory of the sky and the atmosphere.

Constable's contemporary J. M. W. Turner (1775–1851) pushed the exploration of light and atmosphere even further. "Airy visions, painted with tinted steam," said Constable of his work, which sought to capture how color and light actually look.

Other British artists of note include John Sell Cotman (1782–1842), a landscape artist best known for his watercolors; John Martin (1789–1854), who created romantic, apocalyptic visions in paint; and Edwin Landseer (1802–1873), who specialized in painting portraits of animals, usually presenting them as if they were almost human.

The Pre-Raphaelite Brotherhood, founded in 1848, dominated English art during the last half of the 19th century. Its chief exponents were Dante Gabriel Rossetti (1828–1882), William Holman Hunt (1821–1893), Edward Burne-Jones (1833–1898), and John Millais (1829–1896). The Pre-Raphaelites rejected the materialism of their time and tried to capture what they believed to be the simplicity and truthfulness of the Medieval world—a time before Raphael and the High Renaissance. Their paintings are, for the most part, precisely rendered interpretations of moralistic and spiritualistic themes.

Throughout the world—in France, America, and Germany, as well as in England—painting and sculpture in the 20th century remain in a state of flux. Notable British artists include Philip Wilson Steer, Stanley Spencer, Ben Nicholson, Henry Moore, John Davies, Paul Nash, Eric Ravilious, Graham Sutherland, Francis Bacon, John Piper, and David Hockney.

English Literature

One of England's greatest glories is its rich literary heritage, stretching from *Beowulf* to the present day, and consisting of the work of such writers as William Shakespeare, Geoffrey Chaucer, Alexander Pope, John Milton, Jane Austen, Charles Dickens, Samuel Johnson, and Henry Fielding.

English literature is often broken into three phases: Old English (Anglo-Saxon) literature, dating from the middle of the fifth century to the 11th century; Middle English literature, starting with the Norman Conquest in 1066 and ending with Chaucer around 1500; and Modern English literature, beginning in 1500 and extending to the present. This division is somewhat arbitrary, for periods merge and overlap, especially after 1600, yet it is helpful in sorting out the profusion of talent that has contributed to Britain's cultural heritage.

Anglo-Saxon Literature

The most important surviving work in Old English is *Beowulf,* a heroic epic poem based on Norse legends and recorded during the early eighth century. Two important early figures are the poets Caedmon, who died in the late seventh century, and Cynewulf (late eighth to early ninth century). Caedmon wrote religious poetry, supposedly after receiving divine inspiration, and Cynewulf sang of Christianity, saints, and the Last Judgment.

Alfred the Great, who ruled from 871 to 899, began a long tradition of English prose translation when he had Latin writings translated into the vernacular.

Middle English Literature

The Norman Conquest in 1066 brought with it the influence of French literature, which enriched England's traditions by introducing romantic themes and subjects, including those based on the Arthurian legends. Gradually, Old English evolved into Middle English. John Wyclif (1324?–1384) was responsible for the first English translation of the Bible. John Gower (c. 1325–1408), a poet, is best known for his *Vox Clamantis* and *Confessio Amantis.* But it is Geoffrey Chaucer (c. 1343–1400), the so-called Father of English Literature, who stands at center stage in the literary England of the 14th century. A public servant for most of his life, Chaucer's writings began under the sway of French literature, then gradually became influenced by the work of the Italians. His *Canterbury Tales* etches a sharp picture of how men and women of his time actually lived. William Langland (c. 1332–1400), Chaucer's contemporary, gave us *The Vision of William Concerning Piers Plowman,* a moralistic poem that presents a more somber portrait of the times.

Modern English Literature

It was under Queen Elizabeth that the great flowering of English letters took place. Hers was the age of William Shakespeare (1564–1616), Edmund Spenser (1552?–1599), and Christopher Marlowe (1564–1593). Other writers of note include Sir Philip Sidney (1554–1586), a favorite courtier of the Queen; the dramatist Thomas Kyd (1557?–1594); the poet and playwright George Peele (1558–1597); and the philosopher and statesman Francis Bacon (1561–1626). John Milton (1608–1674), writer of both prose and poetry, published his masterpiece, *Paradise Lost,* in 1667, and Samuel Pepys (1633–1703) began his famous *Diary* in 1660, in which he candidly recorded his everyday life. John Donne (1572?–1631), the greatest of the metaphysical poets, first published his poems in 1633. Active at about the same time was Robert Herrick, author of pastoral and love lyrics. John Dryden (1631–1700), a poet, dramatist, and critic, is the literary master of the Restoration. John Bunyan, author of *The Pilgrim's Progress,* was born in 1628 and died in 1688.

The supreme poet of the Age of Reason is Alexander Pope (1688–1744). Pope's friend, John Gay (1685–1732), was a noted poet and playwright of the period. Both Jonathan Swift (1667–1743), author of *Gulliver's Travels,* and Daniel Defoe (1660–1731), who wrote *Robinson Crusoe,* are noted for their satirical commentary on man's condition. Samuel Johnson (1709–1784) is noted for both his monumental *Dictionary of the English Language,* and for his fascinating life, so ably recorded by his friend James Boswell (1740–1795). Other important writers of the time include Richard Sheridan (1751–1816), author of *The School for Scandal,* and Oliver Goldsmith, the novelist and playwright who wrote *The Vicar of Wakefield.*

The modern novel is said to have begun in the 18th century in the works of Samuel Richardson (1689–1761). The genre grew under Henry Fielding (1707–1754), best known for *The History of Tom Jones, A Foundling.* Tobias Smollett (1721–1771) and Laurence Sterne (1713–1768), Fielding's contemporaries, are other major novelists of the period. Jane Austen (1775–1817), much beloved by readers today, wrote of a gentler, more gentrified world than did Fielding and Smollett. It was Charles Dickens (1812–1870) who brought the novel to new heights, writing of social ills and stifling conventions and, at the same time, painting a full, rich picture of his England. Among the works of noted novelist George Eliot (1819–1880) is *Silas Marner.*

Moving backward in time, the poems of William Wordsworth (1771–1850) and Samuel Taylor Coleridge (1772–1834) ushered the Romantic Movement into England. Later poets working in this vein include Lord Byron (1788–1824), Percy Bysshe Shelley (1792–1822), John Keats (1795–1822), and, to a degree, the visionary William Blake (1757–1827). Alfred, Lord Tennyson (1809–1892) was the very spirit of Victorian England, while Robert Browning (1812–1899) and his wife, Elizabeth Barrett Browning (1806–1861), are known for their lyrical love poems.

Important essayists working at the end of the 19th century include Thomas Carlyle (1795–1881) and John Ruskin (1819–1900), noted for his writings on art and aesthetics. Edward Lear (1812–1888) is known as the master of "nonsense" literature; Lewis Carroll's (1832–1898) beloved *Alice in Wonderland* remains a favorite today, among both children and adults.

A flood of noted novelists, poets, dramatists, and essayists were active in the late 19th century, and their numbers continue to grow in the 20th century. What follows is merely a sampling of the talented men and women who have contributed to British literature in the past one hundred years: George Meredith (1828–1909), author of *The Egoist;* Algernon Charles Swinburne (1837–1909); Oscar Wilde (1856–1900), a major figure in the aesthetic movement; Thomas Hardy (1840–1928); Rudyard Kipling (1865–1936); H.G. Wells (1886–

1946); John Galsworthy (1867–1933), Nobel-Prize winner for literature in 1932 and best known for his *Forsyte Saga;* George Bernard
Shaw (1856–1950), winner of the Nobel Prize for literature in 1925;
the Irish poet William Butler Yeats (1865–1939), one of the most gifted
writers of recent years; John Masefield (1878–1967); James Joyce
(1882–1941), Irish author of the revolutionary novel *Ulysses;* George
Orwell (1903–1950); Sir Arthur Conan Doyle (1859–1930), Sherlock
Holmes' creator; T. S. Eliot (1888–1965), poet and recipient of the
Nobel Prize for literature in 1948; D. H. Lawrence, author of *Lady
Chatterley's Lover,* the publication of which rocked the literary world;
Aldous Huxley (1894–1963); Virginia Woolf (1882–1941); W. H.
Auden (1907–1973); Stephen Spender (b. 1909); Ezra Pound (1885–
1972); W. Somerset Maugham (1874–1965); Iris Murdoch (b. 1919);
Agatha Christie (1890–1976); Graham Greene (b. 1904); Harold Pin-
ter (b. 1930); and Samuel Beckett (b. 1906).

English Architecture

Europe's most spectacular, fascinating, and mysterious prehistoric
remains are at Stonehenge in southern England, and date from 3,500
years ago. No one today fully understands why man erected these giant
stones, but they may have once served as a temple to the sun.

Architecture Under the Romans

During their long occupation of England, the Romans built ambi-
tiously, and a number of their works have survived the centuries. In
Lincoln, you can see what is left of Roman gates and walls; in Chester,
an amphitheater; and stretching across northern England, the huge
fortified wall (125 km., 75 miles, long) built by Hadrian, who began
the awesome task around A.D. 122.

The Anglo-Saxons

Until the middle of the 11th century, the simple building style of the
Anglo-Saxons dominated English architecture. Early Anglo-Saxon
architecture shows the influence of the Romans and is characterized by
simple round arches. Its building techniques derive from and mimic the
wood structures common at the time. Little of this work survives today.

The Norman Style

When the Normans conquered England in 1066, they brought with
them knowledge of French architecture and quickly began an impressive building campaign. The basic elements of the Norman style are

Anglo-Saxon Style   Norman Style

Romanesque—thick columns, rounded arches, arcades, and buttresses. Many buildings are adorned with geometric stone carving that is distinctly Norman.

The Chapel of St. John in the Tower of London, built by William the Conqueror, is the best remaining example of early Romanesque architecture in England. Larger, more exciting examples of the style can be found in the churches of Ely (begun 1083), Durham (begun 1093), and Peterborough (begun 1118). In the churches at Kilpeck and Barfreston, you can see the intricate stone carving that is a keynote of the Norman architecture.

A fine example of Norman secular building is the castle in Norwich, constructed in the 12th century, then in the 19th century refaced with stone that mimics the original Norman arcading. In Kent, at the early 12th-century Rochester Castle, you can climb the massive Norman keep then look down at the town and the surrounding Medway countryside. In Lincoln, see the Jew's House and St. Mary's Guildhall, both from the 12th century.

The Gothic Style

Beginning in the late 12th century, the Norman Style started to give way to the Early English Style (1180–1250), the first step in the evolution of Gothic architecture. The rounded arches common to Romanesque building were replaced by pointed arches and ribbed vaulting came into use, giving the churches the grace, visual excitement, and engineering innovation that points the way to a fully developed Gothic Style.

Salisbury Cathedral, begun in 1220, and built almost totally in the 13th century (its famed spire dates from the 14th century), is an outstanding and homogenous example of the Early English Style.

The Decorated Style (late 13th–14th centuries) strongly emphasized ornament: characteristic of it are larger windows with beautifully interwoven tracery and columns with tightly connected shafts. Its sculptural elements are naturalistic and include leafy branches and clusters of flowers. At the cathedrals of Exeter, York, Wells, and Lincoln you can see the innovations of the style.

The Perpendicular Style (14th–early 16th centuries) is characterized by straight vertical lines, large windows embellished with elaborate tracery, and magnificent fan vaulting. King's College Chapel in Cambridge, founded by Henry VI in 1440, is a glorious example, as are the Henry VII Chapel in Westminster Abbey and St. George's Chapel in Windsor.

Throughout the Middle Ages, there is a distinct progression from feudal halls to manor houses. When Henry VIII broke with the Roman Catholic Church and dissolved the monasteries, the importance of religious architecture was forever diminished. Secular building became increasingly important, and as the aristocracy demanded fine mansions, a growing class of prosperous businessmen built more modest homes. Hampton Court (1514) is one of many palatial homes built during the period, and at the same time, countless half-timbered houses arose to satisfy the needs of the more modestly well-to-do.

Decorated Style

Renaissance Style

Classicism in England

The architect Inigo Jones (1573–1652) ushered in the classical princi-
ples of the Renaissance style. A fervent admirer of the works of the
Italian Renaissance architect Andrea Palladio, Jones styled his buildings with classic restraint and balance. The Banqueting House in
Whitehall (London) is a magnificent example of Jones's work.

When the Great Fire consumed much of London in 1666, scores of
buildings were destroyed. The architect of London's reconstruction was
Christopher Wren (1632–1723). He is given credit for rebuilding more
than 50 churches in London alone—St. Paul's Cathedral is his masterpiece.

Among those who followed Wren are Nicholas Hawksmoor (1661–
1736) and Sir John Vanbrugh (1664–1726), noted for his country
houses and for Blenheim Palace, a Baroque mansion in Woodstock near
Oxford, designed in 1705.

Restraint runs through the work of a number of 18th-century architects, who worked primarily in a Palladian fashion as they built formal
country homes for their well-to-do clients. Best known are Lord Burlington (1695–1753), James Gibbs (1682–1754), and William Kent
(1684–1748).

As elaborate formal homes sprang up over the English countryside,
town planning became increasingly important in the cities. John Wood I
(1704–1754) and John Wood II (1728–1781) worked in Bath and John
Nash (1752–1835) in London.

Neoclassicism

In the second half of the 18th century, a wave of classicism swept over
England, inspired in part by contemporary finds at Pompeii and Her-
culaneum. Robert Adam (1728–1792), known today as the Father of
the Classical Revival in England, studied in Italy and published his
findings in 1763. Others associated with the movement include George
Dance II (1700–1768), Sir William Chambers (1726–1796), and Sir
John Soane (1753–1837).

The Gothic Revival

A taste for the picturesque arose in the late 18th century, and nowhere
can you see it more clearly than at Horace Walpole's (1717–1797)
decidedly Gothic Strawberry Hill (c. 1750) in Twickenham. A more
restrained interpretation of the style can be seen in London's Houses of
Parliament, designed by A. W. N. Pugin (1762–1832) and Sir Charles
Barry (1837–1867).

The Industrial Revolution

The new materials introduced by the Industrial Revolution opened avenues of exploration for architects and engineers. Iron, glass, and steel (after 1860) enabled man to build higher, span wider distances, and pierce walls with more and more windows. The Crystal Palace, built by Sir Joseph Paxton (1803–1865) for the Great Exhibition of 1851, is the best example of the advances of the age.

The Twentieth Century

The International Style that has dominated 20th-century architecture is just as common in England as it is in the United States. At its best, it is clean, elegant, and built to accommodate the needs of man. At its worst, it is bland, conventional, and poorly planned. Unfortunately, it is the latter type of architecture that threatens to overshadow England's past achievements. In London, plain, monolithic, uninspired high rises stand next to distinguished examples of the best in English building. Prince Charles himself leads an active campaign to reverse this trend and improve the standards of modern building.

***London

See color map.

London, the most populated (7.5 million inhabitants) and arguably the most cosmopolitan of all European cities, is actually a diverse conglomerate of many small villages that stretch along both sides of the River Thames within an area twice the size of New York City.

These "villages" have retained much of their distinctive character over the centuries even though, inevitably, some splendid buildings and entire streets have been lost to war and real-estate developers, and modern architecture has changed the look of skylines and façades. The changes have not necessarily been for the worse, however. Many long-neglected buildings, most recently the warehouses along the Thames, have been restored, and London's modern, efficient public transportation system makes it easier than ever to explore the many sides of this endlessly fascinating city—a rewarding pursuit, for, as Samuel Johnson said, "If a man is tired of London, he is tired of life."

On the following pages we lay out four walks that take in many of the city's important sights; we also list other places that do not lie directly on the walks but are of great interest as well. Nevertheless, it is not our intention to reduce your visit to London to a dutiful plod through important attractions. Rather, we encourage you to wander at leisure through the streets and parks of the many different villages that are London.

London in Brief

The hub of ancient London is known as *The City*. Barely a mile square, The City is the commercial center of London, where nearly a million people are employed in the banking, insurance, and commodities industries. At one end of The City rises Sir Christopher Wren's masterpiece, historic St. Paul's Cathedral. The other end is marked by the beginning of Fleet Street, almost a synonym for newspaper publishing—these days the headquarters of London's sensational tabloids—and the Temple Bar, the bastion of Britain's legal profession.

Westminster, where the famous landmarks Big Ben, 10 Downing Street, and Westminster Abbey are located, is the formidable seat of British government. Extending from the west of Westminster is *St. James's Park* and the district of the same name, a stronghold of gentlemen's clubs, shirtmakers, and haberdashers. These sedate blocks border the adjoining greenswards of St. James's Park and Green Park,

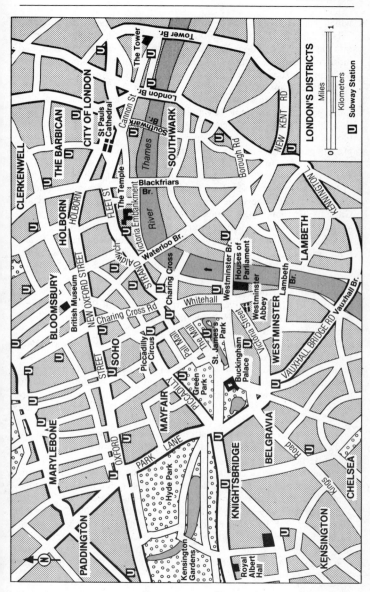

which surround the British monarch's London home, Buckingham Palace. *Piccadilly,* a lively thoroughfare of shops and restaurants, leads into the heart of London's West End, a district of theaters, cinemas, and more restaurants. The area's Leicester Square is the center of operations for nightlife. Beyond Piccadilly lies *Mayfair,* once primarily the architecturally elegant territory of aristocratic households and now a neighborhood of the city's finest shops. The posh terrace houses of nearby *Belgravia* are now occupied by many embassies. Straight on to the west lies *Knightsbridge,* a concentration of shops, hotels, and apartment blocks whose most celebrated commercial institution is Harrod's, the great department store. The area's smartest promenade is Sloane Street, which extends toward the distinctive and equally stylish area of *Pimlico.* Neighboring *Kensington* is another elegant residential district of lovely terraced houses. Some of London's best museums, including the Victoria and Albert, are here, as is the green expanse of Kensington Gardens, surrounding Kensington Palace.

Historic *Chelsea,* much favored by the well-connected young set, is a lively mix of historic houses—once the homes of such British literary luminaries as George Eliot and Oscar Wilde—and trendy shops. *Soho,* the cosmopolitan center of London nightlife, lies just to the north of bustling Piccadilly Circus. Across New Oxford Street, the capital's busiest shopping thoroughfare, is *Bloomsbury,* of literary fame and also the home of London University and the monumental British Museum. Next to Bloomsbury lies *Holborn,* famous for its two bastions of legal London, Gray's Inn and Lincoln's Inn.

The residential quarter of *Paddington* is on the north side of Hyde Park. It adjoins *Marylebone,* a district of 18th-century houses and the home turf, on Baker Street, of that most famous of all detectives, real and fictional, Sherlock Holmes. The London Planetarium, Madame Tussaud's (the renowned wax museum), one of Britain's tallest structures—the British Telecom Tower—and above all, Regent's Park are among the neighborhood's present-day attractions.

The regions of London that stretch east of the Tower of London are known as the *East End,* traditionally a refuge for immigrants and a colorful, mostly waterfront district where dockworkers, many of whom speak in an accented, cockney-like English that may be incomprehensible to American ears, meet after work in noisy pubs. Junk and antique dealers sell their wares at numerous markets in the area.

Among the many neighborhoods on the south side of the Thames are *Southwark,* with its beautiful Gothic cathedral, and *Lambeth,* where Lambeth Palace (open only to groups), the residence of the Archbishop of Canterbury, is located. The South Bank Arts Centre is a concentration of the National Theatre, three concert halls, the National Film Theatre, and the Hayward Gallery.

Seeing London

Unlike their Continental neighbors, Londoners do not flee the city *en masse* in the heat of the summer, perhaps because of its less-than-tropical climate. In fact, the city has a lively summer season of art exhibitions, concerts, theater premieres, film programs, and athletic events. British winters are not as damp or as dismal as many Americans believe them to be. True, there are likely to be frequent showers, and London fog is a romantically gloomy reality. But temperatures only rarely dip below the freezing point, and the infamous "pea soup" fogs went out with the introduction of coal-emission standards in the 1950s.

Whatever time of year you visit London, there is no easier or more pleasant way to see it than from the top of a double-decker bus—either one of the coaches of the city's extensive public transportation network or one of the capital's ubiquitous tourist coaches. (Many of them depart from Piccadilly Circus.) The fastest if least picturesque way to get around town is on the subway, commonly known as the "underground" or the "tube" (see color map).

Just as impressive as London's historic monuments, world-famous shops, well tended parks, and street after street of lovely houses is its cultural life. The lights of the city's 50-plus theaters, many of them located in the West End around Shaftesbury Avenue, burn as bright as those on Broadway—some say brighter. The venerable Royal Shakespeare Company now graces the stages of the new Barbican Centre in The City. The Old Vic has been renovated, and the imposing, modern National Theatre on the South Bank is the new headquarters of the National Theatre Company. No night in London is without music, be it at the South Bank halls, the Royal Albert or Wigmore halls, jazz clubs in Soho, or the opera house in Covent Garden.

History

A.D. 60: London, a thriving Roman settlement, is plundered and burned by the Iceni tribe of East Anglia, led by Queen Boadicea. The Romans regain control and fortify the settlement, which prospers as a trading center and hub of the Roman road network.

Fifth century: The Romans withdraw, and London is occupied by the warlike Anglo Saxons.

604: King Ethelbert appoints the cleric Mellitus as the first Bishop of London. A short time later, St. Paul's Cathedral is founded as the bishop's see.

Eighth century: Vikings from Norway and Denmark repeatedly attack and plunder London, by this time a provincial market town of increasing importance.

884: Alfred the Great, king of all of England that is not under Danish rule, makes London his capital.

1017–1035: The Danish King Canute the Great rules over all of England.

1066: During the Norman Invasion, London submits when its food supplies are cut off. The city thrives under William the Conqueror, the first English king to be crowned at Westminster Abbey.

11th–12th centuries: Devastating fires rage through the growing city. Wooden walls and thatched roofs are prohibited.

1217: A stone bridge, the only span between the two shores of the Thames until 1750, replaces the wooden London Bridge.

1263: Trade guilds, still in existence today, take control of commerce and crafts.

1269: Construction of Westminster Abbey begins.

1280: The old St. Paul's Cathedral is completed.

1338: Westminster becomes the regular meeting place of Parliament.

1348: Some 30,000 Londoners, half of the city's residents, die in an outbreak of the plague.

15th–16th centuries: London becomes one of the most powerful cities in Europe. The population swells to nearly 300,000.

1582: London receives its first modern water supply.

1665: The Great Plague claims 90,000 victims.

1666: The Great Fire of London destroys four-fifths of the structures in the city. Sir Christopher Wren builds a new St. Paul's and some 50 other churches.

1689: King William III names Kensington Palace the residence of English kings.

1749: Westminster Bridge, the second span over the Thames, is built.

1750: London's population reaches 675,000.

1830: London's first police force comes on duty. With no central government, London is ruled by 300 separate administrative bodies.

1836: The first railroad train rolls from London to Greenwich.

1839: The Palace of Westminster is rebuilt after a fire.

1851: The Great Exhibition, celebrating British technology, is held.

1889: The formation of the London County Council gives the city a unified municipal government.

1906: The first underground, between Baker Street and Waterloo Station, opens.

1914–1916: German air raids during World War I damage London and take 640 lives.

1940: During the Blitz of World War II, The City is reduced to rubble. St. Paul's survives the nightly bombings, which kill some 30,000 Londoners.

1951: The Festival of Britain, a great fair and exhibition, is held on the south bank of the Thames.

1965: The Post Office Tower (Telecom Tower), 190 meters (623 feet) tall, then the highest of London's modern structures, is erected.

1986: The Greater London Council, founded in 1963, is dissolved, leaving London without a central city government.

WALK 1: **Piccadilly Circus–St. James's Palace– *Buckingham Palace–*Parliament–***Westminster Abbey–Whitehall–Trafalgar Square–***National Gallery–**Piccadilly Circus

See map on page 35.

P.D. James, perhaps England's greatest living writer of detective fiction, once wondered how many secrets of British state have been whispered on Birdcage Walk, the path that leads through St. James's Park toward the Houses of Parliament. It is rather difficult not to think of the men and women who have set the course of British history as you follow Walk 1 from busy Piccadilly past Buckingham Palace and down Birdcage Walk to Whitehall and British officialdom. Many of the Kings, Queens, and statesmen the walk evokes are portrayed at the National Portrait Gallery, at the end of the route, next to one of the world's foremost art museums, the National Gallery.

Piccadilly Circus (1) (Piccadilly Circus underground stop), known at the height of the British Empire as the "center of the world," is still a bustling and brightly lit hub, where some of London's busiest thoroughfares, including theater-laden Shaftesbury Avenue and regal Regent Street, come together. The traffic circle surrounds the *Shaftesbury Monument,* on which a statue of a naked Eros, the Greek god of love, seemingly casts his spell on the crowds. The statue, installed in 1893, actually represents the Angel of Christian Charity. Even so, its nakedness so shocked Edwardians that its creator, Sir Alfred Gilbert, was forced to leave England.

Piccadilly, a sunny and open boulevard that skirts *Green Park,* leads west from the Circus past the austerely elegant **church of St. James's** (2). The distinguished structure, built by Sir Christopher Wren from 1676–1684, was severely damaged during the air raids of the Second World War but was restored to its original splendor in 1954. **Burlington House** (3), just across the avenue from the church, was built in 1665 as the London residence of the First Earl of Burlington, but it has long been the home of the *Royal Academy of Arts,* whose first president, Sir Joshua Reynolds, is commemorated by a statue in the neo-Renaissance courtyard. Constable, Turner, and Millais are a few of the famous alumni of the Academy, which is still an art school. Works by many of the Academy's esteemed graduates hang in the Burlington House galleries. A white marble relief of the Virgin and Child in the collection is the only work by Michelangelo on British soil. The Academy's temporary exhibitions, including an annual summer program of contemporary art, are highly praised.

The *Royal Society,* founded in 1660, occupies the eastern wing of Burlington House. Sir Christopher Wren, Samuel Pepys, and Sir Isaac Newton are among the past presidents of this august scientific body. Backing onto Burlington House is the **Museum of Mankind,** the Ethnography Department of the British Museum. Its remarkable, frequently changing exhibits dramatize the lives of ancient and modern non-Western peoples.

A bit farther along Piccadilly is the famous **Burlington Arcade,** the largest of London's covered shopping promenades, laid out in 1819 and now housing 72 shops. War veterans, known as "beadles" and garbed in natty uniforms and top hats, patrol the exceptionally well-heeled crowds. The very genteel *Fortnum and Mason,* across the street, is one of London's finest and best-known shops. The ground-floor grocery department is a popular stop for Londoners and tourists alike, who cherish the goods and the attentive staff. Tea at Fortnum's is a London institution.

As you approach the very Edwardian *Ritz Hotel,* just past Bond Street, internationally famous for its exclusive shops and art galleries, turn left into St. James's Street and walk to the wide boulevard known as *Pall Mall,* still a male-dominated enclave of gentlemen's clubs. The most imposing building on the Mall is the red brick, turreted ***St. James's Palace** (4), which Henry VIII had built from plans by Holbein in 1532. St. James's became the royal residence after Whitehall Palace burned to the ground in 1699. To this day the palace is the statutory seat of the sovereign, and ambassadors are still named to the Court of St. James. The guard changes every day at 11:15 A.M. in front of the imposing four-story gate house, also called the Clock Tower, which faces St. James's Street.

Walking eastward on the Mall, you soon come to **Marlborough House** (5), a mansion of red brick that Sir Christopher Wren built from 1709–1711 for the Duke of Marlborough after the commander's victories over the French. Ironically, the lavish decorations include murals by Louis Laquere, godson of Louis XIV of France. Just to the west of St. James's Palace is ***Lancaster House** (6), which Benjamin Wyatt built for the Duke of York in 1825. The sumptuous palace, long the center of London society, is so lavishly decorated that Queen Victoria once remarked to

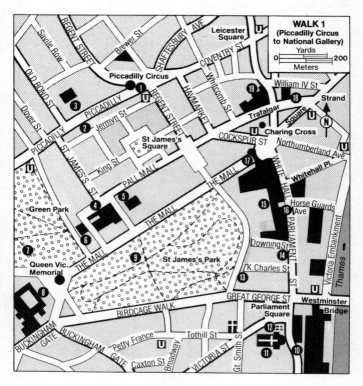

WALK 1
(Piccadilly Circus to National Gallery)

her hostess, "I have come from my house to your palace." One of the salons is fitted with a ceiling painted by Veronese, the Italian master of the early Renaissance.

From Lancaster House, the Mall leads through *Green Park* (7) to ***Buckingham Palace** (8), built as the residence of the Duke of Buckingham in 1703. Court architect John Nash remodeled and expanded the palace from 1824–1830, although eventually he was dismissed from the job for allegedly squandering public funds. Despite the minor scandal, Queen Victoria moved her court to the palace in 1837; and it has remained the London residence of the monarch. The sedate, classicist façade is a 1913 addition, and the monument to Queen Victoria in front of the palace was erected in 1911. Although the palace is closed to the public, most visitors to London come to pay their respects from outside the gates, hoping to catch a glimpse of the royal residents (who are at home when the flag above the palace is flying) or to watch the changing of the guard, which takes place every morning at 11:30.

Buckingham Palace faces **St. James's Park** (9), a lovely expanse of greenery that owes its existence to Henry VIII, who in 1536 had a swamp drained to create a hunting preserve. Under Charles II, the French landscape architect Andre Le Nôtre laid out public gardens here in the style of the Tuileries in Paris. John Nash remodeled the park again in 1829, digging a natural-looking lake that is much frequented by waterfowl and Londoners out for a stroll. The bridge across the lake affords a fairytale view of Whitehall's castellated towers.

Birdcage Walk leads along the western edge of the park to *Westminster* and the ***Houses of Parliament** (10), which occupy the site of the old Westminster Palace, where Edward the Confessor took up residence in the 11th century. The palace was expanded under William the Conqueror, rebuilt in 1099, destroyed by fire, and rebuilt in 1299 under Richard II. The only portions of the building to survive an 1834 blaze that engulfed the Medieval palace were ****Westminster Hall,** where British kings and queens have met with noblemen since the 13th century; the crypt of the cha-

Parliament and Clock Tower

pel of St. Stephen, the first meeting place of the House of Commons; a cloister; and the Jewel Tower, built in 1365 to store royal valuables. Incorporating the remnants of the old structure, Sir Charles Barry and Augustus Pugin built the new Westminster Palace in a flamboyant neo-Gothic style between 1840–1888. Parliament convened for the first time in its new quarters in 1852.

The *House of Commons* occupies the northern wing of the palace, and the *House of Lords* occupies the southern wing. (Tours of Westminster have been suspended for security reasons; however, you can watch sessions from the Strangers' Gallery by lining up at the entrance to St. Stephen's Hall, south of Westminster Hall, Monday–Thursday at 4:15 P.M. or Friday at 10:00 A.M. for a session of Commons, and Monday–Wednesday at 2:30 P.M., Thursday at 3:00 P.M., or Friday at 11:00 A.M. for Lords.) The public rooms are lavishly decorated, although most of the palace is divided into offices where the day-to-day workings of British lawmaking take place. The monarch's wardrobe room, with a Victorian throne and frescoes depicting the legend of Sir Arthur, is where the sovereign is dressed in the state crown and crimson parliamentary robes. The *Royal Gallery,* lined with statues of British kings and queens and their heraldic shields, is the monarch's official passage-

way to the House of Lords, which is reached through the *Prince's Chamber,* decorated with portraits of Tudor monarchs and their consorts, including the six wives of Henry VIII. The House of Lords is a riot of gold and crimson and is lined with red leather benches. At one end are three thrones—for the king, the queen, and the Prince of Wales—and looking over the grand chamber in its sumptuous splendor are statues of the 18 barons who witnessed King John sign the Magna Carta. Members of the public wait to meet their MPs in the adjoining, 23-meter- (75-feet-) high *Central Lobby.* The *Corridor, Commons Lobby,* and *House of Commons* were destroyed in a 1941 air raid and, unlike the rest of the palace, rebuilt in a plain style. ***Westminster Hall,* the scene of many famous and infamous trials of such notable Britons as Sir Thomas More and Richard II, has also witnessed the grand Christmas feasts of England's Medieval kings and once served in the 13th century as a rowing pond when the Thames was in flood. It is now divided into court chambers. A stairway leads from the southeastern corner of the chamber to *St. Stephen's crypt,* a chapel that Edward I built between 1292–1297 and which, for several centuries, was used for meetings of Parliament.

The famous clock tower known as *Big Ben,* 97.5 meters (320 feet) tall, dominates the northern end of Westminster Palace. The name actually refers to the huge bell, which commemorates Sir Benjamin Hall, a rotund man who was serving as Britain's Commissioner of Works at the time of its installation in 1859. The blockish *Victoria Tower*, a hair taller than Big Ben, is at the southern end of the palace. It houses the Parliamentary Archives, with its 3 million volumes.

***Westminster Abbey (11), known formally as the Collegiate Church of St. Peter, is the church of Parliament and the official church of Great Britain. Although St. Paul's is much larger, it is here, in the comparatively modest abbey, that the nation's kings and queens are married, crowned, and laid to rest. In its 2,500 tombs lie the remains of England's greatest statesmen and men of letters. Henry VII lays in his own elaborate, fan-vaulted chapel, flamboyantly decorated with the

Westminster Abbey

carved statues of saints. Elizabeth I and her rival, Mary Queen of Scots, rest, peaceably at last, on opposite aisles. In *Poet's Corner* are the tombs and memorials of Chaucer, Shakespeare, Browning, Milton, and other great English writers and poets. Perhaps one of the most visited memorials in the abbey is that of the Unknown Warrior, surrounded year-round by Flanders poppies.

Founded in 616 and dedicated to Mellitus, the first Bishop of London, the abbey as we now know it began to take shape under Edward the Confessor in 1050 as the minster of the west (as opposed to the minster of the east, St. Paul's; hence the name, Westminster). Edward, canonized in 1163, is buried in a large, marble shrine, erected in 1268 behind the main altar; for centuries, his shrine has been a popular pilgrimage destination. Near the tomb is the coronation throne on which British monarchs of the past six centuries have been crowned. It rests atop the Stone of Scone, the coronation stone where Scottish kings, including Macbeth, were once crowned and which Edward I brought to England in 1297. According to legend, the stone is the Jacob's Pillow of Biblical note, imbued with both mystical and magical powers. Whatever the true nature of the stone may be, it is a powerful symbol of both Scottish and British history.

The abbey is a soaring structure that is 170 meters (557 feet) long, 25 meters (82 feet) wide, and 34 meters (111 feet) high. Henry III is largely responsible for the church's appearance. Inspired by the Gothic cathedrals of France, he rebuilt the church from 1503–1519 in the purest form of the style. Thankfully, the architects of later additions have maintained the Gothic spirit of the place. The last major additions to Westminster Abbey were the west towers, designed by Sir Christopher Wren and Nicholas Hawksmoor and completed in 1745.

The 13th-century *Chapter House,* just to the east of the Abbey, is an octagonal structure that was once the royal treasury; many times in the past it has been used for meetings of Parliament. Beneath it, the church's history comes alive in painstaking displays in the *Abbey Museum.* The grounds also house the *Westminster School,* an elite public (that is, private) school that Elizabeth I instituted in place of the monastery school after the Church of England's break with Rome.

In the 11th century, Edward the Confessor founded the **church of St. Margaret's** (12) as a parish church for the neighborhood, preserving nearby Westminster Abbey for the more important personages among the faithful. So beloved was the little church, rebuilt and remodeled many times over the centuries, that it was saved from demolition in the 16th century by locals who attacked the workmen with clubs and bows and arrows. Nowadays, St. Margaret's is the preferred place of worship—and booked solidly for weddings—of the British aristocracy.

The Flemish *stained glass* in the east window was commissioned in 1501 by Ferdinand and Isabella of Spain in celebration of the marriage of their daughter, Catherine, to Prince Arthur. Soon thereafter Arthur died, the doomed Catherine married Henry VIII, and the window was stored outside of London until 1758, when the House of Commons presented it to the church. Sir Walter Raleigh, who was executed nearby in 1618, is buried beneath the high altar.

A wide, rather formidable avenue begins at Westminster in *Parliament Square,* in which stand statues of such famous statesmen as George Washington and Winston Churchill; under the name of Whitehall, the avenue leads to the heart of London, *Trafalgar Square* (see page 40). Just off Whitehall on King Charles Street, you'll find the **Cabinet War Rooms** (13) where Winston Churchill and his cabinet met during the World War II air raids. This living museum seems to have stopped in time at the year 1945. In the middle of Whitehall, lined with buildings housing the various British government ministries, is the **Cenotaph** (14), a memorial erected in 1919 to commemorate Britain's war dead. On Remembrance Sunday, the Sunday nearest November 11 (when the armistice ending World War I was signed), the Queen lays a wreath at the memorial before an audience of statesmen, citizens, and visitors.

The little lane just past the memorial to the left is **Downing Street,** where, at number 10, British prime ministers have lived since George II gave the house to Sir Robert Walpole in 1732. A bit farther along Whitehall is the **Horse Guards** (15), the 18th-century barracks of the royal cavalry, topped by a lovely bell tower. The guard, in bright uniforms and plumed helmets, changes every weekday morning at 11:00 on the adjacent Horse Guards Parade. ***Banqueting House** (16), across the street, is the only surviving portion of the old Whitehall Palace, which burned to the ground in 1698 shortly after the court moved to Kensington Palace (see page 46).

Henry VIII seized Whitehall from Cardinal Wolsey in 1529 and greatly enlarged it. In 1622, Charles I commissioned the architect Inigo Jones to rebuild the Banqueting House in Palladian style. The King also commissioned ceiling paintings from Rubens and knighted him for his efforts. In 1649, Charles was executed just beneath the windows of the hall, an event commemorated by a bust of the ruler that stands above the doorway.

The handsome, brick *Old Admiralty Building* is fronted by a portico and a screen that depicts its function with figures of winged sea horses. The building stands at the foot of the wide boulevard known as *The Mall,* which leads along the borders of St. James's Park and Green Park to Buckingham Palace. The **Admiralty Arch** (17), erected in honor of Queen Victoria in 1910, spans the Mall. Just behind it is a bronze statue of James Cook, the 18th-century British naval officer and explorer.

Whitehall ends at **Charing Cross,** a square graced by an equestrian statue of Charles I, erected in 1675, and by a 19th-century copy of the 13th-century cross that Charles placed here in homage to his dead queen. A bronze tablet imbedded in the pavement in 1955 denotes this busy intersection as the geographic center of London. Charing Cross adjoins **Trafalgar Square,** laid out by court architect John Nash in the 1820s and, since then, the scene of innumerable public demonstrations. No

Trafalgar Square

doubt the protesters are inspired by the figure of fiery Admiral Nelson, whose victory over Napoleon at Trafalgar in 1805 gave the square its name and whose statue is perched atop the 55-meter- (180-foot-) high *Nelson's Column,* erected in 1843. An equestrian statue of King George IV rides closer to earth in the northeast corner of the square, surrounded by a pleasant medley of fountains, pigeons, and sightseers.

Trafalgar Square's famous **church of St.-Martin-in-the-Fields** (18), its name recalling London's status as a village, was built in 1222, remodeled in 1544 for Henry VIII, and rebuilt between 1721–1726 by James Gibbs, a student of Sir Christopher Wren. It was Gibbs who added the graceful spire, 56 meters (184 feet) tall. The other famous building on the square is the huge *****National Gallery** (19), completed in 1838 to house the paintings of William of Orange and enlarged many times since then to house a constantly expanding collection of masterpieces—4,500 in all, only a third of which can be hung at one time. (Queen Victoria bequeathed her splendid canvases by Dutch and Flemish masters to the gallery.) The gallery's most prized possessions are its canvases by Rembrandt, Rubens, and the Italian masters of the 16th and 17th centuries. Among the painters represented here, and their works, are: Botticelli, *Mystic Nativity;* Leonardo da Vinci, *Virgin and Child with St. Anne and St. John;* Titian, *Bacchus and Ariadne;* Rubens, *Judgment of Paris;* Rembrandt, two self-portraits; Turner, *Rain, Steam and Speed;* Cézanne, *The Bathers;* and the list goes on and on, through the museum's 46 tasteful, well-lighted galleries. The gallery publishes an excellent guide to its collection that is available in the bookshop.

The National Portrait Gallery, just around the corner on St. Martin's Place, houses images—paintings, drawings, photographs, sculptures—of great Britons from all walks of life, from science and letters to business and finance. The portrayals are not always flattering, but they are invariably illuminating in their revelations of character, as well as period decor and costume.

The best route back to Piccadilly is via Haymarket, a lively street noted for two famous old theaters, *Her Majesty's Theatre* and the *Haymarket Theatre* (or *Theatre Royal*). The *Design Centre,* a shop that sells and displays the best in British-designed products, is on Haymarket, too.

WALK 2: **Piccadilly Circus–Regent Street–Portland Place–*Regent's Park (Zoo)–*Madame Tussaud's–*Wallace Collection–Grosvenor Square–**Piccadilly Circus

See map on page 43.

As you cross busy Oxford Street at the beginning of this walk, you will get a glimpse of a London that seems to be swelling with crowds. You will see the famous figures that crowd the pages of British and world history at the waxworks of Madame Tussaud, and then come to two quiet oases: Regent's Park and the serene galleries of the Wallace Collection, the largest assemblage of French masters outside of France.

Of the major avenues leading out of **Piccadilly Circus** (1) (Piccadilly Circus underground stop; see page 33), Regent Street is surely the most architecturally elegant, as it has been since it was laid out as a fashionable promenade in the 18th century. *Liberty, Jaeger's, Garrard's* (the Crown Jeweler), *Aquascutum,* and the other well-known commercial establishments behind the graceful façades—many of them arcaded—cater to an international carriage trade. For a study in contrasts, walk up Regent Street to **Oxford Circus** (2), where it crosses Oxford Street. Few streets anywhere in the world are more crowded than Oxford Street, thronged with shoppers bustling in and out of the area's many reasonably priced department stores, of which *Selfridge's* is the largest, busiest, and best known. It is also the most handsome, with its grand, pillared façade.

Press on across Oxford Circus and continue north on Regent Street, which soon becomes Langham Place, punctuated by the engaging *All Soul's Church,* with its circular, columned portico. Langham Place then becomes Portland Place, laid out as a fashionable promenade entry to Regent's Park in 1774. The street now has a sedate, official air, lined as it is with embassies, scholarly institutes (including the *Royal Institute of British Architects*), and the imposing headquarters of the BBC (3). A monument to Lord Lister, the pioneer of antiseptic surgery, is at the end of the street, near **Park Crescent** (4), laid out in 1821 by John Nash and a superlative example of the residential "half circles" that are so common in London's residential neighborhoods.

Regent's Park (see below) is just beyond, across Park Square, but if you turn left at the end of the crescent into *Marylebone Road,* you will soon come to the large, colonnaded *church of St. Marylebone,* built in 1817, and just beyond it, on the right, **Madame Tussaud's** (5). The renowned wax museum, founded in 1776 by the talented French-woman who learned her trade making death masks for the vic-tims of the Reign of Terror, opened at this location in 1884. Famous personages past and pre-sent are depicted here with star-tling realism. Heavenly bodies are the attraction at the adjoining *London Planetarium,* Britain's first, opened in 1958. Laser-beam magic, accompanied by music, is on show at the adjoining *La-serium.*

York Gate, behind the museum, opens into ***Regent's Park** (6), a bucolic expanse of greenery that

was originally one of Henry VIII's hunting grounds. The park in its present-day form is the work of that great urban designer John Nash, who, between 1812–1827, created the hillocks, the lake and the gardens (the lovely *Queen Mary Rose Gardens* among them) and surrounded his man-made landscape with clusters of stately terrace houses. Nash incorporated into his design the *Regent's Canal,* which rises from Little Venice in Paddington and flows, via 12 locks, through Regent's Park to the Thames. Noted resi-dents of the park include the American ambassador, whose official residence overlooks it, and the 6,000 animals in the ****London Zoo,** which leads the world in animal research and con-servation.

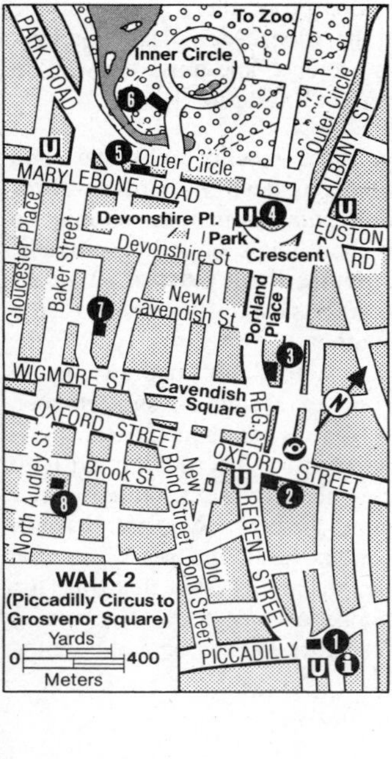

From Marylebone Road, turn left into Baker Street (where fic-tional detective Sherlock Holmes lived) and follow it south to George Street; then turn left to Manchester Square, where in Hertford House hangs the re-markable ***Wallace Collection** (7). In 1897, the widow of Sir Richard Wallace bequeathed to Britain the French paintings that her husband (the Marquis of Hertford) and his family had col-lected for years. The galleries that went on view to the public for the first time in 1900 house the larg-est collection of paintings by French masters outside of France as well as masterpieces of vir-tually every other European painting school, plus decorative objects, furniture, and armor.

WALK 2
(Piccadilly Circus to Grosvenor Square)

Yards
0 ⊢————⊣ 400
Meters

From Hertford House, Duke Street leads south to **Grosvenor Square** (8), an American enclave in London. A monument to Franklin Delano Roosevelt presides over the north side of the square; the house at number 20 was General Eisenhower's headquarters during World War II; and the architecturally out-of-place, fortress-like structure on the west side of the square is the *American Embassy*. Brook Street—where, at number 25, Handel lived for 40 years until his death in 1759 and where he composed the *Messiah*—leads from the square to New Bond Street. A right turn will bring you back to Piccadilly Circus.

WALK 3: Marble Arch–Hyde Park Corner–*Hyde Park–*Kensington Palace–Royal Albert Hall–*Natural History Museum–**Victoria and Albert Museum

See map on page 45.

This walk provides a view of monumental London. You begin at Marble Arch, built as an entryway to Buckingham Palace, then pass Apsley House and its Wellington Arch, built to honor the Duke of Wellington after he routed the French at Waterloo. From there you continue through the greenery of Hyde Park to the Albert Memorial, London's tribute to the Prince Consort of Queen Victoria, and finish the walk in the enormous museums along Kensington's Exhibition Road.

Marble Arch (1) (Marble Arch underground stop) is the monumental archway that John Nash built for the entrance to Buckingham Palace in 1828. In 1851, it was moved to the northeast corner of Hyde Park, where, until 1783, stood Tyburn Gallows, London's execution ground. Those who take advantage of Speaker's Corner, established just behind the arch in 1872, are in no danger of being arrested for their freely expressed opinions. The corner is designated as an official forum where citizens have been able to speak their minds about political, social, religious, and other issues, no matter how unpopular their opinions may be with officials or fellow citizens.

Hyde Park Corner (2), London's busiest traffic circle, is at the southeast corner of Hyde Park. Fortunately for pedestrians, a complex system of subterranean walkways pass beneath the whirling traffic. Those who wish to stay above ground, though, get a good view of ***Apsley House,** which the Duke of Wellington bought in 1817. At that time the mansion was the westernmost residence in London and bore the impressive address "Number 1, London." The Duke's descendants, who still maintain apartments here, presented Apsley House to the nation in 1947, and the ground floor is now a richly decorated museum, with an impressive art collection and the Duke's personal mementos. In 1828, a grateful nation erected the *Wellington Arch* to honor the Duke for his victory over Napoleon at Waterloo. In 1883 the monument was moved to the front yard of Apsley House and crowned with a statue of the Duke and his steed Copenhagen, who is buried at Wellington's country estate, Stratfield Saye (see page 155).

The beckoning greenery beyond the Duke's domain is ***Hyde Park,** which adjoins Kensington Gardens (the two parks are separated by a road that links Kensington and Bayswater) to form the largest expanse of parkland in London. These are two of London's favorite recreation grounds.

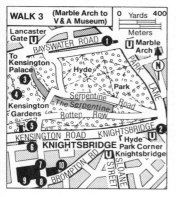

WALK 3 (Marble Arch to V & A Museum)

The Serpentine, a winding, narrow lake dug in 1730 (in which Harriet Westbrook, the first wife of the poet Shelley, drowned herself) is popular with swimmers, boaters, and ice skaters, depending on the season. Rotten Row is a bridle path that has been *the* place to be seen for the equestrian set since the 18th century. Among the popular monuments in the park are the *Peter Pan Statue* (3) and the bronze equestrian statue called *"Physical Energy"* (4), sculpted by G. F. Watts in 1903. The *Serpentine Gallery* is a pleasant place with changing exhibitions of contemporary art.

London's most Victorian monument is the **Albert Memorial** (5), which, in 1876, a grieving Queen Victoria commissioned Sir Gilbert Scott to build in honor of her deceased husband, Prince Albert of Saxe-Coburg Gotha. A bronze statue of the Prince Consort, holding one of the four volumes of the catalog of the 1851 London World's Fair, sits beneath a 58-meter– (190–foot–) tall Gothic canopy. The marble relief encircling the pedestal depicts 178 scientists and artists. (Alas, the memorial is now in danger of collapsing, and saving it will require an expenditure of several million pounds.) Just opposite the Albert Memorial, through the *Alexandra Gate*, is another tribute to the popular prince, the circular **Royal Albert Hall** (6), an 8,000-seat concert hall capped by a massive glass dome, built in 1871. Next to the hall, on the corner of Exhibition Road, is the gabled, brick headquarters of the *Royal Geographical Society* (not open to the public), with a collection of 30,000 historic maps. The *Royal College of Art,* the *Royal College of Organists,* and the *Royal College of Music* are also here.

Several of Victoria and Albert's descendants, including the Prince and Princess of Wales, live nearby in ***Kensington Palace,** a pretty, relatively unpretentious dwelling that has been home to royalty since William and Mary acquired it in 1689 and asked Sir Christopher Wren to enlarge it. The young Victoria received the news of her succession to the throne here. A statue of the queen is on Broad Walk, outside the palace. Some of the staterooms are open to the public.

The first of the world-class museums along Exhibition Road is the ***Science Museum** (7), which, in its seven acres of galleries, houses working models of 18th- and 19th-century machines, weights and measures from the 14th century B.C., space vehicles, and a day's visit worth of other exhibits. The star attractions at the **Geological Museum** (8) are the rooms full of precious gems. An ambitious and highly successful permanent exhibit, "The Story of the Earth," does indeed put things

into perspective. The dinosaurs that greet visitors at the door of the cavernous ***Natural History Museum** (9) are a hint of what's in store. This museum's five divisions—zoology, entomology, paleontology, mineralogy, and botany—grow by about 300,000 objects a year, and there are fascinating videos and slide shows as well.

The best place to begin a tour of the ****Victoria and Albert Museum** (10), officially known as the *National Museum of Art and Design* and popularly called the "V and A"—is the bookshop, where you may purchase a catalog to the extensive holdings of the world's largest museum of decorative arts. In its 11 km. (7 miles) of galleries are 15th-century Italian sculptures, Indian miniatures, Raphael drawings, and a costume collection—to name but a few of the holdings. Plan to spend at least the better part of a day, although it would be difficult to exhaust the museum's riches in a year of visits.

From the nearby South Kensington underground station (at the corner of Exhibition Road and Thurloe Street) you may board a train for Hyde Park Corner (two stops) or Piccadilly Circus (four stops). A bus from the stop just outside the museum reaches Hyde Park Corner in a few minutes.

WALK 4: ***British Museum–*Lincoln's Inn–*The Temple–Fleet Street–**St. Paul's Cathedral–Bank of England–*Monument–**Southwark Cathedral– ***Tower of London

See map on page 48.

The best of old London lies along this walk, which begins, appropriately, in the antiquity-filled galleries of the British Museum. From there you walk through The City, its modern towers throwing shadows over London's oldest streets and its great cathedral, St. Paul's. You end the walk in the environs of the Tower of London, the stone bastion that rises alongside the Thames on the site where William the Conqueror built a fortress 900 years ago.

***The British Museum** (1) (on Great Russell Street; Tottenham Court Road underground stop) is rooted in the 80,000-piece collection of curiosities that Sir Hans Sloane, a physician and naturalist, bequeathed to the nation in his will. Opened to the public in 1753 in Montague House, in Bloomsbury, the museum (once called "The Old Curiosity Shop" for its random holdings) soon outgrew its quarters, which were greatly expanded from 1823–1852. In addition to the vast and priceless collections on view here—many with a strong archaeological bent—the British Museum also oversees the *Museum of Mankind* (see page 34) and the *Natural History Museum* (see page 46), and incorporates in its main building the *British Library*. The library has a copy of every book printed in England. Karl Marx and Charles Dickens are but two of the scholars who have hunched over their books beneath the huge dome of the main reading room, which is surrounded by 40 km. (25 miles) of shelves and 1.3 million books.

Even the most cursory tour of the museum should include the following exhibition sections and special treasures.

Egyptian antiquities: On exhibit here is the Rosetta Stone, a black basalt slab, discovered by French archaeologist Jean-Francois Champollion in 1797, on which is inscribed Egyptian hieroglyphics with a Greek translation. The stone, which provided the first key to Egyptian languages, came into British hands with the fall of Alexandria in 1801. The museum's outstanding collection of mummies includes the remains of human beings, cats, and a crocodile.

Greek antiquities: The friezes and statues that comprise the Elgin Marbles once decorated the Parthenon in Athens. Brought to Britain from 1801–1803 by Lord Elgin, the largest portion of the treasure depicts a procession up Mount Olympus and is a splendid example of the art of Greece during her Golden Age.

Roman antiquities: The Portland Vase is an exquisite piece of Roman glasswork in which white figures appear on a blue background. Acquired by the Duke of Portland in the 18th century, the vase inspired the blue-and-white china patterns of Wedgwood.

Middle Ages: The Sutton Hoo Treasure is from a seventh-century sailing vessel in which Redwald, King of the Angles, was buried, alongside the weapons, helmets, cookware, and other objects he would need in his next life. The treasure takes its name from the town in Suffolk where it was unearthed in 1939.

Of course, such a brief list hardly begins to do justice to this enormous, varied, and unique collection. The *Khorabad Entrance* is a gateway, inscribed with human-headed bulls to ward off evil, that guarded an Assyrian city 2,600 years ago. A superlative collection of Chinese ceramics is here, as is the world's largest collection of European drawings.

From the southern end of the museum, walk across Bloomsbury Square to High Holborn Street, where a right turn leads to ***Lincoln's Inn** (2), historically one of London's four great law schools and now a society for the legal profession. The Old Hall was built in 1420. The Inn's "new" buildings date from the 1600s.

A trek to the north side of *Lincoln's Inn Fields,* the largest open square in London—notable for its ancient and huge plane trees—brings you to the ***Sir John Soane Museum** (3). This eclectic hodgepodge of art and artifacts collected by Soane, a prominent architect who died in 1837, is housed in the equally eccentric residence he bought in 1792 and continually enlarged. His will stipulates that nothing should ever be moved, so the fas-

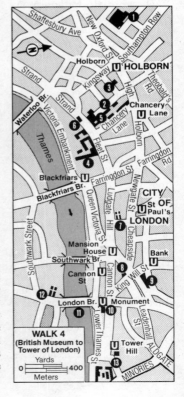

cinating jumble, ingeniously displayed, is intact, with fossils and sarcophagi nestling beneath canvases by Turner, Hogarth, Reynolds, Watteau, and others.

The *Cancer Research Institute* and the *Hunterian Museum,* with an assemblage of historic medical instruments, are on the south side of the square. From the east side of Lincoln's Inn, Chancery Lane leads south to Fleet Street—the "Street of Ink"—for almost five centuries the center of the British publishing industry and where many of London's newspapers are produced. ***The Temple** (4), the headquarters in the 12th century of the Knights Templar, a crusading order founded in Jerusalem in 1119, is best entered from Middle Temple Lane at the foot of Chancery Lane. In the 14th century the ancient buildings and gardens, which extend to the Thames, became a law school, and ever since then the Temple has been a sanctuary for London's legal profession. Modern London's lawyers (or solicitors) now occupy the Georgian buildings that surround a 12th-century church, one of London's finest Medieval buildings and one of only five round churches in Britain. This is the Temple itself, and it is modeled on the Church of the Holy Sepulchre in Jerusalem. Nine marble effigies of Knights Templar lie in solidly eternal rest on the floor of the nave.

Another showcase of legal London, the *Law Courts* (5), is just across Fleet Street. Officially known as the *Royal Courts of Justice,* they were built between 1874–1882 in an exuberantly Victorian version of High English Gothic style.

St. Clement Danes Church (6), which figures in the familiar old song "Oranges and lemons, say the bells of St. Clement's" is halfway across the street, in the middle of the intersection of Fleet Street and The Strand. A creation of Sir Christopher Wren in 1681, this elegant church was completely destroyed during the bombings of World War II and rebuilt in its original style in 1958.

From here, follow Fleet Street east, past Ludgate Circus and up Ludgate Hill to ****St. Paul's Cathedral** (7). The surrounding office towers may rise higher, but the 111-meter- (364-foot-) high dome of this majestic church, whether it is viewed from up close or from such vantage points as Waterloo Bridge, still seems to be the loftiest structure in London.

St. Paul's Cathedral

In 1675, Sir Christopher Wren began to build St. Paul's on the site of the old cathedral, an enormous Gothic structure (with a spire even higher than the new dome) that burned to the ground in the Great Fire of 1666. (The first St. Paul's, founded in 604, burned in 1087. London almost lost St. Paul's a third time, during the blitz of World War II when bombs rained on the church night after night, but brave citizens brushed the bombs from the roofs and put out the fires.)

Wren watched the building of his cathedral (it took 33 years) from his house across the river. He was buried within the walls of his creation in 1723, 13 years after its completion. His tombstone reads, "Readers, if you seek his monument, look around you." The best place to observe the grandeur of the cathedral is from the *Whispering Gallery,* at the base of the painted dome, where a whisper travels full circle back to the whisperer, a curious acoustical phenomenon. A climb of another 542 steps brings you to the *Golden Gallery,* at the base of the lantern, and an unparalleled view over The City.

Other memorials in the cathedral commemorate the Duke of Wellington, Admiral Nelson, General Gordon, and Lord Kitchener, to name but a few of the illustrious Britons honored here. An effigy of John Donne, the poet and dean of the old St. Paul's, presides over the choir. He is wrapped in the death shroud he took to wearing before his death in 1631. The new high altar honors the 335,451 Britons who lost their lives in the two world wars.

From the rear of St. Paul's, follow Cannon Street east to its intersection with Victoria Street, where, on the left, you'll see *St. Mary Aldermary Church,* built by Sir Christopher Wren from 1681–1682 to replace an older structure destroyed in the Great Fire of 1666. The austere, imposing building with the colonnaded porch up the street on the right is **Mansion House** (8), built from 1729–1763 as the official residence of the Lord Mayor of London. Of the ornately decorated rooms, none is more elaborate than the Egyptian Hall, where official dinners are held. Since the Lord Mayor is autonomous in his control of The City, his house is equipped with law courts and cell blocks. The best time to see this important London personage is the second Saturday in November, when he parades with great ceremony to the Royal Courts of Justice on Fleet Street to be sworn in. The event is called the Lord Mayor's Show.

The *church of St. Stephen Walbrook* is just behind the Lord Mayor's residence. Built by Wren between 1672–1679, it served in part as a model for St. Paul's. The **Bank of England** (9), at the junction of eight busy streets across from Mansion House, is known simply as "The Bank," and the name applies as well to the financially oriented neighborhood. The Bank is Britain's central reserve and as such issues its notes and sets the nation's exchange rate. Its banal headquarters date from 1924–1939, although the building incorporates portions of a much more interesting bank that Sir John Soane erected on the site in 1788. The *Royal Exchange,* across the street, is the busy hub of Britain's futures market. Following King William Street south from The Bank, you will come to the imposing ***Monument,** (10) a column that Wren built from 1671–1677 to commemorate the Great Fire, which started in the nearby shop of the Royal Baker in Pudding Lane on September 2, 1666. A winding staircase in the center of the column, 67 meters (220 feet) tall and crowned by a gilded flame, leads to an observation platform, but the tiring climb merely brings you face to face with the glass walls of the surrounding office towers, which obscure the view in most directions.

From the Monument you may cross the Thames on the new *London Bridge* (11), built from 1967–1973 to replace the historic span of children's-song fame, which was indeed falling down under the weight of modern London's traffic. The famous bridge, built in 1749 to replace a 12th-century structure, is now the incongruous main attraction at a shopping center in Arizona. The roads and railroad tracks that surround

**Southwark Cathedral (12), at the south end of the bridge, make it difficult to appreciate the beauty of this impressive structure, which was founded in 606 and rebuilt in 1206 as one of Europe's great Gothic cathedrals. John Harvard, the founder of the American university, was baptized here in 1607. Chaucer's friend and fellow poet John Gower is one of the many notable Londoners of the past who are buried here.

Returning to the north shore of the Thames, turn right on Lower Thames Street and follow it past Wren's *church of St. Magnus the Martyr* to the *****Tower of London** (13). This massive enclosure of 13 towers and massive fortifications replaces the wooden fort that William the Conqueror built here on the banks of the Thames in 1066. Although the Tower was the residence of British monarchs until 1603, it is best known as the prison where the likes of Sir Walter Raleigh, Anne Boleyn, and, as recently as the last world war, Rudolf Hess were confined, and where many a royal head was lopped off on the executioner's block.

A tour of the Tower (London's most popular tourist attraction, so arrive early) begins at the drawbridge near the river, guarded since 1485 by Yeoman Warders, or Beefeaters. Visitors then continue through *Traitors' Gate,* so-called because it was here that prisoners returning from trial at Westminster learned their fates.

(Guards turned their swords toward the accused and away from the innocent.) The *Bloody Tower,* opposite, is where Richard III, eager to secure the throne, allegedly murdered his young prince-nephews in 1485. Sir Walter Raleigh spent 13 years here, filling his days by writing his ambitious history of the world. A passageway through the Bloody Tower leads to the large, grassy enclosure at the center of the fort. Here, in the half-timbered *Queen's House,* Guy Fawkes was questioned and tortured for his involvement in the Gunpowder Plot of 1605, which is commemorated every November 5. The Crown Jewels are kept in the *Jewel House* in the 19th-century *Waterloo Barracks.* Among the most awesome of these royal treasures are the heavy crown made for the coronation of Charles II in 1660 and worn by monarchs ever since, and the crown that the Queen Mother wore at her coronation in 1937. The latter contains the 109-carat Koh-i-Noor diamond, a 14th-century stone presented to Queen Victoria. The *White Tower,* the oldest structure in the Tower, houses behind its thick, 900-year-old stone walls an amazing collection of arms and armor. *St. John's Chapel,* on the second floor, dates from 1080. It is London's oldest preserved church and a perfect example of Norman architecture, a place used in Medieval times for pre-coronation vigils and lying in state. The gruesome history of the

White Tower

Tower of London, though, is best seen in *Beauchamp Tower,* its walls covered with the scribblings of the legion of prisoners confined there over the centuries, and in *Bowyer Tower,* where there is a macabre exhibition of torture devices.

Tower Bridge

The Tower looks especially imposing from the river and the suspended walkway between the two towers of the *Tower Bridge,* built from 1886–1894. The two 990-metric-ton (1,100-ton) sections of the drawbridge can be raised in a mere 90 seconds. The fastest way back to the center of the city from here is by underground, from the London Bridge station on the south bank of the river or the Tower Hill stop, on the north side of the Tower.

Other Sights in London

What follows are many of the other sights of interest in London that are not located on the routes of the previous four walks. They are, nonetheless, fascinating places to visit and well worth a detour. You may want to incorporate them in one of the four walks outlined above. The underground stations closest to each are given in parentheses ( ).

*Barbican Center (Barbican, Moorgate): London's newest art center is set beside a rather formidably dark residential complex very close to the Museum of London. It is the present home of the *Royal Shakespeare Company* and incorporates auditoria for theater, music, and cinema, conference suites, restaurants, snack bars, and exhibition galleries. The best spot in the complex is a pleasant terrace for outdoor eating that overlooks a fountain pool and beyond that one of London's beautiful old churches. The *Guildhall School of Music and Drama* is also located in this complex.

*Chelsea Hospital, Royal Hospital Road (Sloane Square): The history of this retirement home for veterans, built by Sir Christopher Wren between 1682–1692, is summed up in a Latin inscription in the Figure Court at the center of the compound that translates "For the relief and support of maimed and superannuated soldiers, founded by Charles II, expanded by James II and completed by King William and Queen Mary." The hospital is still home to 400 Chelsea pensioners, who take meals in the paneled Great Hall and worship in the barrel-vaulted chapel, as have generations of British soldiers.

Cheyne Walk (Sloane Square): The quiet, elegant streets of Chelsea are at their best on this elegant terrace of the late 17th century. Artistic temperaments seem to be especially susceptible to Cheyne Walk's charms: George Eliot lived at number 4, Dante Gabriel Rossetti lived at number 16, J.M. Turner at 119 . . . and so on. (The houses are marked with plaques honoring the famous past occupants.) While you're in the neighborhood—one of London's most desirable—walk around the corner to 24 Cheyne Row and tour the *home of Thomas Carlyle* (1795–1881), the Scottish historian. This, one of the oldest houses in Chelsea, is crammed with his memorabilia.

Cleopatra's Needle, Victoria Embankment (Charing Cross, Embankment): This obelisk, rising incongruously beside the Thames, was erected in ancient Egypt 3,500 years ago under Thutmose III. There is a companion obelisk in New York's Central Park.

**The Courtauld Institute Galleries, Woburn Square (Russell Square, Goodge Street): This relatively small assemblage of art bequests to London University is a very choice one. Almost every work at the Courtauld is a masterpiece: 32 paintings by Rubens, 12 by Tiepolo, and one of the world's best collections of works by Impressionists and Post-Impressionists.

Covent Garden (Covent Garden): This neighborhood has kept its famous name, although its character has changed considerably from the time when it was the center of the wholesale food market. Visitors will think of George Bernard Shaw's *Pygmalion*, of Eliza Doolittle, and Henry Higgins when they visit, and indeed, there is still a young woman who dresses in Eliza costume and hawks posies as the fictional girl did. The Garden, as the covered marketplace that adjoins the Royal Opera House is called,

is now a center of dozens of smart, trendy shops of every description (also see page 312). There still remains an aura of street-market character in parts of the neighborhood, though, and street entertainers provide a variety of diversions for the onlooker. The Strand marks the southern boundary of the Garden. The area abounds in pubs, restaurants, and theaters, as does the adjoining West End, and as a result, streets here are always very lively. Historic buses, trolleys, and other vehicles of the *London Transport Museum* are now parked in an area adjacent to the old market.

Charles Dickens' House, 48 Doughty Street (Russell Square): Dickens lived here only two years, from 1837–1839, but during that time he wrote *Oliver Twist, Nicholas Nickleby,* and several other works. Letters, manuscripts, and other memorabilia are on display.

Docklands: For centuries the miles of Thames-side docks that stretch east of the town were jammed with goods and humanity. Colorful their past may be, but the docks have seen better days. They have seen worse days, too, and are now rebounding from their post-war slump with a great burst of redevelopment, overseen by the London Docklands Development Corporation. One of the best ways to see the new *Billingsgate Market* on the Isle of Dogs and other signs of rebirth is from the deck of a Thames cruise boat on your way to Hampton Court or Greenwich (see page 58).

*Gray's Inn, High Holborn (Chancery Lane): This ancient society of lawyers, one of London's four Inns of Court, was founded in the 14th century and was the scene, in 1594, of the first performance of Shakespeare's *Comedy of Errors.* The Inn's architectural treasures include 16th-century glass windows in the hall, and the gardens, designed by Sir Francis Bacon (1561–1626), a famous member of the Inn.

*Guildhall, Aldermanbury (Bank): The administrative headquarters of the City of London was built between 1411–1425 and has undergone many changes since then. The mixed Classical and Gothic façades are late 18th century. The banners of the 12 historic trade guilds of London (grocers, drapers, etc.) hang in the Great Hall, which retains more of its Medieval character than most of the Guildhall. The work of one of these guilds, 700 timepieces, is on display in the adjoining *Museum of the Worshipful Company of Clockmakers.* The curios include a silver clock in the shape of a skull that opens its jaws to reveal the time.

Hampstead Heath (Hampstead): These days the view of London from this magnificent expanse of heath is not very much like the one painted by John Constable. Little matter, because a ramble over the heath—seemingly as wild as the Yorkshire moors—can still happily fill the better part of a day, all the more so if you have had your fill of London traffic and crowds. The heath has man-made attractions, too, foremost among them *Kenwood House,* an 18th-century mansion with restaurants, a teahouse in the garden, and an incredible collection of paintings by the likes of Rembrandt and Turner. The village of *Hampstead* is a delight in itself, with quaint old streets lined with shops and pubs (the most notable ones are *Jack Straw's Castle* and the *Spaniard's Inn*) and, in *Keats' Grove,* the house where the poet lived with his lover, Fanny Brawne.

**Hayward Gallery, South Bank Arts Centre (Waterloo): This gallery, built in 1968 on terraced levels facing the Thames, houses changing art exhibitions of particular interest.

*The Imperial War Museum, Lambeth Road (Lambeth North): Housed in an early-19th-century building that was once an insane asylum, this remarkable collection contains uniforms, weapons, warship models, and other artifacts from the two world wars.

London Toy and Model Museum, 23 Craven Hill (Queensway; Bayswater): A Victorian house is the perfect setting for this amazing collection of toys. Play forts, models, Dinky toys, model railroads, and the like make this a favorite London stop for kids and for serious toy collectors.

**Museum of London, 15 London Wall (St. Paul's, Barbican). Some of London's oldest artifacts, including Stone Age tools and Roman sculpture, are displayed in the most up-to-date fashion. Special lighting effects allow visitors to watch a re-creation of the Great Fire engulfing the old City. Entire streets are brought back to life in painstakingly accurate reconstructions. The Lord Mayor's ceremonial coach, trotted out but once a year for his parade (see page 50), is on permanent display here.

*The Percival David Foundation of Chinese Art, 53 Gordon Square (Russell Square, Euston Square): This museum seems to be bursting with cabinet after cabinet of beautiful ceramic Chinese artworks, some of them from the Imperial collection in Peking.

*Royal Festival Hall, South Bank Arts Centre (Waterloo): This concert hall, one of the best in Europe with its 3,400 seats, superb acoustics, and a stunning location on the banks of the Thames, was built for the Festival of Britain and completed in 1956.

Royal Mews, Buckingham Palace Road (Victoria): The royal stables house the monarch's coaches, carriages, and landaus, many of them still in use.

Somerset House, The Strand (Aldwych): This long, impressive, 18th-century riverfront building occupies the site of a palace built by the Duke of Somerset in the 16th century. Previously the headquarters of the British Navy and the Registry of Births, Deaths and Marriages, the building now houses the Board of Inland Revenue; its staterooms are open for temporary exhibitions.

**St. Bartholomew-the-Great, Little Britain (Barbican): The second oldest church in London (after the chapel in the Tower) preserves only the 1143 Norman chancel of the once great Romanesque church.

*St. Etheldreda (also known as Ely Chapel), Ely Place (Farringdon): This Roman Catholic church, built in 1290, has changed hands and functions many times and has been a residence, a prison, and a hospital. Largely destroyed during the bombings of World War II, only portions of its Medieval grandeur, including the timber-roofed crypt, survive.

Smithfield Market (Farringdon): London's wholesale meat market is housed in a splendidly characteristic Victorian iron structure. The sight of hundreds of raw carcasses hanging from hooks may not be one of the world's most aesthetically attractive sights, but it is rather an awesome one for those with the stomachs to take it. You can turn away and partake of a delicious meal (which often includes some of the best available meat!) in one of the local pubs or cafés. Definitely not an experience for vegetarians.

*Staple Inn, Holborn (Chancery Lane): Two black-and-white timbered Elizabethan houses form the façade of this 14th-century complex. Built for the guild of wool merchants and home to Dr. Johnson from 1759–1760, it is now headquarters for the Society of Actuaries. The Inn strikes an enchanting note on this commercial and otherwise modern street.

**Tate Gallery, Millbank (Westminster): Sir Henry Tate, a sugar tycoon, gave his sizable collection of British paintings to the nation in 1892. Since then the Tate has grown into one of the world's finest museums. Its collections can be divided into two parts: British art from the 16th–20th centuries, with works by Hogarth, Reynolds, Gainsborough, Constable, Millais, Whistler, Moore, and virtually every other British artist of note; and the modern collection, with works by Picasso, Mondrian, Munch, and an exhaustive collection of other 20th-century artists. The new (1987) *Clore Gallery* displays a marvelous collection of paintings by Turner with great panache and reverence.

*Westminster Cathedral, Ashley Place (Westminster, Victoria): The major Roman Catholic church in England was built of red-and-white-striped brick in the Byzantine style from 1895–1903 and is modeled after Santa Sophia in Istanbul. The striking interior walls of the cathedral are decorated with mosaics, though the lower portions are faced with white marble and granite. The view from the top of the 94-meter- (308-foot-) high campanile (elevator) is marvelous. So are the cathedral's acoustics. This is a popular setting for concerts.

Day Trips from London

Visitors to England and armies that over the centuries have planned invasions have something in common: They both find that the country is so compact that it is easy to get from one point to another. London is close enough to other parts of England—and roads and public transportation are so good—that you can get there and back in a day. All of the following places are included in more detail in our Travel Routes. However, since the Routes are geared to automobile travel, here we also tell you how to get to these destinations by public transportation.

Bath (see Travel Route 7; page 153): There was a time when every grand tour included a stop and a rest cure at this elegant Georgian city, whose baths were popular even among the Roman legions. By train, from Paddington Station (about 70 minutes); by bus, from Victoria Coach Station (about three hours).

Brighton (see Travel Route 5; page 132): Combine sea air with one of the world's most eccentric palaces, Brighton Pavilion, and a lively boardwalk, and you have a good day's outing. By train, from Victoria Station (about one hour); by bus, from Victoria Coach Station (about one hour 45 minutes).

Cambridge (see Travel Route 13; page 184): One of England's greatest seats of scholarship also happens to be one of its greenest, most charming cities. By train, from Liverpool Street Station (about one hour); by bus, from Victoria Coach Station (two hours).

Canterbury (see Travel Route 1; page 113): This magnificent cathedral city was a pilgrimage sight for centuries; it still is. By train, from Victoria Station, (80 minutes); by bus, from Victoria Coach Station (two hours).

Greenwich (see Travel Route 1; page 113): The old buildings of this ancient port city tell the history of Britain's naval power. By train, from Charing Cross (10 minutes); by bus, number 53 from Piccadilly Circus (about one hour); by boat—the best way, providing a good look at the gentrified docks and warehouses of London—from Westminster Pier (45 minutes).

Hampton Court (see Travel Route 7; page 153): This palace is so charming that Henry VIII felt compelled to steal it from Cardinal Wolsey. By train, from Waterloo (35 minutes); by bus, Green Line coaches number 715, 718, and 728 from Eccleston Bridge; by boat, from Westminster Pier (45 minutes).

Kew Gardens (see Travel Route 7; page 153): Even non-gardeners are taken in by this exuberant and expert display of blossoms and foliage. By underground, District line to Kew Gardens stop (about 50 minutes); by boat, from Westminster Pier (about 85 minutes).

Knole (see Travel Route 8; page 160): England's largest private home has 365 rooms and grounds as big as all outdoors. By train, from Charing Cross to Sevenoaks (about 30 minutes); by bus, Green Line numbers 705 or 706 to Sevenoaks, from Buckingham Palace Road near Victoria Station (about 90 minutes).

Oxford (see Travel Route 16; page 196): One of the world's greatest universities occupies some of the world's finest buildings. By train, from Paddington Station (one hour); by bus, from Victoria Coach Station (two hours).

Rye (see Travel Route 5; page 132): A Medieval town for the romantically minded that was the adopted home of Henry James.

By train, from Charing Cross, change at Ashford (two hours).

Stratford-upon-Avon (see Travel Route 19; page 215): The hometown of William Shakespeare is a literary mecca. By train and bus, "The Shakespeare Connection," from Euston Station (about two hours).

Winchester (see Travel Route 3; page 123): The former capital of England is still steeped in history. By train, from Waterloo (about one hour): by bus, from Victoria Coach Station (about two hours)

Windsor Castle (see Travel Route 7; page 153): The royal residence is also the world's largest inhabited castle. By train, from Paddington, with change at Slough (about 30 minutes); By bus, Green Line number 700 from Eccleston Bridge (about 90 minutes).

**Cambridge

96 km. (60 miles) north of London; by train, frequent service from Liverpool Street Station; by bus, from Victoria Coach Station; by car, Routes A 10 or M 11.

Cambridge is a small city of about 100,000 inhabitants that is famous above all for its distinguished university. For 800 years, Cambridge, along with Oxford, has been the breeding ground of British intellectuals, who in turn have not always been kind to their alma mater. "For Cambridge people rarely smile, being urban, squat, and packed with guile," wrote the poet Rupert Brooke in 1912. His classmate and fellow poet A. E. Housman once said, "I find Cambridge an asylum, in more senses than one." These statements hardly do justice to Cambridge, which, with its Medieval streets and sedate college buildings and its quiet, lovely river, the Cam, has charmed generations of students and visitors.

Cambridge is at its best in spring and summer, when its many ancient trees are in full leaf and the college gardens are in bloom. May Week, which actually occupies ten days in June, is a time of boat races, concerts, formal balls, and much unabashed merrymaking, all of it repeated again a month later during the annual Cambridge Festival. A different, and perhaps more typical, view of Cambridge is to be had on a winter's day, though, when the wind blows across the surrounding fens and students crowd the pubs and tearooms for some truly serious chatter.

History

Despite its Roman origins, the history of Cambridge really begins in the 12th century, when a *universitas scholarium* in Cambridge began to be recognized throughout England. From that time on, the history of Cambridge tells the story of the university that has educated some of the greatest minds in England and Europe. Erasmus, the Dutch scholar, was Cambridge's first teacher of Greek. Samuel Pepys (d. 1703), Britain's famous 17th-century diarist, attended Cambridge, and his journals are on display in the Pepysian Library at the university's Magdalene College. Sir Isaac Newton taught at Cambridge from 1669–1701. William Wordsworth studied here in the late 18th century, as did Lord Byron and Alfred, Lord Tennyson, in the 19th century. (Byron shared his rooms at Trinity College with a pet bear.) Since 1869, Cambridge has admitted women, who now number prominently among the 700 professors, readers, and lecturers and 10,000 students at the university's 25 colleges.

Bridge of Sighs over the Cam River

Attractions

See map on page 62.

As large as modern-day Cambridge is, it has the look and appearance of a market town, as indeed it has been for the past 1,000 or so years. Appropriately, the center of Cambridge is **Market Hill** (1), where a lively market, with goods as diverse as apples and Wellingtons, is held weekday mornings. The imposing, English-Gothic *church of St. Mary's the Great,* built between 1478–1514, is here, as is the *Guildhall,* Cambridge's town hall.

Wherever you are in Cambridge, you are never far from the university, and the buildings of some of Cambridge's most famous and interesting colleges surround Market Hill. Many of them can be reached on the town's major thoroughfare, Kings Parade, which changes its name as it winds through Cambridge to Trinity Street, St. John's Street,

and Trumpington Street. Following is an itinerary that will take you to some of Cambridge's most impressive colleges and other sights. Should you have only a short time to spend in Cambridge (it is an easy excursion from London) you will not want to miss these quintessential Cambridge sights: *King's College Chapel,* Cambridge's favorite place of worship; *The Great Court* at Trinity College, the most imposing and famous of the university's many famous courtyards; *King's Parade,* the town's main street which always bustles with students and their professors; and *The Backs,* as the expanse of greenery behind the colleges and along the River Cam is called. The only way to see Cambridge is on foot (beware, however, of the ubiquitous bicycles), and no place in the world is better suited to a leisurely ramble.

Senate House (2), at the junction of Market Hill and King's Parade, is the stately administrative headquarters of the university and the scene of elegant balls and other formal functions. It was built by architect James Gibbs from 1722–1730. Beyond it, on the west side of King's Parade, stretch the *Old Schools,* which house the university's first lecture rooms, some of them dating from as early as 1350. Behind the Old Schools is **Clare College** (3), founded in 1338 by Lady Elizabeth de Clare, who was three times widowed by the age of 29 and subsequently

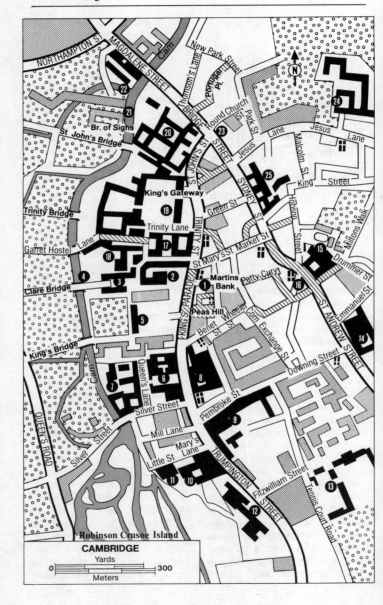

NORTHAMPTON ST.

MAGDALENE STREET

Cam

New Park Street

Thomson's Lane

Portugal Pl.

22

21

MAGDALENE BRIDGE

Round Church ST.

Park St.

23

Jesus Lane

24

Jesus Lane

Malcolm St.

Br. of Sighs

St John's Bridge

20

ST. JOHN'S ST.

Jesus

SYDNEY STREET

King Street

25

Hobson Street

Trinity Bridge

King's Gateway

Green St.

Miltons Walk

19

Trinity Lane

TRINITY ST.

St Mary's St.

Market St.

15

Drummer St.

Garret Hostel Lane

17

18

St Andrew's

4

3

2

1

Martins Bank

Petty, Cury

16

Clare Bridge

Cam

5

Peas Hill

Benet St.

Wheeler St.

Corn Exchange St.

Downing Street

14

ST. ANDREW'S

King's Bridge

QUEEN'S ROAD

Queen's Lane

7

6

8

Emmanuel St.

Silver Street

Pembroke St.

9

QUEEN'S ROAD

Cam

Silver Street

Mill Lane

Little St. Mary's Lane

11

10

TRUMPINGTON STREET

Fitzwilliam Street

13

Tennis Court Road

12

Robinson Crusoe Island

CAMBRIDGE

Yards

0 — 300

Meters

devoted her energies to good works. **Clare Bridge** (4) leads from the lovely, 17th-century Renaissance buildings of the old college on one side of the Cam to *Clare Gardens* on the other, where there is a bronze sculpture of the *Unknown Warrior* by Henry Moore and the *New Court of Clare*, built from 1924–1929.

***King's College** (5) is south of Clare on King's Parade. The King in question is Henry VI, who in 1440 leveled most of Medieval Cambridge and set about building the largest, most impressive college in the land. The War of the Roses put an end to the King's plans, although he did manage to start **King's Chapel*, which Henry VIII completed in 1515. This, the most famous of Cambridge's many chapels, is one enormous room, 96 meters (315 feet) long, 15

King's College Chapel

meters (49 feet) wide, and 25 meters (82 feet) high, lit by 25 stained-glass windows that depict the life of Christ. Rubens's painting *The Adoration of the Magi* adorns the altar. The poet William Wordsworth, an alumnus whose brother taught at Cambridge, described the chapel's vaulted, honeycombed ceiling as "ten thousand cells where light and shade repose."

St. Catherine's College (6), just south of King's College, was founded in 1473, rebuilt from 1674–1757, and added onto from 1932–1951. **Queens' College* (7), behind St. Catherine's, is reached through a gateway off Queens' Lane. Although Margaret of Anjou, wife of Henry VI, founded this picturesque college in 1448, Elizabeth Woodville, the wife of Edward IV, saw the brick buildings, which surround unaltered Tudor courtyards, through to their completion in 1456. From 1510–1513, the scholar Erasmus lived in the tower now known as *Erasmus Tower*, which is just to the south of *Cloister Court*, with its sundial and half-timbered façades. From here, the *Mathematicians Bridge* (so called because the structure was held together by gravity alone until a curious, 19th-century scholar took the bridge apart to discover the principle and was able to get it back together again (only by using steel pins) crosses the Cam to *Queens' Gardens*.

**Corpus Christi* (8) is across King's Parade from St. Catherine's. The Medieval *Old Court,* begun in 1377, is the oldest courtyard in Cambridge. It is a sobering thought indeed that the court and its surrounding buildings were already 200 years old when Christopher Marlowe, who many consider to be England's second greatest playwright, studied here in the 16th century. The college *library* houses England's oldest and best collection of Anglo-Saxon manuscripts, bequeathed by the Archbishop of Canterbury in 1575, and Thomas à Becket's prayer book. The college *Hall* is hung with canvases by Poussin, Reynolds, and other masters.

Corpus Christi is surrounded by two churches: *St. Bene't's,* with a Saxon tower from 1050 that is said to be the oldest structure in Cambridge, to the north; and *St. Bodolph's,* built in the 15th century, to the south. Just beyond St. Bodolph's is ***Pembroke College** (9), founded in 1347 by the Duchess of Pembroke. The college is known as the *Collegium Episcopale,* because of the large number of bishops it has educated. (The college has also produced several poets, among them Herbert Spencer.) In keeping with its reputation, Pembroke's most famous building is its chapel, Christopher Wren's first building, completed in 1664.

The oldest college at Cambridge is ***Peterhouse** (10), also known as St. Peter's, founded in 1281. Thomas Gray, the poet, was a student at Peterhouse in the early 18th century, and he wrote his famous "Elegy in a Country Churchyard" here. (Actually, the poet, who was deathly afraid of fire, left the college for Pembroke in anger when his fellow students set off a false alarm that sent him scrambling down the rope ladder outside his rooms.)

Cambridge is also a city of museums, and several of its finest are nearby. The science museums and laboratories on Downing Street are known collectively as the ***New Museums.** The *Museum of Archaeology and Anthropology* (11) houses a fine collection of artifacts from faraway lands, including the Americas and the Pacific Islands, and from as near as Cambridge itself. The nearby *Museum of Zoology* houses a fine, though poorly displayed, collection of wildlife specimens. The *Sedgwick Museum of Geology* is one of the world's finest. Cambridge's premier museum is the ***Fitzwilliam** (12), on Trumpington Street. Based on the pieces that the Viscount Fitzwilliam bequeathed to the university in 1816, the museum now houses an extensive collection of Egyptian, Greek, Roman, and Chinese art; a large and eclectic array of European paintings, with works by Leonardo da Vinci, Hogarth, Reynolds, Whistler, Monet, Gauguin, Tintoretto, and many, many others; and many historic documents, including Keats's original manuscript of his poem "Ode to a Nightingale."

From the front of the museum,

Emmanuel College

Fitzwilliam Street leads through *Downing College* (13), with somber Neoclassical buildings that surround an enormous court, to **Emmanuel College** (14). It was founded in 1584 on the site of a Dominican monastery, some of which has been incorporated into its buildings. Americans have a special affinity for this college, which graduated John Harvard, founder of the most Cambridge-like university in the United States, and several other Pilgrim fathers. The educator, who died in 1638 at age 31, just one year after his arrival in the colonies, is commemorated by a stained-glass window in the chapel, built in 1677 to designs by Sir Christopher Wren. The spacious gardens of Emmanuel, built around a pond, are among the loveliest in Cambridge. The largest and most celebrated gardens at Cambridge, though, are those of nearby ***Christ's College** (15), founded in 1505 by Lady Margaret Beaufort, the mother of Henry VII. John Milton was a student

here from 1625–1627. Two of his best-remembered accomplishments at Christ's are planting a mulberry tree, which still grows in the garden, and the composition of a college exercise that has come to be considered one of his finest works, "Hymn on Christ's Nativity."

In the *church of St. Andrew's* (16), across St. Andrew's Street from Christ's College, there is a chapel honoring the family of British seafarer Captain Cook, whose voyages took him as far from home as Tahiti and Hawaii, where he was killed by natives in 1779, at the age of 51. St. Andrew's is just a short walk down Petty Curry, a narrow lane, from *Market Hill* (1), where you can begin a tour of the colleges on the northern end of Cambridge.

The large, imposing gate facing the Senate House is the *Gate of Honour,* which opens into Cambridge's medical school, **Gonville & Caius College** (17). Next door is *Trinity Hall* (18), Cambridge's only college to retain the "Hall" in its name and the university's foremost school for lawyers.

Just beyond is ***Trinity College** (19), Cambridge's largest and perhaps most famous college. A statue of Henry VIII, who founded Trinity in 1546, presides over the imposing *Great Gateway.* Trinity's famous literary alumni include Alfred, Lord Tennyson, Lord Byron (who bathed nude in the fountain in the enormous Great Court, where Isaac Newton measured the speed of

Trinity College

sound for the first time under the surrounding arcade), A. E. Housman, and Vladimir Nabokov. It has also graduated the statesman Lord Acton, the composer Ralph Vaughan Williams, the philosophers Ludwig Wittgenstein and Bertrand Russell, the kings Edward VII and George VI, and the current Prince of Wales, Charles. Isaac Newton taught at Trinity from 1669–1701. Statues of many of these august fellows populate Trinity's imposing courts. The *library*, facing Cloister's Court on one side and the Cam on another, was built by Christopher Wren from 1676–1695. Its elaborately carved bookcases, by Grinling Gibbons, house some of England's rarest manuscripts, including those by Milton, Tennyson, and other literary alumni.

*St. John's College (20), just to the north of Trinity College, was founded by Lady Margaret Beaufort, mother of Henry VII, in 1511. The college's most dramatic work of architecture, the **Bridge of Sighs** (21), built across the Cam in the style of its Venetian namesake in 1831, leads to another architectural curiosity, the gaudy *New Court,* finished at the same time as the bridge, and the new (1966) but lovely riverside *Cripps Building.* St. John's also has many fine, old courts and halls, including the Elizabethan, rose-colored *Second Court,* which the essayist John Ruskin praised as the finest in Cambridge. A door on the north side leads to the *Combination Room,* a handsome paneled hall with a painted ceiling.

Magdalene College (22) was the recipient of the library of Samuel Pepys, the greatest of all British diarists. The books, including his diary, are on display in the *Pepysian Library* in the Second Court, arranged in their

View of St. John's College

book presses just as Pepys left them when he died in 1703. Other sights at Magdalene, which was founded in 1542, are the *Hall* (1519) with a magnificent double staircase and the timber-roofed *chapel* (late 15th century).

Crossing the Cam again and heading back toward the center of town on Bridge Street, you will soon come to the ***church of the Holy Sepulchre** (23), also known as the Round Church, of which it is one of five in England. Built in 1130 as a replica of its namesake in Jerusalem, the church has been restored many times since then. Just down Bridge Street, Jesus Lane leads off toward ***Jesus College** (24), which the Bishop of Ely founded on the site of a nunnery in 1496. Since the Bishop left most of the original buildings intact (he sim-

ply added to the Cloister Court and made the nun's refectory the Hall), Jesus is Cambridge's most Medieval college, even though its chapel, which incorporates remains of a Norman church, is lit by flamboyantly 19th-century stained-glass windows by William Morris, A. C. Pugin, and others. Samuel Taylor Coleridge was already writing verse when he arrived at Jesus in 1790.

Back toward Bridge Street, which has now become Sidney Street, is **Sidney Sussex College** (25), founded in 1596 in the buildings of another religious order, Franciscan monks. The place was redone in Gothic style in 1832. A portrait of the college's most famous graduate, Sir Oliver Cromwell, graces the Hall. From here, Sidney Street leads back to Market Hill.

**Canterbury

98 km. (61 miles) southeast of London, near the coast of Kent; by train, frequent service from Victoria Station; by bus, from Victoria Coach Station; by car, A 2 and M 2.

History has unleashed fires, civil strife, and bombings on Canterbury, but this pretty town of 33,000 inhabitants has withstood well the ravages of the ages. Indeed, the past is in glorious evidence in Canterbury—in the Roman remains, the Medieval walls and towers, and above all, in the magnificent cathedral.

History

Pilgrims—as celebrated in Chaucer's 14th-century masterwork, *The Canterbury Tales*—have made their way to Canterbury in homage to Archbishop Thomas à Becket since 1170, when knights of Henry II burst into the cathedral and murdered him. (The first of these pilgrims was the penitent Henry himself. As the bells tolled, the King walked down St. Peter's Street to the cathedral, where he received five lashes from every bishop and three from each of 80 monks for his frightful deed.)

Canterbury was an important place long before Thomas's murder. A commercial outpost of the Roman Empire, the town became the capital of Saxon Kent in 560. Shortly thereafter, Saint Augustine arrived at the court of King Ethelbert; he soon established an abbey and became its first Archbishop. Since then, Archbishops of Canterbury have been the chief primates of England, first among subjects of the Monarch, and members of the House of Lords. Even so, the relationship between the Archbishop and the Crown has not always been an easy one. Thomas à Becket's insistence that the Church came before the state cost him his life. When Henry VIII broke with the Church in 1535, he destroyed much of the cathedral, taking special vengeance on Thomas's tomb, and its gold and gems, as well as on the saint's bones, which vanished into obscurity. Puritan fanatics ravaged Canterbury and the cathedral again in the 17th century. The most fervent of them, "Blue Dick" Culmer, scaled the church's soaring stone walls to smash as many windows as he could—"Proud Becket's glassie bones," he called them. Some 10,000 German bombs rained down on Canterbury on the night of June 1, 1942. The cathedral was spared only because of the bravery of townsfolk, who climbed to the roof to brush away incendiary bombs.

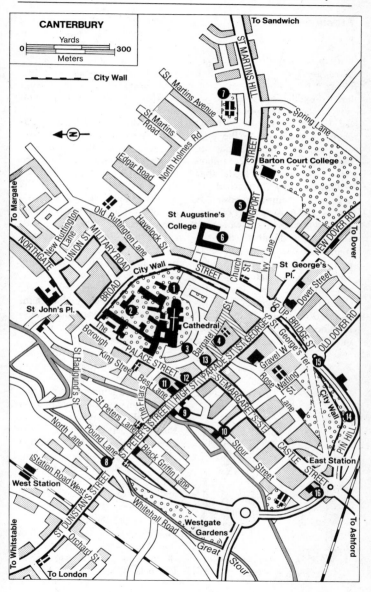

CANTERBURY

Yards
0 — 300
Meters

City Wall

N

To Sandwich

ST MARTINS HILL

St Martins Avenue

St Martins Road

North Holmes Rd

Edgar Road

Old Ruttington Lane

Havelock St

To Margate

New Ruttington Lane

NORTHGATE

UNION ST

MILITARY ROAD

BROAD

City Wall

St John's Pl.

The Borough

PALACE STREET

King Street

St Radigund's St

St Peters Lane

North Lane

Pound Lane

West Station

St DUNSTAN'S STREET

Station Road West

Orchard St.

To Whitstable

To London

Whitehall Road

Great

Stour

Westgate Gardens

Spring Lane

Barton Court College

St Augustine's College

LONGPORT

Ivy Lane

St George's Pl.

New Dover Rd

To Dover

Cathedral

STREET

Church St

Dover Street

STOUR ST

BRIDGE ST

St George's St

St George's Ter

Gravel W

Rose Lane

WATLING ST

OLD DOVER RD

Old Dover Rd

ST MARGARET'S ST

Castle Street

Stour Street

City Wall

PIN HILL

East Station

To Ashford

Best Lane

The Friars

ST PETER'S STREET

HIGH ST

PARADE

Bargate

Black Griffin Lane

St John's Pl.

7

5

6

1

2

3

4

13

11

12

9

10

8

15

14

16

Attractions

See map on page 69.

Little has changed in Canterbury since Becket's murder. Before Henry VIII did away with sainthood altogether in 1540, Thomas was England's favorite saint. By the 16th century there were 63 churches dedicated to the popular martyr, though none of these places was more important, and more visited, than ***Canterbury Cathedral** (1). This massive edifice, whose gray towers (the most famous of them is the central one, known as Bell Harry) still dominate the surrounding countryside, was begun in 1070 and not completed until 1503. Though Canterbury ranks only ninth in size among the cathedrals of England, its many admirers consider it to be the most beautiful and architecturally interesting. Canterbury is unique

Canterbury Cathedral

among British cathedrals in that it is "rounded off" at its east end. This peculiar configuration allowed 14th-century architect William de Sens to preserve two Norman side chapels, one to Saint Anselm and the other to Saint Andrew.

Cathedral tours depart regularly from the main entrance, where a useful floor plan pinpoints the many details of the interior. While the intricately designed and decorated cathedral is worthy of a week-long study, visitors with limited time should be sure to see the following:

The stone-floored *nave,* broken by columns, slopes gently upwards toward a staircase leading to the *choir,* from which it is separated by a 15th-century *screen.* The figures of Henry V, Richard II, Ethelbert, Edward the Confessor, Henry IV, and Henry VI decorate the screen.

Trinity Chapel, with its stained-glass windows depicting the miracles of Saint Thomas, once housed a magnificent shrine to the martyr. Dismantled in 1538, all that remains of the shrine is a depression in the pavement, worn down by generation after generation of kneeling pilgrims. The chapel is also the final resting place of King Henry IV and Edward, the Black Prince. Among the other *tombs* in the cathedral are those of six Archbishops of Canterbury, located in the choir. The most interesting of them is that of Archbishop Chichele (1414–1443). Statues depict the holy man naked and in Bishop's robes.

The *Great Cloister,* which dates from 1397–1414, is surrounded by an arcade with remarkable painted vault-bosses, which include 40 shields. On the night of December 29, 1170, knights burst through a door on the north side of the cloister, surrounded Thomas à Becket, who was saying Vespers in the northwest transept (now called the *Martyrdom Chapel*), and murdered him. A blood-stained paving stone, allegedly sent to Rome as a relic, has been replaced by a slab that marks the spot where the slain saint is said to have fallen. The cloister also opens onto the *Chapter House,* the oldest part of which dates to 1320. The poet T. S. Eliot's play of Becket's martyrdom, *Murder in the Cathedral,* was performed here for the first time in 1935. "For where a saint has dwelt . . . there is holy ground, and the sanctity shall not depart from it," wrote Eliot of the cathedral.

Much of the cathedral's *stained glass,* carefully stored during World War II, dates from the 13th century. Among the earliest glass is that in a window known as the *"Poor Man's Bible,"* because the illiterate once learned their catechisms from its vitreous depictions of such Bible stories as Noah's Ark and the Wedding Feast at Cana.

French protestants, Huguenots, who fled their homeland during 16th-century persecutions took

Crypt

refuge in the *crypt,* which dates to the 11th century and is the oldest part of the cathedral. Their descendants still worship in a side chapel, known as "The Temple." Some of the best close-up views of the cathedral are to be had from the grounds of adjacent **King's School** (2), which occupies the buildings of a former monastery founded in the seventh century. The cathedral and the school still draw their water from a Norman *water tower* built in 1161. King's is an elite public (which means private in England) school for boys, and it counts among its alumni the 16th-century playwright Christopher Marlowe and 20th-century novelist W. Somerset Maugham. Maugham paints a dreary picture of the rigid life at King's in his autobiographical novel, *Of Human Bondage.* From the square on the west side of the cathedral, ***Christ Church Gateway** (3), a lovely Tudor

Christ Church Gateway

building built from 1507–1517, opens into Burgate Street. A left turn soon brings you to Butchery Lane and the **Roman Pavement** (4), as the ruins of a villa, once the home of a prosperous Roman family, are known. An intricate, mosaic floor and traces of a central heating system buried beneath the streets of Canterbury were unearthed during an air raid in 1942. They suggest that Roman Canterbury was a civilized and prosperous outpost. Farther along Burgate, past the Medieval city walls, is **St. Augustine's Abbey** (5), founded by the saint in 597 and until the 12th century one of the three most important Augustinian monasteries in Europe. King Ethelbert, Queen Bertha, Saint Augustine, and nine other early Archbishops of Canterbury are buried here. **St. Augustine's College** (6), a school for missionaries, now occupies several of the old abbey buildings, including

Cemetery Gate, built in 1369, and the *Entrance Gateway,* dating from 1300. Farther along Longport Street you will come to **St. Martin's Church** (7), of Saxon origin and built on the site of a fourth-century church of Roman Britain, which in turn replaced a Roman temple. Augustine baptized Saxon King Ethelbert at the baptismal font in the sixth century.

*West Gate (8), across town at the foot of St. Dunstan's Street on the banks of the River Stour, is the only one of Canterbury's original seven Medieval gates that wasn't reduced to rubble in the blitz of World War II. This is especially fortunate, because it is perhaps the most beautiful gate of its kind in England. Its massive towers, once a gruesome prison and place of execution, now house a pleasant museum of arms and armor, and from the top,

West Gate

you'll enjoy a magnificent view of the cathedral and town.

The *Weavers,* a group of houses where Huguenot refugees from France took up residence in the 16th century, stretch along the Stour tributary near Best Lane. The name, not surprisingly, refers to the trade with which the Huguenots earned their keep in their adopted country. Just beyond the *main post office,* on Stour Street, is the **Hospital of St. Thomas** (9), which was welcoming droves of pilgrims, come to Canterbury to worship at the shrine of slain Thomas, as early as the year 1180. The faithful were given bread, beer, and a bath in the river, which flows gently beneath the hospital's windows. Nearby is the *Poor Priests Hospital* (10), home to indigent priests during the Middle Ages. The restored building now houses the *Canterbury Heritage Exhibition,* which brings to life the city's history from Roman times up to 1942.

The Medieval buildings on and around *High Street* house the shops and offices of modern Canterbury, though they still speak strongly of the town's past. *Queen Elizabeth's Guest Chamber,* a lovely Tudor house from 1573, is now a tea shop. Debenham's department store was once the Chequer of Hope, where Chaucer used to stay when he was in town. The town library, the Slater Art Gallery, and a museum of antiquities (including a magnificent fifth-century silver hoard) occupy the *Beany Institute* (11) on High Street. The nearby *Guildhall* (12) went up in the 18th century. The souvenir shops along **Mercery Lane** (13)— which turns off High Street, passes the War Memorial, and leads to the cathedral—are no less gaudy now than they were 700 years ago, when they did a brisk business in Saint Thomas medallions and bottles of healing water from the well in the Cathedral crypt. (The wonder-giving pump is now affixed to the wall of H. V. Bacon and Sons, Leather Goods.)

Canterbury's pleasant city park, **Dane John** (14), was laid out on both sides of the old walls in 1790. *Invicta* (15), a steam locomotive from 1836, has been put out to pasture here, not too far from another remnant of the past, an imposing and solemn Norman castle from the year 1175, of which little remains but one massive tower.

Excursions

Sandwich (19 km., 12 miles, east of Canterbury on Route A 257): Among Americans, this lovely, unspoiled Medieval town is best known for one of its enterprising 18th-century earls, who ordered his cook to put a piece of meat between two slices of bread and in so doing invented the universally popular concoction. The town's more noble history includes the arrival here of many important personages: the Romans, who first set foot in Britain in A.D. 43, just up the River Stour at what is now Richborough Castle; the doomed Thomas à Becket, who landed here in 1170 after his self-imposed exile in France; and Richard the Lion-Hearted, who landed here in 1190 after his imprisonment in Austria. Sandwich was one of Britain's five major ports, called the Cinque Ports, though it is now a full 2 km. (1.2 miles) inland.

Many of the town's most impressive structures date from its seafaring days, among them the *Custom's House* on the Upper Strand, the Medieval *Fisher Gate*, and the old *quay*. Henry VIII built another gate house, the dank *Barbican*, to guard the Stour riverbank.

Canterbury is also near *Ramsgate, Margate,* and other popular English Channel resorts (see Travel Route 1; page 113).

**Lincoln

213 km. (133 miles) north of London; by train, frequent service, with connections at Newark North Gate, from King Cross Station; by car, Route A 1 to Newark and Route A 46 to Lincoln.

Lincoln's majestic cathedral soars high above the surrounding fens, yet, impressive as this holy edifice is, somehow it doesn't overshadow other reminders of the town's rich and important past. Indeed, the 74,000 residents of modern Lincoln hold a deep appreciation of all the generations, Romans and Normans among them, who have walked their steep streets, and as a result visitors are rewarded with a dazzling view of British history.

History

Ancient Britons were fighting for control of what they called "Lindcoit" long before the Romans arrived, in A.D. 47. The empire billeted its retired soldiers here, and these pensioners were an industrious lot. Before long the settlement could boast of city walls and fortifications, straight city streets, canals and fields on the surrounding plain, and an aqueduct. The town the Romans called Lin-Coln emerged as the most beautiful in Britain.

The town slumbered under the Anglo-Saxons, but under the Danes it became an important trade center—coins of the period, struck around Lincoln, have turned up in Scandinavia. The Normans, who conquered Britain in the 11th century, were Lincoln's most aggressive builders, putting up its mighty cathedral and massive castle. Their King, William the Conqueror, called Lincoln the "Fourth town in Britain;" only London, Winchester, and York were more important.

Lincoln made its Medieval fortune in wool, which it sent to Flanders to be woven into fabrics. Agriculture was the town's mainstay in the 19th century, when the surrounding, swamplike fens were drained, and since then industry (primarily machinery manufacture) has taken over. The tank was invented in Lincoln during the First World War and was used for the first time in the Battle of Flers-Courcellette, in France, in September 1916.

Attractions

See map on page 76.

By its sheer size and position atop a high hill, **Lincoln Cathedral** (1) makes itself known to visitors long before they have passed through the old city gates.

First built as a Norman church in the late 11th century, then devastated by an earthquake and resulting fire in 1185, Lincoln Cathedral as we know it today was rebuilt in the 13th–14th centuries. It is largely the work of Bishop Hugh of Avalon.

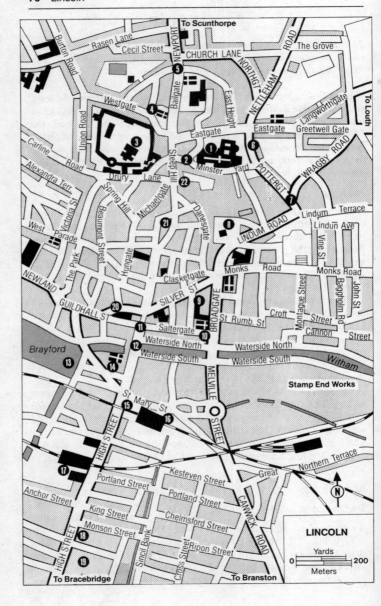

Lincoln Cathedral

Its three towers create much of the illusion of the fortlike cathedral's bulk. The central tower (lost in a wind storm long ago) was once the world's tallest spire, though its five-ton bell, *"Great Tom of Lincoln,"* still rings on the hour.

Despite its size, the cathedral has a friendly, human quality that may well be due to the copious figures that grace its façades and interior. Statues of 11 kings of England surround the main doorway on the *west façade.* Edward I and his two queens, Eleanor and Margaret preside over the flying buttresses on the *south façade.* A nearby gargoyle that glares menacingly upon the city is known as the "Devil looking over Lincoln." Inside, the Presbytery is called the *"Angel's Choir,"* because 30 seraphim, allegedly blown into the cathedral on a gust of wind, have alighted on the triforium. In their midst is the famous *Lincoln Imp,* a small devil who the vexed angels turned to stone.

Even the cathedral's magnificent *stained-glass windows* have been imbued with human qualities. There are two stunning rosettes, one called the *Bishop's Eye* (from 1325), because it looks out toward the Bishop's Palace, the other called the *Dean's Eye* (from 1220), because it overlooks the deanery. Among the noble and famous who are buried and commemorated in the cathedral are Catherine Swynford (longtime mistress of John of Gaunt, a warlike 14th-century Duke of Lancaster) and her daughter, the Countess of Westmoreland. A monument below the lovely east window honors Queen Eleanor I, whose final resting place is in Westminster Abbey. She died near Lincoln in 1290, and during the funeral procession to Westminster her mourners left the famous "Eleanor Crosses" at 12 places between Lincoln and Charing Cross, in London. A 14th-century shrine to Saint Hugh, the Bishop responsible for the cathedral, still stands proudly, a little the worse for wear, in front of the *Burghersh Chapel.*

The most striking of the cathedral's architectural treasures is the *main choir,* one of the earliest and best examples of pure English Gothic style. Its canopied and carved pews date from 1300. Beyond the 13th-century *cloister* is the ten-sided *Chapter House* dating from the same period. It occupies a special place in English history because the parliaments of Kings Edward I and Edward II met beneath its lovely vaulted roof, which fans out from a central column. One of the four original copies of the Magna Carta, the backbone of British government, is in the *Cathedral Library,* most of it built in the 17th century by Sir Christopher Wren.

If you leave the cathedral through the main entrance and pass through the 14th-century *Exchequer Gate* (2), you will be on *Castle Hill.* A short climb brings you to the ruins of **Lincoln Castle** (3), which stretches across two pleasantly planted hills. Only some walls and mounds remain of the once mighty fortress that William the Conqueror began to build around 1068, but *Cobb Hall,* a later, 13th-century tower that was for years a place of execution, still stands. The *Observatory Tower* is built over the base of a Norman tower; the view of the cathedral from its 19th-century turreted top is worth the climb up the steep, ladderlike steps. The *Assize Court,* from 1826, is also within the thick, herringbone-patterned Norman walls, as are the gloomy brick buildings that 19th-century Lincoln used as a prison. The prison *chapel,* with brick stalls designed so repentant prisoners could see the pulpit but not each other, is especially forbidding.

Bailgate Street, which cuts north and south between the cathedral and the castle, leads through Roman Lincoln. Circles on the pavement mark the spots where columns once stood. The house at number 29 is built over the ruins of a Roman basilica. The remains of the church of **St. Paul's** (4), on Bailgate at the foot of Westgate, is also an important site in Lincoln's religious past, for these stones mark the site of the church of St. Paulinus, who brought Christianity to these parts in 628. Bailgate continues north to yet another reminder of Lincoln's Roman past, ***Newport Arch** (5). Erected in the second century as the northern gate of the Roman city, it is the only Roman arch in Britain that still spans a road. Beyond the arch, in the Old Barracks on Burton Street, the *Museum of Lincolnshire Life* paints an interesting picture of county history from the Middle Ages to the present. A right turn at Newport Arch puts you on East Bight Street, which follows the remains of the *Roman city walls.* Turn left on Eastgate and you will shortly come to Pottergate, where another left turn will bring you to two other city gates. The first, **Priory Gate** (6), is actually a triumphal arch built on the site of a Medieval city gate that was demolished in 1815. Farther along is **Potter Gate** (7), a well preserved structure from the 14th century. At the end of Pottergate, turn left on Lindom Road; it will bring you to the **Usher Art Gallery** (8), which James Ward Usher, a jeweler and onetime sheriff of Lincoln, bestowed on the town. Usher's collection of jeweled watches is here, as are the works of local watercolorist Peter de Wint; the hats and gloves that William Tom Warrener, another local painter, wore when he posed for Toulouse-Lautrec's famous poster, *The Englishman at the Folies-Bergere;* and a collection of fine porcelain. Broadgate leads south from the gallery to another interesting museum, the **City and County Museum** (9), which occupies the 13th-century Grey Friars Priory, the oldest Franciscan church in Great Britain. The museum houses a valuable collection of antiquities from Lincoln and its environs, including many Roman artifacts, as well as a natural history collection and a collection of weapons. A right turn at *St. Swithins Church* (10) into Saltergate brings you to ***Stonebow** (11), a massive Medieval gate built during the 15th–16th centuries as the southern entrance to the town. The *Guildhall* now occupies an upper floor, beneath the Mote Bell, made in 1371 and still rung before every session of the town council.

High Street, Lincoln's busy shopping thoroughfare, leads south from Stonebow to **High Bridge** (12), one of the few Medieval bridges in Europe that is still lined with houses. (The shore path along the River Witham provides a good look at the bridge's Medieval construction.) In the Middle Ages, when Lincoln was an important inland port, the quays along *Brayford Pool* (13), just beyond the bridge, were piled high with wool bound

for the Continent. The *National Cycle Museum,* filled to the rafters with historic bicycles, some of them built 150 years ago, now occupies a building on Bayford Wharf North.

Beyond High Bridge, High Street leads south to the early Medieval churches of *St. Benedict's* (14) and *St. Mary-le-Wigford* (15), both with Saxon-Norman towers. Lincoln's railroad termini, *Central Station* (16) and *St. Mark's Station* (17), are nearby.

Farther south along High Street is the *Guildhall of St. Mary's* (18), a fine, 12th-century Norman building that is now used as a storehouse. Many locals still call this former headquarters of Lincoln's most famous Medieval guild "John of Gaunt's stables," because the duke's palace once stood across the street. Just beyond, the 12th-century *church of St. Peter-at-Gants* (19), boasts a lovely Saxon tower.

To the north of Stonebow, High Street passes the *main post office* (20) and the *Theatre Royal,* then ends at a fork. The street on the right, The Strait, leads to the so-called **Jew's House** (21), built early in the 12th century and one of the most beautiful and best-preserved Norman houses in England. It is now a restaurant. Steep Hill leads from here to another splendid example of Norman architecture, the **House of Aaron the Jew** (22), which also dates from the 12th century. Exchequer Gate and the cathedral are just up Bailgate.

**Oxford

91 km. (57 miles) west of London; by train, frequent service from Paddington Station; by bus, from Victoria Coach station; by car, Routes M 40 and A 40.

Take a great Englishman—a poet, a statesman, or maybe a 19th-century explorer—and try to determine where he was educated. There are really only two answers to that question, Cambridge and Oxford. If a well-bred Englishman didn't go to one, chances are he went to the other, if only for a short time before he was booted out ("sent down" is how they say it here), as the flamboyant poet Shelley was from Oxford.

Oxford is a great university, and with its gray towers and green lawns, it looks the part. Bear in mind, too, that Oxford, the town of some 100,000 residents, is an important manufacturer of cars (British Leyland, for one, is here) and other goods, and the place has its fair share of shopping centers, traffic, and the other trappings of modern life. Even so, with the university's buildings and sheer grandeur, Oxford overwhelms. Few visitors will be as inspired as Henry James, the American novelist, was. He wrote of his visit, "There are no words for these colleges. . . . I thought the heart of me would crack with satisfied desire. . . . The whole place gives me a deeper sense of English life than anything yet." Then again, maybe Oxford will strike you the same way.

Prestigious as Oxford is, it goes fairly crazy quite frequently. If you don't enjoy dancing in the streets with besotted young members of the British aristocracy, you will probably want to avoid Oxford on May Day. Eights Week, at the end of that month, is a more sedate celebration in which spectators watch crews from the different colleges compete on the River Isis, as the Thames is poetically called as it flows through town, or on the well-groomed cricket greens that abound in Oxford. The colleges hold their formal Commemoration Balls in spring, at the end of summer term, and the rowdier St. Giles Fair takes over the streets in early September.

History

Oxford tends to cloud its origins in mystery. Some historians say that King Alfred established a university here in 872, and Alfred did at least build the old city wall that now runs through the gardens of New College. Others attribute the origins of the university to the legendary King Memphric. Still others say that the first students came to Oxford when Henry II ordered them back home from Paris, to make sure that his rival France wouldn't drain England of all its bright young minds.

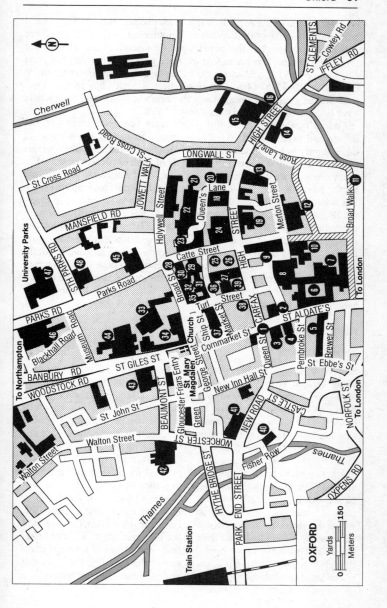

Even the origin of the name is in question, one argument holding that it quite literally means "ford for oxen," another camp agreeing that there was indeed a ford, but that it belonged to a man named Osca. Some facts are certain. The name Oxford does appear in the Anglo-Saxon Chronicles of 912, and monastic colleges did begin to spring up at Oxford in the 13th–14th centuries. The university has moved away from its religious beginnings over the centuries—slowly, as teachers have been allowed to marry only since 1858.

Oxford's otherwise peaceful quads have been the scenes of hot debate and even bloodshed over the years. Townsfolk haven't always taken kindly to having learned fellows in their midst, and bloody riots between "town and gown" left hundreds of students dead in 1355. (For every student killed, the town paid a penny to the university every year for the next 100 years.) King Charles I and his court took up residence in Oxford during the Civil War, from 1642–1646. Among the many intellectual movements that have taken root at the university, few were more hotly contested than the so-called Oxford Movement of the mid-19th century, in which Oxford theologians attempted to restore Roman Catholic doctrine and practices to the Anglican church. Methodism was born at Oxford in the 18th century. These days, much of Oxford's pugnacious energies are channeled into preserving the university's magnificent architecture, greenswards, and of-another-age atmosphere—a most worthwhile cause, as visitors will agree.

Attractions

See map on page 81.

The only way to really get to know Oxford is to be a student here—to dine in its Medieval halls, to study in its many libraries, to walk across its mist-shrouded meadows on your way to a morning lecture. Short of that, the best way to see the university is to walk through it at your leisure—unobtrusively, please. Oxford is, after all, a place of learning. The hours at which the various colleges permit visitors to stroll through their quads and gardens vary widely, though as a rule of thumb afternoons are usually better for touring. The worst time to visit is late May and June, when the students are immersed in their grueling examinations and many colleges shut their premises to outsiders.

The following itinerary can be done in half a day, though given the fact that there's a story behind practically every stone at Oxford, such a short visit is all too hurried. By all means, if you're pressed for time, be sure at least to walk down High Street, to visit Henry VIII's *Christ Church College* and its *cathedral,* beautiful, riverside *Magdalen College,* and the lush gardens of *St. John's College,* and to see at least the exterior of the *Radcliffe Camera.* But really, a cursory look would be a crime; plan to spend at least the better part of a day strolling through this learned place. The *Tourist Information Centre* near Carfax (see below) can supply additional information and may be able to tell you where to find a student guide. The porters at many colleges are walking encyclopedias of Oxford-related knowledge and are happy to show off the premises; be sure to tip them for their services. Punting—as taking to the river in one of the local flat-bottomed boats is called—is popular on Oxford's two rivers, the Isis (local name for the Thames) and the Cherwell. As you punt down the Cherwell near the University Parks you may come across a river full of naked men, exercising their right to bathe in the buff at the beach known as *Parson's Pleasure.* Women can swim alongside men at *Dame's Delight* (wear a suit) and at several beaches along the Thames.

The best place to begin a tour of Oxford is at the busy intersection of **Carfax** (1), where most of Oxford's main streets converge. All that remains of the *church of St. Martin's*—which was demolished in 1896 to widen the street, a desecration that Oxford hasn't repeated often—is the 13th-century *Carfax Tower.* There's barely a piece of earth in Oxford that hasn't at one time or another been trod upon by the feet supporting the world's greatest minds, and this spot is no exception. William Shakespeare is said

to have attended services at the church and was wined and dined across Cornmarket at the *Crown Tavern.* If you walk south on St. Adlate's Street, you will pass a cluster of Oxford's civic buildings—the *town hall* (2), the *Tourist Information Centre* (3), and the *main post office* (4)—then come to **Pembroke College** (5), founded in 1624, just in time to educate that great writer with the famous gift for gab, Samuel Johnson. He is remembered by his desk in the Library and a portrait by Reynolds that hangs in the Commons Room. Another famous alumnus is James Smithson, who, though he never set foot in America, bequeathed upon his death in 1829 the then-unheard-of sum of half a million dollars in silver coins to the U.S. Government to establish the Smithsonian Institution in Washington, D.C. Pembroke has what many visitors find to be the most quaint of Oxford's many quads, formed in part by reconstructed old cottages along Pembroke Street. Across St. Aldate's Street is ***Christ Church College** (6), which is usually referred to in superlatives. It is the largest college in Oxford, with about 350 undergraduates; it has the largest courtyard, *Tom Quad* (which surrounds a lily pond topped by a statue of Mercury); and it has the biggest and loudest bell, a seven-tonner called "Great Tom." You will hear the monster nightly, beginning at 9:05, when from *Tom Tower,* erected by Sir Chris-

Christ Church

topher Wren in 1680, it clangs 101 times as if calling the college's original 101 students in at curfew. The imposing, rather gloomy *College Hall* is hung with portraits of famous alumni, who count among their ranks 13 prime ministers and 20 archbishops. What else would you expect from a college that was founded by Cardinal Wolsey and again by Henry VIII? America's William Penn also attended Christ Church. He was sent down (expelled) in 1661 for his ardent religious views for which he was later imprisoned. He eventually set sail for the colonies, where he founded Pennsylvania.

One of the college's few claims to modesty is **Christ Church Cathedral** (7), which serves both as the college chapel and the city's cathedral—the smallest in England. The little cathedral, much of which dates from the 12th century, is famous as the scene of Cranmer's humiliation. Cranmer was a 16th-century

Archbishop of Canterbury who helped nullify several of Henry VIII's marriages, then fell out of favor with the crown and was brought here, shorn, stripped of his vestments, and burned at the stake. The murder of another ill-fated Archbishop of Canterbury, Thomas à Becket, struck down by knights of Henry II, is illustrated in the stained glass of the east window in *St. Lucy's Chapel*.

If you walk from the cathedral to the opposite side of Tom Quad, you will come to a passage known as *"Kill Cannon,"* so-called because a killer wind usually rushes through it. A statue of a 17th-century dean is inscribed with the verse by the poet Tom Burns, "I do not love thee, Dr. Fell." Kill Cannon opens onto **Peckwater Court** (8), built in 1705 on the site of an old inn of the same name. Nearby *Canterbury Quad* is so called because on its site once stood a college belonging to the monks of Canterbury. (Sir Thomas More studied at the college in the 16th century.) *Christ Church Picture Gallery* is in Canterbury Quad. In it hang works by Leonardo da Vinci, Raphael, and other masters, most of them of the Italian, Dutch, and Flemish schools.

Leaving Christ Church by *Canterbury Gate* you will see on the left **Oriel College** (9), founded in 1326. Within its pleasant buildings, most of them from the 17th and 18th centuries, raged the pitched battle of what has come to be called the Oxford

Oriel College

Movement. It was orchestrated by Oriel theologian John Newman and John Keble, of nearby Corpus Christi, who argued that the Church of England should move closer to the doctrines of the Church of Rome—fighting words for Anglicans. Another famous Oriel fellow was Cecil Rhodes, the great colonist who settled vast tracts of Africa and who established the esteemed Rhodes Scholarship, which allows students from the Commonwealth, America, and Germany to study at Oxford. Just opposite Oriel you'll find **Corpus Christi College** (10), founded in 1516. This college is a must for visitors from Georgia, for it is the alma mater of General James Oglethorpe, who founded the colony and the city of Savannah in 1733. The 400-year-old *sundial* in the Front Quad was already an antique when the General walked past it

in his student's gown. The altarpiece in the *Chapel* is by Rubens.

From the south side of Corpus Christi you can walk across *Merton Fields* to **Christ Church Meadow** (11). This bucolic, grassy expanse stretches to the Isis. Oxford's oldest, and to many observers, most picturesque, college is ***Merton College** (12), founded in 1264 as a school for scholastic—as opposed to monastic—studies, a rarity in those days. Actually, Merton's claim that it is the oldest college is debatable, as Balliol and University colleges were both endowed earlier. Whatever, Merton's buildings from the 13th–14th centuries are beautiful, and its central court, curiously named *Mob Quad,* is unquestionably the university's oldest. The college *Library,* built from 1377–1378, is also the oldest at Oxford—in fact, it is the oldest library in England and the first to keep books on shelves, rather than in presses. The *Chapel,* too, is the university's oldest, built between

Merton College "Mob Quad"

The High

1290–1450, with much of its original stained glass intact.

If you leave the college and follow Merton Street north, you will soon come to the **Examination Schools** (13), a Victorian edifice that strikes dread in the hearts of students, for this is where exams are administered. When the ordeal is over, the students return to celebrate with great quantities of champagne, of which Oxford's well-heeled student body is inordinately fond. The Examination Schools front *"The High,"* as Oxford's **High Street** is known locally. This busy, graceful street, lined with shops and college buildings, crowded with students and townsfolk, is the epitome of what the main street of college towns everywhere should be. If you follow High Street to the west from the Examination Schools, you will soon come to the **Botanic Garden** (14), established in 1621 and England's oldest. A peaceful retreat today, it was built for the utilitarian purpose of supplying Oxford's medical faculty with healing herbs. Fittingly, a rose garden near the entrance honors the Oxford researchers who, in 1941, established the effectiveness of penicillin. The best time to visit ****Magdalen College** (15), across High Street from the Botanic Garden, is at 6:00 on the morning of May 1. Choir boys sing to usher in the month from atop the 15th-century college tower, which rises from the banks of the River Cherwell near the *Magdalen Bridge* (16). The scene evokes all the glory of the English spring, which is in full evidence at Magdalen. The college is bounded by a lovely deer park, *The Grove* (17), and riverside meadows, which you can cross on *Addison's Walk,* named after the poet and statesman Joseph

Bell tower and
bridge over the Cherwell

LONDON
UNDERGROUND
SYSTEM

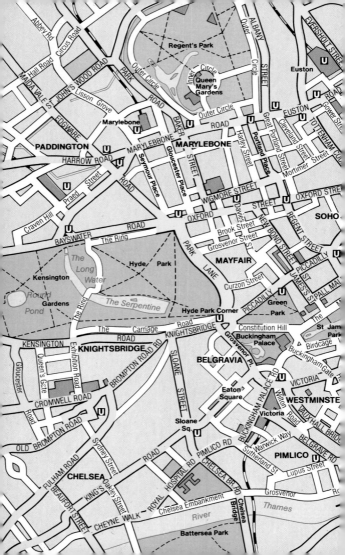

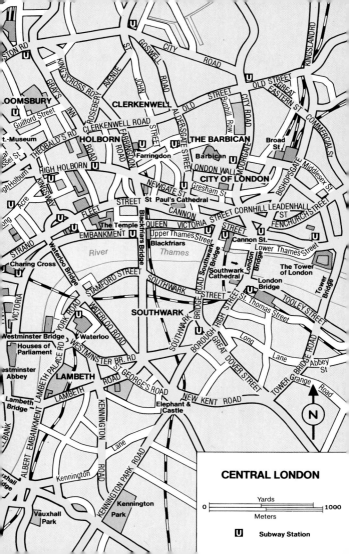

CENTRAL LONDON

```
Yards
0 |————————————————| 1000
Meters
```

U   Subway Station

Big Ben, in the clock tower at the north end of Westminster Palace, is among the best-known sights in London.

For centuries, the Tower of London served simultaneously as a fortress, royal palace, and jail. Today, the Tower houses the well-guarded Crown Jewels in its Waterloo Barracks.

The "Weavers," a group of Tudor houses in Canterbury, are located on the River Stour. The homes were occupied by Huguenot refugees from France during the 16th century.

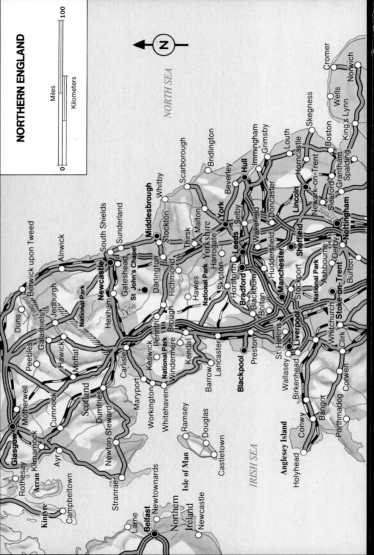

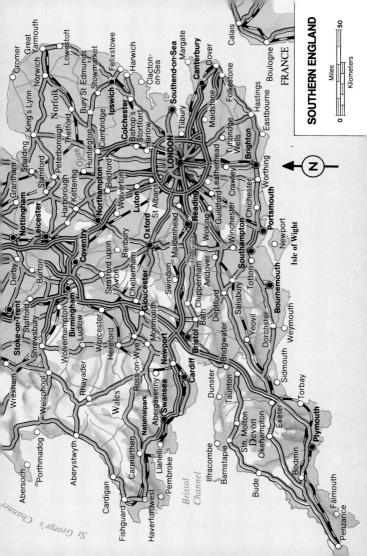

SOUTHERN ENGLAND

Miles

Kilometers

0   50

N

Christchurch is Oxford's largest college. The inner courtyard boasts a lily pond that features a statue of Mercury.

Addison, a 17th-century Oxford student.

Few of Magdalen's famous alumni are more flamboyant than Oscar Wilde, though a contender may be an anonymous student of at least a century ago who wrote the doggerel, "There once was at Magdalen Hall/A man who knew nothing at all/He took his degree/At Seventy-Three/Which is youngish for Magdalen Hall." This verse says something about the history of the university. It wasn't until the 19th century that a law limited the time a student could study at Oxford to 10 years. Until then, many men spent their entire lives studying here.

Magdalen has plenty of indoor treasures, too, notably its *Chapel,* where the choir sings at evensong, its *Cloisters,* and its oak-roofed, portrait-lined *Hall.*

Leave the college and walk back toward the center of town on High Street, stopping to admire the view of "The High" from the curve it makes at Queen's Lane. You are now in front of ***Queen's College** (18), which Chaplain Robert de Eglesfield founded in 1340 in honor of Queen Philippa, the wife of Edward III. Queen's was established with the rather quaint notion that its mission was to educate 12 fellows, representing Christ and the apostles, and 70 "disciples." Old customs have a way of lingering on at Oxford, especially at Queen's. A trumpet still summons students to dinner; a boar's head dinner is still served on Christmas Day, said to com-

memorate a student who killed an attacking boar by stuffing a copy of Aristotle down its throat; and on New Year's Day, the bursar distributes needle and thread, *aiguille* and *fil* in Latin, a spot of Medieval humor that puns on de Eglesfield's name. Queen's has its share of serious-minded history, too, including the fact that Nicholas of Hereford made the first translation of the Bible into English here, in 1380. Christopher Wren designed the *Chapel* and *Hall,* and his student, Nicholas Hawksmoor, is responsible for the elegant front *quadrangle,* completed in 1710. A statue of Hawksmoor's patron, Queen Caroline, stands at the entrance.

University College (19), across High Street from Queen's, was allegedly founded by Alfred the Great in 872. Although there's not much evidence to back up this claim, the college is very old indeed and was officially founded in 1249. The college's most famous alumnus is Percy Bysshe Shelley. The poet was sent down in 1810 for publishing his pamphlet "The Necessity of Atheism," but he is honored nonetheless by the *Shelley Memorial,* a much-visited domed building that houses a lifelike statue of the poet, who drowned off Italy in 1822. Just across Queen's Lane is **St. Edmund's Hall** (20), founded by Archbishop of Canterbury Edmund of Abingdon in 1220. It is the last of Oxford's Medieval colleges to still bear the name "hall." The small, well-proportioned quadrangle was begun in 1650 but not completed until 1934. Farther up Queen's Lane is the **church of St. Peter's in the East** (21), built over an old Norman church, of which little remains but the crypt. The most famous tenant of the church's tombs is James Sanders, an Oxford scientist who, in 1784, was the first Englishman to make an ascent in a hot-air balloon. Follow Queen's Lane around its sharp bend to **New College** (22), which is officially called the "College of St. Mary the Virgin of Winchester" and which isn't new at all. It was founded in 1379 by William of Wykeham, Bishop of Winchester and Chancellor of England. Much of the college buildings—those in the first *court,* the *Chapel,* the *Dining Hall,* the *Cloister,* and the *Bell Tower*—remain just as the Bishop left them upon his death in 1404. Through a gate in the *Garden Quad* you may enter the lovely college garden, a quiet oasis and all the more remarkable because a part of Oxford's old city wall runs through it. From New College follow New College Lane to the corner of Catte Street, where you'll see **Hertford College** (23). The old buildings of this college, founded in 1284 as Hart Hall, are connected to the newer buildings by the so-called *Bridge of Sighs*—a reminder of just how much Venice has captured the imagination of generations of British architects. Walking on

All Souls' College

Catte Street back toward High Street, you will pass ***All Soul's College** (24), the souls to whom the college was dedicated in 1437 being those who lost their lives in the bloody wars that Henry V and Henry VI waged against France. The architect Christopher Wren, who seems to have built at least half of the important buildings in England, was a student here, and his acclaimed protégé, Nicholas Hawksmoor, built one of its quadrangles, the so-called *Second Quad.* The 100,000-volume *Library* houses Wren's designs for St. Paul's Cathedral in London.

Just opposite All Souls is the ***Radcliffe Camera** (25), camera being an antiquated term for a round building, which this magnificent example of Anglo-Italian architecture is, and Radcliffe being the Oxford alumnus and court physician who, upon his death in 1714, left his sizable library to his alma mater. Today this amazing structure, the most accomplished work of architect James Gibbs, is part of the nearby Bodleian Library (see below). The **church of St. Mary** (26), on the south side of Radcliffe Square, opposite the Camera, was founded by Alfred the Great on the site of a Saxon church. Its 13th-century tower still provides the best views of Oxford. On the west side of the square is **Brasenose College** (27), founded in 1509. The origin of its name still sparks controversy at Oxford. It may refer to the brass knocker, in the shape of a lion's head with a prominent snout, that was once affixed to the door of the Hall (it is now given a place of honor inside). Or it may have originated from the "brasen-haus," or brewery, that once stood here.

If you return to Catte Street and walk north, you will soon find yourself in a square lined with some of Oxford's most prominent buildings. Nicholas Hawksmoor built the distinguished **Claren-don Building** (28), on the north side of the square, in 1713. It is now the administrative headquarters of the university. On the south side of the square is the **Bodleian Library** (29), which owes its origins to a 15th-century bequest from the Duke of Gloucester but was actually founded in 1602, by Sir Thomas Bodley. Every book published in Great Britain finds its way to the Bodleian, one of the oldest and

most important libraries in the world. As a result its shelves fairly groan under the weight of two and a half million volumes. Oxford students receive their diplomas in the **Sheldonian Theatre** (30), a grand arena that Christopher Wren, then teaching astronomy at Oxford, built from 1664–1668 in imitation of the theater of Marcellus in Rome. No doubt the matriculating students have one eye on the future and the other on the flamboyantly painted ceiling. The Bodleian spills over to an upper story of the **Divinity School** (31), a noble 15th-century structure that now houses temporary book exhibitions but has been pressed into such ig-noble uses as a storehouse for corn and a hog market (the swine occupied only the vestibule or Proscholium). Oxford takes greater pride in the fact that Parliament met here in 1681.

Just to the north of the *Sheldo-nian Theatre* you will come to Broad Street. Turn to the left and you will soon come to the

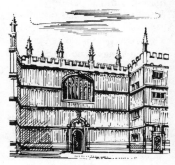

Proscholium

Museum of the History of Science (32), notable both for its fascinating collection of microscopes, cameras, and other scientific equipment and for its 17th-century structure. It once housed the collections that Elias Ashmole bequeathed to the university (the Ashmolean collections have since moved to larger quarters (see page 91). Across the street is a passageway leading to ***Trinity College** (33), a pleasant array of buildings and gardens where Lord Baltimore, who founded the state of Maryland, was educated. Peaceful as Trinity seems to be, it has a long roster of quarrelsome alumni. Walter Landau, the poet, was sent down for firing shots into the room of a fellow 18th-century student; Sir Richard Burton, the famous 19th-century explorer who mastered no fewer than 40 languages, was asked to leave when he challenged another student to a duel. Even today, Trinity students are by unwritten charter the sworn enemies of students at neighboring **Balliol College** (34), founded in 1262 and one of the oldest colleges in Oxford. The Victorians put up most of the present buildings. The gates are the originals, though, dating to 1288 and still bearing the scorch marks from the fires that engulfed Protestant martyrs in the 16th century. The victims are officially commemorated in the college's 19th-century *Martyr's Memorial,* designed in the style of the Eleanor crosses that were erected across the English countryside in 1290 to mark the funeral procession of Queen Eleanor from Lincoln to London. A left turn into Turl Street soon brings you to ***Exeter College** (35), one of the largest colleges at Oxford, founded in 1314 but largely rebuilt in the 19th century. England's famous 19th-century founders of the Pre-Raphaelite movement, the artists William Morris and Sir Edward Burne-Jones, went to Oxford, and a stunning example of their work, a tapestry depicting the Magi, hangs in Exeter's *Chapel.* Just across Brasenose Lane—still edged with its Medieval gutters—is **Lincoln College** (36), with many buildings that date from its founding in 1427. Lincoln is the birthplace of the Methodist Church. The church's founder, John Wesley, was at Lincoln from 1726–1751. Early on in his university career his rooms became the meeting place for a group of devout Christians who came to be known as "Methodists," a reference to their rigidly methodical habits. On the other side of Turl Street from Lincoln is **Jesus College** (37), which Queen Elizabeth I founded in 1571. A fine portrait of the queen, by Zucchero, hangs in the *Common Room;* though the place to see likenesses of British monarchs is really the *Hall,* which is lined with royal portraits, including one of Charles I by Van Dyck.

Heading south on Turl Street you'll come to High Street and the

17th-century *Mitre Hotel* (38), where generations of Oxford's distinguished visitors have bedded down. The church across the way is *All Saints* (39), built in 1708. You are now only a few steps from *Carfax*, the beginning of the tour, though there is still much of Oxford to be seen. Follow High Street to the west. It becomes Queen Street, then New Road, and comes to Oxford's Medieval **Castle** (40), where Richard the Lion-Hearted was allegedly born in 1157. About all that remains of the once mighty fortress is its *crypt* and the imposing 11th-century *St. George's tower,* though these Medieval remains are enough to form a dramatic contrast with the modern buildings of **Nuffield College** (41), across the road. The college went up in 1937, with funds from the Viscount Nuffield, born William Morris. He founded Oxford's Morris Motor Company and in so doing put the town on the map as a major center of automobile manufacture. Worcester Street runs north from Nuffield (the Oxford Canal is just to the west) to **Worcester College** (42), which has long been called "Botany Bay" because of its isolated location. (Botany Bay is the inlet near Sydney where Captain Cook first set foot on Australian soil.) Its isolation as well as its large gardens and lake lend Worcester a rather romantic air, which is probably why over the years it has attracted such dyed-in-the-wool romantics as Thomas

De Quincey, the decadent writer and opium addict who, in 1821, penned *Confessions of an English Opium Eater* for a London magazine, and Richard Lovelace, the swashbuckling 17th-century poet.

From Worcester, Beaumont Street brings you to the acclaimed **Ashmolean Museum** (43), Britain's oldest public museum and one of its finest. The foundations of this massive and eclectic museum are the artifacts John Tradescant collected in the 17th century and settled on Elias Ashmole, who gave them to Oxford. The 50 galleries are crammed with skeletons, sketches by Leonardo, Greek antiquities, Uccello's masterpiece *Hunt in the Forest,* many Impressionist paintings, 250 casts of Greek sculptures, and one of England's greatest treasures, the gold and cloisonné *Alfred Jewel,* found near one of the ninth-century King's monasteries. Just across St. Giles, a broad avenue, from the museum is **St. John's College** (44), one of Oxford's most attractive, founded in 1555. Its colonnade is modeled after the famous one at the Hospital in Milan. You may walk across the large gardens, designed by Capability Brown—the famous landscape architect who also laid out the gardens at Blenheim (see page 215) and Kew (see page 58)—to **Wadham College** (45), founded in 1610. Christopher Wren studied here, and the place is little changed since then. Parks Road leads north past these north-ernmost reaches of the university toward the playing fields known as *University Parks.* Just to the south of the fields are the brick Victorian buildings of **Keble College** (46), which opened its doors in 1870 in memory of the Reverend John Keble, one of the forces behind the Oxford Move-ment. On the other side of Parks Road is the **University Muse-um** (47), which houses a vast array of artifacts relating to the natural sciences. Next door is the *Pitt-Rivers Museum,* named after the so-called father of British archaeology, Augustus Henry Pitt-Rivers. The former army officer made many of his famous excavations close to home, on his estate in Wiltshire. He left his findings to Oxford upon his death in 1900. The museum also dis-plays thousands of other items from around the world of anthro-pological interest. The **Rhodes House** (48), across South Parks Road from the museum, is the headquarters of the acclaimed Rhodes Trust. A left turn here on Parks Road will take you back to the heart of the university and High Street.

**Stratford-upon-Avon

149 km. (93 miles) from London; the "Shakespeare Connection" makes the two-hour trip by train and bus from Euston Station; by car, Routes A 40 and M 40 from London to Oxford, Route A 34 from Oxford to Stratford.

The 20,000 inhabitants of this pretty market town may bless (or curse) the day, April 23, 1564, that their most famous son, William Shakespeare, was born. Some half a million visitors come around every year to pay their respects to the Bard, and, after London, the little hamlet is probably the second best-known place in England. Few visitors are disappointed by the memorabilia—birthplace and grave site included—with which Stratford commemorates Shakespeare, or with the charm, complete with old houses and window boxes, of what is still essentially a typical English country village.

History

No doubt, as a student at the Stratford grammar school the young Will Shakespeare learned that his hometown had been a Roman outpost, that a monastery stood at this important road junction in 693, and that "Streatford" was already an important market town in the 13th century. Little did the teachers realize that this boy would grow up to put their town on the map. At 18, Shakespeare married Anne Hathaway, seven years his senior, and not long afterward the couple moved to London, where the young man joined a troop of actors, began writing plays, and opened his prosperous theater, The Globe. Rich and famous, Shakespeare returned to Stratford around 1597 and purchased New Place, the largest house in town, where he died in 1616, at the age of 52.

It was another thespian, David Garrick, who established Stratford as a pilgrimage site. In 1769, he staged the first Shakespeare festival here. About all we know of this event is that James Boswell, the man of letters and biographer of Samuel Johnson, attended and that the weather was terrible. Shakespeare's house became a national monument in 1847 and is now maintained by the Birthplace Trust, which is responsible for several other historically important properties in Stratford.

Attractions

See map on page 95.

It's not surprising that most visits to Stratford begin on Henley Street at ****Shakespeare's**

Birthplace (1), a typical and well-preserved Elizabethan house that the playwright's father, a solidly middle-class glover and agricultural trader, bought in 1552. The house was commodious

Shakespeare's House

enough to accommodate the Shakespeares and their seven children comfortably, and visiting these rooms, furnished much like they were in the 16th century, it is easy to imagine the family sitting around the kitchen hearth (the strange contraption in front of it is a 17th-century child guard, which kept small fries from falling into the flames.) The room where the Bard was born is also furnished in typical period fashion, though the signatures, scrawled across windows and walls, of Sir Walter Scott, Thomas Carlyle, Ellen Terry, and other famous past visitors give the place a shrinelike air. Obviously the flora in the large garden left its mark upon young William, for he referred to these plants and trees in many of his plays.

Several tourist attractions, quite tasteful, have sprung up around the birthplace, among them *Tussaud's Shakespearean Waxworks* and an exhibition of costumes used in BBC productions of the plays. The sedate *Shakespeare Centre* is geared to scholarly research. Henley Street ends at High Street, on the corner where Shakespeare's daughter Judith lived with her husband, the vintner Thomas Quincey. Their house is now Stratford's *Information Centre* (2). The Tudor building just across High Street is ***Harvard House** (3), so called because this is where Katherine Rogers, mother of John Harvard, the American colonist who founded the prestigious university, grew up. Even without its Ivy League connections, the house, owned by Harvard University since 1909, is noteworthy as one of the grandest in Stratford. It has two lovely half-timbered Tudor neighbors at the corner near Ely Street, the *Garrick Inn* (4) and the *Old Tudor House* (5).

David Garrick commemorated the Shakespeare Jubilee he sponsored by presenting Stratford with a statue of the Bard to put in front of its *Town Hall* (6), then only three years old. The place was restored after a fire in 1946.

Old Tudor House

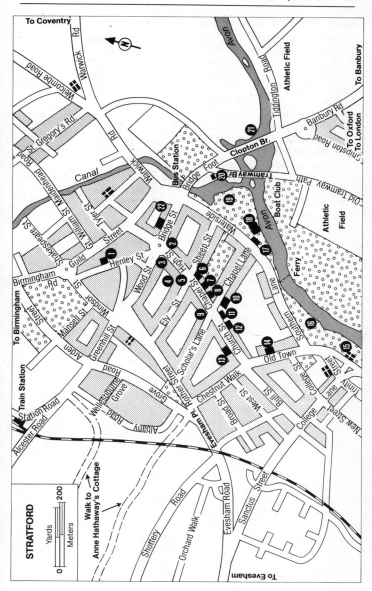

Nearby **Nash's House** (7) was the home of Shakespeare's granddaughter Elizabeth and her husband, Thomas Nash. It is now a museum that divides its display cases into local Roman and Saxon archaeological finds and Shakespeare memorabilia, including knickknacks from the playwright's day and mementos of the 1769 Jubilee. Shakespeare lived next door, in **New Place** (8), a fine house that he bought, for £60, in 1597. Only the foundations remain, because the Reverend Francis Gastrell, who bought New Place in 1756, tore the house down three years later after a dispute with the city fathers over taxes. The cranky reverend also took an axe to a mulberry tree that Shakespeare planted, because he was tired of literary pilgrims trespassing on his property to see it. A new mulberry, grown from a slip of the original tree, still flourishes, as does the beautiful Elizabethan knot garden, much like the one that grew here in Shakespeare's day and in which he is said to have written *The Tempest*. Across Chapel Street on the corner of Scholar's Lane is the **Falcon Inn** (9), where Queen Henrietta Maria, the wife of Charles I, lived in 1643. It is worth dropping into the nearby *Guild Chapel* (10) to see the lovely mural of the Last Judgment, painted around 1500, and other Medieval frescoes. The **Guildhall** (11), next door, was already 300 years old when the young Shakespeare came here to

Guildhall

watch strolling players perform. Actually, he spent quite a bit of time here, because the King's New School of Stratford-upon-Avon occupied an upper floor. Pensioners still occupy the adjoining 15th-century **Almshouses** (12), just as they did in the Bard's day. The *Shakespeare Institute of Birmingham University* (13), a center for Shakespearean scholarship, is across the street. At the end of Church Street, a right turn brings you into the street known as Old Town and to ***Hall's Croft** (14), the lovely 16th-century house where Shakespeare's daughter Susanna and her husband, the physician John Hall, lived until they moved to New Place in 1616. Dr. Hall's pharmacy, its walls lined with vials and other equipment typical of an Elizabethan surgeon, looks so authentic that you expect the good doctor to walk in and begin an examination. By the same token, it's hard to visit the bedroom, with its diamond-paned leaded windows and lovely Tudor bed, without feeling you are invading the couple's privacy.

Old Town ends at the Avon riverbank, and here, beneath beautiful lindens, is **Holy Trinity Church** (15), where Shakespeare was baptized, married, and buried. (The church register in the corner records his baptism and death.) For many visitors, the most remarkable attraction here is a bust of the Bard, commissioned seven years after his death and, though a bit clumsy, said to be a very close likeness. Shakespeare's tomb, in front of the altar, is a modest affair. Popular belief holds that the poet himself wrote the doggerel inscribed upon it, though it's little wonder that his respectful followers tend to deny this claim:

Shakespeare's Tomb

> Good Frend for Jesus sake forbeare
> To digg the dust v heare;
> Blese be ye man yt spares these stones
> And curst be he yt moves my bones.

Shakespeare's wife and other family members rest nearby.

An expanse of greenery, the *Avonbank Garden* (16) stretches north along the river from the church, and it runs into the *Theatre Garden* (17). Walk through it to the **Royal Shakespeare Theatre** (18), home stage of the prestigious Royal Shakespeare Company. The Bard's plays have

been performed on this spot since 1879, first in the old Memorial Theatre, which burned in 1926, and since 1932 in this dignified playhouse. Even when the house is dark, Shakespeare is center stage in the upstairs gallery, whose holdings include the playwright's gloves, painted scenes from the plays, and portraits of prominent Shakespearean actors. If memorials to Shakespeare have become rather tiresome at this point, take a riverside seat at the pleasant terrace restaurant. Then, continue north through another greensward, the *Bancroft Gardens* (19) and follow the rim of the basin of the *Stratford-upon-Avon Canal*. This scenic waterway, dug in the early 19th century, has recently been restored and is usually plied with boats that cruise from the basin into the countryside. The *Gower Memorial* (20), Lord Ronald Gower's tribute to Shakespeare, is on the far side of the basin. From here, the stone *Clopton Bridge* (21) crosses the Avon. It was built in 1490 by Hugh Clopton, a prominent architect and onetime mayor of London. Bridge Street leads away from the river to the **Red Horse Hotel** (22), once a favorite haunt of writers. Washington Irving, the American author, spent some time here in the early 19th century and he recorded his impression of Stratford in his *Tales of a Traveler.* Henley Street and Shakespeare's birthplace are just beyond.

Excursions

Tourist agencies have taken to calling the delightful countryside around Stratford "Shakespeare Country." This is accurate enough, because practically every village seems to have a house that is somehow connected to the playwright. Even so, the neighborhood is perfectly beautiful even without its famous son. **Shottery** (1.6 km., 1 mile, from Stratford): You can follow a path from Stratford through pleasant meadows to the birthplace in 1556 of Shakespeare's wife, Anne Hathaway. The stone cottage, with its thatched roof and simple furnishings, is terribly authentic, so a visit here really is a step into the past. The beautiful garden completes the picture. **Wilmcote** (6 km. 3.5 miles, northwest of Stratford): Those who want to experience what Shakespeare's rural life was like can hike across the meadows to Wilmcote from Stratford and Shottery. Shakespeare's mother, Mary Arden, was born at this simple Tudor farmstead, and she lived here until she married John Shakespeare in 1557. The farm buildings, milking room, and crudely furnished cottage depict the harsh reality of Medieval farm life. **Charlecote Park** (6 km., 3.5 miles, east of Stratford): It is said that Shakespeare made his fateful move to London in haste, after he was caught poaching deer on this Elizabethan estate built in 1558. The grounds are now a nature preserve.

**Winchester

104 km. (65 miles) southwest of London; by train, frequent service from Waterloo Station; by bus, from Victoria Coach Station; by car, Routes M 3 and A 33.

The poet John Keats lived in Winchester around 1818–1819, and he called it the "pleasantest town I ever saw." That's true, no doubt, as not many of England's old cities can match Winchester for charm and beauty. However, there was a time when Winchester was mighty, too— the capital of all England, the center of Medieval industry, the birthplace and final resting place of kings and queens. Little evidence of Winchester's glory days has come down through the ages, but what has survived—most notably its famous cathedral—gives an idea of what once was Winchester's grandeur.

History

In 519, when it became the capital of Saxon Wessex, Winchester had already been occupied for more than 1,000 years—first by Iron Age Celts, then by the Romans. Egbert was crowned the first king of a united England here in 827, and for the next five or six centuries Winchester enjoyed its status as the greatest city in the land. In the late 11th century, William the Conqueror put up a castle and witnessed the construction of the city's great cathedral. William also planted the seeds of Winchester's decline when he made London co-capital, though 12th-century Winchester flourished as a wool market and royal residence. London supplanted Winchester as sole capital in the middle of the 13th century, relegating the city to relative obscurity—which may account for what many visitors consider to be its greatest asset, its quiet charm.

Attractions

See map on page 100.

Winchester's picturesque *High Street* meanders up a steep hill from the River Itchen. The best place to begin a tour of the town is at the top, at the 13th-century **West Gate** (1). Sir Walter Raleigh, the gallant seaman, was imprisoned behind these massive walls in 1603, on charges of conspiring against King James I. Now, about all that reminds us that this was a defensive gate, complete with slots for arrows and boiling oil, is a *museum of arms and armor.* Just to the west of the gate is the **Great Hall** (2), the last remnant of a once mighty

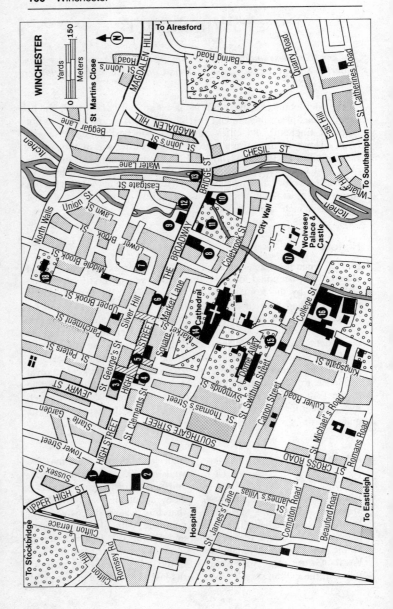

fortress begun by William the Conqueror and completed by Henry III in 1235. Cromwell's troops demolished the castle during the Civil War four centuries later, leaving only this splendid example of Medieval architecture. The Hall's most notable furnishing is a round table rumored to have been the very one around which King Arthur and his knights sat. Impressive as the huge table is, it was built in the 14th century, a full 800 years after Arthur's legendary Camelot.

Return now to *High Street,* and for a good look at Winchester walk down its length. Many of the buildings along High Street have witnessed the intrigues, pageantry, and disasters of early English history. The 16th-century **God Begot Hostel** (3), at number 101, stands on the site of the house that the weak-willed Saxon King Ethelred the Unready presented to his queen, Emma, in 1012. Just across the street is the old **Guildhall** (4), which is now a bank, though Winchester's Medieval curfew bell still hangs in its tower. The building's large clock, with a figure of Queen Anne, went up in 1713 to commemorate the signing of the Treaty of Utrecht, which brought an end to the wars the Queen waged on the Continent. The power-hungry Cardinal Beaufort, who was as much a statesman as an ecclesiastic and who virtually ran Henry VI, erected the **City Cross** (5) (also known as the Butter Cross)

in the middle of the 15th century. The architect Gilbert Scott restored the cross in 1865 and replaced many of the figures, though the one of John the Baptist in the south niche is the original. Only a tower remains of Norman Winchester's *St. Maurice's Church* (6), which stood opposite the cross when Beaufort erected it. Continuing down High Street—past the main post office (4), just off to the left on Middle Brook Street—is the city's new **Guildhall** (8), built in 1873 to designs by Sir Gilbert Scott and restored after a fire in 1969. Winchester's *Tourist Information Centre* is located here. The 13th-century *chapel* (9) of St. John's Hospital is on one side of High Street, and the *hospital* (10) itself is on the other. The greenery surrounding the Guildhall is called the **Abbey Grounds** (11), all that remains of a Benedictine convent that Alswitha, the wife of King Alfred, founded in Wincester at the end of the ninth century. The King was good to Winchester, making it the most important city in the land, and he is honored by a *statue* (12) nearby in High Street, not far from where it spans the River Itchen on *City Bridge* (13). Winchester's 18th-century city mill, now a youth hostel, is on the opposite riverbank.

To visit the city's biggest attraction, head back up High Street as far as the Cross. Turn left into *The Square,* where the palace of William the Conqueror

Winchester Cathedral

once stood. You will see in front of you ****Winchester Cathedral** (14), which some observers find surprisingly uninspiring because of its low towers—or rather, because of its lack of a high tower. Actually, it had a high tower that collapsed in 1170 and was never replaced. What Winchester Cathedral lacks in height, it makes up for in length: 180 meters (526 feet) of it. Winchester is England's fifth-largest cathedral and Europe's longest Medieval church.

The cathedral is second only to Westminster Abbey in London when it comes to the number of important baptisms, weddings, coronations, and burials of British monarchs that have transpired beneath its roof. It is, after all, the cathedral of a town that was once the capital of England.

One of the most famous personages to lay at rest here is Saint Swithun, the tutor of King Alfred, the patron saint of weather, and the subject of the popular verse "St. Swithun's Day if thou doest rain/ For forty days it will remain." The doggerel refers to 40 days of particularly soggy weather in 971, which delayed the transfer of the saint's remains from outside the cathedral to a proper tomb inside. Rain on St. Swithun's Day (July 15) still portends 40 days of rain to come, though inclement weather is hardly unusual here in southern England. The cathedral is also the final resting place of novelist Jane Austen, who died in Winchester at the young age of 37 in 1817, and Izaak Walton, whose masterpiece, *The Compleat Angler,* was probably inspired by the superb trout fishing in the River Itchen.

The history of this ancient church begins on the site of the *Roman Forum* just to the north, now being excavated. This is where the Saxon King Chelwah built Winchester's first cathedral, in the middle of the seventh century. (The nearby *City Museum* displays other archaeological finds from Winchester and vicinity.) The present cathedral went up in just 14 years, from 1079–1093, though it was greatly enlarged in the 14th–15th centuries. The best way to capture the spirit of the cathedral is to walk its awesome length, taking in the many tombs, shrines, and side chapels. The most highly regarded chapel is the *Wykeham Chantry,* halfway down the nave. It is dedicated to William of Wykeham, the Bishop of

Wykeham under whom the cathedral rose to its present form. A modern monument honors William Walker, who at the beginning of this century spent most of his working life replacing the decaying wooden foundations of the cathedral, which its Norman builders had set into the boglike soil. The old Norman crypt is accessible only in fair weather, because it tends to fill with water when it rains.

One of the cathedral's greatest treasures is its *Library,* which houses the famous, brilliantly illuminated 12th-century Winchester Bible. The green *cathedral close,* surrounded by the walls of an ancient monastery that once stood here, encloses several historic buildings, among them the 14th-century *Pilgrim's Hall.* It is a reminder that for centuries this was one of the stops on the well-traveled pilgrimage route to nearby Canterbury (see page 68), the final resting place of old England's favorite martyr, Thomas à Becket. Leave the close by **King's Gate,** the 13th-century entrance to the city. The tiny chapel of *St. Swithun* (15) occupies an upper story. King's Gate opens on College Street. A left turn presently brings you in front of the house where Jane Austen died and just beyond, ***Winchester College** (16), England's oldest public school. Public school means private school in England, and few are more elite than this noble institution, little changed in appear-

ance since Bishop William of Wykeham founded it in 1382. Winchester students, many of whom go on to Oxford's New College, which Wykeham also founded, are called "Wykehamists." Just across College Street are the ruins of **Wolvesey Castle** (17), the original bishop's palace, built in 1138 and torn down by Cromwell's troops during the Civil War in 1646. Present-day bishops of Winchester live in the adjacent Bishop's Palace, though this building, too, is a ghost of what it once was, merely one wing of the palace that architect Christopher Wren built in 1646.

Winchester's other noteworthy old churches include *Holy Trinity* (18) and *St. John's* (19). By all means make the trek to the ***Hospital of St. Cross,** about 1.5 km. (a mile) south of the cathedral. To get there, take a pleasant stroll on College Walk, which runs behind Winchester College and becomes a path through the riverside meadows. St. Cross Road, which runs into Cannon Street a few blocks north of King's Gate, also goes there. St. Cross is England's oldest functioning almshouse, founded in 1136 by Bishop Henry of Blois, grandson of William the Conqueror. Cardinal Beaufort enlarged the hospital in 1446, and it's Medieval buildings still house 25 brethren, who dish up a very modest dole to visitors who ask for it. If you're hungry, you're better off returning to the pubs on and around High Street.

***York

320 km. (200 miles) north of London; by train, regular service from King's Cross Station; by car, M 1 north to Sheffield, M 18 to Doncaster, A 1 and A 64 to York.

If you were to conjure up a vision of a classic old European city, it would probably be pretty close to what modern York actually looks like. It's hard to visit York without feeling that the whole town is an extraordinarily authentic museum reconstruction, and York does indeed have a few such places. However, York is real, all right, with such real-life attractions as England's largest Medieval cathedral, *York Minster,* with acres of Medieval stained glass; miles of narrow streets and old city walls; a Viking neighborhood; Roman ruins—and enough charm to stir the imagination and fill a storybook, which is why York has turned up in so many fictional accounts over the centuries. Robinson Crusoe was "born in the year 1632, in the city of York," and in *Ivanhoe,* the character Isaac of York lived here in Castlegate.

All this is not to say that the 100,000 inhabitants of York live in a museum of yesteryear, for their city is an important commercial center and the informal capital of northern England. Before you set out on a tour of York, it's important to know a couple of things about the local topography. For one thing, streets are called "gates" (a leftover from its past Scandinavian occupants) and gates are called "bars." For another, whatever they're called, streets in York tend to be very narrow. Lady Holland, a 19th-century diarist, recorded a conversation between her father and a resident of York: "Why, Mr. Brown, your streets are the narrowest in Europe; there is not actually room for two carriages to pass," said the father. "Not room!" said the indignant Yorkist. "There's plenty of room, sir, and above an inch and a half to spare."

History

Roman York, known as Eboracum, was the headquarters of the Sixth Legion, the capital of Roman Britain, and from its settlement in A.D. 79 to the Saxon invasion in 417, among the most important of all Roman outposts. The Emperor Hadrian paid an official visit in 120, the Emperors Septimus Severus and Constantius Chlorus both died here, in 211 and 306, respectively. Upon the death of Chlorus, Constantine the Great was proclaimed Emperor of the Romans in York.

Under the Saxons, York (then known as Eoforwic) was one of the bright spots of Dark Age Europe. Paulinus preached Christianity in this capital of Northumbria in the seventh century, and from here Christianity spread throughout the north. Under the scholar Alcuin, Eoforwic was one of Europe's most important centers of learning (so renowned that the Emperor Charlemagne entreated Alcuin to found schools throughout his kingdom).

Danish raiders leveled Eoforwic in 867, but built a prosperous trading center, Jorvik, on its ruins. The city fell again in 1067, this time to the Normans, who leveled it and rebuilt another city in its place. Norman York proved to be more permanent than its predecessors. William the Conqueror put up castles; construction on England's most impressive Medieval cathedral, York Minster, began in the 13th century; new ramparts, pierced by massive gates, replaced the Roman walls. The might of Medieval York, a prosperous city of 40 churches and nine guildhalls, is in abundant evidence today.

Attractions

See map on page 106.

Like most of Europe's great Medieval cathedrals, ***York Minster** (1) was built to inspire and so it does, even to our jaded, secular, 20th-century eyes. It stands on important piece of real estate for 2,000 years. The headquarters of the Roman legion stood on this spot. Here, too, Constantine the Great was crowned emperor in A.D. 306 and here Paulinus, who brought Christianity to York, built a wooden chapel for the baptism of Edwin, King of Northumbria, on Easter Day, 627. The cathedral that rose here, from 1220–1440, can only be described in superlatives—all the more so since the completion of a successful restoration program undertaken in the 1970s. York Minster is the largest Gothic cathedral in England and one of the largest in all of Europe—145 meters (485 feet) long, 30 meters (100 feet) high, 67 meters (225 feet) across. It contains, in its 120 windows, almost half of the Medieval stained glass in England. Its *Great East Window* in the *Choir* is the world's largest expanse of stained glass. The *Five Sisters,* as the lancet windows in the *North Transept* are called, are among the world's finest examples of *grisaille,* a painting technique with a rather gloomy effect in which gray tones are dominant. (Releaded in 1925, the windows

York Minister

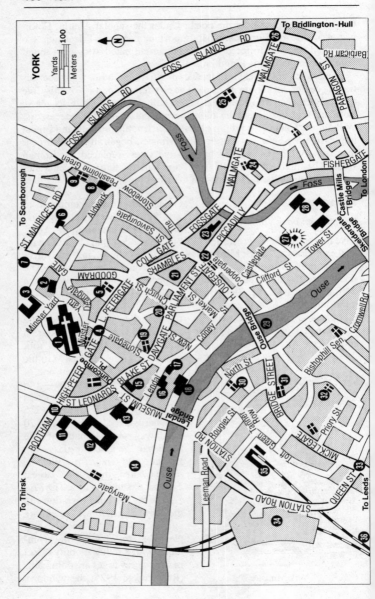

were dedicated to the women who lost their lives in the First World War.) Even the most sonorous of the cathedral's 13 bells is outsized—the humongous, ten-ton *Great Peter* is rung every day at noon.

The best way to organize a tour of the cathedral is from the bottom up, starting in the *Undercroft Museum and Treasury*. Side by side down here are the remains of the Roman military headquarters and the very modern superstructure installed in the 1960s to keep the old walls from toppling and wreaking havoc on the good citizens of York. Pillars from an eighth-century Norman stone church still stand in the adjoining *crypt,* which has also become the repository for the curious *Doom Stone,* carved with primitive scenes that depict the eternal damnation that lies ahead for sinners. In the Middle Ages, the stone stood in front of the cathedral as a sort of advertisement— no doubt a highly effective one— to come in and be saved.

Upstairs, York Minster's greatest virtue is, quite simply, its Gothic grandeur. If soaring expanses of stoney splendor are to your taste, York Minster is the place for you. The *nave,* with its acres of wooden ceiling painted to look like stone, is England's best example of the Decorated Style, the *choir* is one of the best examples of English Gothic, and the octagonal, timber-roofed *Chapter House* is considered to be one of the best of its kind. This lofty

cathedral appears to be indestructible, though disaster, in the form of a lightning bolt, struck in July 1984. The resulting fire engulfed the *South Transept,* but fortunately was confined there. Repairs are underway and should be completed soon.

As you leave the cathedral through the main entrance, the half-timbered building facing you across the cathedral yard is **St. William's College** (2), built in the 15th century to house priests attached to the ministry. The building was pressed into use for secular service in the 17th century, when Charles I, in the grips of a Civil War, set up the royal printing press and mint here. It would perhaps have been more logical for him to have used the nearby ***Treasurer's House** (3), so called because Medieval treasurers of the Minster lived here. The house shelters much history within its handsome walls. The remains of a Roman road runs through the basement,

Treasurer's House

about all that's left of the original structure from 1137. Upper stories date from the 13th, 17th, and 18th centuries, and are furnished with fine old period pieces. The small church of **St. Michael-le-Belfry** (4), just south of the cathedral, is lit by stunning stained-glass windows from the 13th–16th centuries. This peaceful church was the site, in 1570, of the baptism of Guy Fawkes, destined for a stormy life here on earth and for whom there must be a special place in Anglican hell. On the night of November 4, 1604, the Roman Catholic extremist crawled through the cellars of the Houses of Parliament in London and attempted to blow British government to kingdom come. Fawkes was executed for his attempted deed, but not before he was tortured into revealing the names of his co-conspirators in what came to be known as the "Gunpowder Plot."

The quaint, picturesque *Holy Trinity Church* (5) is a little farther east on Goodramgate. It, too, has good stained glass, from the 15th century. Heading north on Goodramgate—notice the houses along the stretch known as *Lady's Walk;* they are some of the best old York has to offer—you will come to the Medieval *town wall* and, in its shadow, what remains of a Roman *bastion*. A little farther along the wall is a reminder that York was a thriving Medieval commercial city, the 14th-century **Merchant Taylors' Hall** (6). The largest and most

grim of the city gates that Edward III built in the 13th century, **Monk Bar** (7), is just opposite the Roman bastion. Edward had reason to be security conscious—though looking at these massive gates and ramparts it's hard to imagine how anyone would even think of sacking York—because he made at least three bloody campaigns into nearby Scotland during his reign. Monk Bar is a good place to climb to the top of the walls and make a circuit of the Medieval town. The *views,* especially those of the bulky cathedral, are stunning. (The Minster looks especially imposing at night, under floodlights.)

Aldwark runs parallel to the wall and you can follow it from the Monk Bar and the Merchant Taylors' Hall to another Medieval guildhall, **St. Anthony's Hall** (8), built from 1446–1453 and used since then as an arsenal, prison, school, and now, the headquarters of the Borthwick Institute of Historical Research. The *church of St. Cuthbert* (9) is just to the north of the guildhall.

Going west from the Minster, High Potter Gate leads to another Medieval gate, **Bootham Bar** (10), built over the foundations of a Roman gate. York's *Tourist Information Centre* is nearby, in Exhibition Square, near the **York City Art Gallery** (11). What began, in 1879, as a showcase for local artists is now one of Britain's finest art museums, with many works by Old Masters. Nearby *King's Manor* (12) was once the house of the abbot of *St. Mary's Abbey* (see below) and after that the reception hall where York greeted its most distinguished visitors, among them the Kings Henry VIII, James I, and Charles I, and Charles Dickens. (The poet Shelley and his first bride, Harriet Westbrook, who visited York in the early 19th century, stayed across town in the *Black Swan Inn,* on Peaseholme Green. Harriet drowned herself not long afterwards when the poet ran off with Mary Wollstonecraft, the teenage daughter of a friend.)

York's *municipal library* (13) is also on Exhibition Square, as is the *Yorkshire Museum.* The museum exhibits a fine collection of antiquities, with some excellent Roman reliefs and a Viking bowl, but its most popular attractions are outdoors, in the **Museum Gardens** (14). *St. Mary's Abbey,* an important Benedictine monastery established in 1089, stood here. Only several walls of its once prestigious church still

St. Mary's Abbey

stand, though its guest house, the *Hospitum,* has survived to display a good array of Roman antiquities. The garden walls also enclose the imposing *Multangular Tower,* a Medieval lookout built on a portion of York's Roman wall.

Leave Exhibition Square on Leonard Place, which soon becomes Blake Street. On your left you will pass a lovely Georgian building known as the **Assembly Rooms** (15). The Earl of Burlington built this imposing public building from 1731–1732, lavishing as much care on interior details as he did on the façade. No doubt the Duke took special care with the murals in the rotunda; they depict Roman York, a subject close to the heart of this Renaissance man who also translated Pliny. Blake Street soon comes to *St. Helen's Square,* the heart of York's shopping district and as busy now as it has been for centuries. If you walk to the far end of the square you will be in front of York's *main post office* (16) and next to it, *Mansion House* (17), also built by the Earl of Burlington, in 1724. It is the residence of the Lord Mayor, whose official domain is York's Medieval **Guildhall** (18), just behind Mansion House on the River Ouse. This near-perfect Gothic building, built between 1447–1453 and restored after it was severely damaged in World War II air raids, has witnessed many important events in York's civic life. Few days in its important history, though, are more momentous than the one in 1647 when the Scots came here to turn the rebellious British King Charles I over to Parliament for a bounty of £20,000. Charles was eventually beheaded at Whitehall Palace in London, though regarding the peaceful Ouse from the Guildhall's riverside terrace, it is easy to forget that British history tells an essentially bloody story. Walk across St. Helen's Square to the church of the same name, which is dedicated to the mother of York's "native" Roman emperor Constantine the Great.

A right turn into Davygate soon brings you to *St. Sampson's Square* (20). You are now surrounded by a York that really hasn't changed much since the Middle Ages. Actually, the neighborhood goes back much further, as evidenced by the ruins of Roman baths that are visible in the cellar of the nearby *Mail Coach Inn*. Parliament Street, the only broad avenue in Medieval York, begins in the square. It's width still accommodates a lively fruit and vegetable market. The narrowest of this neighborhood's many narrow streets is the **Shambles** (21), just to the north. Looking at the Shambles you will probably think the name refers to the confusing architecture of its buildings, their gables overhanging the pavement and leaning haphazardly toward one another. Actually, the name "Shambles" refers to the Medieval meaning of the word,

"slaughterhouse," and that is just what this quarter was, as many as 1,000 years ago. Even now, the Shambles is a good place to buy cold cuts, though antiques dealers and galleries do a brisk business, too.

The Shambles begins, off Market Street, at the old *Whip-ma-whop-ma-gate* (the key syllables being "whip" and "whop," for this gate was once the municipal whipping post) and ends in a street called The Pavement, a reminder that for most of York's history, its streets, with a few exceptions, were rutted tracks, usually either very muddy or very dusty. The 15th-century *church of All Saints* (22) is south on The Pavement at the beginning of a street called Coppergate, which leads farther south through what was once a neighborhood of Viking Jorvik.

Fascinating remains of Jorvik, recently excavated, have been incorporated in the new and very modern *Jorvik Viking Center,* where visitors climb aboard a train for a ride through a reconstructed Viking town, complete with cooking smells—a unique experience, but after the sights of real York, it may seem rather contrived.

All Saints Church also marks the beginning of Piccadilly, which leads to the ***Merchant Adventurers' Hall** (23), built between 1357–1368 and the oldest and most beautiful of York's Medieval guildhalls. This fine timbered building was the headquarters of the Merchant Adventurers, who traded in cloth. Like members of most guilds, the Adventurers were a civic-minded crew and also, as recently as 1900, provided shelter in their building to needy men and women. The guild is no longer active, though relics of its admirable past are on display in a small museum.

If, just outside the Merchant Adventurers' Hall, you cross the River Foss on Piccadilly and turn left, you will be on Walmgate. Passing two distinctive churches—*St. Denis* (24), with a Norman portal and beautiful 14th-century stained-glass windows, and *St. Margaret* (25), also with a remarkable Norman portal, you will come to the Medieval city's eastern gate, *Walmgate Bar* (26).

From the Merchant Adventurers' Hall you can also walk south a short distance to the **Castle grounds** (27), where William the Conqueror built a wooden fort near the confluence of the rivers Ouse and Foss in 1069. Of this massive fortress not much but the moat remains, though Clifford's Tower, built by another embattled king, Henry III, is still as imposing as it was when it went up around 1250. In one of the bleaker episodes of York's past, the city launched a pogrom on members of its influential Jewish community, many of whom were money lenders, and they took refuge on the castle grounds when the mobs set fire to their houses. Many perished

when the fire spread to the castle, too. A women's prison built on the castle grounds in 1780 now houses the ***Castle Folk Museum** (28), the best of its kind in England, thanks to one Dr. Kirk. The physician hated everything modern, and confronted with a rapidly changing England (he lived from 1869–1940) he preserved as much of the old ways as he could. The results of his labors can now be seen in the remarkable period rooms, in "Kirkgate," a painstakingly authentic Yorkshire business street of the Victorian era, cobblestones included, and in the Edwardian "Half Moon Court."

From the castle grounds follow the Ouse riverbank north and cross the *Ouse Bridge* (29) then turn right into North Street. After several blocks you will come to York's second church with the name *All Saints* (30), this one built between the 13th–15th centuries, its magnificent Medieval stained glass still intact. This is a neighborhood of fine churches, among them *St. Martin's-cum-Gregory* (31), on Martin Lane, also with beautiful Medieval glass, and *St. Mary's Younger* (32), on Bishophill Junior, with a remarkable Saxon tower.

For another view of York's secular past, follow Micklegate (which begins at Bridge Street at the foot of the Ouse Bridge) to ***Micklegate Bar** (33), the well-preserved southern approach to town, with a good stretch of Medieval walls on either side of

Micklegate Bar

it. The year 1746 was an especially gruesome period in the gate's history: The heads of Jacobite rebels, who supported the restoration of the Stuarts to the throne of England and were defeated near York at Culloden Moor, were strung up here for public view.

Queen Street follows the Medieval walls west and north from the bar to York's main *railroad station* (34). This is a good place to visit even if you're not going anywhere. The terminal houses **Rail Riders World** (35), where 500 meters (1,640 feet) of model railroads are a dream come true for kids and adult train buffs. In a spruced-up railyard shed there's an even bigger surprise in store, the **National Railway Museum** (36). Railroading is a great national pastime in Britain, which may explain the extraordinary care with which the museum's vintage rolling stock has been restored. Queen Victoria's private car is here, as is a 1797 locomotive, the clock from London's old Euston Station, a fascinating collection of old signals, and enough railroad paraphernalia to make this, in the opinion of many aficionados, the best of Britain's many railway museums.

From the front of the station, you can follow Station Road across Lendall Bridge, where it becomes Museum Street then Duncombe Place, to the Minster.

Excursion

Bishopthorpe, 5 km. (3 miles) south of York: The Archbishop of York, Britain's second-most important ecclesiastic (after the Archbishop of Canterbury), has lived in this important dwelling since 1226, though only the original chapel remains after an 18th-century restoration. Getting here, via boat on the River Ouse, is half the fun. Check with York's *Tourist Information Centre* in Exhibition Square for opening hours.

English Channel Ports

The following four Travel Routes lead to the English Channel and North Sea ports of Dover, Folkestone, Newhaven, Portsmouth, Southampton, and Harwich. All of these places have been gateways to the Continent and other continents for centuries. Roman legions, religious pilgrims, and armies have trod these paths to and from London, but this point of history might be a little hard to appreciate as you barrel down the highways alongside trucks and buses headed for the rest of Europe. However, these Travel Routes take you off the main roads into a quieter, more picturesque England—a good way to go if you're on your way to a Continent-bound ferry or just out to see the British countryside and soak in the local scenery and history.

TRAVEL ROUTE 1: ***London–*Dover–Folkestone (125 km.; 75 miles)

See color map.

To get from London to the seaport towns of Dover and Folkestone, you can choose between two equally interesting routes.

The coastal route is the frequent choice of Londoners yearning for a day at the beach. The route follows the coastline of the peninsula of Kent that juts into the North Sea on the north and the English Channel on the east, and it passes through many of England's most popular seaside towns; some of them—like Margate—big resorts with all the trappings, others—like Broadstairs—relatively quieter seaside retreats, and still others—like Deal—seaside bastions that have played prominent roles in England's history.

The inland route (see page 117) to the ports and resorts of Dover and Folkestone passes through the very heart of Kent, an agricultural region that is as beautiful as it is bountiful. Kent is historic, too—amazingly so—and there's hardly an old village or town on this route that won't tempt you to linger.

The Coastal Route

Leaving London on Route M 2, drive east as far as the historic city of *Faversham* (see page 120), then drive northeast on Route A 299 to the ancient coastal town of **Whitstable,** famous for its oys-

ters since the Romans first cultivated them here 2,000 years ago. Even the town's 15th-century *All Saints Church,* on Church Street, is connected with the mollusks—townsfolk used to keep an eye on their extensive oyster beds from the church tower. The busy seaport also has a colorful religious past, for it was here, in 597, that Saint Augustine baptized 10,000 Saxons in the River Swale. During the Middle Ages, Whitstable was an important port of entry for Europeans who crossed the Channel to make the pilgrimage to the shrine of Thomas à Becket in nearby Canterbury (see page 68).

Follow A 299 along the coast to **Herne,** a popular resort famous both for its lovely seaside promenade and its Roman past. The legions built a fort just to the east of the present-day town, at **Reculver.** You can walk there, or drive, about 5.5 km. (3.5 miles), along the coast. Although the sea has engulfed much of the once mighty fortress, some walls remain. *Reculver Church,* built inside the fort in 669, hasn't fared much better—only two 12th-century towers survive.

From Herne, Route A 299 swings inland. When you come to Route A 28, turn north toward the northwest corner of the pen-

insula, across which stretch **Margate** and a conglomerate of other resorts fronting a 14-km.-(9-mile-) long strip of fine sandy beach. In 1753, Margate witnessed the use of the world's first bathing machine, a small boathouse mounted on wheels that could be pushed to the water's edge so the bather could climb in and out of the water in absolute privacy. Looking at these crowded beaches on a warm summer's day, though, you may find it hard to believe that such modesty ever existed in these parts. Aside from the beach, Margate's biggest attraction is *Dane Park,* where a series of caves, discovered in 1835, has been elaborately decorated with seashells. Charles Dickens came to this part of the world frequently and stayed at the quieter resort of **Broadstairs,** just around the point from Margate on Route B 2052. Queen Victoria stayed at Broadstairs, too, in a house that is now occupied by the town offices. Dickens called the town "one of the freest and freshest little places in the world" and he aptly named his novel *Bleak House* after a house atop the cliffs. The town's most historic attraction is *York Gate,* a towerlike structure built on Harbour Street in 1540 to protect the coastline.

Just south of Broadstairs is **Ramsgate,** whose southern exposure affords it a pleasant, mild climate. One of Ramsgate's biggest admirers was A. W. Pugin, the architect who created

Reculver

many of the designs for London's Houses of Parliament, and he built the town's *church of St. Augustine* at his own expense. Ramsgate's greatest hour came in World War II, when the townsfolk ferried thousands of stranded troops across the English Channel from Dunkirk in France. **Pegwell Bay** and its town of **Cliffsend,** just to the east, are also famous for Channel crossings. Cliffsend is England's first hoverport, from which jet-propelled hovercraft skim just above the water to make the trip in a mere 40 minutes. The area has, in fact, witnessed several other historic landings. The Vikings Hengist and Horsa set foot on English soil in 449 at a site that is now marked by the *Hugin,* a reproduction of their ship that, in 1949, was sailed here from Frederiskund, Denmark to commemorate the 1,500th anniversary of the historic landing. Saint Augustine, who brought Christianity to England, also landed nearby, in 559. *St. Augustine's Cross,* erected on a side road to Minster (follow signs), marks the event.

Viking ship *Hugin*

Rejoin Route A 256, which takes you south and inland through *Sandwich* (see page 73), where you can get on Route A 258 and head back toward the coast and **Deal,** famous for its golf links at the Royal Cinque Ports Golf Course and for its illustrious past. Julius Caesar and his legions are said to have landed here in A.D. 55. Beginning in the 13th century, Deal was known as a "limb" of the Cinque Ports, which, by royal decree, provided ships and men to serve England in return for exemption from taxes and for other privileges. Deal prospered in other ways, too. Just offshore lie the treacherous and feared Goodwin Sands, where capricious winds have grounded many a ship over the years. As a result, Deal has been a bustling port in the storm for seamen awaiting favorable winds. Dangerous as the sands are, there is a bit of romantic myth about them, too: According to legend, the sandbar is all that remains of a thriving island that slipped beneath the waves in a fierce 11th-century storm.

Henry VIII built three castles in Deal, two of which survive much as he left them 400 years ago. The remarkably well-preserved *Deal Castle* is built in the shape of a Tudor Rose. *Walmer Castle,* practically a stone's throw down the beach in the adjacent town of *Walmer,* has been the official residence since 1730 of the Lord Warden of the Cinque Ports. Although this is now

Deal Castle

largely an honorary title, it comes with rights to the seaside castle and has in recent years been bestowed upon the likes of Winston Churchill and the Queen Mother. There was a time, though, when the Lord Warden played an important role in Britain's maritime policy.

From Walmer, Route A 258 crosses the downs to ***Dover**. Over the ages this busy seaport has hosted Roman legions, the knights of Richard I who assembled here in 1190 to embark on the Crusades, French marauders who pillaged the town in 1295, and American and British seamen who formed the Dover patrol to guarantee safe passage for some 12 million soldiers on their way to the battlefields of World War I. All of these visitors have no doubt gaped in awe at the famous White Cliffs. The chalk heights overlook the Straits of Dover, in which England decimated the Spanish Armada in 1588 and whose 27 km. (17 miles) of watery expanses between England and France have been a challenge for the adventurous for centuries. The Frenchman François Blanchard became the first man to float across in a balloon, in 1785. Exactly 90 years later, Captain Matthew Webb became the first man to swim across, in 21 hours and 45 minutes, a record that has been broken many times since. (Captain Webb drowned in 1885, however, when he attempted to swim the rapids beneath Niagara Falls.) The most famous of the cliffs is *Shakespeare's Cliff* (so-called because in Shakespeare's *King Lear,* Edgar leads his blind father to the precipice), just to the west of town. Dover's future lies at the foot of this cliff, for this is to be the British terminus of the "Chunnel," the tunnel that will eventually link Britain with the Continent (See page 308).

The best reminder of Dover's turbulent past is its *castle*, which

Dover Castle

rises a sheer 400 feet to the east of the center of the city. The castle is said to capture England's history in stone. Its 35 acres shelter a Roman lighthouse, the seventh-century *church of St. Mary de Castro,* built of Roman stones, and walls 8 meters (24 feet) thick that Henry II built to protect England against a French invasion. The castle has withstood the ravages of storms and invaders for centuries and provided protection to residents of Dover during the almost continual shellings of World War II. These days the castle is a popular excursion spot, with outrageously good views of the town, the cliffs, the Channel, and, on a clear day, France.

Down below, Dover bustles with the comings and goings of ferry and hovercraft passengers. A good place to watch the action in the busy harbor is *Admiralty Pier,* a waterfront promenade. Medieval pilgrims who crossed the Channel on their way to **Canterbury (see page 68) also landed in Dover, and often they bedded down at the 13th-century *Maison Dieu,* now part of the Town Hall on Biggin Street. A reminder of Dover's ancient past is the *Painted House,* nearby on New Street. The obviously prosperous Roman residents had the building covered with frescoes and installed central heating. As you leave Dover, you may want to make a short excursion of about 4 km. (2.5 miles) up the old road to Canterbury to the spot where the 12th-century *abbey of St. Rade-*

gund lies in wonderfully romantic ruin.

Route A 20, slightly inland, follows the top of the cliffs south to the fashionable resort of **Folkestone,** a flower-filled town of 44,000 inhabitants that may have been the headquarters of the Roman fleet. Relaxation is clearly the main business here today. Virtually anyone who comes to Folkestone makes the promenade along the *Leas,* a grassy walk lined with fine hotels on one side and on the other, hanging gardens laced with paths that lead down to a pleasant beach. The Leas ends at the *church of Saints Mary and Eanswith,* founded in the 12th century on the site of a seventh-century church. A window commemorates the physician William Harvey, who was born in the town in 1578 and during his distinguished career discovered the circulation of blood.

The Inland Route

Leaving London through the rather grimy East End, you will soon come to the pleasant town of **Greenwich.** In the days when Britainnia ruled the waves, Greenwich was the country's most important port. So, it is hardly surprising that the town is dominated by the *Royal Naval College,* a Baroque palace that is largely the work of Christopher Wren. The best place to review the town's seafaring past is at the *National Maritime Museum,*

Royal Naval College

filled with seascapes by Turner, relics of Admiral Nelson, and other nautical memorabilia. Greenwich is the berth for two important ships, too—the *Gypsy Moth IV,* the ketch in which Sir Francis Chichester circumnavigated the globe from August 1966–May 1967, and the speediest masted clipper of the China trade, the *Cutty Sark.* Greenwich is also home to the *Royal Observatory,* for years the source of Greenwich Mean Time. The floor is marked to show the division of the hemispheres, so you can stand in both at once. A recent addition to the town's maritime importance is the nearby *Thames Barrier,* a moveable flood gate that prevents ocean tides from causing the Thames to swell its bank and inundate London and other riverside places.

Continue east on Route A 20 to **Dartford,** one of London's easternmost suburbs. Dartford has been a busy center of commerce since the early 17th century, when a German named John Spilman came to town and built one of England's first paper mills here on the banks of the River Darent. The term "foolscap" supposedly comes from a jester who is pictured on the Spilman coat of arms. Another famous figure of local history is Wat Tyler, who in 1381 supposedly assembled a mob of farmers at an inn on High Street (the inn now bears his name) and marched on London, where the Lord Mayor promptly killed him.

A side road, Route 225, leads 5 km. (3 miles) south to the *church of St. John's Jerusalem,* founded by the 12th-century Knights of the Templar. From Dartford, Route A 2 continues east to **Cobham,** a quiet little village with a surprisingly rich history. The little *church* has 18 old brasses (memorial tablets, very popular among the Elizabethans, that are usually fashioned from copper or zinc), the largest collection in England. The *Leather Bottle Inn* has a remarkable collection of relics relating to Charles Dickens, who lived in and around nearby Rochester (see page 119) and set many of his novels in these parts. Cobham's most renowned structure, though, is its estate, **Old Cobham Hall,* built by the renowned architect Inigo Jones from 1662–1672. The place is now a girls' school, but in its more glorious past was the country seat of the Duke of Richmond and later the Duke of Darnley. A magnificent park of rhododendrons still flourishes.

Owletts, to the west of the village, is another fine 17th-century house, once home to Charles II.

Route A 2 continues on to **Rochester,** a pleasant town that also has a long history and—a boon for Charles Dickens buffs— many associations with the novelist. The Romans settled Rochester, though its name comes from its Saxon conquerors: Hfrof's *caestre* (castle). Indeed, the *castle* is one of Rochester's big attractions—and big it is, one of the largest in England, its massive walls rising almost 40 meters (120 feet). A climb to the top affords a good view of Rochester's river, the Meadway.

Saint Augustine brought Christianity to Rochester around 600 and founded a modest church that soared to the present heights of *Rochester Cathedral* in the 12th and 13th centuries. The Norman builders outdid themselves at Rochester and included in their design a stunning West Front,

Rochester Cathedral

with a recessed *doorway,* that is said to be one of England's best examples of Norman architecture.

Over the years Rochester has attracted many great personages—some of them unwelcome—including the Dutch admiral De Ruyter, who sank part of the English fleet not far from here in 1667. James II fled to Rochester after his abdication in 1688, and it was here, in 1540, that Henry VIII met Anne of Cleeves, his fourth wife. The most popular lore, though, surrounds Charles Dickens, who spent much of his childhood in Rochester and returned at the height of his success to live at *Gad's Hill Place.* Get acquainted with Dickensian Rochester by visiting the *Charles Dickens Centre* in Eastgate House, on High Street. The chalet the author used as a study at Gad's Hill has been transferred to the garden. Inside, displays pinpoint the various locales that crop up on the pages of Dickens' novels. Eastgate House itself makes an appearance in *The Mystery of Edwin Drood* and *The Pickwick Papers.* The *Restoration House,* where Charles II spent a night in 1660, figures in *Great Expectations.*

Leave Rochester through the adjoining city of *Chatham* (a port and important naval headquarters since the days of Henry VIII) and get on Route A 229 which dips south. (You may also proceed directly east to *Faversham,* see below, on Route A 2.) On A 229, you will come first to **Aylesford,**

Aylesford

with a beautiful 14th-century bridge across the Meadway and an interesting monastery, *The Friars*, which the Carmelites founded in 1240, then repossessed 700 years later. The road continues to **Maidstone**, the capital of Kent, an agricultural center, and a lively market town. Maidstone has its fair share of paper mills along the Meadway, but it is also crisscrossed by lively old streets lined with beautiful houses and shops. The town's most venerable pieces of architecture are from the 14th century: the *church of All Saints* and the *Tithe Barn*, which now houses an extraordinary carriage museum. The writer William Hazlitt was born in Maidstone in 1778, and his memorabilia is displayed in the *Museum and Art Gallery*, in *Chillington Manor House*, a 16th-century mansion.

Weather and time permitting, take a nice walk about 3 km. (about 2 miles) upriver to

*Allington Castle,** built in the 13th century and the home of the 16th-century poet Sir Thomas Wyatt.

From Maidstone head north again on Route A 249, which after 11 km. (9 miles) comes to *Sittingbourne*, a manufacturing center whose famous attraction is the 14th-century *church of St. Michael*, just to the north of town in *Milton Regis*. Route A 2 now continues east to the fascinating old town of **Faversham**, which was chartered in 812 and where Witenagemore, the Anglo-Saxon version of Parliament, convened in 930. King Stephen founded an abbey here in the 12th century, though little remains of it but a few stones. The bones of Stephen and his queen, Mathilda, lie in the 14th-century *church of St. Mary of Charity*. Faversham has another abbey, too, this one built in the 16th century and now splendidly restored. The town has many other old buildings as well, including the *Guildhall*, from 1574, which rises above the old marketplace on 19 oak pillars, and the *Old Grammar School*, now a Freemason's Hall, built in 1567.

You can now continue directly to **Canterbury* (see page 68) on Route A 2. If you have time, you may want to explore the countryside around this fascinating pilgrimage city. Route 28 leads southwest along the River Stour through *Chartham*, with a 14th-century, timber-roofed church that is noted for its stained glass, to *Chilham*, 8 km. (5 miles) from Canterbury. A 17th-century governor of Virginia, Edward Diggs, was born in Chilham on an estate built by Inigo Jones and landscaped by the equally esteemed Capability Brown.

From Canterbury, Route A 2 continues south for 36 km. (22 miles) through a countryside planted with hops to Dover (see page 116). From here you may complete Travel Route 1 as described on pages 116–117.

Chilham

TRAVEL ROUTE 2: ***London–Reigate–Brighton– Newhaven (100 km.; 60 miles)

See color map.

It's been said that there's nothing closer to an Englishman's heart than his garden. This may or may not be true, but it might account for the care lavished on Leonardslee and the other gardens that dot the already scenic Surrey countryside along this route to the port of Newhaven, a major departure point for France.

Leave London through its southern suburbs and follow the signs for Route A 217. You will pass through *Banstead* and after another 16 km. (10 miles) come to **Reigate,** a pretty, ancient town nestled at the foot of a hill of the same name. Any one of 55,000 inhabitants is likely to tell you that barons met in a cavern beneath the castle keep, now called "Baron's Cave," to draw up the Magna Carta. Popular as the story is, there's not a grain of truth to it, although Reigate does have a 12th-century castle, now in ruin, and it is indeed built over a series of subterranean vaults.

Lord Howard of Effingham, who routed the Spanish Armada in 1588, lived just south of town on the estate of *Reigate Priory,* and he is buried in the 12th-century *church of St. Mary Magdalen.* The church has long been popular among Reigate's literary populace, for it houses the *Cranston Library,* England's first lending library founded in 1701.

Route A 23 continues south for another 10 km. (6 miles) to *Horley* and the 13th–15th-century *Charlwood Church,* famous for its wall paintings. Continue south another 7 km. (4 miles) to *Crawley,* a sprawling residential town near London's second major airport, Gatwick. For a look at a quieter country town, turn east on Route A 264 just before you get to Crawley for a short side trip to **East Grinstead,** about 16 km. (10 miles) away. There's not too much here to remind you of the 20th century—certainly not High Street, lined with timbered houses, or the magnificent alms-house from 1619, *Sackville College.*

From *Crawley,* Route A 23 continues south for about 11 km. (6.5 miles) through *St. Leonard's Forest,* one of the most scenic parts of this lovely Sussex coun-tryside, to *Handcross,* a typical English country village. After about 10 km. (6 miles), Route B 2114 turns off to the east and soon leads to **Nymans Gardens,** 30 acres of rare conifers and shrubs planted early in this century. The mild Sussex climate and fertile soil make this region a gardener's paradise. About 8 km. (5 miles) farther down A 23 you'll come to the town of *Bolney* and the nearby ***Leonardslee Gardens.** Leonardslee is an absolute must if you're making this trip in the spring. In fact, the gardens are only open from April–June, because they are planted only with camelias, rhododendrons, and other spring-flowering shrubs and trees. *South Lodge Gardens,* in the nearby village of *Lower Beeding,* are also famous for their rhododendrons.

You are now nearing *Brighton* (see page 138). Before you get into town, though, you may want to get off A 23 and explore some of the surrounding sights. About 10 km. (6 miles) before you get to Brighton, Route A 281 takes you west past two magnificent man-sions. *Danny,* built in 1595, was the home of the Campion family, whose members stare down from centuries' worth of portraits. *Newton Place,* just down the road, is a spectacular 17th-cen-tury house surrounded by a moat.

As you drive south into Brighton, you will cross the South Downs, a line of stark hills that run for about 100 km. (60 miles) along the coast. From *Brighton,* Route A 259 heads west between the sea, the downs, and a seemingly endless row of bungalow colonies to **Newhaven,** a port town that bustles with ferry traffic to and from the Continent, primarily Dieppe in France. The town owes its prominence to a fierce storm that lashed the coast in 1579 and changed the course of the River Ouse so it ran right through the village, then called Meeching, to form a good harbor. Making the most of this act of nature, the townsfolk changed the name of the town to Newhaven—exactly what it was—and built up the port. About all that remains of old Meeching is the 12th-century *church.* A more modern reminder of the port's past is its *fort,* one of 72 along this stretch of coast that Britain fortified to repel an inva-sion by Napoleon.

TRAVEL ROUTE 3: ***London–*Guildford–**Winchester–Southampton (123 km.; 77 miles)

See color map.

Had you made the Grand Tour of Europe even half a century ago you would probably have taken this trip from London by train down to Southampton to connect with your Transatlantic liner. Travel may no longer be quite as romantic as it once was, but this trip across the downs, past thatch-roofed villages, old market towns, and grand country seats, is still a pleasure, and besides, Southampton is more interesting viewed on foot than it looks from the railings of an outbound ship.

You can drive directly, and rapidly, from London to Southampton, a trip of 123 km. (77 miles) on Route M 3 to Winchester (see page 99) and from there Route A 3 south to Southampton. You can also take Route A 3 directly from London to Guildford (see below) and pick up the rest of this Travel Route from there. However, a trip on the less travelled route described here is actually shorter and far more enjoyable. If you leave London through its southern extremes on A 24, you will pass through **Epsom,** famous for its mineral springs that once yielded the widely acclaimed, healing Epsom Salts and for its racetrack, Epsom Downs. The most famous of all horse races, the Derby Stakes, has been run here in late May or early June since 1780, when the Earl of Derby wagered a bet on a swift horse. Continue south to **Leatherhead,** a pleasant town whose greatest attraction—aside from a colorful history that includes the fact that John Wesley, founder of the Methodist Church,

preached his last sermon here, in 1792—is its fine location on the edge of the North Downs. These gentle, dunelike hills stretch all the way from Leatherhead across the rest of Surrey and Kent to the White Cliffs of Dover. Weather permitting, walkers take to these hills in droves, and Leatherhead is especially popular among Londoners out for some nearby country air. You can see a nice bit of the Downs as you drive west from Leatherhead toward *Guildford* on Route A 246. As you near Guildford, you will come to a turnoff for **Polesden Lacey,** a lovely Edwardian house surrounded by woods and gardens. This peaceful setting was home to the sharp-tongued Irish politician and dramatist Richard Sheridan (1751–1816), who penned such ripping comedies of manners as *The School for Scandal.*

In just a few minutes' time A 246 comes to another mansion, *Hatchlands,* built in 1758 by the formidable Admiral Edward Boscawen (a.k.a. "Old Dreadnaught"). The distinguished architect Robert Adam designed the interior—his first work in England. Route A 246 next passes the Duke of Sutherland's country seat, *Sutton Place,* a Tudor mansion dating from 1525 (not open to the public), then comes to the neighborhood's finest estate, **Clandon Park.** Venetian architect Giacomo Leoni built the estate in 1731 for the Onslow family—a breed of fiery politicians that sent three Speakers of the House to Commons. The pink, rectangular house, a perfect example of Classical style, looks more typical of the Veneto than of Surrey, but its very British gardens were designed by landscape architect Capability Brown, who also laid out the gardens at Kew (see page 58).

After 4 km. (2.5 miles) on A 246 you'll enter **Guildford,** a pleasant town of many attractions. The least impressive of them is no doubt the depressingly austere, red brick *Cathedral of the Holy Spirit,* a modern effort consecrated in 1961. Not all of Guildford's modern buildings are as unsuccessful, though. Take a look at the stunning *Yvonne Arnaud Theatre* in the meadows along the River Wey. If it's old world charm you want, head over to cobbled *High Street,* one of the steepest in England. Climb to the top to see the *Royal Grammar School,* which Edward VI founded in 1553. Its ancient library, from 1573, still has 89 chained books. *Abbott's Hospital,* across the street, is an almshouse built in

Yvonne Arnaud Theatre

1619. The large clock projecting over High Street about halfway down its length belongs to the 17th-century *Guildhall.* Nearby *Trinity Church* was rebuilt in the 18th century after the tower of an earlier church collapsed. The much older *church of St. Mary's,* built from 1160–1180, is on Quarry Street. Just beyond, the Medieval *Castle Arch* opens to Guildford's public gardens. The pile in the middle of the greenery is the keep of the Norman *castle* that once defended the town and today provides a good view, well

Royal Grammar School

worth a climb to the top. Surrey's antiquities can be seen in the *museum* adjoining the Castle Arch, which also displays relics of Charles Lutwidge Dodgson, the Oxford mathematician who under the name of Lewis Carroll wrote *Alice's Adventures in Wonderland*. He lived in Quarry Street for a time and is buried in Guildford.

In addition to the historic houses that you passed on the way into town, you may want to visit ***Losely House,** 3 km. (about 2 miles) to the south. Sir William More, a relative of the statesman and saint, Sir Thomas More, built this mansion and its park from 1561–1569. He filled it with exquisite furnishings and fittings—including paneling from Henry VIII's Nonesuch Palace, which is somewhat ironic given that Thomas's quarrels with the King cost him his head. The Mores' descendants still live in the house. **Albury Park House,** 5 km. (3 miles) southeast of Guildford, has been broken into apartments for retired gentlefolk, though its magnificent reception rooms—the result of the combined genius of designer A. W. Pugin and architect Sir John Soane, who rebuilt the ancient house in 1847—remain intact. Gardening enthusiasts may want to take A 3 about 35 km. (21 miles) north to the town of *Ripley*. (If you take A 3 directly from London to Guildford, you'll speed by it on your way down.) ***Wisely Gardens,** a showcase of the Royal Horticultural Society, is located in Ripley. You'll find a visit at any time during the growing season rewarding because the garden always has something in bloom—the rock garden and alpine meadow in April; the rhododendrons in May; the heather in September.

Continuing to Southampton, leave Guildford on Route A 31 for a view-packed drive along a ridge known as Hog's Back. After about 16 km. (10 miles) you will come to **Farnham,** a pretty old town dominated by a Norman *castle*. For eight centuries Farnham was the seat of the bishops of Winchester. These two aspects of Farnham come together in the fact that the bishops of Winchester took up residence in the castle in the 12th century and lived there until 1927, when the bishops of Guildford moved in for a short time. More modest dwellings, but nonetheless exquisite, line West Street and Castle Street. Mementos of the town's most famous citizen, the radical journalist and essayist William Cobbett (1763–1835), are displayed alongside other antiquities in *Willmer House,* built in 1718 and one of the town's finest.

As you continue east on Route A 31, you will cross into Hampshire and come to **Alton,** a pleasant market town that once lay on the Pilgrim's Way, the track on which the Medieval faithful made their way across the Downs to the shrine of St. Thomas à Becket in Canterbury. Alton has two good museums: the *Allen Gallery,* featuring paintings by W. H. Allen

(1863–1943) and some fine ceramics and silver, and the *Curtis Museum*, which displays a nice mix of old farm implements, geological specimens, and the like.

After just 2 km. (a little more than a mile), A 31 comes to **Chawton,** the small town where the novelist Jane Austen lived from 1809–1817. Her house, where she wrote *Emma, Persuasion*, and *Mansfield Park*, is now a museum filled with mementos. Turn south here onto Route B 3006, which in 8 km. (5 miles) comes to **Selborne,** a picturesque village of thatch-roofed houses where Gilbert White, the naturalist and author of the classic *Natural History and Antiquities of Selborne*, was born in 1720 and died in 1793. His house, *The Wakes*, is now a museum filled with his personal effects and those of Antarctic explorer Captain Lawrence Oates. (Oates reached the South Pole in 1912, but, when he became ill on the return trip, he walked across the ice to his death so that he wouldn't delay the expedition.) White is buried in the yard of the town's Norman church, which his great-nephew helped restore in the 19th century.

Return to Route A 31, which in 25 km. (15 miles) comes to **Winchester* (see page 99), then drops south to Southampton.

Southampton

See map on page 127.

About 200 years ago Southampton struck the novelist Daniel Defoe as a "truly ancient town." This probably won't be your first impression of Southampton, which today is a sprawling, busy port city of 200,000 people and vast tracts of docklands and industrial zones. If you are sailing for New York on the *Queen Elizabeth II*, you'll leave from Southampton. As the ship slips out of the harbor, you may want to remember that it was from here that Richard the Lion-Hearted set sail for the Crusades, in 1189; the troops of Henry V boarded a ship here in 1415 and went off to war with France at Agincourt; and the pilgrims sailed for America from the town quay in 1620. The Romans and Saxons built settlements here, and enough reminders of Southampton's Medieval heydays remain to get you thinking about the past.

The best place to begin a tour is at the *Tourist Information Bureau* (1) at the corner of Canute Road and Above Bar Street (the corner is known as The Junction). The buildings just north on Above Bar went up in the 1930s and comprise Southampton's **Civic Centre** (2), a bastion of municipal offices and civic culture. You'll find not only the town *library* here, but also the town *art gallery*, which is hung with a good collection of British paintings from the 18th–20th centuries. The **Titanic Memorial** (3), at the top of Above Bar in East Park, is a gift from survivors of the disaster to commemorate those who died when the liner sank on its way from Southampton to New

York in 1912. Edward Lutyens's *War Memorial* to those who fell in the two world wars faces the park from the other side of London Road. Walking south from the park on Above Bar Street you will pass Civic Centre Road, which leads west to *Central Station* (4), then come to ***Bargate** (5), a 12th-century gate that was the most important entrance to the Medieval city. It was here that customs officials levied their tolls on goods going in and out of Southampton—a profitable enterprise for the town government, whose meeting hall, *Bargate Guildhall*, is just above the gate's archway. The Hall is now a *town museum*.

You are now in the heart of Medieval Southampton. Follow Bargate Street west to **Arundel Tower** (6), a remainder of the 13th-century city wall. Actually, a good bit of the wall remains, and you can climb to the top and walk to **Catchcold Tower** (7), its name a reference to the discomfort of keeping watch from its drafty heights. Remains of Southampton's old castle adjoin the walls here, though most of it—and certainly the spirit of the place—has been usurped by an apartment block.

Follow the walls south to Blue Anchor Lane and the **Tudor House** (8), a picturesque structure built between 1510–1518 that now houses a museum displaying old furnishings. Its garden, overshadowed by the town wall, has been planted as a Tudor knot garden. The adjoining

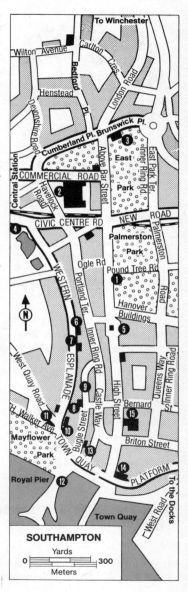

Bargate

church of St. Michael (9) was built in the 11th century and is one of Southampton's most ancient buildings. However, you may find it a little hard to appreciate the few Norman components that survived a clumsy restoration in 1826.

From the church, walk toward the walls on Westgate, a street that takes its name from the 14th-century **West Gate** (10), which was once the entrance to Southampton's quays. The pilgrims who settled America walked through this gate on August 15, 1620, an event that is commemorated across the way at the *Pilgrim Fathers' Memorial* (11). Modern-day travellers, most of them vacationers, set out for the *Isle of Wight* (see page 142) from the end of nearby *Royal Pier* (12). Just across the Western Esplanade at the foot of Bugle Street stands the 14th-century **Wool House** (13), a stone warehouse that was once filled to its beautiful rafters with what has long been one of England's major exports. In subsequent years it has housed French prisoners captured in the Napoleonic wars and now ship models and other artifacts of the town's maritime museum. Heading south on the Town Quay you will soon come to **God's House** (14), as the 12th-century *Hospice of St. Julian* is called, and next to it, *God's House Tower*, which must be one of the town's most utilitarian structures. It has been used for fortification, as a piggery, as a warehouse, and now as a museum of local archaeology. Many of the surrounding 12th- to 14th-century houses still show the damage they incurred in the bombings of World War II. If you follow Winkle Street one block and turn left, you will be on High Street, Southampton's major avenue, which will take you north past the *main post office* (15) and Bargate to The Junction.

TRAVEL ROUTE 4: ***London–Colchester–Harwich (118 km; 73 miles)

See color map.

If you are leaving England for northern Europe, chances are you will be boarding a ship in Harwich or its sister port of Felixstowe. This route allows you to take in some of the great scenery of Essex on the way there. After a side trip to Southend-on-Sea, London's busy seaside playground, you can proceed north across the quiet, historic countryside to Colchester, a must stop for connoisseurs of oysters—England's finest come from its nearby beds—then head north to Harwich, with a possible side trip to the fine beaches of nearby Clacton.

Leave London on Route A 12, which soon comes to *Romford.* From here, Travel Route 4 continues north, though you may want to detour east on Route A 127—if it's a hot day, just follow the stream of cars—to **Southend-on-Sea.** This is London's closest (just 73 km.; 44 miles) seaside resort—a lively place at the mouth of the Thames. The city attracts about six million visitors a year, a good many of them Londoners who come in droves on weekends and for longer summer holidays to swim, golf, take in the sun and surf from 8 km. (5 miles) of promenades, attend shows at the famous *Palace Theatre,* and the greatest pleasure of them all, walk the length of Southend's *great pier,* at 2 km. (1.2 miles) the longest in the world.

Southend has its quieter attractions, too. Much of *Prittlewell Priory,* including its refectory, dates to 1110, and the museum it houses displays artifacts from an even older Southend, many from the Iron Age. The *Beechcroft Art Gallery,* in the most fashionable part of town, Westcliff, has an outstanding collection of European paintings, with an emphasis on British works. For a good view of the Thames as it flows into the North Sea, go to *Hadley* just to the west of town and climb to the top of the tower of its Norman church. The adjoining *castle* was refurbished from 1359–1370 as a residence for King Edward III; it may look familiar, because it was one of painter John Constable's favorite subjects.

From *Romford,* Route A 12 continues north for 14 km. (8.5 miles) to **Ingatestone,** a village with many fine old houses, including *The Bell,* a 16th-century inn. The town's showplace *Ingatestone Hall,* also from the 16th century, now houses a museum of local history. In another 10 km. (6 miles), Route A 12 comes to **Chelmsford,** the county seat of Essex and famous in the annals of technology. It was the first town in England to be lit electrically, and it was here, around 1896–1897, that the Italian physicist Guglielmo Marconi did some of his first experiments with wireless telegraphy. The town's 15th-century *Cathedral Church of St. Mary* collapsed in 1800, though many old elements, including its original tower and an 18th-century spire, survive. Continue up Route A 12 through *Witham,* where you may want to stop for at least a quick look at its 13th-century *church.* Mystery fans will definitely want to stop, for Dorothy Sayers lived in Witham at 24 Newland Street. About 5 km. (3 miles) up Route A 12 you will come to *Kelvdon,* whose High Street is lined with fine, 17th-century houses. You may make a short side trip here by following Route B 1024 about 5 km. (3 miles) to ***Coggeshall** and **Paycocke House,* the ornately decorated, 15th-century home of a wealthy merchant family. Follow B 1204 for 7 km. (4 miles) to the village of *Mark's Tey,* where you will rejoin Route A 12. In about 8 km. (5 miles), you will come to ***Colchester** (88 km., 53 miles). As you drive into this town of 77,000 inhabitants, you will probably be struck, first, by just how many old houses there are—literally hundreds of them from the 18th century and earlier—and second, by the number of signs advertising oysters. The mollusks have been cultivated in the nearby tidal waters of the Colne since the Romans settled the town in A.D. 43. (Colchester is also famous for roses and for textiles, the latter an import that Dutch refugee weavers brought to the town several centuries ago.)

The Romans were relative latecomers to Colchester, for there was probably a settlement of the earliest Britons here in the fifth century B.C. By the first century A.D., Colchester was the residence of King Cunobelinus, chief of the powerful Catuvellauni tribe and, by virtue of might, the king of all Britain. Cunobelinus was

the model for King Cymbeline in Shakespeare's play of the same name. Under Queen Boadicea, the Britons pillaged Colchester in A.D. 60, killing the Roman inhabitants. The Anglo-Saxons, the Danes, and finally the Normans also conquered Colchester. One of Colchester's most famous "modern" citizens is William Gilbert, who was born here in 1544. The physician managed to find time between administering to Queen Elizabeth I and King James I to experiment with magnetism and electrical force, and his efforts won for him the sobriquet "Father of Electricity."

Quite a bit of this event-filled past is still in evidence in Colchester, which is in part surrounded by its Roman wall. The *castle*—which William the Conqueror built with Roman bricks over the ruins of the Roman temple—still stands, too. Its keep shelters one of Britain's finest **museums of archaeology* (a leg of the Colchester and Essex Museum, which also occupies several other historic buildings in town), with many reminders of Colchester's Roman past.

The castle isn't Colchester's only structure to have been built of Roman bricks: so were *St. Botolph's Priory,* founded in 1095 and now in ruin, and the tower of *Holy Trinity Church,* which is 1,000 years old. The church houses an interesting collection of items relating to shipping, part of the Colchester and Exeter Museum. *Holly Trees,* a mansion from 1781 near the Castle Park, houses a museum of local history. *St. John's Abbey* gateway is all that remains of a Benedictine abbey built in 1415.

Leave Colchester to the west on Route A 604. At the town of *Hare Green,* you may either take Route A 20 directly northeast into Harwich, about 35 km. (21 miles) away, or you may go a roundabout route by dropping south on Route A 133 for a drive of 30 km. (18 miles) to **Clacton-on-Sea,** the most popular seaside resort in Essex, featuring many hotels, restaurants, and other trappings. Good beaches extend about 16 km. (10 miles) north of Clacton, past *Frinton,* whose seaside cliffs are popular with walkers, to *Walton-on-the-Naze*. The Naze is a sandy headland where amateur paleontologists still find arrowheads and other artifacts from the Pliocene period.

From Clacton you can take Route B 1027 west about 6 km. (3.5 miles) to the village of **St. Osyth.** The picturesque ruins of its 13th-century *priory* mark the spot where the Danes executed the Anglo-Saxon Queen Osyth in 870. The 15th-century gatehouse has survived and now has a good collection of paintings and Chinese jade and ceramics. From Clacton, Route B 1414 goes north about 44 km. (26 miles) into **Harwich** (118 km.; 73 miles), an old port city on a point of land bounded by the River Stour, the River Orwell, and the North Sea. It is no surprise that

Harwich has a long nautical past: Admiral Nelson used to throw back a few brews at the old *Three Cups Inn,* and Captain Jones, who sailed the *Mayflower* to America, lived in King's Head Street. The town's most important structures include its old *lighthouses* and the earthwork *fort* built in 1818 to repel a possible invasion by Napoleon. Today, Harwich and Felixstowe (see page 191), across the harbor, are important ports that handle ferry traffic to and from the Hook of Holland, Zeebrugge in Belgium, Hamburg and Bremerhaven in Germany, and Esbjerg in Denmark.

The beautiful countryside inland from Harwich along the River Stour was a favorite haunt of painter John Constable (1776–1837). He painted the landscape constantly, and one of his favorite subjects was the *Flatford Mill,* about 20 km. (12 miles) west of Harwich on Route B 1352.

Flatford Mill

Southern England

It is no accident the land south of London was the first in England to be settled. The Channel coast has long been alluring to Britain's continental neighbors, and the landscape, with its rolling hills, is certainly hospitable. The civilizations that have taken root in southern England are much in evidence today. Richborough, where the Romans first set foot on English soil in A.D. 43, is not too far from Cliffsend, where the Vikings came ashore in A.D. 449 and Saint Augustine landed in 597. The great southern cathedral cities of Canterbury, Chichester, Winchester, and Salisbury bear witness to the region's Medieval importance. All of these places are quite near London; the following Travel Routes will tell you how to explore them.

TRAVEL ROUTE 5: *Dover–Brighton–Portsmouth–Isle of Wight–Bournemouth (274 km.; 170 miles)

See color map.

Although England's southern coast is best known as the departure and arrival point for travelers to the Continent, the region is rich in history and scenery and well worth a tour for its own sake, which this Travel Route provides. From Dover, it takes you across Romney Marsh, past Henry VIII's Camber Castle to Hastings, where the battle that determined Britain's future was fought in 1066. From there the route leads through picturesque seaside towns to the most famous of all British resorts, Brighton, and on to the important port cities of Portsmouth and Bournemouth.

Dover, (see page 116), the largest of the Channel ports, is well known for the white cliffs that shelter it on the east and west. Leave the city from the west on A 20 and, at *Folkestone* (see page 117), take A 259 west. Just past the small town of *Sandgate*, you can take a short detour north to *Sandgate Caste*, built by Henry VIII to protect the area.

Continue on A 259 to **Hythe,** an ancient port town that is now a popular seaside resort, with well-tended public gardens and a beautiful pebble beach. Hythe's contributions to England's military history date back over five centuries. In 1278, Edward I expressed appreciation for the town's supplying warships to the Royal Navy by absolving it from paying taxes. Until World War II, Hythe was the point of departure for Imperial Airways' flying boat service to the Empire. (After the war,

Imperial Airways became BOAC, which is now part of British Airways.)

The 12th-century Norman *parish church* in the old village rises above a crypt containing many human skulls and bones, probably transported there from the old churchyard. Lionel Lukin (1742–1832), inventor of the lifeboat, is buried in the cemetery.

Northwest of Hythe are *Sandling Park,* famous for its magnolias, rhododendrons, and azaleas; and ***Lympne Castle,** overlooking Romney Marsh to the French coast. Built on the site of Norman and Saxon castles, Lympne was owned until 1860 by the archdeacons of Canterbury.

Continue southwest on A 259 from Hythe through *Romney Marsh*. This extensive coastal marsh is especially beautiful in the spring, when it is blanketed by acres of cultivated flowers. Deep dikes divide the flat expanse into smaller fields, where the famous Romney Marsh breed of sheep graze peacefully. Drive through the marsh at sunrise or sunset for the most perfect effect.

In the 18th century, smugglers landed in isolated harbors here and carried their cargo of brandy, tobacco, silk, and lace inland along secret forest tracks. It is said that these old smuggler's paths are still used by illegal immigrants.

Since 1927, a miniature steam railway, now powered by replicas of historic locomotives, has traversed the marsh, connecting Hythe with the peaceful beach resorts of *Dymchurch* and *New Romney*. You can also follow footpaths that wind through the marsh. The most scenic paths follow the *Royal Military Canal,* dug to provide a safe waterway between Hythe and Rye when Napoleon's armies threatened the security of Britain.

Continue southwest on A 259 to **New Romney,** site of the miniature railway's main station and a *museum*. The town has a *parish church* built in Norman and Early English style. From New Romney it is an easy drive to the nearby beach resorts of *Littlestone* and *Greatstone*. ***Rye,** the next stop on A 259, was once a port, but the sea has long since receded, leaving it high and dry except for a link provided by the River Rother. Rye is a beautifully preserved Medieval town with steep, cobbled streets and many old buildings. On Mermaid Street you'll find the 15th-century *Mermaid Inn,* once a notorious haunt for local smugglers. Further along the street is the lovely Georgian *Lamb House,* where the American novelist Henry James lived for the last 18 years of his life. For a panoramic view of the town and marsh, climb *Ypres Tower* (pronounced "Wipers" by the locals). Built in 1200 to protect the town from the French, it now houses a museum of local history.

Before continuing on A 259, take a short trip to ***Smallhythe Place,** 12 km. (7 miles) to the north on B 2082. This beautifully

Smallhythe Palace

preserved timbered house, built in 1480, was the home of Ellen Terry, a famous 19th-century Shakespearian actress. Since her death in 1928, it has been a theatrical museum exhibiting mementos of her career.

From Rye you might also visit ***Great Dixter,** a 15th-century house in Northiam, 12 km. (7 miles) to the northwest on Route A 268. The estate is noted for its magnificent *Great Hall* and the extensive *gardens,* laid out in the early 20th century by Sir Edwin Lutyens, an architect who is most famous for the country houses he built. Lutyens also made a small addition to the house. Continue several miles farther along A 268 to ***Bodiam Castle,** a 14th-century fortress whose outer walls and towers still stand, surrounded by a moat full of water lilies and vividly evocative of the Middle Ages.

Continue south from Rye on A 259, past *Camber Castle,* a fortification built under Henry VIII, to the town of **Winchelsea.** Here you can see underground *wine cellars* remaining from the Middle Ages, when the town was the center of a thriving wine trade with Gascony in France. Stop off at *Manna Plat* in Mill Road to take in the *art gallery* and refresh yourself at the café. Don't miss the *church of St. Thomas,* considered by many to be the most important Decorated-style church in Sussex. Built in 1290, it was dedicated to Thomas à Becket of Canterbury, the archbishop who was brutally murdered by Henry II's followers in 1170. At the altar are the graves of the Alard family, some of whom were the first admirals of England. ***Hastings** is the next sizable town on Route A 259. It has given its name to perhaps the most momentous battle of British history. In October of 1066, William the Conqueror landed south of town and began the Norman conquest of England with the ensuing battle of Hastings. His landing marked the

Bodiam Castle

beginning of a dramatic change in English society, government, language, and architecture. William met England's King Harold northwest of town, on a field near the present-day town of *Battle,* at 4:00 P.M. on October 16, 1066. Harold was struck by a French arrow, and Norman knights broke through his bodyguard and killed him. Within an hour, the battle was over. William had vowed that if he was victorious, he would build an abbey on the site. Ruins of this ****abbey** still stand, and its high altar is placed on the spot where Harold died. Adjoining the original abbey are a 14th-century *abbot's lodge* and *library,* an elaborate **gatehouse* built in 1339, the ruins of a *banqueting hall* and of a 13th-century *dormitory,* and a *cloister* in Gothic style. The town of Hastings erected the **Triodome** in 1966 to honor the 900th anniversary of the battle. The large, round *exhibition hall* contains an enormous hand-

Battle: Abbey Gatehouse

embroidered tapestry depicting the history of Hastings since 1066, and a model of the battlefield. If you climb on a steep cliff between the old and new parts of Hastings, you'll see the ruins of the first Norman-style *castle* in England, built by William. The *Conqueror's Stone,* on the seafront, is said to be the table at which William sat for his first meal on British soil.

Today, Hastings and its twin town, *St. Leonards,* are lively seaside resorts with many inviting tourist facilities. A walk through Hasting's old town takes you back to a 16th-century port city. The twisting lanes are lined with timbered houses and Medieval façades, and many 18th-century Georgian houses face the sea across a shore promenade. The Medieval *church of St. Clements* is where the Pre-Raphaelite painter and poet Dante Gabriel Rossetti was married in 1860. Be sure to see the *White Rock Gardens,* where there is a clock with a face made of more than 30,000 flowering plants.

Take a short drive 10 km. (6 miles) north of Hastings on A 28 to ***Brede Place,** a 14th-century mansion with a beautiful chapel and a collection of Medieval weapons. Just to the northwest of Hastings is *Beauport Parks,* where lovely terraced gardens contain rare varieties of plants.

Return to A 259 and continue to **Bexhill,** a beach resort with a charming esplanade at the foot of the Sussex Downs. The parish *church of St. Peter* was built by the Normans just four years after their landing, and its churchyard has a unique old Saxon tombstone. There is much more modern history in Bexhill as well—it was the home of J. L. Baird, a pioneer of television. There is a plaque at his former residence at 1 Station Road.

A 259 will take you to **Pevensey,** the exact spot where William the Conqueror landed in 1066. The town is the site of a Norman *castle,* which is surrounded by Roman walls dating to A.D. 250. The Roman fortress that stood here was sacked by the Saxons in the fifth century. The present castle's *keep* was built in 1080 and its *gatehouse* in the 13th century. You will also want to see Pevensey's 14th-century *Mint House*.

Several miles north of Pevensey is **Herstmonceux Castle,** a 15th-century turreted brick structure that has been the home of the *Royal Observatory* since it moved

Herstmonceux Castle

here from Greenwich (see page 58) in 1948. The Observatory's astronomers will take you on a tour of the exhibition rooms.

Continue south to **Eastbourne,** one of England's most popular seaside towns. It was a small fishing village until 1834, when the seventh Duke of Devonshire inherited it. He transformed Eastbourne into a Victorian resort of parks, gardens, elegant houses, and shops. Visitors still stroll along the long esplanade to admire the shorefront buildings, just as Lewis Carroll probably did on his frequent vacations here. Duck into the *Towner Art Gallery,* now filled with paintings of the Sussex area.

From Eastbourne, take the coastal road that curves southwest to *Beachy Head,* where chalk cliffs tower 190 meters (623 feet) above the sea. Hike the footpaths that lead along the cliffs for spectacular views all the way to the *Isle of Wight* in the west and Dungeness in the east. Following the scenic coastal road to Brighton you will pass through the small seaside towns of *Seaford, Newhaven,* and *Rottingdean* (where there is a charming toy museum in the Grange).

You may want to detour to *Charleston Manor,* north of Seaford, to get a glimpse of seven centuries of history. The oldest section of this manor—surrounded by vast gardens—belonged to William the Conqueror's cup bearer. The manor was enlarged and later became a monastery. Its varied architecture includes Romanesque windows in the north, a Tudor addition constructed during the 15th–16th centuries, and a Georgian addition built between 1710–1730.

There is another, inland route from Eastbourne to Brighton that offers more history and art, if less seaside scenery. Leave Eastbourne on A 22 north and turn west at *Polegate* onto A 27. (A 22 continues to *Michelham Priory;* see page 164.) Just past *Wilmington,* take the access road leading south to **Alfriston,** site of an early Gothic parish church called the *Cathedral of the Downs.* The 14th-century *Alfriston Clergy House* is now a museum. Rejoin A 27 and continue to *Firle Beacon,* a high hill (on the left side of the road) that you can climb for the excellent panoramic views. At the foot of the hill you'll find *****Firle Place,** a 15th-century country estate set in a lovely garden. Its rooms are now filled with Italian, Dutch, and English paintings, a collection of Sèvres porcelain, and French and English furniture from various periods.

Continue on A 27 to the turnoff for *****Glynde Place,** which is just north of the highway. Art lovers will revel in this 16th-century building's display of works by Rubens and other artists, as well as its remarkable cache of historic documents. The nearby **Glyndebourne Opera House** is the site of the famous Glyndebourne

Glynde Palace

Festival Opera every June and July. The occasion is formal— during the long intermissions, opera goers in evening dress picnic on the edge of the Sussex Downs and stroll through the lovely gardens.

Rejoin A 27 and continue west to *****Lewes.** Beautifully designed, Lewes affords views of the Downs from every street. It is built around the few remains of an 11th-century Norman castle constructed by William de Warenne, the first Earl of Surrey. Visit the 16th-century *house of Anne of Cleves,* fourth wife of Henry VIII (divorced, rather than beheaded). The house is now a museum displaying period art and furnishings. There is more history in the city museum, located in the 14th-century *Barbican House.* There you will see prehistoric Roman and Saxon objects and regional paintings. The ruins of the *Priory of St. Pancras,* built in 1078, are south of town. Continue on A 27 to Brighton.

Brighton

Brighton was a poor fishing village until 1782, when the Prince Regent (later George IV) brought his court here. They made sleepy Brighton into one of England's major seaside resorts, a distinction it retains today. Many of the Regency terraces and hotels built at that time have been preserved, and they provide a pleasing contrast to the city's more modern buildings and modern attractions. Brighton's 2,000 slips make it one of the largest man-made harbors in the world; its long beach of coarse-grained sand is backed by a seaside promenade lined with shops, restaurants, gardens, and good hotels.

Brighton's chief attraction, though, is still the ***Royal Pavilion,** built in 1787 for Prince George and later used as an occasional summer residence by Queen Victoria. The fantastic palace in Indian Mogul style is

Royal Pavilion

always striking, but is especially dramatic in the evenings, when its domes and minarets are illuminated by floodlights. Inside, some of the magnificent state and festival rooms are furnished in Chinese style. The Pavilion's valuable art collection includes 19th-century British paintings, watercolors, and some works by Old Masters. Brighton's second most popular attraction is the *Palace Pier,* an amusement park, built between 1891–1899, perched on iron pillars above the sea.

Brighton is famous for flowers, too. Its magnificent *stone garden* is one of the largest in the world; the *Floral Boulevard,* which stretches from St. Peter's Church to Old Steime, is illuminated at night. The old town, where many antiques stores are now located, is a labyrinth of narrow lanes and courtyards dating to the 17th century. Other sights include the *Booth Bird Museum,* which has more than 1,900 animals on display; and the 18th-century *Preston Manor,* which has retained its period furnishings.

From Brighton, choose one of the two routes to *Chichester.* The first follows A 259 along the coast, passing through many seaside resorts. The second goes inland, taking in some charming Norman and Medieval architecture. On the coastal road, you'll pass through a good starting point for exploring the *Downs,* and the location of *Highdown* in *Goring-by-Sea,* a lovely garden. Travel on to *Littlehampton*, popular for its miniature railroad and amusement park. Pass through *Middleton* to *Bognor Regis*, another resort.

To follow the inland road, leave Brighton to the west and, shortly before the bridge over the River Adur, turn north onto A 283 *to Bramber*. Here you will find *St. Mary's*, a 15th-century timbered house that is generally regarded to be the most beautiful of its kind in southern England. It is now a crafts museum. Bramber's other famous house is the *House of Pipes*, a museum devoted to smoking. Continue on A 284 to *Steyning*, where there is a remarkable *parish church* with an early Norman nave, and the *Chantry Green House*, where W. B. Yeats wrote some of his poems.

Return to A 27 and continue west through *Sompting* to ****Arundel**, a picturesque country town on the River Arun. Its *church of St. Nicholas*, built in 1380, is the only church in England where Roman Catholic and Protestant services are held under the same roof (the two areas of worship are separated by a glass panel and a gate). ****Arundel castle**, built under Edward the Confessor, has been the residence of several kings and was the property of the bishops of Norfolk for more than 500 years. Set in a large, forested park near Swanbourne Lake, it provides breathtaking views of the Downs. Parts of the 12th- and 13th-century structure are still standing,

Arundel Castle

although the castle was rebuilt in the 18th century and enlarged in 1890. Its rooms are furnished with 16th-century furniture and decorated with paintings by Gainsborough, Holbein, and Van Dyck.

Continue west on A 27. Just before Chichester, an access road leads north to **Goodwood House**, with its fine collection of period paintings and Louis XV furniture. The car and horse racecourse are nearby at *Goodwood Park*.

*Chichester

See map on page 140.

One of the most important towns in the area, Chichester lies between the South Downs and the sea. Under the Romans, it was called Regnum and was an important military and commercial center. The Saxons settled here in the fifth century, and their leader Cissa renamed the town Cissa's Ceaster (the castle of Cissa). The 12th-century ***cathedral** (1) has a 15th-century, free-standing belltower, the only one in England, and inside, Romanesque sculptures and windows from the 14th–15th centuries. Several noted modern artists, among them Marc Chagall, have contributed works to the cathedral. The

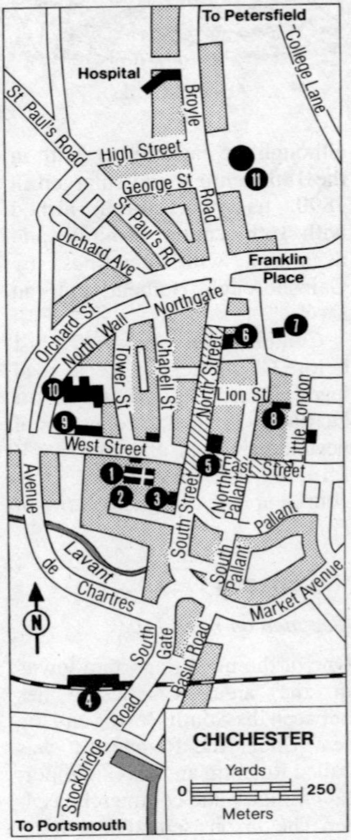

Bishop's Palace (2) has a remarkable Early English chapel and a Medieval kitchen (these buildings are not open to the public).

The 16th-century *Canon Gate* (3) opens to South Street, one of Chichester's two main streets. In the nearby *Pallant quarter* are some well-preserved Medieval houses. South Street leads to the *railroad station* (4) and the *South Gate*. In the middle of town at the site of the Medieval marketplace is one of the finest crosses in England, ***Market Cross** (5), built in 1500 and embellished in 1724. To the east is a bronze bust of Charles I. North Street leads to the *Town Hall* (6), behind which is *Priory Park* and *Greyfriars Monastery* (7), with its noteworthy Early English chapel. Just past *St. Martin's Square* is *St. Mary's Hospital* (8), whose chapel dates to the 13th century and since 1562 has been a home for elderly women. The 17th-century town *library* (9) is on West Street; behind it is the modern *County Hall* (10). You can walk along the top of the nearby Medieval *North Walls*, built on Roman foundations. A more modern attraction in Chichester is the *Chichester Festival Theatre* (11), located in *Oaklands Park*. Since 1962 a festival has been held here every summer. Chichester is a good starting point for excursions to mansions and castles in the area, and to the *South Downs*.

CHICHESTER

Yards

0 ⊢⊢⊢⊢⊢⊣ 250

Meters

To Portsmouth

Continue west on A 27. Just outside Chichester, and north of the road, is ***Fishbourne**

Roman Palace. Built in the first century, and excavated between 1961–1969, it is the largest single Roman building ever discovered in Great Britain. The palace may have belonged to Cogidubnus, the Briton whom the Romans made viceroy at the time of the invasion under Vespasian. Although the palace burned down in A.D. 285, extensive ruins remain. Several floor mosaics in the north wing have survived, including a large one depicting a boy on a dolphin. Archaeologists have recreated the garden according to an ancient design, and a small museum is open to visitors.

*Bosham, farther west on A 27, is one of the oldest towns in England. Vespasian began his invasion of Britain here in A.D. 43. The remains of a *Roman house,* a *bath,* and an *amphitheater* survive from that time. There is more recent—only slightly so—history in the ruins of an 11th-century Anglo-Saxon *church* and *tower* in the town. Its 13th-century *crypt* was once a popular hiding place for smugglers. Look in the cemetery for the grave of the 18-year-old daughter of Canute, a Danish king who lived here in the year 1,000.

In 1066, King Harold II, the last Anglo-Saxon king of England, sailed from Bosham on an ill-fated mission to Normandy to dissuade William from invading. His trip was of no avail; William landed and defeated Harold at the Battle of Hastings (see page 134) ot long afterward.

Today, Bosham, which is set on a peninsula between two tidal creeks, is a busy yacht harbor.

Continue west on A 27 through *Emsworth* and *Havant;* turn south at *Cosham* to *Portsmouth.*

Portsmouth

For centuries, Portsmouth (200 km., 124 miles, from Dover) has been one of England's most important seaports. In the third century, King Alfred left from here to fight the Danes; in the 11th century, King Harold's fleet gathered here to fight the Normans; and throughout the centuries, Portsmouth has defended itself from the French. Near the harbor is the oldest drydock in the world and it houses a collection of historic ships. Lord Nelson's famous flagship *Victory,* on which he died while winning the Battle of Trafalgar in 1805, is here, along with H.M.S. *Warrior,* the

Nelson's flagship *Victory*

first iron warship ever built, and H.M.S. *Foudroyant,* a wooden frigate built in 1817. In the nearby *Victory Museum* many objects that belonged to Lord Nelson and his men are on display, as are model ships, figureheads, and a collection of marine paintings.

The city was badly damaged by bombs in World War II; its *Guildhall,* destroyed completely in 1941, was rebuilt in 1959 as a concert and convention hall. Charles Dickens was born in Portsmouth, in the small house at *393 Commercial Road.* It is now a museum displaying mementos of his life and first editions of his books. **Southsea,** the resort adjoining Portsmouth, has a good sand and shingle beach. At one end of the *South Parade Pier* is *Southsea Castle,* built by Henry VIII. In its tower is a military museum. From Southsea, you can take a ferry to the Isle of Wight.

Isle of Wight

See map on page 143.

The Isle of Wight, part of the county of Hampshire, is separated from the mainland by the Solent Channel. Ferries run daily from Southampton to Cowes, and from Portsmouth to Ryde; car ferries run from Portsmouth to Fishbourne, and from Lymington to Yarmouth. The trip takes about an hour. Hydrofoils also run regularly from Southampton and Portsmouth to Cowes, and from

Portsmouth to Ryde, taking only about 20 minutes for the crossing.

The island is 35 km. (21 miles) from east to west, and 20 km. (12 miles) from north to south. Along the Solent Channel are a beautiful series of bays, many of which are thickly forested. Ship traffic is heavy here, however. In the south, lowlands stretch to seaside chalk and sand cliffs interspersed with sandy bays. The most beautiful of these cliffs are at the western end of the isle. They form knife-edged tips referred to as *"The Needles."* Charming rural villages, such as *Godshill* (3) and *Brightstone* (4) dot the island.

Queen Victoria frequented the isle in the mid-19th century and the publicity she gave it made it a popular resort. Start your tour of the island from **Cowes** (5), a lively port city on the Solent, and Great Britain's most important sailing harbor. From here, you can see ocean liners docking in Southampton (see page 126) on the mainland. Visit ***Osborne House** (2), in East Cowes, which belonged to Queen Victoria and Prince Albert. Their nine children were born here, and Queen Victoria spent the last years of her life in the house. The *Durbar room* was furnished by J. Lockwood Kipling, Rudyard Kipling's father, with statues of the Buddha, Indian portraits, and miniatures. The *Swiss Cottage* was designed by Prince Albert as a playhouse for the royal children. It now contains the Queen's writing table and her personal collection of porcelain. **Newport** (6), the capital of the isle, is situated at the source of the River Medina. It has an old-fashioned market and many interesting buildings. Nearby is ***Carisbrooke Castle** (1), built on the site of a Roman fort. Charles I was imprisoned here after his defeat in England's 17th-century civil war, and his 15-year-old daughter died here in captivity. The castle houses the *Isle of Wight County Museum* and its collection of archaeological objects, as well as mementos from the life of the poet Alfred,

Lord Tennyson, who had a house on the island. **Ryde** (7) is a popular resort with more than 8 km. (5 miles) of sandy beaches. Its long pier (almost one km., half a mile, in length) was built in 1813, and its electric railway, built in 1880, was one of the first in the world. **Sandown** (8) has a sandy beach surrounded by high cliffs and **Shanklin** (9) is an old village surrounded by beautiful gardens. **Bembridge** (10), a yachting center on the east coast with a sandy beach, features a picturesque old *windmill*. At

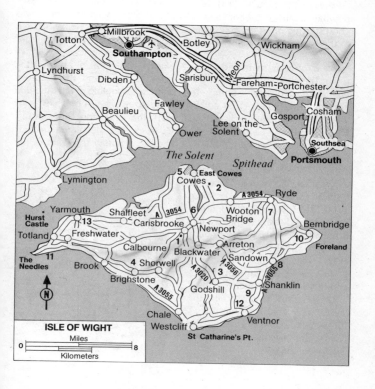

Freshwater Bay (11), a peaceful beach resort on a rocky coast, there is a golf course and deep-sea fishing facilities. On top of the nearby *High Down* you will see a monument to Alfred, Lord Tennyson. **Ventnor** (12) is laid out on terraces that zigzag down to the sea. *Saint Boniface Down,* behind the village, is the highest point on the isle. Ventnor boasts sandy beaches as well as a seashore promenade, a lake for boating, a paddleboat pond for children, and an excellent repertory theater located in the *Winter Gardens.* **Yarmouth** (13) is a popular sailboat harbor and a good starting point for excursions to the western part of the island.

Back on the mainland, continue Travel Route 5 from *Cosham* (the turnoff point to Portsmouth). Follow A 27 northwest along Portsmouth harbor to **Portchester.** Called Portus Costra by the Romans, Portchester retains traces of its past in the ruins of the Roman fort *Portus Adurni* on the shore. Henry II built a *castle* on this site between 1160–1172; it was later enlarged by Richard II. Next to the castle is a remarkable *parish church* built in 1133 and behind the city is *Ports Down,* which provides a good view of Portsmouth Harbor and the Solent Channel.

Leave Portchester from the west, and continue on A 17 through *Fareham* and across the River Hamble to *Southampton* (see page 126).

Take a side trip from Southampton to the small market town of ***Romsey,** 10 km. (6 miles) to the northwest on A 3057. Romsey was founded by King Edward the Elder, a son of Alfred the Great, in 907. Its *abbey* is one of the most impressive in England; from a distance, it looks more like a fort than a place of worship. The abbey was founded in 907 in association with a convent of Benedictine nuns. Danish invaders destroyed it in 1004 but it was rebuilt, and for many years served as a home and school for Saxon and Norman princesses and queens. When the abbey was dissolved by King Henry VIII, it became the local parish church. The well-preserved ****abbey church** was built in 1120 on the ruins of 10th- and 11th-century churches. Notable details include a life-sized *crucifix* on an exterior wall, the 13th- and 14th-century *windows,* the decorated *arches,* and the Norman *triforium* in the

Romsey Abbey

choir. Earl Mountbatten of Burma is buried in the churchyard. East of the church is *King John's Hunting Box*, the small, 13th-century house where King John and, later, Edward I, stayed when they hunted in the *New Forest* (see below). The inscriptions and drawings dating from 1306 were discovered on its walls in 1927 and have been attributed to crusading knights. The house is now a museum. Just south of town is *Broadlands*, the country seat of the Mountbattan family. It is open to the public during the summer.

From Southampton, take A 36 west to A 35 and the **New Forest**. A 94,000-acre expanse of oak, beech, and yew trees interspersed with heaths, it is one of the largest areas of open land in the south of England. Wild ponies, donkeys, and cows roam freely. The New Forest was declared property of the crown by William the Conqueror in 1079. At the time, the word forest meant an area set aside for hunting. Until the late 12th century, a commoner could be blinded for merely disturbing the royal deer. Today, activities in the forest are more leniently regulated by the British Parliament. It is a popular hiking and tourist area. One of England's most luxurious hotels, the *Chewton Glen*, is located in nearby *New Milton*.

Follow A 35 through *Millbrook* and across the River Test at *Redbridge*. Continue through *Totten*, to **Lyndhurst**, the capital of the New Forest. Lyndhurst's *parish church* contains paintings by Leighton, Burne-Jones, and other Pre-Raphaelites. From Lyndhurst, you can make excursions to *Minstead* and the *Furzey Gardens; Stoney Cross*, site of the Rufus Stone, where William Rufus was killed (possibly deliberately) by an arrow in 1100; *Beaulieu*, whose beautiful Cistercian Abbey was founded in 1204 by King John; the *Palace House*, the private residence of Lord Montagu since 1538; and *Montagu Motor Museum*, which exhibits historic cars and motorcycles.

From Lyndhurst, take one of two routes to *Bournemouth*. A 337 goes south to *Lymington*, where yachts are docked in a picturesque port. A 35, via *Wilverley Post*, provides a more scenic route. Both roads meet in ***Christchurch**, an ancient town situated in the delta formed by the rivers Stour and Avon. Christchurch has a lovely fishing and sailboat harbor protected by *Hengistbury Head dam*. The town's *Priory Church*, built during the 12th–13th centuries, incorporates some earlier Norman sections. Its 15th-century tower is 40 meters (130 feet) high. Ruins of a Norman *castle* and several *historic houses* stand near the harbor.

Continue west to **Bournemouth**. Because of its mild climate, this elegant beach resort is busy year-round. Set between two pine-covered hills on the warmest and most protected part of

England's southern coast, it has 2,000 acres of parks and gardens, a long stretch of fine sandy beach, and many sports and entertainment facilities. Its symphony orchestra is well known, as are its opera and theater. The *Russell-Cotes Gallery,* housed in a Victorian building, has an impressive collection of paintings by Turner, Corot, and others. Bournemouth is a good starting point for excursions into the *New Forest* and *Dorset* and for travel by boat for the *Isle of Wight* and several coastal towns.

TRAVEL ROUTE 6: ***London–**Stonehenge–*Salisbury–Bournemouth (191 km.; 118 miles)

See map on page 148.

This Travel Route takes in two of the most famous profiles in Britain—Stonehenge, the mysterious Stone Age monument that has intrigued archaeologists for centuries; and Salisbury Cathedral, one of the most beautiful examples of Early English architecture. Along the way you'll discover quaint, lesser-known spots that have remained virtually unchanged through generations of English village life.

From London, take A 4 west to A 30 southwest. Near *Staines,* cross the River Thames; then continue on A 30 along the southern edge of *Windsor Great Park* (see page 154). You'll pass the *Ascot Race Track,* site of the fashionable Royal Ascot race meeting, where, if G. B. Shaw and Lerner and Loewe are to be believed, Liza Doolittle was introduced into society. The horse race has been run every June since 1711.

Continue southwest on A 30 through *Bagshot* to *Camberley.* **Sandhurst,** the royal military academy that has trained great leaders such as Winston Churchill since 1799, is north of Camberley on A 321. A former riding school on the academy grounds houses the *National Army Museum,* founded in 1960. Stop to take a look at the impressive collection of historic arms, flags and banners, helmets, uniforms, and medals. The medical instruments used by Florence Nightingale, the founder of modern nursing, are here, too.

Return to A 30 and continue to *Hartley Wintney.* Don't miss the *West Green House,* just south of town. This 18th-century mansion is surrounded by a beautiful garden. From the town of *Hook,* take the side road that leads south to **Odiham** and *Odiham Castle.* With its wide main street, lined with Georgian buildings, Odiham looks like an English country town of an earlier, more prosperous era. The town also has a *Tudor vicarage* and a beautiful

14th-century *church,* as well as a considerably less attractive but fascinating building called the *pest-house.* Built in 1665 to house victims of the Great Plague, the pest-house came in handy again during the Napoleonic Wars as a prison for French captives. Ruins of the 13th-century *Odiham Castle* are nearby.

A 30 continues southwest to **Basingstoke,** an important market town. Among several interesting 16th- and 17th-century buildings in Basingstoke are the parish *church of St. Michael* and the ruins of the *Holy Ghost Chapel,* near the railway station.

There are two side trips worth taking from Basingstoke—one for lovers of architecture, the other for lovers of nature. A short trip north of town leads to the beautifully preserved ***Vyne mansion.** Built for Lord Sandys, the Lord Chancellor for Henry VIII, it was expanded and embellished in the 17th century by the famous architect Inigo Jones. Highlights include a classical *portal* built in 1664 by John Webb; Tudor paneling in the *Long Gallery;* a richly decorated Renaissance *stairway;* 16th-century windows in the *chapel;* and exquisite private rooms, most of them furnished in Rococo style.

A short drive south of Basingstoke leads to *Herriard Nature Park.* Wander through the extensive rose gardens and greenhouses to refresh your senses.

From Basingstoke, you can take one of two routes to *Salisbury.* The quickest, but least interesting, is southwest via A 30, through *Wheat Sheaf, Sutton Scotney,* and *Stockbridge.* A slightly longer but far more enjoyable drive begins on B 3400 west from Basingstoke. The first sizable town along the way is *Whitchurch,* whose parish church boasts a tombstone dating from Saxon days. Continue west on B 3400 to **Andover,** an important market town that was once a favorite royal hunting spot. In A.D. 994, King Olaf, great grandson of the first king of Norway, was baptized here by Saint Alphege. Just south of Andover are two charming old villages, *Upper Clatford* and *Wherwell.*

From Andover, follow A 303 west toward *Amesbury* (see page 148). Just before Amesbury, look for the access road leading north to *Bulford,* site of a mill and an Elizabethan mansion. Continue a few miles on this road to *Dur-*

The Vyne

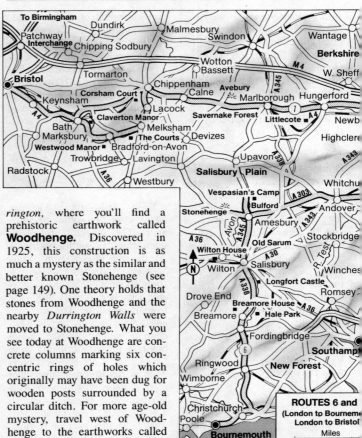

ROUTES 6 and
(London to Bourneme
London to Bristol

Miles

Kilometers

rington, where you'll find a prehistoric earthwork called **Woodhenge.** Discovered in 1925, this construction is as much a mystery as the similar and better known Stonehenge (see page 149). One theory holds that stones from Woodhenge and the nearby *Durrington Walls* were moved to Stonehenge. What you see today at Woodhenge are concrete columns marking six concentric rings of holes which originally may have been dug for wooden posts surrounded by a circular ditch. For more age-old mystery, travel west of Woodhenge to the earthworks called *Vespasian's Camp.* Although named after the Roman emperor, they date from prehistoric times. The camp marks the center of *Salisbury Plain,* a chalk downland of low grassy hills, clear trout streams, and many prehistoric stone circles, earthworks, and artificial mounds.

From here drive back down into **Amesbury,** a small town situated on the Wiltshire and

Avon rivers. Its *abbey church,* built in Norman and Early English style, is said to stand on the site of a priory to which Queen Guinevere withdrew when she learned of King Arthur's death. It was in Amesbury in 1727 that John Gay wrote *The Beggar's Opera,* the famous

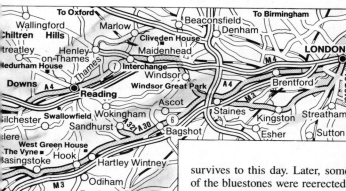

satire of society. Just west of Amesbury is *Stonehenge*.

**Stonehenge (130 km.; 80 miles from London), the largest Stone Age monument in Europe, is a powerful symbol of prehistoric man's intellect and ingenuity. To this day, researchers have not been able to unravel its meaning, or even explain how such monstrous boulders were transported and erected almost 4,000 years ago. Stonehenge consists of two concentric circles of huge standing stones, the largest of which weighs more than 40 tons. The outer ditch is the oldest part of the monument, probably dating to before 2150 B.C. The stone circle was erected about 500 years later with bluestones from the Prescelly Hills in southwest Wales, more than 200 miles away. In 1650 B.C., the bluestones were replaced with two rings of sarsen stones in the formation that survives to this day. Later, some of the bluestones were reerected, and the largest, the so-called Altar Stone, was set at the center of the circle.

Some scholars believe Stonehenge was a burial place; others speculate that it was a sun sanctuary. One theory that does not hold up is that it was built by the Druids. This is impossible, since the Druids migrated to southern England 1,000 years after the monument was completed.

Return to Amesbury and take A 345 south to *Salisbury* (141 km.; 87 miles from London).

Stonehenge

*Salisbury

See map on page 151.

Salisbury, the capital of Wiltshire, is one of England's most beautiful cathedral towns. Located at the confluence of the rivers Avon, Nadder, Bourne, and Wylye, and at the edge of the Salisbury Plain, it is a town of narrow streets with long rows of timbered houses, many dating from Medieval times. The city, moved to its present site in the 13th century, originated two miles to the north under the name Old Sarum—which was, successively, an Iron Age hill fort, a Roman camp, and a Norman stronghold. It had two cathedrals, the first of which was struck by lightning five days after its consecration. The second was abandoned in 1220 because of the lack of water at the site and conflicts with a military garrison stationed

Salisbury Cathedral

nearby. The stones of this second church were moved to present-day Salisbury and used to build ****Salisbury Cathedral** (1). Built between 1220–1258, the great church is a classic example of the Early English style and is beautifully situated in a grassy field. Massive proportions contribute to the overall effect. The church *tower,* added in 1320, is the tallest in England (130 meters- ; 426 feet-high) and the **cloister,* dating from 1270, is the largest in all of Great Britain. Many handcrafted details inspire awe, particularly the *windows* in the southern lateral nave. Among the tombstones from the 12th–16th centuries is one marking the grave of William Longespee, King John's half-brother, who died in 1226. Be sure to see the *Triforium,* the *choir,* and the *Lady Chapel* at the eastern end—the oldest part of the cathedral. In the 16th-century *library,* located on the east side of the cloister, is one of four surviving original editions of the *Magna Carta,* as well as several hand-decorated Anglo-Saxon bibles. In the octagonal *Chapter House,* its roof supported by a graceful central column, are the sculptured biblical scenes dating from the 13th century.

The best way to appreciate the cathedral's architecture is from a distance. Walk northeast to *St. Ann's Gate* (2) for the most spectacular view. Go across the cathedral square to the Medieval *Harnham Gate* (3) to get a different perspective. Visit some of the picturesque old houses, many of them Medieval, that surround the cathedral. Among them are the 15th-century *Wardrobe House (4), which is now the bishop's residence; *Mompesson House (5), built in 1701; and the *Old Deanery* (6) and *King's House* (7), both built in the 14th century. King's House is now the *Salisbury and South Wiltshire Museum*, home of a fascinating collection of prehistoric objects. The old *Bishop's Palace* (8) is now the cathedral school.

On the Medieval *High Street Gate* (9) there is a statue of Edward VII, eldest son of Queen

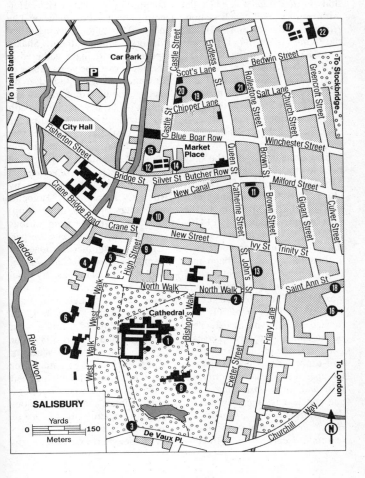

SALISBURY

0   Yards   150
Meters

Victoria. Henry III and James I were also represented here at one time. From religion and royalty you can turn your attention to places meant for relaxation, beginning with the 14th-century *Bay Tree Restaurant* (10) to the right of High Street Gate. In this area of Medieval inns you'll also find the *Red Lion Inn* (11), the 14th-century mail-coach station, *Haunch of Venison Inn* (12), and the *King's Arms Inn* (13). It was at the King's Arms, the oldest inn in Salisbury, that Charles II hid after he was defeated in the Battle of Worcester. North of here, at the end of Silver Street, is the 14th-century hexagonal *Poultry Cross* (14), marking the site of the original marketplace.

The cathedral is not the only notable church in Salisbury. The Medieval *church of St. Thomas* (15) is noted for its striking Tudor roof and the wall painting of the Last Judgment, executed in 1410. *St. Martin's Church* (16), built in the 15th century, incorporates a 13th-century tower and baptismal font. Salisbury's art center since 1975, *St. Edmund's Church* (17) was founded in 1269 and rebuilt in 1407. *Joiners' Hall* (18), is located on St. Ann Street. This old guildhall for woodworkers is a good example of the Elizabethan half-timbered house. Follow Chipper Lane past the *library* (19) and main *post office* (20), and consider resting your feet at the 16th-century *Shoemaker's Guildhall* (21), which is now a tearoom. Nearby, the 17th-cen-

tury *Council House* (22) was originally called the College of St. Edmund.

From Salisbury, you may take a side trip west to ****Wilton House,** built in the 16th century on the site of a Benedictine convent. Henry VIII gave the land to the future Earl of Pembroke, who supposedly consulted Hans Holbein about the mansion he planned to build. Distinguished visitors, among them Shakespeare himself, have gathered at the house over the years. Some of England's most celebrated architects, including Inigo Jones and James Wyatt, have designed additions to the mansion, creating the large, castlelike structure that stands today. The magnificent house is a suitable environment for the priceless *art collection* that hangs there, with paintings by Rubens, Rembrandt, Holbein, and others and exquisite sculptures and furniture from various periods. The *staterooms* are particularly magnificent. One of them, the *Double Cube Room*, displays 10 paintings by Van Dyck. In the *gardens* are dramatic cedars of Lebanon and a Palladian bridge, built in 1750.

About 8 km. (4.5 miles) west of Wilton House on B 3089 near *Teffont Magna* lies **Wessex Shire Park,** a large nature preserve crisscrossed with marked trails. The park also has domestic farm animals and an outdoor museum depicting the history of farming in the area.

Another short excursion northwest of Salisbury will take you to *Figsbury Ring*. On this hill overlooking the city are the remains of a prehistoric settlement.

Leave Salisbury from the south on A 338. Just outside the city, you'll pass **Longford Castle,** the residence of the Earl of Radnor. This mansion, built in 1591 and added to over the years, contains one of England's largest private galleries. Unfortunately, it is closed to the public. But if you continue south on A 338 to ***Breamore House,** you'll find another Elizabethan mansion, built in 1583, whose considerable

collections of paintings, tapestries, furniture, and other works of art are open to visitors. From Breamore, a side road leads west to **Hale Park.** Built in 1715 by architect Thomas Archer, and altered by Henry Holland in 1770, this beautiful Georgian mansion houses a collection of *Aubusson tapestries*.

Return to A 338 and continue to *Fordingbridge,* where you'll find an interesting 13th- to 15th-century *parish church,* through *Ringwood,* and on to *Christchurch* (see page 145). Then continue west to *Bournemouth* (191 km.; 118 miles from London; see page 145).

TRAVEL ROUTE 7: ***London–*Bath–Bristol (–*Cardiff) (189 km; 117 miles).

See map on page 148.

This travel route takes you from London to Wales. On the way, you'll pass through two of the most striking cities in England—Bath, a spa since Roman times; and Bristol, the point of departure for many early American settlers.

Leaving London to the west on Route A 4, you will come to ****Kew,** a pretty village (actually, it's a nearby suburb) on the River Thames, built around a magnificent green. Here, in the late 18th century, Sir Joseph Banks established a botanic garden on the grounds of a royal residence, Kew Palace. Today the 286-acre Royal Botanic Gardens are, perhaps, the most famous horticultural display in the world. Bamboo,

rhododendrons, perfectly clipped hedges and magnificent architecture—a *Chinese pagoda; Palm House,* one of the world's largest greenhouses, in which a dense rain forest flourishes beneath acres of glass; and remnants of the palace itself—all vie for visitors' attention. Across the Thames from the gardens is **Synon House,** a castlelike structure built as a nunnery in 1415. Over the years, the estate has been put to more secular uses, as the home of Edward Seymour (brother of Jane Seymour, third wife of Henry VIII) and since 1594, as the seat of the Dukes of Northumberland. Built around a central courtyard, the house was modernized by the architect Robert Adams in 1762 and many consider it to be his masterpiece. The grounds were designed by Capability Brown and are a fair match for the grandeur of Kew across the river. Following the Thames south on Route A 307, in *Richmond* you will come to another great riverside mansion, **Ham House,** built as a modest country retreat in 1610 and remodeled to its present Baroque extravagance later in the century by a minister of Charles II. In addition to fine paintings by Van Dyck and others, there are rich tapestries and textiles, elaborate plaster work, and many original furnishings. The greatest of the Thames-side residences, though, lies farther upriver.

Hampton Court was once the estate of the powerful minister Cardinal Wolsey, but his king, Henry VIII, was so covetous of the Tudor palace and its grounds that Wolsey presented it to him. Already one of the most spectacular houses in the land in Henry's time, it was a later king, William III, who expanded the palace to its present greatness. He commissioned Sir Christopher Wren to embellish the façade, the courtyard, and the apartments. Much remains of the palace's noble occupants—Wolsey's study; Henry's Great Hall, wine cellar, and tennis courts; William's Banqueting House and Cartoon Gallery. The palace houses one of England's finest collections of art—with works by Titian, Correggio, and others—and is surrounded by magnificent gardens, in which Henry himself was known to toil. Still farther upriver is another royal palace, ****Windsor Castle, begun by William the Conqueror in 1070 and still one of the residences of Britain's Royal family. This massive structure is best viewed from the seemingly endless green expanses of Windsor Great Park. Inside the gates, the most notable edifice is ***St. George's Chapel,* a Gothic masterpiece that is the final resting place of many British monarchs. Queen Victoria rebuilt an adjoining, 13th-century chapel as the *Albert Memorial Chapel,* in memory of her husband, Prince Albert. The architect Edward Lutyens designed *Queen Mary's Dolls' House,* a spectacular miniature replica of a 20th-century house, in 1923 and furnished it with tiny works by famous authors and painters of the day. Real works appear throughout the rest of the castle, most notably the Leonardos in the galleries collectively known as the *Exhibition of Drawings* and the spectacular furnishings of the state apartments.

Continue on A 4 to **Maidenhead** which occupies one of the loveliest stretches of the river. Its shops are popular with tourists and Londoners alike, and it is a good base from which to explore the surrounding area. Just upriver from town is *Boulter's Lock,* where you'll get a picturesque view of the river valley. North of the lock are the vast *Cliveden Woods,* crisscrossed with hiking trails and the setting of *Cliveden House,* whose formal gardens are laced with 18th-century temples.

From Maidenhead, take A 4 west to **Reading,** an important city of railroads and industry situated at the confluence of the Kennet and Thames rivers. Reading's *Benedictine abbey,* of which only ruins remain, dates from 1121 and is the burial place of Henry I. Some of the first polyphonic liturgical music, including the canon "Sumer is icumen in," was composed by the abbey's monks in 1240. The novelist Jane Austen briefly attended the abbey school in 1786.

Next to the impressive *church of St. Laurence* is the *town museum* where there is a fascinating collection of archaeological finds from the Roman town of Calleva Atrebatum, now Silchester. The town also has, at Reading University, a good, small museum of Greek archaeology, and a large Museum of English Rural Life, which displays an amazing collection of farm implements and other artifacts of rural England.

From Reading you may take a side trip south to the small town of *Swallowfield,* on A 33. There you will find **Stratfield Saye,** a 17th-century mansion that the nation presented to the Duke of

Wellington after his victory over Napoleon at Waterloo. The practical-minded duke installed plumbing and central-heating systems that are still in use to this day. You may also make a side trip north from Reading on A 4526 to ***Mapledurham House.** This late 16th-century Elizabethan mansion and its magnificent garden overlook the River Thames. The poet Alexander Pope was a frequent guest here, and the house figures in John Galsworthy's series of trilogies, *The Forsyte Saga.*

Leave Reading from the west on A 4. For the next 40 km. (25 miles), A 4 skirts the southern edge of the *Berkshire Downs,* a gentle, hilly landscape that has been inhabited since prehistoric times. Few roads traverse the Downs, making the area a paradise for hikers, especially in the spring. Prehistoric paths, artificial mounds, and walls built by ancient Britons are concrete reminders of the area's long history.

A 4 follows the River Kennet through the villages of *Theale, Woolhampton,* and *Thatcham,* to **Newbury,** a busy market town with a well-known horse-racing track and the town's 16th-century parish *church of St. Nicholas.* The Jacobean latticework *Cloth Hall*—now a museum of British Civil War relics—and Newbury's many old weaver's houses recall past times when the city was a center of Britain's clothing industry. In the old part of the city, streets are lined with Georgian houses and old-fashioned inns. The 14th-century *Donnington Castle,* in the northern part of town, was the site of a Civil War battle in 1644.

Continue on A 4 to **Hungerford,** a popular fishing village on the River Kennet above which rises *Inkpen Beacon,* a 300 meter- (984 foot-) high hill that affords a panoramic view of the area. Tulips and lilies imported long ago from the Continent now grow wild all around. Just west of Hungerford, follow an access road to *Littlecote Manor.* This long, low, brick building, built between 1490–1520 in meadows along the River Kennet and surrounded by magnificent gardens, is said to be haunted by the ghost of William Darrell's newborn baby, whom he threw on the fire in a fit of madness in 1578. Another mystery surrounds the manor: an 18th-century servant found a Roman villa, with a magnificent mosaic floor, on the grounds, then died soon afterwards, carrying the secret of the villa's location to his grave. The site was subsequently rediscovered and archaeologists continue to excavate it. The mansion is furnished with valuable paintings, panels, furniture, carpets, tapestries, and porcelain. The *Great Hall* houses a collection of Cromwellian arms.

Marlborough, on A 4, is named after Maerl's Barro, a prehistoric mound on the grounds of Marlborough College that is said to be the grave of the magician Merlin. High Street, the city's wide, curved main street, is lined with elegant 17th- to 19th-century houses and colonnaded shops notable for their colorful, tiled façades. *Marlborough College,* founded in 1843, is one of England's leading public (i.e., private) schools. The poet, designer, and social reformer William Morris was a graduate.

Continue west on A 4. Near *West Kennet,* take A 4003 north to *Silbury Hill.* At 40 meters (130 feet), Silbury Hill is the largest artificial earthwork in Europe and one of the largest in the world. Researchers know it was laid out in prehistoric times, but its origin and purpose remain a mystery.

You'll find more inscrutable earthworks in the small town of **Avebury.** Among several massive prehistoric stone and earth rings and ditches is *Avebury Circle.* Dating from around 2000 B.C., this monument is older than Stonehenge (see page 149). The outer ring encircles more than 28 acres. Inside are two rows of unhewn Sarsen stones, a deep trench, and an avenue of stones leading to the northeast. Jump ahead 35 centuries to *Avebury Manor,* a 16th-century building with magnificent wall and ceiling decorations and a famous collection of porcelain, furniture, and miniatures. The beautiful garden is ablaze with tulips every spring.

Continue west on A 4 through the villages of *Beckhampton,* site of the ruins of *Oldbury Castle,* and *Calne,* a town noted for its bacon since the 18th century. Just past *Chippenham* take A 350 south to ***Lacock Abbey,** an Augustinian abbey founded in 1229. The building was converted into a mansion in 1540, but the handsome Medieval cloisters have been preserved. The mansion's barn houses a museum dedicated to William Fox Talbot, who experimented with photography here in the 1830s. The village of *Lacock* rates among the most beautiful in England and has been given landmark status. Its many well-preserved houses date from the 15th–18th centuries.

Return to A 4 and continue west to ***Corsham Court.** This Elizabethan mansion, set in a lovely park and gardens, was built in 1582 and altered between 1760–1770 by Capability Brown. The house is splendidly furnished with period furniture, including pieces by Chippendale, and famous paintings by Fra Filippo Lippi, Joshua Reynolds, and Thomas Gainsborough.

From here, you can continue on A 4 directly to Bath via *Box*. However, a little backtracking to Lacock (see above) takes you to several architectural treasures. Take A 350 south from Lacock, and just outside *Melksham*, follow A 3053 to *Holt*, where you can visit two mansions, *The Courts*, so-called because disputes among local weavers were once settled here, and *Great Chalfield Manor*. Part of Great Chalfield Manor is built of stone that was quarried near Box in 1480. Continue to **Bradford-on-Avon,** a peaceful country town of elegant stone buildings. Its *church of St. Lau-*

rence is one of England's best-preserved Anglo-Saxon churches, and its *parish church* is an amalgam of Norman, Decorated, and Early Gothic styles. Nearby *Kingston House,* built in 1580 in Italian style, is surrounded by lovely gardens. Just to the southwest is *Westwood Manor,* a two-story house that has been occupied since the 15th century and contains lovely period furniture. Continue to *Bath* (170 km.; 105 miles from London).

*Bath

Cupped in the sheltered valley of the River Avon, Bath looks much the same as it did in its 18th-century heyday, when fashionable ladies and gentlemen retreated there to "take the waters"—and to see and be seen. Residents and visitors included Jane Austen, Henry Fielding, Lord Nelson, William Wordsworth, William Pitt, Samuel Johnson, James Boswell, and Beau Nash, an 18th-century gambling dandy who was the town's social lion. Built on the only natural hot springs in Great Britain, the town has been a spa since the Romans built extensive baths here in A.D. 50. They named the town Aquae Sulis for the goddess Sul. When the Romans left three centuries later, Aquae Sulis slowly sank into the marshy ground. The ****Roman baths** were excavated in 1882, and they constitute some of the most fascinating Roman ruins in England. In the *museum* next to the baths you can see remains of

Baths and Bath Abbey

the temple of Sul, and many Roman art and cult objects.

Today Bath is an elegant and distinctive city, a masterpiece of British town planning. In the 18th century, John Wood and his son designed much of the present city in Georgian style. The buildings rise in tiers from the valley floor, giving the effect of a colossal wedding cake. The best examples of their work are the *Royal Crescent,* often called the most magnificent crescent-shaped street in the world; the *Queen Square and Circus; Pulteney Street;* and *The Parades.* In 1964, Bath was designated the most beautiful flower town in England for its well-designed and meticulously tended parks and gardens.

One of the city's most magnificent buildings belongs to its religious, not secular, past: ***Bath Abbey** was founded in 1499 and has been restored many times over the centuries. Today the abbey is noted for its beautiful western portal, stained-glass windows, fan vaulting, and intriguing tombstones. Among its plaques commemorating Bath's distinguished citizenry is one to Sir Isaac Pitman, a past resident and the inventor of shorthand. Bath's *Assembly Rooms* now house an historic costume museum. Other historic buildings include the *Guildhall,* with its *Banqueting Room.* Its magnificent furnishings include three large crystal chandeliers. You can still ingest the city's famed mineral waters at the 18th-century **Pump Room. Pulteney Bridge,* built in Florentine style, is lined with shops on both sides and illuminated at night. *Sham Castle* overlooks the town. One of the most popular excursion spots is the mansion called *Prior Park of John Wood,* just south of Bath. Built in 1743 by the elder architect of Bath, it is a masterpiece of the Palladian Renaissance style. The building now houses a Roman Catholic boarding school, but the chapel and the garden are open to visitors.

*Claverton Manor, just south on Route A 36, is a Classical style manor nestled amid a lovely garden on a hill above the River Avon. In its *American Museum,* rooms are furnished with 17th-, 18th-, and 19th-century objects brought here from the United States. Other rooms are decorated in the Spanish

Calverton Manor

Colonial style of New Mexico. The museum also displays American and Indian ethnic art and old mail coaches, and has a reconstructed country store.

From Bath, take A 4 west to *Keynsham* past *Frye & Sons'* chocolate factory and across the street from the remains of a Roman house, west to *Bristol* (189 km.; 117 miles from London).

Bristol

In 1497, John Cabot sailed from Bristol to North America, forging a transatlantic link of great significance to American history. A year later, his son Sebastian followed, exploring the coast of North America from Newfoundland to Florida. Over the next 200 years, many of the first emigrants to America, including William Penn, sailed from this important port at the mouth of the Avon.

Today Bristol is a modern business center, but visitors can still see traces of its seafaring history.

The city's shipbuilding past is nicely evoked at the *Bristol Maritime Heritage Center,* opened in 1985. Its modern displays tell the story of shipbuilding in Bristol from the Middle Ages to the present, and include an ocean liner dating from 1843. There is an old pirate hangout on the paved quays of the old town dock called the *Llandoger Trow.* Robert Louis Stevenson fans may know this tavern as the "Spyglass," as the novelist called it in *Treasure Island.* Across the street is the *Theatre Royal,* the smallest theater in England, which has operated continuously since 1766. The nearby merchant seamen's *almshouses* date to 1699. *Cabot Tower* on Brandon Hill pays tribute to the father and son who paved the way for English explorers of North America.

Bristol's ***cathedral** stands on the spot where Saint Augustine met with early British Christians in the fourth century. Founded in 1142, it was originally the abbey church of an Augustinian monastery. The cathedral is known for its many Norman components, including the well-preserved *chapter house* and doorway, and the *nave,* which was destroyed in the 16th century and not rebuilt until 1888. The *central tower* was built in 1450. The cathedral's interior is unique in that it has no triforium or upper gallery. As a result, arches soar to the full height of the interior, giving a dramatic effect. The beautiful east window in the *Lady Chapel* was constructed in 1320 and still contains some of the original glass. The ***church of St. Mary Redcliffe,** built in the 13th century by wealthy merchants on the site of an earlier church, is an outstanding example of Early Gothic style. Inside is the tomb of William Penn and a wooden statue of Elizabeth I, made during her lifetime. Here, in 1795, the poets Robert Southey and Samuel Taylor Coleridge were married in a double ceremony to Edith and Sara Fricker. Another important Bristol church is *St. Mark's,* better known as *The Lord Mayor's Chapel.* This secular appellation derives from the fact that the mayor owns the chapel and it has been the official place of worship for city officials since 1721. The most striking features of the Gothic building are its numerous monuments, its profusion of stained glass, and the fan-vaulted, tile-floored Poyntz Chapel.

Two of Bristol's old city gates, *St. John's Gateway* and *Abbey Gateway,* remain as do several residences from its prosperous seafaring days, among them *Georgian House* and *Royal York Crescent.* The city's *stock exchange,* on Corn Street, is not what 20th-century visitors might expect—four brass pillars mark the spot where the town's merchants used to make their payments. Bristol also has some admirable museums: *The City Museum and Art Gallery* on Queen's Road has extensive collections of antiquities, including mummies and early glass and porcelain. *The Bristol Industries Museum* on Prince's Wharf honors the region's important industrial past. One of the city's greatest technological accomplishments is the *Clifton Suspension Bridge* which opened in 1864 and crosses the River Avon in a single span.

If you are in Bristol in July, don't miss the international wine festival where 2,000 wines from 30 countries are tasted.

From Bristol, M 4 goes west, over the mouth of the River Severn, and on to *Cardiff,* the capital of Wales (see page 279).

TRAVEL ROUTE 8: ***London–Royal Tunbridge Wells–Hastings–Eastbourne (107 km.; 66 miles)

See map on page 161.

Even if you have only a short time to spend in England and don't plan on venturing much beyond London, you may want to take at least part of this Travel Route through the rolling fields and woods of Kent—certainly the first part, to England's most magnificent estate, Knole, and the other country estates and villages in the vicinity. From London, you can easily drive this route as far as Royal Tunbridge Wells—the spa of royalty for centuries—and back for a leisurely day of sightseeing.

Leave London to the south on Route A 21 and continue to **Sevenoaks** (38 km.; 23 miles). For many residents, this small and picturesque village is too close to ever-sprawling London for comfort. To date, though, Sevenoaks has managed to retain its charm, and the town takes good care of its treasures. These include a 13th-century *church* where the great poet John Donne was rector from 1616–1631 and a *school*, founded in 1431, which occupies a Palladian-style building from 1727. Even the town's cricket field, *The Vine*, is said to be the oldest in England. Sevenoaks's major attraction, though, is its great estate, ***Knole**, the largest house in England. Built by the Archbishop of Canterbury in 1456, the house then passed to Henry VIII, then to Elizabeth I, and finally to the Sackville family, whose home it has been for four centuries. With its 365 rooms, 52 staircases, and seven courtyards (the resemblance to calendar demarcations is not accidental), Knole is not everyone's idea of a cozy home. Vita Sackville-West, the popular writer, was born here in 1892, and she remembered dinners during which footmen stood on the carpets to keep them from flying ceilingward in the enormous drafts. Knole is now administered by the National Trust, and a dozen of its rooms—

filled with magnificent tapestries, paintings, and other furnishings—are open to the public. You can also visit the beautiful 1,000-acre park, where tame red deer roam freely and are likely to nibble at your unattended picnic hamper.

Sevenoaks is surrounded by many other estates. About 9 km.

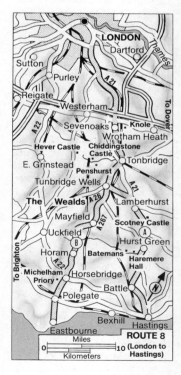

ROUTE 8
(London to Hastings)

(5 miles) to the east is **Ightham Mote,** which takes the first part of its name from the nearby village and the second part from the moat that surrounds this stone and timbered mansion built in the 14th century and rebuilt many times since. Notice the *newel post* on the staircase; it is carved in the form of a Saracen head, part of the family crest of Ightham Mote's residents, the Selby family. A 17th-century Selby, Dorothy, looks down from a nearby portrait. She is said to have learned of the Gunpowder Plot and exposed it to the authorities, putting an end to Roman Catholic extremist Guy Fawkes and his plans to blow up the Houses of Parliament.

Old Soar Manor, 11 km. (7 miles) east of Sevenoaks near the village of *Plaxtol,* is a knight's house from the 13th century. From Sevenoaks, Route A 21 crosses lovely countryside, much of it planted in forest that for centuries supplied the oaks used to build British ships, then comes to *Sevenoaks Weald,* a small village that is a sort of pilgrimage site for admirers of the Bloomsbury Group. Vita Sackville-West (see Knole, above), lived here for a time, and in her house, *Long Barn,* Virginia Woolf wrote part of *Orlando* and Roy Campbell wrote *The Georgiad.*

Route A 21 continues through fields and orchards to **Tonbridge,** an old market town on the River Medway. What's left of Tonbridge's old *castle*—a gatehouse and some walls—is said to be England's best example of Norman architecture. Tonbridge has a good share of timbered buildings, too, none more beautiful than the 15th-century *Chequers Inn.* Take time to drive east about 8 km. (5 miles) through the fields on Route B 2176 to the picturesque village of ***Penshurst.** Sir John De Pulteney, a prosperous wool merchant, built his country estate, *Penshurst Place,* here in 1340. The estate later passed to the Sidney family, whose members include Philip Sidney, the poet, soldier, and embodiment of a perfect 16th-century gentleman. The estate is still in the family, now the country seat of the Viscount De L'Isle. The Viscount opens his house to the public, so you may see the magnificent, chestnut-timbered *Great Hall,* the amazing furniture and armor, and the gardens, so beautiful that they inspired the great Ben Jonson to write a poem about them. Tea is served in the old kitchen.

From Penshurst you can walk or drive the 3 km. (2 miles) to **Chiddingstone,** a village that is so lovely and has so many timbered buildings that the whole place is administered by the National Trust. From the village there is a remarkable view across a lake to ***Chiddingstone Castle,** an 18th-century version of an old castle that is built around a much older house. Inside this quintessentially British structure you'll be surprised to see an amazing collection of Egyptian art, Japanese lacquer, and representations of Buddha—as well as a well-known collection of Stuart and Jacobite paintings and manuscripts.

*Herne Castle, the girlhood home of Henry VIII's second wife, Anne Boleyn, is about 6 km. (about 4 miles) northwest of Chiddingstone in the old village of *Herne.* William Waldorf Astor, of the prominent American family, bought the castle in 1903 and restored it to its Tudor glory. He also made a magnificent addition—an Italian-style garden, filled with the classical sculpture he collected when he was American ambassador to Italy.

From Tonbridge, follow Route A 26 south for about 9 km. (6 miles) through rolling farmland to **Royal Tunbridge Wells** (57 km.; 35 miles from London). The wells refer to the therapeutic springs that Dudley, Lord North, stumbled upon in 1606 while out for a walk during his stay at nearby *Eridge Castle.* Almost immediately, the health-giving springs attracted royalty. One of the first visitors was Henrietta Maria, the queen of Charles I, who camped out in the countryside. Another queen, Anne, built the graceful promenade known as the *Pantiles.* The *church of King Charles the Martyr* went up in 1676, and, ironically, the first child to be baptized in its font was a gypsy baby whose mother gave

birth while passing through this spa of royalty. Queen Victoria came to Tunbridge Wells often, staying with her mother at *Calverley House,* now a hotel. In 1909, King Edward VII made the spa's royal connections official by adding the "Royal" to the town's name. Modern visitors can take time out from their regimens at the Wells to attend concerts, play golf, shop, and partake in all the other attractions of this still popular resort. For a look at the town's illustrious past, pay a visit to the *Museum and Art Gallery.* Route A 21 continues south from Royal Tunbridge Wells for another 13 km. (8 miles) to **Lamberhurst,** which the essayist William Cobbett described in his 1830 work *Rural Rides* as "one of the most beautiful villages that man has ever set his eyes upon." This is quite a claim, especially for a village that was Medieval England's center for iron smelting (the surrounding forests supplied fuel). Lamberhurst is still beautiful—surrounded as it is by gardens and fine old houses. One of the most colorful—in terms of its present appearance and its past—is *Owl House,* a 16th-century cottage that sits amid splendid rose gardens and was once a haven for smugglers. After just 2 km. (a little more than a mile), Route A 21 comes to **Scotney Castle,** an enchanted-looking place that was built in 1377 and is surrounded by forests and a moat. A garden of narcissus and azaleas adds to its charm. At the village of *Flim-*

Scotney Castle

well, Route A 21 crosses into Sussex, then shortly comes to the village of *Hurst Green,* where you can take a short side trip of 3 km. (2 miles) west on Route A 265 to *Haremere Hall,* a 17th-century mansion with terraced gardens that cling to the side of a steep hillside. A few minutes' drive farther west on A 265 will bring you to the village of *Etchingham,* whose old church is lit by beautiful stained glass. Just beyond it the road comes to the village of *Burwash,* where Rudyard Kipling lived from 1902–1936 in *Bateman's,* a 17th-century mansion. The mementos on display include the citation for the Nobel Prize he won in 1907 (he was the first Englishman to do so).

From *Hurst Green,* Route A 21 continues south for 8 km. (5 miles) to *Battle* (see page 134) then in another 10 km. (6 miles) comes to *Hastings* (see page 134). From Hastings, you can drive on Route A 259 into *East-bourne,* as described in Travel Route 5 (see page 136).

You can also drive directly from Royal Tunbridge Wells to Eastbourne. Leave Tunbridge Wells on Route 267, which after 15 km. (9 miles) comes to **Mayfield,** where Saint Dunstan, one of the first archbishops of Canterbury, built a *palace* in the 10th century. The town was a favorite residence of his successors for centuries. What remains of the magnificent palace they built in the 14th century— with a glorious *Great Hall* that the designer A. W. Pugin restored as a chapel from 1863–1866—is now a school. In another 13 km. (8 miles), Route A 267 comes to **Horam,** where the bounty of its surrounding orchards is pressed into fruit wine that is exported around the world. The local great house, *Horam Manor,* now serves as a winery. Some 8 km. (4.5 miles) south, Route A 267 joins the larger Route A 22. About 4 km. (2.5 miles) beyond the junction there is a turnoff to **Michelham Priory,** which the Augustinian order founded in 1229. The priory was fortified by a moat and a gatehouse a century later, and it was restored as a country house in the 16th century—which explains the profusion of fine furnishings and tapestries. A drive of 14 km. (10 miles) down Route A 22 brings you to *Eastbourne* (107 km.; 66 miles; see page 136).

The West Country

The West Country begins in the county of Somerset and stretches to the westernmost tip of England, Land's End. Between those two geographic extremes lies some of the best scenery in England, be it rolling countryside or rocky headlands. The Celts, Romans, and most of the other peoples who have inhabited England have left their marks upon this pleasant landscape, though few of the historic residents are more appealing than King Arthur himself, who was supposedly born in the West Country, at Tintagel on the Cornish coast.

TRAVEL ROUTE 9: Bournemouth–Dorchester– Exeter (132 km.; 82 miles)

See map on page 170.

This Travel Route begins in Bournemouth, where Travel Routes 5 and 6 end. It passes along England's southern coast through County Dorset, a beautiful part of England that is well-known to readers of Thomas Hardy.

Leave Bournemouth from the west on A 35 and drive to **Poole,** which has been an important working port since the 12th century. The old harbor is lined with piers and warehouses that evoke its history. The town is also famous for its pottery and you may want to take the time to tour the pottery works or the *Guildhall Museum* which has an extensive collection of ceramics and glassware. Gardening enthusiasts should consider a side trip north from Poole to *Yaffle Hill Mansion* and its lovely gardens.

Continue on A 35 to *Bere Regis,* a town featured as Kingsbere in Hardy's *Tess of the d'Urbervilles.* Near the city, a side road leads south to *Clouds Hill,* which was the home of T. E.

Lawrence—better known as Lawrence of Arabia. The upstairs sitting room is as simple and spare as he left it. Return to A 35 and continue west to ***Athelhampton,** one of England's most beautiful Medieval man-

Athelhampton

sions. It was built by Sir William Martyn, Lord Mayor of London in 1493 on the site of an older palace. The great open hall has a timbered ceiling and bow windows glazed with heraldic symbols. The rooms are furnished in Tudor style, and there is a wine cellar and a secret staircase. The nearby River Piddle forms refreshing waterfalls in the mansion's 12 gardens.

Just west of Athelhampton, an access road leads off A 35 to *Hardy's Cottage* in *Higher Bockhampton*. The novelist was born in 1840 in this cottage built by his grandfather. The forest behind it, threaded with footpaths, has been set aside as a nature park by the National Trust. Here Hardy wrote *Under the Greenwood Tree* and *Far From the Madding Crowd.* Many of his novels and poems are set in a county he called Wessex, which is really a thinly disguised Dorset. Particular houses and villages in the novels can be identified as actual places in Dorset. For example, Casterbridge, as in *The Mayor of Casterbridge,* is really the city of Dorchester (46 km.; 28 miles from Bournemouth), just west on Route A 35.

Dorchester

Modern Dorchester is a bustling county seat whose many Georgian and Victorian buildings give it the air of a 19th-century market town. The Romans founded a city called Durnovaria here in the third century, and traces of their occupation remain. *The Walks,* a promenade around the town, follows the original Roman city wall. South of town, the *Maumbury Rings* are the remains of a Roman amphitheater, which, with 10,000 seats, is the largest one built in England. You can see artifacts from the prehistoric and Roman periods at the *Dorset County Museum,* on High Street. Nearby, you'll also find the *Tutankhamen Exhibition,* a reconstruction of the Pharaoh's grave, which also houses the *Dinosaur Museum.*

The 15th-century *church of St. Peter's* on High West Street holds the tomb of Reverend John White, the founder of Dorchester, Massachusetts.

A short drive a few miles south of the city will take you to ***Maiden Castle,** the best-preserved prehistoric fortified camp in Europe. It was first used in 2000 B.C. Continue 13 km. (8 miles) south of Dorchester on A 354 to **Weymouth,** a popular beach resort since the 18th century. George III, enemy of the American colonists, was a frequent visitor, and his statue stands on Weymouth's promenade. The armed forces from the United States left from Weymouth for the D-Day invasion of France in 1944.

From Weymouth, you can ferry to the *Channel Islands* of Guernsey and Jersey (see page 293). Or you can cross the unique stretch of pebbles called the Chesil Bank to the *Isle of Portland,* a navy base. The island is the source of the famous Portland stone used in many London buildings, including St. Paul's Cathedral.

Also near Weymouth is **Abbotsbury,** 13 km. (8 miles) to the west on A 3157. Its subtropical garden contains plants from all over the world and the town is also known as a breeding ground of wild swans.

From Dorchester, continue on A 35 west to **Bridport,** a center for the manufacture of rope and fishing nets for centuries. In the Middle Ages, the "Dagger of Bridport" was a popular term for the hangman's noose. Today, the harbor town is one of the prettiest in Dorset. Its wide streets, once hung with drying ropes, are now lined with well-preserved houses dating from the 15th–19th centuries.

Follow A 35 to *Charmouth,* and then take A 3052 south to **Lyme Regis,** a lovely beach resort on the border of Dorset and Devon counties. An ancient curved stone jetty, *the Cobb,* shelters its port. In 1685, the Duke of Monmouth landed here in his attempt to conquer the throne. Jane Austen set part of her novel *Persuasion* here, and 20th-century author John Fowles used the town and the Cobb in his novel *The French Lieutenant's Woman.* The coastal cliffs around Lyme Regis are exceptionally beautiful and laden with fossils. The icthyosaurus was discovered here in 1811.

Continue on A 3052 to *Sidford,* just north of the beach resort of *Sidmouth,* a trim town set in the hills. From Sidford, A 3052 continues to *Exeter,* but it's better to take A 376 for a pretty detour south along the coast. You'll go through *Budleigh Salterton,* a popular beach resort at the mouth of the River Otter. A quick jog to the north leads to the marvelous *Bicton Gardens,* designed by Andre le Nôtre, creator of the Tuileries in Paris and the gardens at Versailles. **Exmouth,** situated—not surprisingly—at the mouth of the River Exe, has a wide, sandy beach. The town's *Strand Gardens* are a sea of flowers for nine months of the year. Leave Exmouth on A 377. Just past town, take Summer Lane to a remarkable mansion called **A La Ronde.* Built in 1798, it was designed after the church of San Vitale in Ravenna, Italy. Return to A 377 and go north to **Exeter** (132 km.; 82 miles from Bournemouth).

This historic city is beautifully situated on a hill overlooking the River Exe. Now capital of the county of Devon, the city was settled before the birth of Christ. In the first century A.D., the Romans conquered the town and renamed it Isca Dumnoniorum. Ruins of the second- and third-century Roman city *walls,* as well as many Medieval buildings, have survived the ravages of time, and of a German bombing in 1942.

Exeter's most important building is the *Cathedral of St. Peter.* It is built almost entirely in the Decorated style, but two massive towers survive from an earlier

Roman church, as do several tombstones in the churchyard. Inside the cathedral are works of art dating from the 14th–17th centuries, including the 14th-century *bishop's chair* and the *stone pews* in the choir, the 15th-century frescoes at the entrance to *Lady Chapel,* and the 15th-century ceiling of the *Chapter House.*

North of the cathedral are the ruins of *Rougemont Castle,* built under William the Conqueror and mentioned in Shakespeare's *Richard III.* Only its moat, gatehouse, and Athelstan's Tower remain, surrounded by a lovely park. The handsome façade of the city's 15th-century *Guildhall* fronts High Street. The Medieval Benedictine *St. Nicholas Priory* with its 11th-century Norman crypt, is located on The Mint, a street named for the small assay-furnaces once used there to determine the amounts of gold and silver contained in alloys. The 300-year-old *Mol's Coffee House,* northeast of the cathedral now houses an art shop.

TRAVEL ROUTE 10: Exeter–Plymouth–Penzance– *Land's End (226 km.; 140 miles)

See map on page 170.

The variety of southern England is astonishing. This Travel Route explores much of its landscape from the old seafaring town of Plymouth to the ancient and mysterious land of Cornwall.

If you don't have much time, A 30 provides a quick but scenic route from *Exeter* to *Penzance.* It traverses the romantic heath of *Dartmoor* and *Bodwin Moor,* and passes through several interesting towns, among them *Okehampton,* site of the ruins of a Norman castle, and *Launceston* which also has Norman castle ruins, the Medieval South Gate and the 16th-century church of St. Mary Magdalene with its beautifully carved granite. A 30 continues through *Bodmin,* the capital of Cornwall, which boasts the largest parish church in Cornwall, and *St. Petroc,* which contains a Norman baptismal font and interesting Medieval woodcarvings.

Lanhydrock House, a few miles south of Bodmin on B 3268, is a 17th-century building with a 35 meter- (115 foot-) long picture gallery, whose stucco ceiling depicts Old Testament themes. A 30 also passes through *Redruth* which is at the center of Cornwall's rich tin and copper mines.

However, we recommend you take a more leisurely trip via *Plymouth.* There are two routes from Exeter (see page 167) to Plymouth.

The shortest route leads inland on A 38 through *Kennford* and *Chudleigh* to **Ashburton,** a pretty village of 17th- and 18th-century houses, and the location of a 14th-century granite parish church. Ashburton is a good center for excursions into *Dartmoor,* a landscape of broad, hilly heaths and moors where wild ponies still roam freely and many signs of prehistoric inhabitants remain. Dartmoor is the largest remaining tract of open land in southern England, and much of it is now national park. Today, the moor has turned into farming country, with sheep and cattle farms on the uplands.

From Ashburton, take A 38 southwest where, just outside of town, an access road goes north to **Buckfast Abbey.** The abbey was established in the 10th century by Benedictine monks, later destroyed, and then reestablished in the 11th century by the Cistercians. In 1882, the Benedictines returned to the abbey, and, at the beginning of this century, they built a larger chapel. Today, the monks sell the honey, fruit, wine, and stained glass that they produce.

Continue southwest on A 38 through *Buckfastleigh,* where there is a racetrack, to **South Brent** with its Norman parish church. *Brent Hill* is just outside of town; from its 300 meter- (984 foot-) high summit, a panoramic view of surrounding moors can be had. Lovely hiking trails thread through *Harford Moor, Ugborough Moor,* and *Brent Moor.*

Ivybridge, on A 38, is picturesquely located on the River Erme. The village provides a good starting point for excursions into southern Dartmoor, where there are many prehistoric mounds and stone circles.

Continue to **Plympton,** birthplace of the painter Sir Joshua Reynolds (1723–1792). The grammar school that he attended still stands; it dates to 1671. Southwest of the town, an access road leads south from A 38 to ***Saltram House,** a Georgian mansion built in the mid-18th century. The mansion's drawing rooms and dining room were designed by Scottish-born architect Robert Adam. Other noteworthy features include its stucco ceilings and chimneys, 14 portraits by Sir Joshua Reynolds, and a fine porcelain collection. A beautifully landscaped garden surrounds the mansion. Continue on A 38 to Plymouth (see page 172).

The second route from Exeter to Plymouth skirts a section of the southern coast often called the English Riviera. Take A 379 southwest from Exeter.

*Powderham Castle, near the town of *Kenton,* is a stately home built in 1390 and restored and enlarged in the 18th and 19th centuries. Now the family residence of the Courtneys, Earls of Devon, it is furnished with valuable period pieces and family portraits (open to the public). Deer roam the park surrounding the castle.

Teignmouth, on A 379, is a popular beach resort at the mouth of the River Teign. Its red sandstone cliffs, fir trees, and bright blue water are more typical of France's sunny Côte d'Azur than of the rest of the English coast— one reason for the area's lasting

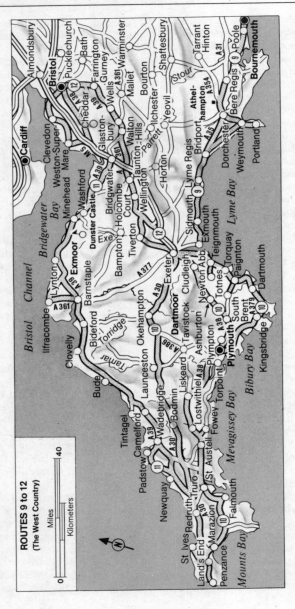

ROUTES 9 to 12
(The West Country)

Miles

0   40

Kilometers

popularity. A worthwhile side trip to *Newton Abbot* can be made from Teignmouth. Take A 381 west to the town of **Newton Abbot**, which, despite its name, is seven centuries old. Two kings—Charles I and William of Orange—stayed in *Forde House*, built in 1610. In 1688, William proclaimed himself King of England at *St. Leonard's Tower*, all that remains of St. Leonard's Church, which was destroyed in 1836. The 15th-century *Bradley Manor* is also worth a visit.

You can reach Torquay either by taking A 380 south from Newton Abbot, or, by following A 379 along the coast from Teignmouth.

The largest and most famous beach resort in this region of beach resorts, ****Torquay** bears a startling resemblance to a resort on the French Riviera, largely because its unusually mild climate supports subtropical vegetation. Its eight beaches are lined with palm trees and brightly colored flowers, and are backed by hills that provide magnificent views of Tor Bay. The town's gardens, many of which are illuminated at night, are famous for their flowers, fountains, ponds, and fauna. The *Abbey Gardens* are particularly beautiful. The abbey itself, *Torre Abbey*, was built in 1196. On its grounds are an 18th-century mansion, which houses the municipal art gallery, and a tropical greenhouse. The monastery granary is called the *Spanish Barn*, because 400 sailors from a galleon of the Spanish Armada were impri-

soned here 1588. A more recent piece of history was the birth here, in 1890, of Dame Agatha Christie, the most famous of all British mystery writers.

In 1968 the adjoining beach resorts of Torquay, Paignton, and Brixham were merged into the community of Torbay.

Three interesting side trips can be made from Torquay. **Kent's Cavern,* close to the town center, is a series of remarkable limestone caves that were inhabited by Ice Age tribes. Wall paintings dating to this time can be seen in the caves, along with some bizarre stalactite and stalagmite formations, and the skull of a saber-toothed tiger.

Cockington, a few minutes west of Torquay, is a village of white-washed, thatched-roof houses. You can see its ancient forge, mill pond, and inn, and ride the horse-drawn carriages that carry visitors from the town to the sea.

Just west of Cockington is the 14th-century *Compton Castle,* home during the 16th century to Sir Humphrey Gilbert, who founded Newfoundland.

Continue on A 379 south along Tor Bay to **Paignton,** another well-known beach resort with subtropical gardens. Its castlelike mansion, **Oldway,* was the retirement home of Isaac Singer, the American sewing-machine manufacturer. Built in pseudo-classical style, the mansion is often called "Little Versailles." Concerts and dances are held here during the tourist season. The town's *Coverdale Tower* was the home of Miles Coverdale, an English priest, who in 1535 made the first English translation of the Bible. Paignton's extensive *zoo* and *botanical gardens* cover more than 74 acres.

If you wish, you can make a detour west from Paignton to **Totnes,** whose many interesting buildings include a well-preserved *Norman castle,* and the *church of St. Mary,* with a 15th-century choir gate. The High Street, lined with colonnades, is interrupted by a series of piazzas.

From Paignton, continue south on A 379. Just past the town, a side road leads south to the little fishing village of *Brixham,* where William of Orange landed in 1688. Continue along the coast to *Dartmouth,* set on the wide mouth of the River Dart.

*Dartmouth is a town of historical and architectural interest as well as a lively beach resort. The town's restored 17th-century **Butterwalk,* an arcade of houses supported by granite pillars is particularly noteworthy. Other interesting buildings in Dartmouth include the *church of St. Saviour,* built in 1372 and added to in the 15th century; the *church of St. Petroc's,* which has some Norman sections; the Medieval *Mansion House;* the nearby *Dartmouth Castle* on the River Dart, one of Henry VIII's strongholds; and *Kingswear Castle,* on the opposite bank. Dartmouth's harbor has been important since

the Roman invasions; today, it is the seat of the Royal Naval Academy. On D-Day in 1944 American troops embarked from Dartmouth to invade Normandy. The Dart's estuary, accessible from Dartmouth by boat, is particularly beautiful.

Continue on A 379 to **Kingsbridge,** an old market town situated at the head of the Kingsbridge estuary. The sailing in the area is excellent and many of the town's sidestreets lead to beautiful beaches. William Cookworthy, who discovered China clay in Cornwall and who was the first to make porcelain in England, was born here in 1705.

A 379 continues through *Aveton Gifford, Modbury,* and *Yealmpton* to Plymouth (114 km.; 71 miles from Exeter).

Plymouth

Most Americans associate Plymouth with the Pilgrims and their historic voyage on the *Mayflower* to the New World in the 17th century. Actually, Plymouth has been one of England's most important harbors for centuries. The city's growth can be attributed to its excellent location at the mouths of the Tamar and Plym rivers, and on Plymouth Sound, a broad estuary that forms a natural harbor. For a time, Plymouth was one of England's largest cities.

Many warships sailed from Plymouth against the French during the Hundred Years' War. Under Queen Elizabeth I, the small fishing village of Plymouth blossomed into one of England's main trading ports and departure points for the country's sailors who set out to explore the New World. In 1577, Sir Francis Drake left Plymouth to begin his three-year circumnavigation of the world aboard the *Pelican* (later named the *Golden Hind*). In 1588, Drake led a fleet of warships from Plymouth Harbor to destroy the Spanish Armada. And, in 1620, the Pilgrims left in their small craft, the *Mayflower,* to settle in the New World. A monument to their voyage stands in Barbican Quay.

Plymouth's city center was all but destroyed by German bombs in 1941, and has since been rebuilt. However, many old sections of the city have survived, notably *Barbican Quay,* lined with well-preserved 16th-century houses built in typical Elizabethan style. The 15th-century *Prysten House* is the oldest house in Plymouth. Nearby is the royal

Plymouth

citadel, built in the 17th century under Charles II. The building is now a marine research station that opens its fascinating aquarium to the public.

From the roof of the city's modern *municipal building,* there is a view that takes in an area from Dartmoor in the northeast to Eddystone Lighthouse, 22 km. (14 miles) out to sea. Also in the new section of town is *Armada Way,* a boulevard running through the new shopping center, with its large park. South of the city center is one of Plymouth's best-known attractions, *the Hoe,* an area of terraced gardens and flowerbeds that date from Elizabethan times. Tradition has it that Sir Francis Drake calmly played a game of bowls at the Hoe before setting out to destroy the Spanish Armada. A statue of Drake stands in the garden. The nearby lighthouse, called *Smeaton's Tower,* was built in the 18th century and was once one of the most important lighthouses in the world.

Three worthwhile side trips can be made from Plymouth. ***Buckland Abbey,** 17 km. (10 miles) to the north, is a 13th-century Cistercian monastery that was turned into a mansion in 1576. Once the home of Sir Francis Drake, it now contains many mementos of his life. The *Tithe Barn,* on the abbey's grounds, is a buttressed gabled building dating to the 14th century. ***Cotehele House,** 20 km. (12 miles) to the north, was built between 1485–1539 on the banks of the River Tamar. It has an

Buckland Abbey

excellent collection of furniture, arms, tapestries, and handicrafts dating from the 17th century. A beautiful view can be had from the top of its *Prospect Tower.* **The Garden House,** near Buckland Abbey, has graceful terraced gardens.

From Plymouth, Route A 38 crosses Plymouth Sound and enters the county of Cornwall. From *Torpoint,* you may follow a narrow, twisting coastal road south to *Polperro,* where there is a *smuggler's museum.* However, this is a time-consuming journey and is not recommended. Instead, we suggest that you take A 38 west to *Liskeard.* Nearby are many prehistoric stone pillars and circles, most notably the *Trevethy stone circle.* Continue on A 38 to *Dobwalls,* where the road crosses the picturesque Fowey river valley.

Pick up A 390 going southwest. In **Lostwithiel,** the capital of Cornwall in the 18th century, are the Medieval *Duchy House* and the 13th-century *Fowey Bridge.* A pleasant 2 km. (just over 1 mile) walk north of the village will take you to the 13th-century *Restormel Castle.* Continue south on A 390; just past Lostwithiel take A 3269 south to *Fowey,* a port city with a rich but not always savory history. The Fowey Gallants were notorious seamen who raided the French coast both during and after the Hundred Years' War. Many of their haunts on the harbor have been preserved, as have some notable 15th- and 16th-century buildings.

From Fowey, continue west back to A 390 and from there, drive southwest to **St. Austell.** This town has been the center of England's porcelain industry since the 18th century, when China clay was discovered in the area. To the south are beautiful sandy bay beaches. Continue on A 390; just past *Grampound,* an access road leads south to the 18th-century *Trewithen mansion,* famous for its 20-acre garden of rhododendrons, magnolias, and camellias.

Truro, on A 390, is situated on the River Truro. Its remarkable *cathedral* was built from 1880–1910 on the site of a 16th-century church. Designed by the architect J. L. Pearson, it is a fine example of the Victorian Gothic revival. The town's *Cornwall County Museum* has interesting archaeological and mineral collections. From Truro follow A 39 southwest. Just outside the town, B 3289 leads south to the *Trelissick Gardens,* with many subtropical plants. Rejoin A 39 and continue to **Falmouth,** a port city since Roman times. It is situated on Carrick Roads Bay, and can be reached by boat from Truro. With the arrival of the steam railway in the 19th century, Falmouth burgeoned into a resort town, made popular by its lovely setting, jagged swimming bays, and shore promenade. Falmouth is a good starting point for excursions by land or by sea to many parts of Cornwall. *Pendennis Castle,* just south of the town, was built by Henry VIII on a knoll guarding the harbor entrance and later expanded by his daughter, Queen Elizabeth. Charles II took refuge at the castle during his flight to France. On the other side of the bay is *St. Mawes Castle,* also built by Henry VIII.

From Falmouth, follow A 394 to *Helston,* where A 3083 leads south through the heather-covered Goonhilly Downs, location of a satellite communications station. *The Lizard* is the southernmost point in England. It takes its name from the Cornish words *lis,* which means "palace," and *ard,* which means "high." It is, in fact, a majestic coastline of soaring cliffs and rock pinnacles. The cliffs are composed of serpentine, a mottled green rock characteristic of the region. There are many lovely swimming bays and coves here, particularly *Mullion Cove* and *Kynance Cove.*

Return to Helston, and continue northwest on A 394 to *Breage.* The village's 15th-century *church of St. Breaca* has interesting wall paintings, one of which portrays Saint Christopher, the patron of travellers. North of *Ashton* is the old Tudor *Godolphin House,* with its colonnade dating to 1635. The Godolphins were a family of local squires who became prominent under Henry VIII.

Continue on A 394 to *Marazion.* From here, boats leave for ***St. Michael's Mount,** an 80 meter- (262 foot-) high granite rock on which stands a castle. Originally a Benedictine abbey founded by Edward the Confessor in 1047, it was ruled by the same order that held Mont St. Michel in France. The abbey was secularized in 1660, after the. Reformation. Continue on A 394 to **Penzance** (210 km.; 130 miles from Exeter), the westernmost town in England. Situated at the center of the so-called "Cornish Riviera," its climate is so mild that palm trees and subtropical plants flourish. The town has picturesque old streets, a Medieval market cross, and many gardens. Sir Humphrey Davy, who invented the miner's safety lamp, was born here in 1778; a statue of him stands in Market Jew Street. Penzance's beach lies east of the town, and is connected via a dam to *St. Michael's Mount.* Many prehistoric stone circles and monuments are nearby, including *Lanyon Quoit,* a neolithic burial chamber; *Nine Maidens,* a line of standing stones; and the Iron Age hut village of *Chysauster.*

Two side trips can be made from Penzance. South of town is the fishing village of *Mousehole.*

Its color-washed and granite houses surrounding the small harbor give it a typically Cornish appearance. Mousehole was the home of Dolly Pentreath, who died in 1777, and was reputed to be the last person to speak the ancient Cornish language as her native tongue. Northwest of Penzance are the *Trengwainton Gardens,* where there are specimens of vegetation from all over the world.

The Isles of Scilly (which actually lie off Land's End) can be reached by boat (three hours) or helicopter (20 minutes) from Penzance. They consist of more than 100 tiny and tinier islands, only five of which are inhabited—St. Mary's, St. Agnes, Bryher, Tresco, and St. Martin's. Their climate is exceptionally mild; in fact, the islands are said to have only two seasons: spring and summer. *St. Mary's* is the largest of the isles. *Hugh Town,* its capital, is hardly a town at all. It does, however, have a *museum,* though the main attractions are the island's rocky and sandy beaches. *Tresco* is famous for its tropical *gardens,* where palms, bananas, lemons, and aloes flourish. The *Valhalla Museum* houses a collection of old galleon figureheads, nameboards, and other curios from ships that were wrecked off Tresco over the past two centuries. Prehistoric remains and Medieval castles also dot many of the isles.

From Penzance, follow A 30 to ***Land's End** (226 km.; 140 miles from Exeter), the farthest point west on mainland England. It is marked by a massive granite rock formation that falls into the sea. Land's End is a highly atmospheric spot, steeped in tales of shipwrecks, smugglers, and mysterious happenings and rife with ancient legend. Even the climate is somewhat mysterious: in just an hour, a walker can traverse the narrow neck of the peninsula from the warm channel shore to the gale-swept Atlantic coast.

Land's End

TRAVEL ROUTE 11: Penzance–*Newquay–Ilfracombe–Bristol (340 km.; 211 miles)

See map on page 170.

Cornwall's dramatic northern coast is a favorite subject for artists, and for good reason. Its towering cliffs, sandy bays, and charming fishing villages provide some of the most breathtaking scenery in England. This Travel Route traces the coast from south to north.

Leave Penzance on B 3311 going north. ***St. Ives,** one of Cornwall's loveliest beach resorts, has long been a haunt for artists, including James Whistler and Walter Sickert among others. Its old town, a labyrinth of steep cobblestone streets, is the site of the 15th-century *church of St. Hia,* dedicated to the Irish saint of that name. In the Lady Chapel are works by the sculptor Barbara Hepworth (d. 1975), who lived in St. Ives. Local fishermen still catch sardines in the old harbor. The new part of town is set near a beautiful sandy beach with a bay where people surf. St. Ives is a good center for excursions to the many prehistoric settlements and beautiful stretches of coast in the area.

Continue north on the coastal road B 3301 to *Newquay* (59 km.; 36 miles from Penzance).

*Newquay is the surfing center of Great Britain and often the site of national championships. A side trip can be made from Newquay southeast to *Trerice Manor,* an Elizabethan house noted for its latticed windows—including one in the main hall that is made up of 576 panes of glass—that is open to the public.

From Newquay continue north to **Padstow.** A pretty little town built around an old fishing port, Padstow was once a major trading port. However, as ships got bigger, they couldn't pass a sandbar that lies outside the harbor. The bar is called Doom Bar, so-named because it is said to be the work of a dying mermaid who was murdered by a local fisherman. Padstow still has some remarkable 15th-century structures, including *Raleigh's Court House, Abbey House,* and the *church of St. Petroc.* Northeast of town are sandy sailing bays.

Drive inland to A 39 and then continue northeast to **Wadebridge,** situated at the mouth of the River Camel on the bay of the same name. A bridge 100 meters (330 feet) long with 15 arches, built in 1485, spans the river. Wadebridge was the terminus for one of the first railroads in England, which ran between here and Bodmin.

Continue north on A 39 to *Camelford;* from there, B 3263 leads northwest to the coast and **Tintagel.** This small legendary village is one of the most famous spots in England. The ruins of a Norman *castle* on a rocky promontory jutting out over the sea stand on an even older foundation. Indeed, excavations have uncovered evidence of a Celtic monastery which existed from A.D. 500–850. Later legend reveals it as the birthplace of famous King Arthur, founder of the Knights of the Round Table. Under the castle is a cave called Merlin's grotto, where the magician is supposed to have lived. In 1145, this building gave way to the Norman castle, which was built for the Earl of Cornwall. The castle fell out of use several centuries later, and has been in ruins since Tudor times. In Tintagel is the parish *church of Sts. Materiana and Marcelliana,* which has Norman and Saxon sections, and the *Old Post Office,* a 14th-century building that has been restored. Sandy beaches dot the nearby bays. The village of *Boscastle* to the north has a pretty harbor surrounded by cliffs.

Return to A 39 and continue north to **Bude,** a resort on a wide, sandy beach. In the 19th century, the town was notorious for the shipwrecks off its coast where, between 1824–1874, more than 80 ships foundered. A cliff walk to the south provides breathtaking views.

Continue north to *Kilkhampton,* location of a beautiful Norman church. Near *Clovelly Cross,* north on A 39 from Kilkhampton, an access road leads north to ***Clovelly,** a fishing village set among coastal cliffs. Its steep streets (from which cars and trucks are banned) and small, brightly painted houses form a picture-postcard Medieval village. Indeed, Clovelly is often portrayed on canvas by local artists.

A 39 continues east to **Bideford,** situated at the mouth of the River Torridge. Sections of Bideford's striking 24-arch bridge over the Torridge date from the 15th century. On the quay is a statue of Charles Kingsley (1819–1875), who wrote his famous novel *Westward Ho!* here

in 1855. In the novel, Kingsley described the climate of north Devon as one that combines the "soft warmth of south Devon with the bracing freshness of the Welsh mountains." Westward Ho! itself is 3 km. (2 miles) to the west. Until the publication of Kingsley's book it was an obscure little town on a sandy beach; today, it is a popular resort.

Barnstaple, northeast of Bideford on A 39, is one of the oldest market towns in England. As early as the tenth century, it was a busy trading center that minted its own coins. Because of its setting at the mouth of the River Taw (spanned by a 13th-century arched bridge) and on the bay of the same name it also became an important commercial port. In fact, until the Taw silted up, Barnstaple was the third largest town in Devon. The 18th-century *Queen Anne's Walk* is a pleasant colonnade which was built to service the stock exchange, a statue of Queen Anne was erected there in 1708. The

Queen Anne's Walk

Tome Stone, on which merchants set their money to make their contracts binding, is also in the colonnade. Other notable sights in town include the 14th-century *church of St. Peter's* with its leaning tower and the *Pannier Market,* which comes to life on market days.

From Barnstaple, there are two routes to *Lynton and *Lynmouth.* A 39 provides the most direct route. It passes through *Arlington,* location of a remarkable 19th-century mansion called Arlington Court, which has a noteworthy collection of model ships, old carriages, and rare shells. Continue on A 39 through *Blackmoor Gate* to Lynton.

A 361 from Barnstaple is a longer but prettier route. It passes through *Braunton* to the coastal resort of **Ilfracombe,** built around its old harbor. Good shingle beaches surround it; some can only be reached through tunnels in the coastal cliffs. The coast around the town is steep and rocky and characterized by many bizarre rock formations.

From Ilfracombe, take A 399 east to A 39 and continue north to ***Lynton** and its twin town **Lynmouth,** the most important coastal towns in the Exmoor National Park. Both towns provide good starting points for excursions into the surrounding hills and forests. *Exmoor National Park* was declared a royal forest more than 1,000 years ago. Today it encompasses 265 square miles of moor, farmland, valleys, and woods, where wild ponies and

deer roam. The novelist R. D. Blackmoor set *Lorna Doone* in this region.

Lynton, set on steep cliffs 150 meters (500 feet) above the sea, is connected by a cliff railway to Lynmouth, at the foot of the cliffs. Its small harbor is situated at the mouth of the River Lyn. The coastal path east from here to *Porlock* is particularly lovely.

A 39 also leads to **Porlock.** This pretty little village is set at the foot of forested hills. Its 13th-century *church of St. Dubricius* has a magnificent Medieval tomb. Just south of the village stands *Dunkery Beacon,* which, at 560 meters (1,836 feet), is the highest point in the Exmoor hills. When the weather is fine, the view from here is extraordinary.

Continue on A 39 to **Minehead.** Until the advent of the railway, Minehead was one of the most important ports in the area. Today, it remains a pleasant place with sandy beaches and lovely gardens, as well as many Medieval houses and the remarkable 14th-century parish *church of St. Michael's* in the old part of town. Minehead is a good base for excursions to nearby coastal towns such as *Somerset,* and the forests of *Brendon Hills.*

East of Minehead, an access road leads to ****Dunster Castle.** The original structure was built in 1070 and added to over the centuries. It is set in a particularly lovely park. Inside the castle, a large oak-paneled *Hall* opens onto a 17th-century carved wooden *stairway.* The beautifully furnished *Banqueting Hall* is also noteworthy. Other rooms are furnished with pieces from the 14th–16th centuries. Charles II was a guest here on many occasions. Many old houses line the wide main street of the nearby village of *Dunster.* Its sights include *St. George's,* its parish church; the *Packhorse Bridge;* and the *Domesday Mill.*

Continue east on A 39 to *Washford* and the nearby ruins of ***Cleeve Abbey.** Founded by the Cistercians in 1188, the abbey has a 14th-century *gatehouse* and a well-preserved 13th-century *dormitory.* The *refectorium* dates to the 16th century.

Near *Dodington* is Dodington Hall, built in the 14th and 15th centuries. **Nether Stowey,** once home to the poet Samuel Taylor Coleridge, is farther east. *Coleridge Manor,* the cottage where he lived from 1797–1800 and wrote "The Rime of the Ancient Mariner" and "Kubla Khan," is open to visitors. William Wordsworth was a frequent guest at the manor.

Bridgwater, the next sizable town on A 39, has many 18th- and 19th-century brick houses.

St. Mary's Church, built in 1420, has a sleek gothic tower. From Bridgwater, there are two routes to *Bristol.* The first and most direct follows A 38 north through *Highbridge.* However, if you can spare the time, the more scenic route leaves A 38 at Highbridge, where you can take A 370 north to **Weston-Super-Mare,** a popular spot on Bristol Bay with a long, sandy beach, a shore promenade, and an amusement park. Continue north along the coast to **Clevedon,** a peaceful resort town that Coleridge frequented. Just outside Clevedon is *Clevedon Court,* a 14th-century mansion set in a beautiful garden. Continue to *Bristol* (see page 159).

Weston-super-Mare

TRAVEL ROUTE 12: Bristol–*Wells–Glastonbury–Exeter (132 km.; 82 miles)

See map on page 170.

Most people associate the southwest of England with two characteristics: its mild climate and its magnificent coastline. However, you'll find much mystery and beauty in the region's interior. From Bristol, through the towns of Wells and Glastonbury, set amidst prehistoric cave settlements, to the bustling commercial center of Exeter, Travel Route 12 provides a course that is both historically fascinating and full of natural beauty.

From *Bristol* (see page 159) take A 37 south to *Farrington Gurney;* from there, follow A 39 southwest through the charming landscape of the Mendip Hills to *Wells* (33 km.; 20 miles from Bristol).

*Wells

This lively market town has retained its Medieval appearance, and houses, inns, and city gates dating from the 14th–16th centuries line its streets. Wells's famous **cathedral** was built between the 12th–13th centuries, and towers were added in the 14th–15th centuries. The cathedral's western façade, completed in 1239, is a splendid example of Early English architecture. It is decorated with more than 300 statues, 152 of which are life size and all of which were originally painted bright red, blue and gold.

Inside, the cathedral's magnificent arched *vaults, column capi-*

tals, richly decorated *triforium,* and Medieval *tombstones* warrant close inspection. The *choir* contains an 18th-century bishop's chair. The **Lady Chapel* dates from 1326, and the *astronomical clock* in the northern transept was built in 1392. Its mechanism, which still works, is on display at the Science Museum in London. The **Chapter House,* built between 1293–1319, is an outstanding example of Decorated style.

Other noteworthy sights in Wells include the **Vicar's Close,* a courtyard lined with Medieval houses that adjoins the cathedral; the *town square,* which has been a marketplace since the Middle Ages; and the *church of St. Cuthbert,* on High Street, with its beautiful Early Gothic tower. The *Bishop's Palace,* built in 1208, is surrounded by a moat populated by well-trained swans that ring a bell to be fed.

Two fascinating side trips can be made from Wells. **Wookey Hole,** a few kilometers west of the city, is actually a series of large caves formed by the River Axe. The caves were home to some of the earliest settlers in Great Britain. Excavations have unearthed artifacts dating to 250 B.C.; many of which are on display in a *museum* near the cave entrance. The museum also contains a cabinet for wax figures with which Madame Tussaud toured England from 1802–1835.

Wells Cathedral

One of the caves contains a huge stalagmite called the "witch of Wookey." According to legend, it was formed when a Glastonbury monk turned a witch into stone. This legend appears to have some basis in fact: the bones of a young woman and a sacrificial knife were found nearby. Near the caves, a *paper factory*, which supplied the Confederate mint in Richmond, Virginia, during the American Civil War, still produces handmade paper. It has been in business since 1600.

Cheddar Gorge, a 3-km.- (2-mile-) long gash in the limestone Mendip Hills, is northwest of Wells. At the bottom of the gorge are caves that were occupied in prehistoric times. Among them, *Gough's Cavern* and *Cox's Cavern* are especially interesting.

From Wells, continue southwest on A 39 to **Glastonbury** (44 km.; 27 miles from Bristol). The area surrounding Glastonbury was once a vast, marshy valley dotted with villages built on islands. Glastonbury was one such village and it was built upon an island called Avalon, where it has stood since the seventh century.

The town grew up around famous **Glastonbury Abbey*, founded in 601 and to which many legends have been attached over the years. The best known concerns Joseph of Arimathea, who brought the Holy Grail here from Jerusalem to convert the English pagans. He is said to have founded a church on the site of the abbey; but, although there is no historical evidence of his particular church, there has been a church of some kind on this site since the fifth century. Another legend has it that King Arthur was brought here after his death, and that he and Queen Guinevere are buried in the abbey.

The abbey fell into ruins after the Dissolution in 1539, though these ruins are richly evocative of all the mystery and romance of the ancient legends of the Holy Grail and King Arthur.

The *George Hotel,* in the town of Glastonbury, was once a pilgrim's inn. On its paneled façade is the heraldic shield of Edward IV. The parish *church of St. John the Baptist* has an exceptionally beautiful late Gothic tower. On Bere Lane is the 14th-century *Abbots Barn,* decorated with symbols of the evangelists.

A worthwhile side trip can be made northwest to *Meare,* where there are traces of villages dating from 150 B.C.

From Glastonbury, take A 39 south to A 361, which cuts west across the low *Polden Hills,* circles the northern edge of *King's Sedge Moor,* and continues through *Othery* to **Taunton.** This thriving market town on the River Tone is also a popular summer resort. Taunton has many historic buildings, notably the *Almshouses* on Middle Street, built in 1637, and the English Gothic *church of St. Mary Magdalene,* with its splendid tower decorated with gargoyles and pinnacles.

The 12th-century *Taunton Castle* houses the *Somerset County Museum,* where prehistoric artifacts are on display.

From Taunton follow A 38 southwest. Just past the town of *Wellington* you will pass an impressive monument to the Duke of Wellington, built on the summit of one of the Blackdown Hills in honor of the Duke's victory over Napoleon at Waterloo.

A little further along A 38, a side road leads north to **Cothay Manor,** one of the best-preserved mansions in Great Britain. Built on the banks of the River Tone in 1309, it was enlarged in 1481. Its decorations include some exceptional 15th-century frescos. Its *gatehouse* is now a chapel.

*Holcombe Court, just north of A 38, is a Tudor mansion dating from the early 16th century. Of particular interest are its *Long Gallery,* 20 meters (65 feet) long, and the stucco chimneys and ceilings in many of the rooms. Much of the furniture dates from the 18th century.

Holcombe Court

Return to A 38 and continue southwest. From *Waterloo Cross,* there are two routes to Exeter. A 38 runs through *Cullompton,* where there are several Medieval houses and a 15th-century church, *St. Andrew's. Killerton House,* south of Cullompton, is surrounded by lovely gardens and houses the National Trust's collection of 18th- to 20th-century costumes. A 38 then continues to Exeter.

However, a more interesting route from Waterloo to Exeter follows A 373 west to **Tiverton,** a small market town picturesquely located on the River Exe. Its castle is now in ruins, though the 14th-century *gatehouse,* built of red sandstone, is well-preserved. Other buildings of interest in Tiverton include the 15th-century parish church, *St. Peter's; Old Blundell's School,* the town's grammar school founded in 1604; and many beautiful Georgian homes. A worthwhile side trip from Tiverton leads northeast to *Knightshayes Court,* a Gothic structure erected in the late 1800s, surrounded by magnificent gardens, and the equally beautiful gardens of *Chevithorne Barton.*

From Tiverton follow A 396 south through *Bickleigh,* with its 15th-century castle, and *Burn,* site of *Cadbury Castle.* The castle, now in ruins, is believed by some to be the site of Camelot, King Arthur's court, because of its proximity to the River Cam and the village of Queen Camel. From Burn, A 396 continues north to *Exeter.*

East Anglia

East Anglia, once a Saxon kingdom, today encompasses a large region stretching northeast from London. The flat landscape is characterized by wide marshes and heaths, whose quiet beauty has been immortalized by the English painter John Constable. The history of its main cities—Cambridge, Ely, and Norwich—parallels that of Britain. Travel Routes 13 and 15 provide a round trip through East Anglia; Travel Route 14 explores some interesting sights off the beaten path.

TRAVEL ROUTE 13: ***London–**Cambridge–**Ely– *King's Lynn–Cromer–**Norwich–(Great Yarmouth) (285 km.; 177 miles)

See map on page 185.

For a crash course in British history, you could do no better than to take this Travel Route. With stops at Cambridge, Ely, and Norwich, some of Britain's most historic cities, a circuit along a stretch of coast that has been settled for centuries, and a scenic tour of the Norfolk Broads, the route perfectly conveys the essential qualities of England.

Leave London from the north on A 10. In the northern suburb of *Enfield* is *Forty Hall,* a mansion built in 1629 that is now an historic museum displaying 17th- and 18th-century furniture and paintings. Route A 10 continues to **Ware** where Lady Jane Grey was proclaimed Queen in 1593; she reigned only nine days. Ware also has the ruins of a 14th-century Franciscan monastery. You can take a worthwhile side trip from Ware by driving west on A 14 to the old market town of *Hertford,* with a 12th-century castle and many Medieval timbered cottages, including one that houses a museum of local history.

Continue north on A 10 to Royston where the highway bears east toward **Cambridge** (see page 60). (Cambridge is just east of Newmarket and Bury St. Edmunds, which are part of Travel Route 15; see page 194.) Take A 45 west to A 1102 north, and continue on to *Anglesey Abbey.** This Augustinian abbey was founded in 1236 and in 1591 became a private home. It now houses a large collection of tapestries, paintings, and sculptures and is surrounded by a magnificent garden decorated with classical statuary including busts of 12 Roman emperors.

Continue on A 142 to **Ely** (110 km.; 58 miles from London). Ely means Eel Island: Until the 17th and 18th centuries, when the fens were drained, the city

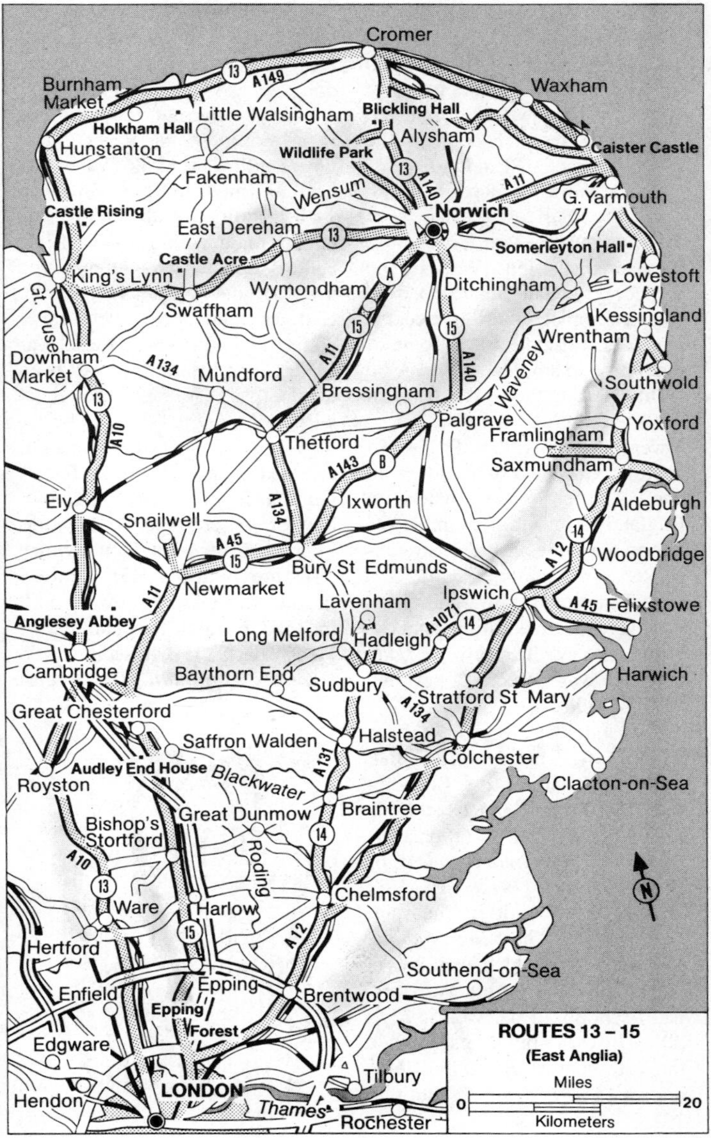

Cromer
Waxham
Burnham Market
13 A149
Holkham Hall
Little Walsingham
Blickling Hall
Alysham
Caister Castle
Hunstanton
Wildlife Park
13 A140
A11
Fakenham
Wensum
G. Yarmouth
Castle Rising
East Dereham
13
Norwich
Somerleyton Hall
King's Lynn
Castle Acre
A
Ditchingham
Lowestoft
Wymondham
Kessingland
Swaffham
15
15
Waveney
Wrentham
Downham Market
A134
Mundford
A11
A140
Southwold
13
Bressingham
Palgrave
Yoxford
A10
Gt. Ouse
Thetford
Framlingham
Saxmundham
Ely
A143
B
Ixworth
A12
Aldeburgh
Snailwell
A134
14
Woodbridge
15
Bury St Edmunds
A45
Newmarket
Lavenham
Ipswich
A45
Felixstowe
Anglesey Abbey
A11
Long Melford
Hadleigh
A1071
14
Cambridge
Baythorn End
Sudbury
Stratford St Mary
Harwich
Great Chesterford
A134
Saffron Walden
Halstead
Colchester
Clacton-on-Sea
Audley End House
Blackwater
A131
Royston
Great Dunmow
Braintree
Bishop's Stortford
14
Roding
A10
Chelmsford
13
Ware
15
Harlow
A12
Hertford
Southend-on-Sea
Enfield
Epping
Brentwood
Epping Forest
Edgware
LONDON
Tilbury
Hendon
Thames
Rochester

ROUTES 13 – 15
(East Anglia)
Miles
0   20
Kilometers

N

was on an island, and eels were of great importance in the local diet. Today, this cathedral city is set on the broad, flat fens of East Anglia. The town is dominated by its massive **cathedral,* the third largest in England. This great cathedral, which rises high above the small town, can be seen for miles away as you drive across the dismal, flat fens. Work on the cathedral began in 1083 and wasn't completed until five centuries later. It incorporates some of the finest examples of Medieval architecture in the world. Its most notable feature is the *Octagon,* a tower built in 1322. The 13th-century *Galilee Porch* opens to one of the longest naves in England, a splendid example of Norman architecture that stretches some 60 meters (about 210 feet). Its painted ceiling, however, is a fairly recent addition from the 19th century. The lovely *Lady Chapel* was erected between 1320–1349.

Just south of the cathedral are several *Medieval buildings* that were once part of the Benedictine Abbey that Saint Etheldreda founded in Ely in 673. Of particular note are the *Great Gateway,* or Ely Porta, and *Prior Crauden's Chapel,* both built in the mid-14th century. The *King's School,* founded in the 11th century, is one of the oldest public (i.e., private) schools in the world. Ely's other historic buildings include the 18th-century *Bishop's Palace* and *St. Mary's Church,* built in 1215.

From Ely, continue north on A 10 through *Littleport* and *Downham Market* to **King's Lynn** (165 km.; 102 miles from London).

This lovely old town at the wide mouth of the River Ouse, where it flows into the Wash, has been an important port since the 14th century. With its narrow streets lined with 14th- to 17th-century houses and churches, the town is distinctly Medieval in character and appearance, especially on and around Nelson, Bridge, and Friars streets. It is an ideal city to wander through at leisure. Among its fine old buildings are: *St. Margaret Church,* founded in 1100; *Trinity Guildhall,* built in 1421 and notable for its checkered flintwork; *Thoreby College,* a 15th-century structure with a 17th-century façade; the *Custom House,* built in 1683 by architect and mayor Henry Bell; the 14th-century *St. George's Guildhall,* the largest

Castle Acre

Medieval guildhall in England, now a theater; the 13th-century *Greyfriars' Tower;* and the 15th-century *St. Nicholas Chapel.*

From King's Lynn there are two routes to Norwich. A 47 leads directly to Norwich, passing through *Swaffham,* an 18th-century market town. A side trip can be made from here to the village of *Castle Acre,* which lies on a Roman road and is now noted for its magnificent ruins of an abbey dating from 1090, and a ruined, 11th-century castle. Its nicely preserved *church of St. James,* built from the 13th–15th centuries, has fared better. A 47 continues through *East Dereham* to Norwich.

The second, and longer, route to Norwich follows A 149 along the coast. Just past King's Lynn is ***Castle Rising,** a small town built around the remains of a Norman *castle* that, in turn, is built on some of the most impressive earthworks in England. These earthworks may date back to the Roman occupation of Britain. In the 14th century, the castle was home to Queen Isabella, wife of Edward II and mother of Edward III. The town's *Trinity Hospital,* a 17th-century Jacobean almshouse, is still a home for elderly women.

Continue on A 149 to the access road to ***Sandringham House,** one of the Queen's country retreats. The house and stunning gardens are open to the public when the royal family is not in residence. Continue north on A

149 to the coast and the pleasant Victorian resort of *Hunstanton.*

The coast of Norfolk extends in a wide arc from here to Great Yarmouth. The beauty of its low, sandy cliffs, pebbly peninsulas, bird sanctuaries, lovely bays, and miles of scarlet sea lavender has been immortalized in paintings by two local artists, John Cotman and John Crome. Many of their works are on view in the Castle Museum in Norwich (see page 189).

Follow the coast on A 149 through *Brancaster,* with its bird sanctuary; *Burnham Deepdale,* where there is a church with a Saxon round tower; Medieval *Burnham Market,* from where an access road leads to *Burnham Thorpe,* the birthplace of Admiral Horatio Nelson; and *Overy Straithe,* a sailboat and yachting center, to **Holkham.** **Holkham Hall,* the sumptuous residence of the Earl of Leicester, which an 18th-century earl, Thomas Coke, built in 1734 in Palladian style to demonstrate how this desolate region of salt marshes could be well utilized. Its staterooms are decorated with valuable collections of paintings, tapestries, and furniture, and the equally glorious grounds were laid out in 1762 by Capability Brown.

Continue to the small harbor of *Wells-next-the-Sea,* where a worthwhile detour leads south on A 1065 to ***Little Walsingham.** This pretty little town of half-timbered houses is also the location of *Walsingham Priory,* a once-prosperous Augustinian abbey and pilgrimage site founded in the 11th century that is now largely in ruin.

Return to A 149 and continue along the coast to *Blakeney,* built around a busy yacht harbor. *Blakeney Point* is a nature preserve where both wild fowl and rare plants are protected. Follow A 149 through *Cley-next-the-Sea,* an Edwardian beach resort with a 14th-century church, and *Sheringham,* famous for its crabs and lobsters, to **Cromer** (248 km.; 154 miles from London). This beautifully situated fishing port and resort has been popular since Edwardian times for its lovely, sandy beaches, high cliffs, and esplanade. Cromer also has a notable 15th-century church.

From Cromer, you can terminate this travel route in either Norwich or Great Yarmouth (see page 190).

To reach Great Yarmouth, you can either take A 1159 along the coast or follow A 149 inland through the famous *Norfolk Broads.* The Broads are a wide, flat expanse, punctuated by windmills, wheatfields, lonely heaths, and small villages. More than 200 km. (130 miles) of boating waterways link the villages, and small cabin cruisers can be hired for tours of the region.

The most beautiful (and direct) connection between Cromer and Norwich is provided by A 140. Leave Cromer from the south and drive through *Roughton* to the old market town of *Aylsham.* From Aylsham, a worthwhile side trip

leads east on B 1354 to ***Blickling Hall,** a Jacobean brick mansion built between 1616–1624 on the site of one of Anne Boleyn's childhood homes and enlarged in 1770. In its large rooms you'll see valuable period furniture, tapestries and paintings. The *Great Gallery's* decorated plaster ceiling is striking. The garden features a small man-made lake that was dug in 1930, and a temple built in 1793.

Return to Aylsham and follow B 1145 southwest to *Cawston,* where a side road leads to the **Norfolk Wildlife Park.** This relatively new nature park is home to birds and other wildlife from all over the world. Species residing at the park include eagles, Malay bears, peacocks, arctic foxes, rare fish and seals, and lynxes. Many of the animals roam freely. The park also contains a good restaurant. Continue on this side road to *Great Witchingham,* and then follow B 1149 to Norwich (285 km.; 177 miles from London).

**Norwich

Norwich, the capital of East Anglia and one of England's oldest towns, has been the See of the East Anglian bishops for 900 years. The town has been ruled in turn by Saxons, Danes, Normans, and even the Dutch. Settlers from the lowlands in Europe introduced silk and wool manufacturing, and Norwich grew prosperous from these industries.

Today, the city is a felicitous blend of modern commerce and historical character, with busy shops and cobblestone streets. Elm Hill is the city's best-preserved Medieval street. Among the town's many Medieval houses is the *Suckling House,* home of a 16th-century merchant. The ***cathedral** is Norwich's showpiece. Built in 1096, it burned down in 1272, and was restored under Edward I. The beautifully decorated rectangular *tower* has a

Norwich Cathedral

15th-century *spire* which, at 103 meters (338 feet), is the highest in England after Salisbury. The cathedral also boasts one of the largest and most beautiful **cloisters* in the country.

Norwich has 32 other Medieval churches; noteworthy among them are **St. Peter Mancroft* and **St. Peter Hungate,* both dating from the 15th century. Norwich's large **castle** built between 1120–1130, has a 19th-century façade and a well-preserved **keep.* Inside the castle are a *museum* of archaeology and natural history and a *municipal picture gallery,* displaying works by painters of the Norwich school.

Norwich's marketplace is surrounded by Medieval buildings, including the *Guildhall* (dating from 1407 and incorporating 15th-century glass) and gabled houses dating from the 15th–16th centuries. The nearby *Maddermarket Theatre,* which has been restored in Elizabethan style, stands on the site of the Medieval marketplace where red madder dye was sold.

From Norwich, A 47 leads east to Great Yarmouth (see page 190).

TRAVEL ROUTE 14: Great Yarmouth–*Ipswich–*Sudbury–Chelmsford–***London (205 km.; 128 miles)

See map on page 185.

England has been called a nation of villages, and the region from Great Yarmouth to London is dotted with many that have been in place since

Roman times. This Travel Route takes you through some of the country's most scenic villages and ends in the largest English village of all, London.

Great Yarmouth is situated at the wide mouth of the River Yare and in recent years has become an important base for oil rigs in the North Sea. Yarmouth is also a vacation resort that is popular for its long sandy beach, promenade, piers, and amusement park. Its old *fruit market* and *Fishermen's Almshouses,* built in 1711, are reminders that the town has long been an important fishing port that was already settled at the time of the Norman Conquest. *St. Nicholas Church,* behind the Almshouses, is the largest parish church in England. Damaged severely during World War II, it has since been rebuilt.

Parts of the *city walls* dating from the 13th century are preserved, as is the 14th-century façade of the *old customs house.* The long quay along the River Yare is lined with fishermen's houses; the house at number 4 South Quay, built in 1596, is particularly interesting and can be visited. The old *Merchant's House* on the quay is now a city museum.

Two worthwhile side trips can be made from Great Yarmouth. *Burgh Castle,* to the west, was once a Roman fort. ***Caister Castle,** to the north of Great Yarmouth, was built in 1432 and belonged to Sir John Falstaff, who appears in Shakespeare's *Henry VI.* Much of the castle still stands, including a 30-meter- (98-foot-) high tower that provides an excel-

lent view of the surrounding area. The castle houses a *museum* of vintage cars.

Leave Great Yarmouth from the south, and take A 12 to **Lowestoft,** a coastal town with broad, sandy beaches that is the easternmost port in England. In the 18th century, Lowestoft was known for its porcelain, though the town has long been a port and ship-building center. Its old town, north of a *swing bridge* that connects the inner and outer ports, is a warren of narrow streets lined with interesting old houses. The *church of St. Margaret's* in this district dates from the 15th century. The point known as *Lowestoft Ness* is the most easterly spot in Britain.

Two side trips can be made from Lowestoft. You can visit the popular sailing waters of *Oulton Broad,* to the west, or **Somerleyton Hall,* an attractive 16th-century mansion set in a lovely garden northwest of Lowestoft.

Somerleyton Hall

Continue on A 12 to *Kessingland,* location of the well-known ***Suffolk Wild Life Park.** The fairly new park occupies several acres of woodland, and is stocked with monkeys, arctic foxes, raccoons, porcupines, and other animals. Its large landscape garden features pathways, picnic areas, and a lake that is home to aquatic birds.

Just beyond Lowestoft A 12 intersects B 1127, which leads east to the coast and **Southwold,** a peaceful, pretty seaside town set on low cliffs above the coast. Its 15th-century *parish church* is a nice example of English Gothic architecture. Return to A 12 via B 1095, and continue south through *Blythburgh,* which has a beautiful 15th-century church, and the towns of *Yoxford* and *Saxmundham.* From Saxmundham, side trips can be made—either to *Framlingham,* to the west, with its remarkable 15th-century church and a 12th-century castle or to *Aldeburgh,* to the east, a pleasant beach resort and site of an annual music festival in June in which works by the 20th-century composer Benjamin Britten, who lived here for several years, are featured.

Continue on A 12 past *Woodbridge,* an old market town with a 15th-century church and several surviving Medieval houses and inns, to Ipswich.

*Ipswich (85 km.; 53 miles from Great Yarmouth) has been a thriving port since Anglo-Saxon times, and has a long and interesting history. Cardinal Wolsey, who served under King Henry VIII, grew up in Ipswich. Novelist Charles Dickens stayed at the *Great White House* on Tavern Street, and wrote about it in *The Pickwick Papers.*

Ipswich's many interesting buildings include **Sparrowe's House,* built in 1567; the 15th-century *church of St. Mary-le-Tower;* and the 14th-century *church of St. Margaret's.* **Christchurch Mansion,* built in 1548 and altered over the next two centuries, now houses a valuable collection of 15th-century English paintings, as well as works by Gainsborough and Constable. Many lovely and well-preserved old houses still stand on Fort Street.

Travellers with a particular interest in the painter John Constable can take a side trip south of Ipswich to *Stratford St. Mary,* in the heart of "Constable Country," a region that he painted often. In the town of *Dedham,* to the south, you'll find *St. Mary's Church,* the subject of many of the artist's works.

Felixstowe, 27 km. (17 miles) southeast of Ipswich, can be reached on A 45. This seaside resort may provide you with a welcome break from historic mansions, Medieval churches, and cobblestone streets. Not only is it a simple, cheerful place without pretension, it is also an important ferry port for connections to the Continent.

Leave Ipswich from the west,

and take A 1071 to *Hintlesham Hall,* a Tudor house built by the Timperley family. It has been altered and is now a hotel with a fine restaurant. The village of *Hadleigh* has a 14th-century church and a 15th-century *Guildhall.* Along High Street are examples of almost every kind of building style in the region. Continue to ***Sudbury** (119 km.; 74 miles from Great Yarmouth) which was once the center of the region's thriving wool trade. Reminders of these prosperous times can be seen in its many *half-timbered houses.* There are also three remarkable English Gothic churches in town; *St. Gregory, All Saints,* and *St. Peter.* The birthplace of painter Thomas Gainsborough (1727–1788) at 46 Gainsborough Street now houses a museum, displaying mementos of his life.

Sudbury is surrounded by some of the most beautiful towns in Suffolk. ****Lavenham** may be the most beautiful Medieval town in East Anglia, with its fine half-timbered houses, 16th-century **guildhall* on Market Square, and 15th-century *grammar school.* Lavenham's **Swan Hotel,* built in the 14th century, was a favorite haunt of American airmen during World War II. Many of them carved their names on a section of the bar which now has been preserved under glass.

*Long Melford has a number of beautiful gabled and half-timbered buildings as well as a lovely parish church. The village's *Bull Inn* (1450) is a popular meeting place. **Melford Hall* houses a small museum with a collection of paintings, furniture, and porcelain. It was once owned by Sir William Cordell, the Speaker of the House of Commons, who hosted Queen Elizabeth here. **Cavendish,** on the River Stour, is set around a wide, grassy field. The *church of Pentlow,* across the river has a round Norman tower. The *Grape Vine House* is a restaurant built in 1647.

Leave Sudbury from the south on A 131 and drive past *Halstead* to an access road leading to *Little Maplestead.* The town's 14th-century round *church of the Knights Templar* is only one of four that remain in England. Return to A 131 and continue south through *Braintree* and *Chelmsford* (see page 129) to *Ingatestone. Ingatestone Hall,* an Elizabethan mansion, houses a permanent exhibit on Essex in the Elizabethan Age. Continue southwest on A 131 to ***London (see page 28).

Lavenham

TRAVEL ROUTE 15: ***London–*Newmarket–**Bury St. Edmunds–**Norwich (187 km.; 116 miles)

See map on page 185.

Horses and country homes go together in England. This Travel Route visits both, from a string of lovely mansions to the city of Newmarket, the birthplace of English horse racing.

Leave London (see page 28) from the northeast following M 11 through *Epping Forest.* This 5,600-acre park is all that's left of a 60,000-acre hunting ground used by Saxon, Norman, and Tudor monarchs. A short side road, A 121, leads to *Waltham Abbey,* burial place of King Harold, who was slain at the battle of Hastings (see page 134). And, after Henry II had Thomas à Becket murdered, he built a great *abbey* here to expiate himself. It is in ruins now, but the Norman nave is still an impressive sight.

Return to M 11 and continue through *Harlow* to **Bishop's Stortford.** This busy market town on the River Stort is the birthplace of Cecil Rhodes (1853–1902), who was part of the British imperialistic presence in South Africa. The house on South Row where he was born is now a *museum.* The town's *parish church* dates to 1400. **Newport** has some beautiful 16th- and 17th-century houses. **Audley End** is known for *Audley End House,* a Jacobean mansion built in 1603 by Lord Howard of Walden, First Earl of Suffolk. Its rooms contain valuable paintings and stucco work, as well as lovely period furniture.

A side road leads from Audley End east to ***Saffron Walden.** Once called Waledana by ancient Britons, the name was combined with Saffron from the yellow crocuses which were grown here. A mound dates from the period of the ancient Britons. Many interesting Medieval buildings in the town have survived, including a 12th-century *castle,* a *parish church* in English Gothic style, and more than 100 old houses, some of them half-timbered structures with overhanging upper floors.

Continue to *Great Chesterford.* Nearby you can take A 130 to *Sawston Hall,* built in the 16th century and on to ***Cambridge** (see page 60). Return to Great

Audley End House

Chesterford, and follow M 11 to *Newmarket (97 km.; 60 miles from London), most famous for horse racing, a sport that was introduced into England by James I. The season lasts from April to October. On Newmarket's High Street you'll find the *Jockey Club,* the organization that controls horse racing in Great Britain, as well as the remains of a *palace* that belonged to Charles II. Other interesting buildings include *Nell Gwynne's House,* where the 17th-century actress and mistress of Charles II lived, and the *Old Q-House,* named for the Duke of Queensbury.

You can take a side trip north from Newmarket to *Snailwell* to see the **parish church* with its Norman round tower.

Leave Newmarket on A 45, and drive east to **Bury St. Edmunds** (119 km.; 74 miles from London). This wonderful

Snailwell Church

old market town boasts a wealth of historic buildings and 18th-century Georgian houses. Until the ninth century, the town was an unimportant backwater. However, when Edmund, the last king of Anglia, died in a battle with the Danes in 870 and a *shrine* was built for his corpse, it became an important pilgrimage site. The Danish King Canute founded an *abbey* here in 1020. Its ruins stand in a public park that is entered through the beautiful **Abbey Gate,* a decorative and defensive tower that was built in the 14th century. In 1214, English barons met here and forced King John to sign the Magna Carta.

Other interesting sights in Bury St. Edmunds include the impressive 12th-century *Norman tower;* the Late Gothic *cathedral of St. James,* dating from the 15th and 16th centuries; the 15th-century *St. Mary's Church;* *Moyses Hall,* a 12th-century Jewish store that is now a museum; the old *Corn Exchange;* and the *Nutshell,* England's smallest pub.

From Bury St. Edmunds two routes lead to Norwich. The first takes you north on A 134 through *Ingham* and *Barnham* to **Thetford,** a market town on the Little Ouse. Thetford was the see of the East Anglian bishops until 1091. The ruins of a *Cluniac Priory* date from the 12th century, as do the ruins of the *monastery of the Canons of the Holy Sepulchre,* built by the Dominicans in 1340. Thetford's *grammar school* was founded in the seventh century. In front of the *King's House* is a bronze *statue*, erected in 1964, of Thomas Paine, the American patriot, who was born in Thetford in 1737. At the eastern end of town is *Castle Hill*, which provides a view of prehistoric earthworks in the area.

From Thetford, follow A 11 northeast through *Attleborough*, whose interesting Norman parish church is decorated with some striking wall frescoes. Continue to **Wymondham.** Its *parish church* was built on the remains of a 12th-century abbey. The Norman nave and choir are of particular interest. Also in Wymondham is the *Market Cross*, a half-timbered building dating from 1616, and the *St. Thomas à Becket chapel*, built in the 15th century and now housing a library. Continue on A 11 past *Hethersett* and across the River Yare to **Norwich** (see page 188).

The second route from Bury St. Edmunds to Norwich runs northeast on A 143, through *Great Barton* to *Ixworth.* Most of the town's 12th-century *abbey* is in ruins; however, a crypt, dormitories, the refectorium, and the prior's apartment still stand.

Shortly past *Palgrave*, A 1066 leads northwest to **Bressingham Gardens and Manor.** The gardens have an astounding variety of flora and fauna, as well as a unique collection of vintage locomotives.

Return to A 143 and continue to *Scole*. From here, take A 140 north through *Long Stratton*, where there is a church with a Norman round tower; and *Swainsthorpe*; to *Norwich* (187 km.; 116 miles from London; see page 188).

The Midlands

When many travellers to Britain think of the Midlands, they think of mines and factories and industrial cities—and the Midlands do have many such places. However, the Midlands also abound in history (William Shakespeare was born here, in Stratford-upon-Avon), in great cathedrals (like the ones in Lincoln and Peterborough), and in the natural pleasures of the Cotswolds and Shropshire Hills.

TRAVEL ROUTE 16: ***London–**Oxford–*Gloucester–*Cardiff (255 km.; 158 miles)

See map on page 198.

This Travel Route takes you across southern England into Wales. There isn't a much more scenic drive to be had—past Oxford, through the beech-covered Chiltern Hills, and on into the Cotswolds. Even if you are not planning to go as far west as Wales, you can still follow the route to the Cotswolds for a day or two of sightseeing.

The Cotswolds are limestone ridges that reach heights of 400 meters (1,200 feet) and run roughly from Bath in the south to Chipping Camden in the north, from the valley of the River Thames in the east to the valley of the River Severn in the west. Rolling hills, stone villages, hillsides dotted with sheep, summarize the attractions of the Cotswolds. What is really special about the region is what you won't find there—namely, much that has to do with the 20th century. This absence of modern trappings makes it quite easy to imagine what life in these parts was like 300 or 400 years ago when wool helped the Cotswolds to become one of England's wealthiest regions. This Travel Route takes you right into the best scenery, though you may also want to explore on your own. The tourist bureau in Cirencester (see page 199) can provide you with good maps and brochures, including information on the *Cotswold Way;* a walking path that crosses 160 km. (97 miles) of this remarkable terrain.

Leave London from the west on Highway A 40, which after 46 km. (28 miles) comes to **High Wycombe,** an old market town that has been producing beechwood chairs for the past 200 years. A good place to see some of the town's finest products is the *Chair and Local History Museum.* American servicemen who fought in World War II may remember the town for its 19th-century *Wycombe Abbey,* once the home of Lord Carrington, Prime Minister from 1894–1895, and during the war the headquarters of the U.S. Eighth Army Air Force. High Wycombe was also home to another Prime Minister, Queen Victoria's favorite, Benjamin Disraeli. He bought ***Hughenden Manor** in 1847 and fitted it out in grand Victorian style. Disraeli died at the manor in 1881 and is buried on the grounds (you'll find a monument to him in Westminster Abbey). The house is now open to the public and is still filled with the statesman's furnishings and personal effects, including portraits of his many political associates. High Wycombe has several other fine old buildings, too, most notably its *Guildhall,* built in 1757, and its large *parish church,* built in the 13th–16th centuries.

Route A 40 continues west for another 4 km. (2.5 miles) to ***West Wycombe,** a picturesque village with a macabre past. The town was a hangout for members of one of Britain's notorious 18th-century Hell-Fire Clubs—groups of young men, usually aristocrats, who held secret rites honoring

Satan. Rumor has it that the clubs often went so far as to offer human sacrifices. Francis Dashwood, the 15th Baron le Despencer, son of West Wycombe's most prominent family, belonged to a Hell-Fire Club, and he and his colleagues used to hold their rituals in the *quarries* that run beneath the town (now open to the public). Despite his reckless youth, the baron went on to a respectable political career and built **West Wycombe Park,* a fine home, complete with a swanshaped lake, on the grounds of the family estate. He entertained Benjamin Franklin here in 1773.

Obviously, the baron never outgrew his eccentric tastes, for he also built the odd *parish church* that sits on a hill above West Wycombe. It is topped by an enormous gilded ball, big enough to hold ten men within its interior, and adjoins a roofless, hexagonal mausoleum.

Route A 40 continues through the lovely *Chiltern Hills,* forested in beech, and in 38 km. (23 miles) comes to ****Oxford** (88 km.; 55 miles from London; see page 80). From Oxford, Route A 40 continues for another 17 km. (10 miles) to **Witney,** a pretty old village at the edge of the Cotswolds on the River Windrush. Witney was once one of England's major producers of wool, and its factories, built in the 18th century, harnessed power from the river to make the wool into blankets. The wealthy merchants met to do business in

Hughenden Manor

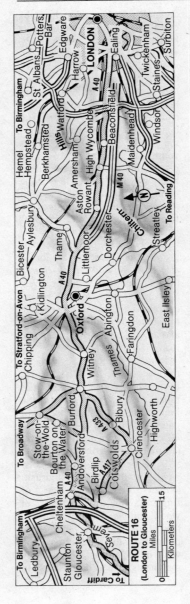

the *Blanket Hall,* built in 1721, on High Street, and they poured their profits into the fine houses you see facing the church green. Route A 20 now follows the Windrush for 12 km. (7 miles) to **Burford,** a typically charming Cotswold village with streets lined with stone cottages. Its *church of St. John the Baptist* practically crawls with stone figures, a tribute to the region's Medieval masons who worked the local stone. The *Tolsey Museum* occupies the 16th-century tolsey (toll house) and displays a comprehensive record of the region's history from the Norman Conquest to the Industrial Revolution.

Burford is a good departure point for a drive through the countryside to some of the Cotswolds' loveliest villages. Follow Route A 424 north to *Stow-on-the-Wold,* a picturesque place that is much visited for its antiques shops. The water of *Bourton-on-the-Water,* just south of Stow on Route A 429, is the River Windrush, and it rushes right down the middle of the main street. About 16 km. (10 miles) beyond Stow, on Route A 424, is *Broadway,* one of the Cotswolds' most popular villages, probably because its warm-colored stone houses are characteristic of the region. This Broadway is a far cry from the New York one of "Give my regards to" fame, though when the village is swarming with visitors on a nice summer's day, you may think otherwise.

From Burford continue west

for 14 km. (8.5 miles) on Route A 20 to **Northleach,** with its impressive 15th-century *church of Sts. Peter and Paul.* Notice especially the vaulted south porch. The grandeur of the church is fairly typical of the Cotswolds. The wealthy wool merchants had to do something with their profits, and what better investment was there than their salvation? In another 21 km. (13 miles), Route A 20 reaches *Cheltenham* (see below).

You can also get to Cheltenham from Burford on the even more scenic Route A 433. About 11 km. (about 7 miles) past Burford, A 433 comes to ***Bibury,** another impossibly picturesque village, all the more so because the River Colne runs through it. The town's 17th-century flour mill is now a *country museum,* with a nice collection of farm implements and crafts. Bibury's 17th-century wool factory occupies *Arlington Row,* a group of stone cottages on the riverbank across from *Rack Island,* so called because the wool was once hung to dry there. The town *church* provides a good slice of local history: it was built by the Saxons, altered by the Normans, rebuilt in Gothic style around 1500, and restored again in the 19th century. Route A 433 continues 11 km. (6.5 miles) to ***Cirencester** (142 km.; 88 miles from London), which tourist brochures often refer to as the "capital of the Cotswolds" because of its central location.

You might want to stop at the *information bureau* in the marketplace to pick up maps and brochures on the area. There's more to Cirencester than scenery, though. The town has a rich history, too. The Roman city here, Corinium Dobunnorum, was the administrative center of the west of Britain, although little of it remains in evidence—aboveground, at least. Recent excavations have unearthed streets and mosaic floors, and many of the finds are on display at the town's **Corinium Museum.* Cirencester did well in the wool trade, and its residents seem to have lavished their wealth on the cathedral-size **church of St. John the Baptist.* With its fan vaulting, elaborate stonework, beautiful windows, and many monuments, the building inspires some observers to call it England's finest 15th–16th-century church. Another manifestation of local prosperity is *Cirencester Park,* a gracious 18th-century estate on which the First Earl of Bathurst spared little expense. The Earl also had refined taste in company—the writers Alexander Pope and Jonathan Swift were frequent guests. The house is closed to the public, but its park is open and is the scene of frequent polo games.

From Cirencester, Routes 417 and 4070 will take you the additional 29 km. (17.5 miles) into **Cheltenham Spa.** Cheltenham seems like the city slicker who has found himself in the middle of beautiful countryside. Although this is certainly the Cotswolds,

Cheltenham is no quaint stone village. Cheltenham's springs yield alkaline waters that do wonders for the digestion, and as a result, the town has flourished as a spa that has greeted the rich, the royal, and the famous since King George III paid a visit in 1788. Cheltenham treats its well-heeled guests royally—with a tree-shaded, flower-bedecked *Promenade* that offers some of the best shopping this side of London; with concerts in the colonnaded *Pump Room;* with walks through *Pittville Park* and many other gardens—and of course, with the waters themselves, which are even administered in the Edwardian *Town Hall.* Day-to-day finance also takes on a rarefied air in Cheltenham: its *Montpellier Rotunda,* modeled on the Pantheon in Rome, now shelters a bank.

Cheltenham has its own colorful history. One John Higgs lays at rest in the 12th-century *church of St. Mary* beneath a tombstone inscribed, "Here lies John Higgs/ A famous man for killing pigs/ For killing pigs was his delight/ Both morning, afternoon, and night." The composer Gustav Holst, whose oeuvre included *The Planets,* was born in Cheltenham, in 1874, and his house is now the *Gustav Holst Birthplace Museum.* The town's *Art Gallery and Museum* has a nice collection of Dutch paintings, Chinese ceramics, and artifacts from Cheltenham's Roman occupants.

From Cheltenham, Route A 40

continues 15 km. (9 miles) south to ***Gloucester** (167 km.; 103 miles from London), a city of 90,000 inhabitants that will bring you back to the 20th century in a hurry. The city has its noble past—settled by the Romans, much loved by King John, the site of the coronation of King Henry III in 1216—but there's not too much of the past in evidence. There are exceptions, of course, most notably the **cathedral,* first built in 670, rebuilt in 1089, and altered countless times over the centuries.

The cathedral still dominates Gloucester, and well it should. Within this almost perfect example of Gothic architecture lie the remains of King Edward II, murdered nearby in Berkeley Castle in 1327, and Robert, Duke of Normandy, the first son of William the Conqueror and heir to the throne—that is, had he not alienated his father and died in prison in 1134. Robert's effigy is

Gloucester Cathedral

painted to look lifelike, a startling effect. The cathedral's real crowd-pleaser is the monk's *lavatorium* in the cloisters, which are surrounded by a magnificent fan-vaulted arcade. The beautiful glass in the church's east window is from the 14th century.

Other remnants of Medieval Gloucester include the timbered building in Westgate Street known as *Bishop Hopper's Lodging,* which now houses a good museum of local history. (Bishop Hopper was burned at the stake for heresy in Gloucester in 1555.) Lady Jane Grey was proclaimed queen at the *New Inn* on Northgate Street in 1553—a sad event, actually, as the Queen's reign lasted a mere nine days and she was executed, at age 17, a year later. (You may have noticed by now that Gloucester's historical figures seem to have all met gruesome ends.) An even older Gloucester is on view at the *City Museum and Art Gallery,* on Brunswick Road, which displays items from the city's Roman past. Also of interest is the *National Waterways Museum,* with displays tracing Channel navigation.

One of Gloucester's biggest events is an ages-old act of nature—at very high tide in the nearby Bristol Channel, a tidal wave known as the *Severn Bore* races up the River Severn.

In addition to the nearby Cotswolds, other popular excursion spots around Gloucester include *Berkeley Castle,* about 26 km. (16 miles) southwest off Route A 38, where Edward II met his brutal end; *Elmore Court,* 7 km. (4 miles) south on Route A 40, a pleasant country mansion built in the 14th–17th centuries, with exquisite furnishings; and *Slimbridge Wildfowl Trust,* 20 km. (12 miles) southwest off Route A 38, the world's largest collection of waterfowl—180 species in all.

To reach *Cardiff* (255 km.; 158 miles from London) you may either take Route M 5 south to Bristol and from there the M 4 into Wales. Or you may drive to Bristol on the slower Route A 48, which crosses the *Forest of Dean,* a royal forest that is now a national park encompassing 34,000 acres—a favorite spot for walkers.

TRAVEL ROUTE 17: *Gloucester–*Worcester– Wolverhampton–*Manchester (210 km.; 116 miles)

See map on page 203.

If you are travelling through Britain in search of the green pleasures of the countryside, this Travel Route is definitely not for you. It takes you north from Gloucester into the heart of the industrial Midlands to England's most industry-oriented city, Manchester. Still, there are sights of interest along the way—the Malvern Hills, for example—and the Travel Route takes you off the busiest roads to many of the fine old estates that dot even this industrial landscape. (If you are interested in bargains, look for outlet shops at the factories along the route; many of them sell their goods at reduced prices.)

Leave Gloucester from the north and follow Route A 38 for 16 km. (10 miles) to ***Tewkesbury,** a picturesque old town at the confluence of the rivers Avon and Severn. Tewkesbury has the distinction of being the scene of one of the bloodiest battles in the War of the Roses, if not in all English history. On a May day in 1471, the Yorkists, supporting Edward IV, met the Lancastrians in a meadow just south of town that is now called "Bloody Meadow." The Yorkists killed the Lancastrians to a man, then marched into town, dragged the remaining Lancastrians out of the Abbey Church, where they had taken refuge, and slaughtered them. The **church,* a splendid example of Norman architecture, commemorates the event with shields and other representations of the victorious Yorkists on its vaulted ceiling. The Lancastrian Prince of Wales, murdered that day, lies beneath a brass in the floor.

Tewkesbury no longer produces the mustard for which it was so famous—even Shakespeare refers to it in *Henry IV, Part 2*—but the High Street is still full of *Tudor houses.*

(From Tewkesbury, Superhighway M 5 speeds north past *Worcester, Wolverhampton, Man-chester,* and many of the other towns on this Travel Route. There are frequent exits on the M 5, so if you are in a hurry, you can take the superhighway and get off near any of the following places you may want to visit.)

Leave Tewkesbury on Route A 38. In about 10 km. (6 miles) there will be a turnoff for Route A 4101, which leads west into the *Malvern Hills,* a dramatically steep range topped by moors. You may also proceed directly into Worcester on Route A 38, but A 4101 provides a much more scenic drive. If you are a walker, by all means bring your brogues, because there's no better walking terrain in England than these flat-topped rises. From the highest point in the hills, *Worcestershire Beacon,* on a clear day you can see 15 counties. The *tourist information bureau* in Great Malvern (see below) can supply maps.

About 11 km. (7 miles) after the turnoff from Route A 38, Route A 4104 comes to *Little Malvern,* the first in a series of towns called Malvern that nestle against the flanks of the hills. The biggest of them is **Great Malvern,** which counts among its attributes a spring, *St. Ann's Well,* which in the past made the town into something of a spa. The

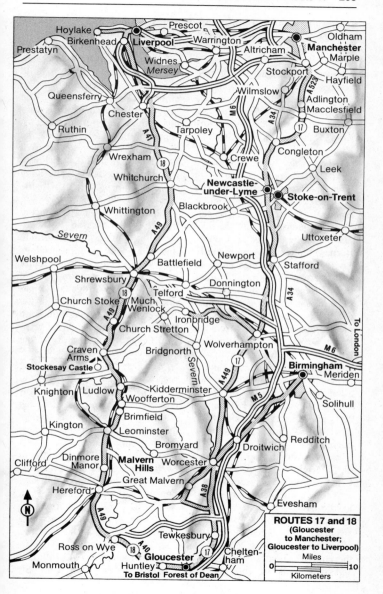

ROUTES 17 and 18
(Gloucester to Manchester;
Gloucester to Liverpool)

Miles

0   10

Kilometers

beautiful, mainly 15th-century *Priory Church of St. Mary the Virgin* has excellent stained-glass windows. You may notice a number of obviously well-bred youngsters walking about town. They attend *Malvern College,* one of England's finest public (private to Americans) schools. Jenny Lind (1820–1887), the "Swedish Nightingale" who thrilled American audiences when she toured with P. T. Barnum, is buried in Great Malvern's cemetery. The town is actually quite popular among the theatrical set, who perform frequently at its *Festival Theatre* (where three of George Bernard Shaw's plays premiered). Route A 449 continues north to ***Worcester** (46 km.; 28 miles from Gloucester), which may be known best for the sauce it produces. There is much more to this picturesque town located on the River Severn than condiments, however. Worcester also makes gloves and fine porcelain, and it has many royal connections, not all of them fortuitous: King Hardicanute plundered the town in 1041 after the citizenry killed one of his tax collectors; and in 1651, during the Civil War, King Charles II stood atop the cathedral tower where he watched Cromwell defeat his troops.

Another king, John, is buried in the great **cathedral,* which went up near the banks of the Severn in the 13th century on the site of several earlier churches. One of the church's greatest benefactors was Saint Wulstan, who was laid to rest here in 1095. A century later the faithful began associating his tomb with miracles, and pilgrims flocked to Worcester, bringing with them funds to build the *Lady Chapel* and to otherwise embellish the cathedral. The tower that gave Charles his vantage point went up in the 14th century; the oldest part of the cathedral is the crypt that Wulstan built in 1084 to house relics of Saint Oswald, the King of Northumbria, killed in battle in 642.

Charles's command post during the Civil War was an 11th-century hospice on Sidbury Road that is now called, appropriately, the **Commandery*. It currently houses a good museum of local history. The city's royalist sympathies are still in full view at the 18th-century **Guildhall* on High Street—a carved head of Cromwell hangs by its ears above the doorway.

Worcester has been making fine porcelain since 1751. You can tour the *Royal Worcester Porcelain Works,* and if you like what you see, buy some place settings at the firm's showroom or in its seconds shop. Some of the best pieces the firm has turned out over the years are on view at the adjacent *Dyson Perkins Museum.* On a riverside walk in *St. Andrew's Gardens,* behind the Guildhall, you will come across a large reminder that Worcester is also a glove-making city—the so-called *Glovers' Needle,* all that remains of the church of St.

Andrew. Many of Worcester's fine old timbered buildings are clustered around *Cornmarket*. King Charles took refuge in *King Charles's House* on New Street, which is lined with several similar half-timbered buildings as it runs south and becomes Friar Street. *Greyfriars* dates from 1480. At the *Tudor House,* just down the street, period rooms show what life in Worcester was like over the ages. The *City Museum and Art Gallery* on Foregate Street is also devoted to local history, with artifacts going back to the first century.

Music lovers may want to make the trip 5 km. (3 miles) west of Worcester on Route A 44 to *Lower Broadheath,* where the composer Sir Edward Elgar was born in 1857. His house is now a memento-filled museum. You may opt for an excursion 10 km. (6 miles) north on Route A 38 to *Droitwich,* a spa with saline springs where even the Romans found relief from rheumatism. *Hanbury Hall,* a fine 18th-century estate with a magnificent interior, is just 4 km. (2.5 miles) to the north of Droitwich.

Travel Route 17 leaves Worcester to the north on Route A 449 and in 23 km. (14 miles) comes to *Kidderminster,* a carpet manufacturing center, and continues for 24 km. (14.5 miles) along the River Stour to **Wolverhampton** (93 km.; 56 miles from Gloucester). This large city of 268,000 inhabitants has been making locks and keys since the 16th cen-

tury and has now branched out to hardware of all types, airplane engines, and just about any other kind of industry you can imagine. Needless to say, Wolverhampton isn't exactly a tourist mecca, but if you do happen to stop here, take a look at the watercolors at the *Art Gallery and Museum,* next to the 15th-century *church of St. Peter* on Lichfield Street. *Wightwick Manor* on the western edge of town is a Pre-Raphaelite showcase: wallpaper by William Morris, paintings by Millais, drawings by Ruskin, the works. Charles II fled to Wolverhampton after his troops were trounced at Worcester (see page 204), and the Whitegrave family hid him at their magnificent Elizabethan mansion, *Mosely Old Hall,* 5 km. (3 miles) north of town. You can see the bed on which the King caught up on his much needed rest and his secret hiding place.

Ironbridge, the birthplace of England's Industrial Revolution, lies 20 km. (12 miles) west of Wolverhampton. The *Ironbridge Gorge Museum* contains five exhibits paying tribute to England's industry, including the first iron railroad bridge (1774), the original furnace (1709) in which black coal was first burned, and a reconstructed blacksmith's shop and manufacturing area. Among the museum's other exhibits are replicas of Victorian workers' homes and pieces from recent industrial history.

From Wolverhampton, Route A 449 continues north through a

dense industrial region that produces, among many other goods, much of England's ceramics. (That's why *Stoke-on-Trent* is called "The Potteries.") About 13 km. (8 miles) past *Newcastle-under-Lyme,* you may want to turn off for **Little Morton Hall** (follow signs), a picturesque Elizabethan mansion, built in 1559, and a riot of half-timbering and leaded windows. Continue north on Route A 34 to *Congleton.* From here you may either proceed directly to *Manchester,* about 45 km. (27 miles) north on A 34, or you may take a slower route past several historic homes. If you opt for the latter, follow Route A 536 for 8 km. (5 miles) north from Congleton to *Gawsworth* and its manor house, ***Gawsworth Hall,** a 16th-century half-timbered mansion that was once home to Mary Fitton, the maid of honor to Queen Elizabeth I and said to have been the "Dark Lady" of Shakespeare's sonnets. Inside, there's a magnificent collection of paintings by the likes of Rubens and Constable. On the grounds you'll find a remarkable array of carriages. In 5 km. (3 miles), Route A 536 comes to *Macclesfield,* the center of England's silk industry. The nearby *Macclesfield Forest* is good walking terrain. Continue north on A 523 for 13 km. (8 miles) to *Adlington.* Its great house, ***Adlington Hall,** dates from 1315, though it has been added on to many times since. The *Great Hall* is from 1450; the

southern façade from 1757. Handel visited Adlington Hall and entertained his hosts on the house's magnificent organ. About 10 km. (6 miles) up Route A 523 you'll come to yet another Tudor mansion—*Bramall Hall,* one of England's best examples of the style.

Route A 253 continues through **Stockport,** an industrial town that specializes in cotton spinning and hat making. Stockport has some fine old *Tudor buildings,* but you're more likely to notice its looming railway *viaduct,* 35 meters (105 feet) high. You are now more or less in the suburbs of ***Manchester** (210 km.; 130 miles from Gloucester), a sprawling industrial city that can be grimmer than grim, though the place makes no claims to be a resort. Industry is what Manchester is all about. There was a Roman settlement in Manchester, though the town didn't really amount to much until the 14th century, when Flemish immigrants introduced textile manufacture. At the height of the Industrial Revolution the major industry here was textiles, earning for Manchester the moniker "Cottonopolis." A good place to see what the city was like in those days is at the huge *Museum of Science and Industry* on Grosvenor Street. Charles Dickens described life in Manchester's Victorian factories in his novel *Hard Times.* Unfortunately, the title also describes what life for many of the city's half-a-million-plus residents is like now that many industries are in decline. Manchester holds its own, though, and in recent years has attracted several high-tech companies.

Manchester does have three very important libraries. The *Central Library,* topped by a huge rotunda, is Europe's largest municipal library; only the reading room at the British Museum in London is bigger. Since 1653, *Chetham's Hospital,* founded in 1421, has been a school and library—one of the oldest free libraries in England. *John Ryland's Library,* on Deansgate Street, has an amazing collection of 700,000 volumes, many of them extraordinarily rare, including Bibles in 300 languages and a fragment of New Testament scripture dating from A.D. 150.

Manchester also has several important collections of art. The *City Art Gallery,* in a beautiful building (1825–1829) on Mosely Street, has a good display of paintings—with works by Corot, Reynolds, Gauguin, and many others—and its annex in Princess Street has pottery and porcelain. The *Gallery of Modern Art* is next door. The museum has also spread its collections among several buildings in outlying reaches of the city. If you're up to venturing outside of the city center, try the *Gallery of English Costume* in *Platt Hall,* an elegant 18th-century house in the Rusholme area to the south. It shows British fashion from the 16th century to the present. *Wythenshawe Hall,* even farther afield in the southern suburb of Northenden, is a fine old country house with a good collection of 17th-century paintings and furniture. The *Fletcher Moss Museum,* in Didsbury, shows a collection of English watercolors, and has an added attraction—a pleasant garden. Manchester University also has an impressive collection of watercolors, at *Whitford Art Gallery* on Oxford Road.

Manchester has several other noble structures, among them its *cathedral,* built in the 15th–16th centuries. *The Town Hall* is a Neo-Gothic pile from 1877, with murals by Ford Maddox Brown illustrating the city's illustrious activities. However, Manchester's most impressive municipal work is probably the *Manchester Ship Canal,* which was dug from 1887–1894 to allow ships to come inland the 56 km. (37 miles) from Liverpool (see page 213).

TRAVEL ROUTE 18: *Gloucester–*Hereford–**Shrewsbury–**Chester–*Liverpool (229 km.; 142 miles)

See map on page 203.

Like Travel Route 17, this Travel Route takes you into the industrial Midlands. Though you can make the trip in well under a day, you will see many sides of England—ancient towns along the Welsh border; historic Shrewsbury, right out of the Middle Ages; Chester, an amazing compendium of Britain's Roman and Medieval past; and Liverpool, an important port that four local boys catapulted into the spotlight in the 1960s.

From Gloucester, cross the River Severn and follow Route A 40 west for 11 km. (7 miles) through *Huntley*. The tall rise on the right is called *May Hill*. Route A 40 skirts the edge of the *Forest of Dean*, a 34,000-acre national park that was for centuries a royal forest, and in 15 km. (9 miles) comes to **Ross-on-Wye,** a pretty place that climbs a hillside above the River Wye. Ross has the good fortune to have been the birthplace in 1637 of one John Kyrle, hailed as the "man of Ross." The public-spirited Kyrle brought in the town's first water supply, laid out the *Prospect Gardens,* and replaced the spire on the 12th-century *church of St. Mary the Virgin*. You can see Kyrle's house, now a bookshop, in the marketplace. From Ross, Route A 49 crosses the Wye on the *Wilton Bridge,* built in 1597, and passes the ruins of *Wilton Castle,* then comes in 24 km. (14.5 miles) to ***Hereford,** a bustling market town whose most famous natives are Hereford cat-

tle and the actor David Garrick, who was born here in 1717. Hereford has been an important place since Saxon times, mostly because it is so close to the Welsh border. Not much remains of its mighty castle, though there are plenty of sights in Hereford that are old and picturesque. Its **cathedral* owes its existence to the ghost of Saint Ethelbert of East Anglia, who demanded that he be buried here, at the site where he was murdered by the father of his bride in 794. A stone church was built in 825, then a larger church that the Welsh burned in 1056, and finally the present building, which has been altered many times over the past nine centuries. The cathedral has two special treasures: the **Mappa Mundi,* a vellum map from 1313 that provides a Medieval view of the world, with Jerusalem at the center and Paradise on top; and the *library,* with 1,500 chained books in their original presses, the world's largest such collection.

Hereford's streets are lined with Medieval houses. You can tour one of them, *The Old House,* on High Town Street, built in 1621 and furnished in period style. The town's 17th-century almshouse is now the interesting *St. John and Coningsby Museum,* with displays that show you how the pensioners lived over the centuries. Leave Hereford heading north on Route A 49. In 10 km. (6 miles) you will come to a turnoff for ***Dinmore Manor,** a 14th-century manor house with a peaceful Medieval chapel that was once headquarters of the Knights Templar of Saint John of Jerusalem. After another 10 km. (6 miles) A 49 comes to ***Leonminster,** an ancient wool center on the River Lugg. Its **church of Sts. Peter and Paul,* an interesting composite of Norman and Gothic architecture, grew around the town's seventh-century monastery. A dunking stool shows what civil order once meant. Of Leonminster's many fine timbered buildings, one of the best is *Grange Court,* built in 1633 as the Market House. Leaving Leonminster, you will come almost immediately to a turnoff for ***Berrington Hall,** an estate built in 1778–1781 by two of the best designers 18th-century money could buy: the house is by Henry Holland, whose work in London includes Sloane Street, Cadogan Place, and the Drury Lane Theatre; and the gardens are by Capability Brown, who laid out Kew. Just beyond, you can turn off Route A 49 to see another mansion, ***Eye Manor,** built for Ferdinando Gorges, a slave trader from Barbados, in 1680. About 11 km. (6.5 miles) beyond Leonminster you can turn west onto Route B 4362 for a short drive to ***Croft Castle,** built to defend the Welsh border and home to the Croft family until 1957. A footpath leads for about 1 km. (half a mile) through the hills to the much older *Croft Ambrey,* with ramparts from as early as 550 B.C. Up to 1,000 people lived inside the defenses—in huts arranged on streets—until they succumbed to the invading Roman legions.

In 7 km. (4 miles), Route A 49 comes to ***Ludlow,** which grew up around the walls of its 12th-century **castle.* The castle has a stormy royal past. Its 14th-century resident, Roger Mortimer, persuaded his mistress, Queen Isabella, to murder her husband, King Edward II, and put her son on the throne. A century later its thick walls confined the two sons of Edward IV. Fearing that the boys threatened his claim to the throne, their uncle, Richard of Gloucester, moved them to the Tower of London, where many historians speculate they were murdered. Prince Arthur and his bride, Catherine of Aragon, spent their brief marriage here in 1501 where he died five months after the wedding. Much of the castle is in ruin, though many of its staterooms and its circular Norman chapel survive. So does the oldest part of the castle, the *keep,* and the views over Ludlow from its heights are amazing. The narrow streets of the old town are lined with timbered houses. One of them, the *Feathers,* an inn from 1603, still takes guests.

Route A 49 continues north through *Bromfield,* where there are remains of a 12th-century priory, and 14 km. (8.5 miles) after Ludlow comes to the stunning ****Stokesay Castle.** Stokesay is really more of a mansion with a moat than a castle. Even so, the house has managed to withstand invaders since the 12th century, and is today considered to be England's best example of a fortified mansion. Route A 49 now passes through *Carven Arms, Church Stretton* (a popular health resort with a good golf course), and *Dorrington,* then enters ****Shrewsbury** (135 km.; 84 miles from Gloucester), an ancient town that is bounded by the River Severn on three sides—a geographic advantage for fending off attackers from over the

Stokesay Castle

Welsh border in the past and helping it prosper to the Medieval splendor you see today. Many of the timbered houses that its wealthy Middle Ages occupants built still stand. Add to this Shrewsbury's beautiful river-bounded location and the charm of the surrounding Shropshire hills, and it's easy to see why the town is so popular among tourists.

The best place to begin a tour of Shrewsbury is its *castle,* built in 1080, modernized many times since, and now the seat of city government. The famous *Shrewsbury School,* just across from the castle, was founded by Edward IV in 1547 and is one of England's oldest and most prestigious public (i.e., private) schools. Though it has since moved to bigger quarters in another part of town, its old buildings now house a *museum of local history.* The pride of its collection is the cloak that Charles I wore at his execution. (Shrewsbury was Charles's headquarters during the Civil War.) A statue of Shrewsbury's most famous native son, Charles Darwin, stands just outside the museum. The naturalist was born in 1809 in a house on the hill just across the river. Shrewsbury's best church, **St. Mary's,* is near the castle on St. Mary's Street. Aside from being a splendid example of Norman architecture, the church also possesses some of the best stained glass in Europe. Notice especially the east window, whose 14th-century glass panels trace the genealogy of Christ. Shrewsbury's other great churches include *St. Chad's,* which is really two churches: the old St. Chad's, of which only the chapel survived when the church tower collapsed in 1788 and crushed the 12th-century building, and the new St. Chad's, built near the river in 1792. The *Abbey Church of the Holy Cross* across the river was founded in 1083.

When you leave the church of St. Mary you are surrounded by some of Shrewsbury's best Tudor houses—*High Street, Butcher Row,* and *Fish Street* are especially good viewing grounds. You will probably want to see what lies behind those timbered walls, and you can satisfy your curiosity at *Rowley's Mansion,* on Bridge Street. The 16th-century warehouse stores a good museum of Roman artifacts. The *Clive House Museum* (with china, silver, and other items of general interest) is housed in a newer, Georgian structure, elegant nonetheless, and once the home of Lord Clive, mayor of Shrewsbury in 1762. *The Lion* is an old hotel that is still in business. Charles Dickens stayed here, and so did Madame Tussaud when she came to town to put on a wax exhibit. Jenny Lind and Nicolò Paganini both performed at the Lion, a tradition that is carried on in monthly concerts.

Just 5 km. (3 miles) beyond Shrewsbury, Route A 49 comes to **Battlefield,** where a *church* built in 1408 commemorates the Battle of Shrewsbury, fought here in 1403. Henry IV emerged the victor, slaying the Earl of Northumberland, his son Hotspur, and the Earl of Worcester. Shakespeare told the story of the bloody battle in *Henry I, Part 1,* in which Falstaff claims that his one-on-one battle with Hotspur lasted "a long hour by Shrewsbury clock." In real life, the hapless Hotspur was dragged back to town, where, in front of the present-day post office, his body was drawn and quartered. In another 21 km. (13 miles) Route A 49 runs into Route A 41, which in 5 km. (3 miles) enters **Whitchurch,** a town that got its name (an anglicization of "Blancminster") from a church that the Normans built here of white stone, which probably came from the surrounding chalky downs. The current *church of St. Alkmund* is the fourth to stand on the site. Route A 41 continues another 32 km. (19 miles) into ****Chester,** a wall-encircled town where the Roman 20th Legion built a fortress (the ***Grosvenor Museum* on Grosvenor Street shows what it must have been like to have been a Roman soldier stationed here), and that in the Middle Ages thrived as a seaport (long since surpassed by nearby Liverpool). Remnants of this noble Roman and Medieval history vie for attention in Chester. The winning attraction, though, is the **Wall*—3 km. (2 miles) long, topped by 26 towers, pierced by four gates—which is both Roman (foundations) and Medieval. Roman ruins are everywhere in Chester: a heating system and *Roman bath* lie beneath the buildings at 39 Bridge Street; the *headquarters of the legion* are in the basement of 23 Northgate; a window in Hamilton Place looks into a Roman strong room. The biggest Roman ruin in Chester is the *amphitheater*, Britain's largest Roman building, which lies just outside New Gate in *Roman Gardens*. The arena was built in A.D. 100 and lay covered until 1939. Much of it still lies beneath centuries of silt.

Medieval Chester's most notable structures are ****The Rows**, timbered houses, built in the 13th century, that are surrounded by a double row of balconied walkways. Chester's best old buildings, The Rows included, are in *Eastgate, Bridge,* and *Watergate streets*. The prize may go to the beautiful *Bishop Lloyd's House* at 29 Eastgate. Chester has a fine Medieval **cathedral*—a beautiful one, built first by the Normans as a church, made into a Benedictine abbey in 1092, and transformed into a cathedral in 1540. The present-day structure has been altered many times over the centuries. Among the best additions are the magnificently carved **choir stalls*, from 1390. Like Lincoln Cathedral (see page 75). Chester has an imp. too—the Chester Imp, a grotesque figure that looks down on the nave. Much of Chester's other great church, *St. John the Baptist*, is in ruin, though many Norman pillars and arcades remain. Given the city's Medieval splendor, you may expect its **castle* to be a towered affair with battlements. You are in for a disappointment. Henry III replaced the Norman timber fort with a stone structure, which gave way to classical-style brick buildings at the beginning of the 19th century.

Leave Chester to the north on Route A 41, which follows the River Mersey for 28 km. (17 miles) to its mouth at **Birkenhead,** which is part of the port for Liverpool, just across the Mersey. Birkenhead has 16 km. (10 miles) of docks, and its shipyards produced England's first iron ship, in 1829. In 1862 the shipyards built the *Alabama* for the Confederate Army in America, a business deal that put a severe strain on England's relationship with Washington. The **Mersey Tunnel*, 4 km. (2.5 miles) long, will take you into Liverpool (229 km.; 142 miles from Gloucester).

The Rows

*Liverpool

See map on page 214.

As you emerge from the tunnel into fresh air, you will be near *St. John's Gardens,* a riverside park crowded with statues of Liverpool's most famous citizens. The park does not have representations of the revolutionary rock group, the Beatles, who put the city on the map in the 1960s—not yet, anyway. Not that Liverpool doesn't appreciate the foursome, who bring untold numbers of tourists here every year. Liverpool's biggest attribute, though, is the River Mersey, which connects to the open sea 5 km. (3 miles) away.

King Henry II was the first to see the advantages of this location. He built a castle here in 1072. King John built the first port 30 years later, and by the 18th century Liverpool was making a fortune in the slave trade. By the time of the Industrial Revolution, the human cargo had been replaced by all the goods that England's Midlands factories were producing. The first Transatlantic steamers sailed out of Liverpool in 1840. These days, although extremely hard hit by Britain's economic crisis, Liverpool remains England's second-largest port.

Liverpool began at the docks along the Mersey, and you should begin your tour there, too, on the riverside at **Pier Head** (1). The floating dock in front of you—the longest in the world, 800 meters (2,534 feet)—is known as the *Landing Stage.* Behind you rise some of Liverpool's grandest buildings. The *Royal Liver Building,* built in 1910, takes its name from the mythological "liver birds" that give the city its name. You can see some affixed to the side of Royal Liver's tower. You can get a good look at Liverpool's historic link with the sea at the brand new **Merseyside Maritime Museum** (2), where you can climb aboard the ships, walk on the restored quays of the **Albert Dock,** and look at exhibits showing what life on the docks has been like over the centuries. Follow Water Street away from the docks and you will come to the city's **Town Hall** (3), a noble structure flanked by columns and crowned by a dome, built from 1749–1754.

Liverpool has several world-class museums. The **Merseyside County Museum and Library** (4), on William Street, originated with a nature collection that the Earl of Derby bequeathed to the city a century ago. The enormous museum now covers the gamut from archaeology, zoology, botany, geology, and astronomy to antiquities, even English decorative arts. It has two stunners: the *Sassoon Collection* of ivories and, in its *Anglo-Saxon Collection,* the Kingston Brooch, a piece of seventh-century cloisonné. The "library" is actually a composite of several specialized collections. Many art lovers consider the ****Walker Art Gallery,** next door, to be England's best art museum outside of London. Its vast holdings include Flemish and Italian Old Masters—Michelangelo, Rubens, Rembrandt—as well as works by British painters. The **Merseyside Museum of Labour History** is a museum with a social conscience. Its fascinating displays—which include an Edwardian classroom—look at labor unions, working conditions, and other topics relating to Liverpool's working classes over the centuries.

Liverpool pays tribute to its most famous sons at the **Beatle City** (5) museum, on the grounds of the 20-acre *Transworld Festival Gardens*. The music that made Liverpool famous blares from opening to closing, adding to the nostalgia for the 1960s you will no doubt feel as you view the group's mementos. **Cavern Walks** (6), at 18 Matthew Street, is another memento-filled place, a reconstruction of the club where the Beatles were discovered. The beat goes on, as do much dancing and drinking, at the *John Lennon Worldwide Memorial Club,* just up the street.

Liverpool's two cathedrals, one Roman Catholic, one Anglican, have much in common. Both are 20th-century creations, both stand on hills (so they are visible from just about anywhere in town) and both are big. There the similarity ends. The Anglican *cathedral, on St. James Mount, is an enormous structure designed by Giles Gilbert Scott in Neo-Gothic style, begun in 1904 and completed in 1978. Scott was 21 when he designed the cathedral, and he was out to impress: the cathedral he built is the big-

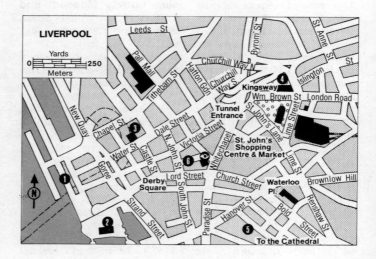

gest in England and second in size only to St. Peter's in Rome. The Roman Catholic **cathedral of Christ the King,** built from 1962–1967, is as distinctly unusual as the Anglican cathedral is big. This cathedral is big, too, a vast cone topped by a multi-colored dome that bathes the circular interior in eerie light.

From Liverpool, the city of Manchester (see page 206), in the heart of Britain's industrial region, is only 35 km. (18 miles) away on Route M 62.

Ten km. (6 miles) to the east of Liverpool on M 62 lies *Knowsley Safari Park*. Behind its 12 miles of wall you can see lions, elephants, giraffes, as well as other exotic creatures.

TRAVEL ROUTE 19: **Oxford–**Stratford-upon-Avon–*Birmingham–*Lichfield (127 km.; 79 miles)

See map on page 217.

If you were to plan a trip so that you could see England at its most varied and best, your itinerary would probably be quite similar to this Travel Route. From Oxford, the seat of one of the world's greatest universities, you drive through rolling green countryside to one of England's finest palaces, Blenheim. From there you cross England's favorite rural landscape, the Cotswolds, to Stratford-upon-Avon, the birthplace of its greatest man of letters. After industrial Birmingham, famous for its modern urban designs, you come to the end of the Travel Route in Lichfield, considered by many to possess the most beautiful cathedral in the land. For a pleasant, sight-filled round trip, you can follow this route as far as Stratford, then return by following Travel Route 20 from Stratford in reverse order.

Leave Oxford on Route A 34, and travel 13 km. (8 miles) north to *Woodstock,* a tiny glove-making village that was once the home of Chaucer's son Thomas and the present home of the *Oxford City and County Museum,* whose good exhibits show what life in Oxfordshire has been like over the past several centuries. These attractions are often overlooked, however, because Woodstock is more or less overshadowed by

Blenheim Palace, which the Duke of Marlborough built with funds that a grateful England presented to him for defeating the French and the Bavarians at Blenheim. Clearly, the Duke was not a man of modest taste, because the manor that he began to build in 1704 is a Baroque extravaganza that wasn't completed until 1722, the year of his death. The palace represents the best work of the leading masters

Blenheim Palace

of the day—Sir John Vanbrugh, Grinling Gibbons, and Nicholas Hawksmoor, among others. Noted landscape artist Capability Brown redesigned the 2,400-acre *gardens* in 1764, damming the River Glyme to create a lake and planting trees to form the plan of the battle that won for the Duke this awesome palace. Brown's landscape delights today's public, who are free to use the grounds and may tour many rooms of the house as well. Winston Churchill was born at Blenheim in 1874 and is buried in the churchyard at nearby *Bladon* alongside his illustrious ancestors—with the exception of the Duke and his Duchess, Sarah, who are buried in an ostentatious tomb in the palace chapel.

Follow A 34 to the village of *Kidlington,* where a side road leads 2 km. (1 mile) to **Ditchley Park,* another mansion inhabited by Winston Churchill, who spent weekends here during World War II. More important to Americans, Ditchley Park is the ancestral home of Robert E. Lee, the famous Confederate general. (Fittingly, the house is now an Anglo-American conference center.) Blenheim Palace may have struck you as being a bit pretentious, vulgar even. Not so Ditchley, which is the masterpiece of architect James Gibbs, who also designed the church of St. Martin-in-the-Fields in London and the Radcliffe Camera in Oxford.

You are now on the edge of the *Cotswolds,* the gentle landscape of hills and valleys that is considered to be the loveliest part of England (see page 196). Some 17 km. (10 miles) beyond Kidlington, Route A 34 comes to ***Chipping Norton,** a charming old Cotswolds wool town that the locals call "Chippy." Like many other Cotswolds villages that grew rich from wool during the Middle Ages ("chipping" once meant "market" in local parlance), Chipping Norton has a fine *Guildhall* and *church,* and—a sign that it took care of its own—a row of 17th-century *almshouses.* To tour other parts of the Cotswolds, drive south from Chipping Norton for 18 km. (11 miles) on Route A 361 to *Burford* (see page 198) or 14 km. (8.5 miles) west of Routes A 44 and A 436 to *Stow-on-the-Wold* (see page 198). From both places you can connect with Travel Route 16 (see page 196).

You have several choices of

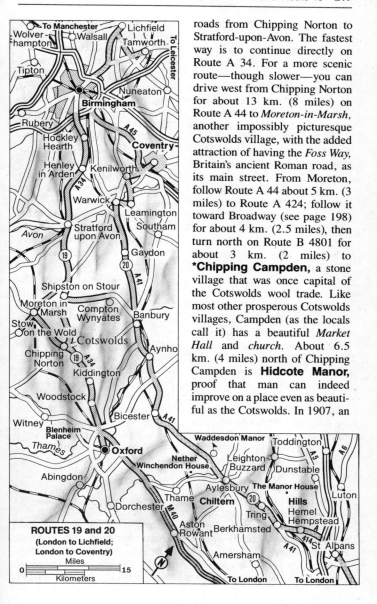

roads from Chipping Norton to
Stratford-upon-Avon. The fastest
way is to continue directly on
Route A 34. For a more scenic
route—though slower—you can
drive west from Chipping Norton
for about 13 km. (8 miles) on
Route A 44 to *Moreton-in-Marsh*,
another impossibly picturesque
Cotswolds village, with the added
attraction of having the *Foss Way*,
Britain's ancient Roman road, as
its main street. From Moreton,
follow Route A 44 about 5 km. (3
miles) to Route A 424; follow it
toward Broadway (see page 198)
for about 4 km. (2.5 miles), then
turn north on Route B 4801 for
about 3 km. (2 miles) to
*Chipping Campden, a stone
village that was once capital of
the Cotswolds wool trade. Like
most other prosperous Cotswolds
villages, Campden (as the locals
call it) has a beautiful *Market
Hall* and *church*. About 6.5
km. (4 miles) north of Chipping
Campden is **Hidcote Manor,**
proof that man can indeed
improve on a place even as beautiful as the Cotswolds. In 1907, an

ROUTES 19 and 20
(London to Lichfield;
London to Coventry)

Miles

0 |====|====| 15

Kilometers

American, Laurence Johnson, bought this estate and began to plant gardens across the rather inhospitable landscape. He planted a series of multicolored hedges to protect his land against the Cotswolds winds, and within their shelter transplanted trees and shrubs from all over the world. The effect is breathtaking, and Hidcote's gardens have rightfully earned the title of the most beautiful 20th-century gardens in the world. From Hidcote you may join Route A 46 and drive the 12 km. (7 miles) into Stratford-upon-Avon (see page 93).

You can make the drive from Chipping Norton to Stratford-upon-Avon directly on Route A 34. About 3 km. (2 miles) north of Chipping Norton, Route A 34 comes to the *Rollright Stones,* a circular arrangement of 100 stones that are thought to predate Stonehenge (see page 149) and are of equally mysterious origin. A grouping of five large stones about 400 meters (a quarter-mile) away is known as the "Whispering Knights." About 14 km. (10 miles) farther north on Route A 34 you will come to *Shipston-on-Stour,* where you should make a side trip about 8 km. (5 miles) east to ***Compton Wynyates,** the Marquess of Northampton's beautiful Tudor home—the finest in England. Driving in, you'll probably gasp at the harmony of it all—yellow brick, stone, and black timbers nestled in a wooded hollow. Inside, you can wind your way in and out of paneled room after paneled room, up and down secret staircase after secret staircase. Outside, the garden is a riot of topiary. Route A 34 continues for another 18 km. (10.5 miles) along the River Stour to the hometown of William Shakespeare, ****Stratford-upon-Avon** (64 km.; 39 miles from Oxford; see page 93). Leaving Stratford to the north on Route A 34, it is only 13 km. (8 miles) to **Henley-in-Arden,** a quaint village surrounded by the ancient Forest of Arden. Stop long enough to take a look at its old *Guildhall,* built in 1448, and its 13th-century *Butter Cross. Hockley Heath,* about 8 km. (5 miles) up A 34 is another old town, with a *church* the Saxons may have built. The little town also has a fine old Tudor manor, ***Packwood House,** about 3 km. (2 miles) east. The 16th-century house is filled with needlework and tapestry, though it is most noted for its amazing yew **garden,* planted around 1650 in shapes that represent the Sermon on the Mount. In another 18 km. (11 miles), Route A 34 comes to Birmingham (103 km.; 64 miles from Oxford).

*Birmingham

See map on page 221.

Birmingham (England's second-largest metropolis after London) is an important city of 1 million people. The city is off the usual tourist itinerary, for it is primarily an industrial center (automobiles, machinery, electronics, brass casting, buttons, gold, and silver). However, Birmingham does have its cultural side, too: several outstanding museums, one of England's leading orchestras, famous libraries, and a good university. Birmingham is rich in history, as many notable buildings attest, and is also one of Europe's most modern cities.

An important military camp during Roman times, Birmingham has been a market center since the 12th century and an industrial hub since the 16th century, when it was already known for its wool processing and metalworking. England's Industrial Revolution took root here as early as the 17th century, and by 1850 many of the city's 250,000 people toiled in foundries and workshops. "An immense workshop, a huge forge, a vast shop," is how the French historian Alexis De Tocqueville described Birmingham after a visit in 1835. A canal has linked the city with the rich coal fields to the south since 1800, and in 1837 Birmingham was connected with London and Liverpool by one of England's first railway lines. Since World War II, the city has rebuilt itself in a bold, energetic style.

The center of Birmingham, and the best place to begin a tour, is *Victoria Square,* over which a statue of the popular queen presides from the middle of a flower bed. The templelike building, fronted by 40 columns, on the

Town Hall

west side of the square is **Town Hall** (1). Indeed, when architect Joseph Hansom (after whom hansom cabs are named) built the structure in 1834, he modeled it after the temple of Castor and Pollux in Rome. Here, in the concert hall that is now the seat of the world-famous Birmingham Symphony Orchestra, Mendelssohn's *Elijah* was first performed in 1846.

The flamboyant **Council House** (2), across the square, was built in Renaissance style

Council House

between 1874–1881. Its bell tower, 52 meters (170 feet) tall, is known affectionately as "Big Brum." The *Central Library (3), just behind Town Hall, is not only Europe's largest library building; it also contains the world's largest Shakespeare collection, with 40,000 volumes in 90 languages.

A statue of native son Sir Roland Hill (1795–1879) keeps an eye on the new *General Post Office* (4), also on Victoria Square. Hill, the son of a schoolteacher who became a teacher himself, was a founder of the Society for Diffusion of Knowledge. He then found his true calling as a postal official. An ardent reformer, he won for the British public guaranteed low postage rates. Just to the west of the post office, across from Easy Row, is the *Hall of Memory* (5), erected in 1925 to honor the 14,000 men of Birmingham who died in World War I.

Beyond the Council House is what many visitors consider to be Birmingham's greatest treasure, the **Corporation Art Gallery and Museum** (6), one of the largest and most valuable collections of art in England. The museum's collection of Pre-Raphaelite drawings and paintings, which include *Blind Girl* by Millais, is considered to be the finest in the world. Among the masterpieces on exhibit are works by Botticelli and other 15th-century Italian masters; canvases by Gainsborough, Hogarth, Rey-

nolds, and other leading British painters; as well as an outstanding, 300-work collection of British watercolors. The museum's archaeological wing houses many important finds from Jericho. The Lysaght Collection of birds in the natural history wing draws ornithologists from around the world.

Another first-class museum is the **Barber Institute of Fine Arts** (7) at Birmingham University, located at the Edgbaston Park Road entrance. Founded by bequest of Lady Barber in the 1930s, this collection of European paintings and sculpture, all of them predating 1900, is small but exquisite. Sculptures by Rodin, Degas, and Giovanni Della Robbia are here. Paintings by Veronese, Rembrandt, Pissarro, Gauguin, and Whistler are among the museum's 90 canvases.

As befits a city that owes its wealth to industry, Birmingham also has a large **Museum of Science and Industry** (8), housed in one of the city's famous old factories on Newhall Street, just to the north of the city center. Locomotives, bottle-making machines, and an eccentric mix of other machinery testify to the city's past.

Birmingham's smallish **cathedral** (9) rises from the pleasant greenery of St. Philip's Churchyard, just down Colmore Row, a bustling shopping street, from Victoria Square. Built in Palladian Renaissance style

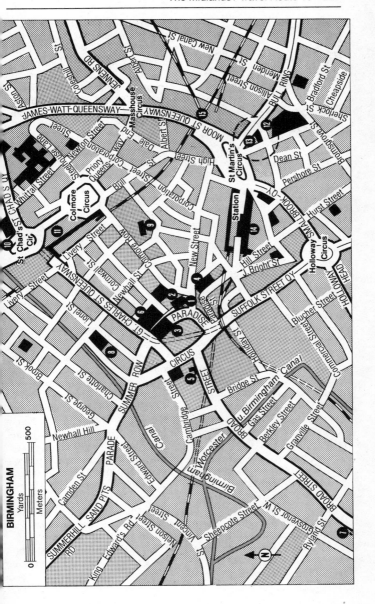

BIRMINGHAM

St. Philip Cathedral

between 1710–1725, the cathedral is noted for four stained-glass windows, representing Christ's birth, crucifixion, resurrection, and last judgment, by Sir Edward Burne-Jones, a native of the area. From here, Colmore Row continues to Colmore Circus and the *Snow Hill Railway Station* (11).

Just beyond is *St. Chad's Circus,* where beautiful gardens and a large mosaic commemorate John F. Kennedy. The nearby Roman Catholic *Cathedral of St. Chad* (10) was built in 1839–1841 by A. W. Pugin, who also designed the Houses of Parliament in London.

The busiest shopping thoroughfare in Birmingham is New Street, which leads from Victoria Square past the *New Street Railway Station* (14) to the ***Bull Ring** (12), an innovative, 23-acre shopping center that houses hundreds of stores and Birmingham's busy bus station. While this district is decidedly modern, it also incorporates such landmarks as the 12th-century *market,* still functioning; the quaint 15th-century *Old Crown Inn,* where Queen Elizabeth I supposedly spent a night; and the parish *church of St. Martin* (13), built in 1873 and incorporating portions of a Norman church from 1285. The Bull Ring adjoins St. Martin's Circus. Birmingham's third railway station, *Moor Street* (15), is at the west end of the circus.

There are several side trips you can take from Birmingham: **Aston Hall,** Aston: The home of Charles I in 1642, this Jacobean mansion, built from 1618–1635, has changed little since then.

Birmingham National Exhibition Centre, 12 km. (7.4 miles) southeast: Britain's largest fairground and exhibition space sprawls over 90,000 square meters (107,000 square yards) near the airport. The nearby *National Motorcycle Museum* houses more than 400 British motorcycles from the past 80 years.

Blakesley Hall, South Yardley: This 16th-century, half-timbered manor house has been converted in part to a small, interesting *Museum of Local History.*

Oratory of St. Philip Neri, Edgbaston: Cardinal John Henry Newman (1801–1890) established this oratory in 1847, the same year he was ordained a Roman Catholic priest. Edgbaston is now a pleasant suburb, with a large botanical garden and several parks.

From Birmingham you can take Superhighway M 5 or Route A 34 the 80 km. (50 miles) north to *Manchester* (see page 206), where you can connect with Travel Route 17. Or you can take Route M 6 for 14 km. (8.5 miles) east to *Coventry* (see page 229) and connect with Travel Route 20.

To continue on Travel Route 19, leave Birmingham to the north on Route A 38 for a short drive of 24 km. (14.5 miles) to ***Lichfield,** a little town where the biggest day of the year is September 18. On that day in 1709, the lexicographer, writer, social critic, and conversationalist Samuel Johnson was born. Lichfield's residents are still basking in Johnson's compliment that they are the "most sober decent people in England," and they treat the man with great honor. Johnson was born in a room above his father's bookshop on Breadmarket Street, and the house is now known as *Dr. Johnson's Birthplace,* and filled with Johnsonian memorabilia and a library of his works. Take a look at the rest of the block, too. Johnson and his biographer, James Boswell, used to stay next door at the *Three Crowns Inn,* and next to that is the birthplace in 1617 of Elias Ashmole, the antiquarian whose famous collections were the nucleus for the Ashmolean Museum in Oxford.

Lichfield has another claim to fame—its magnificent *******cathedral,* built in the 12th–13th centuries with contributions from

Lichfield Cathedral

pilgrims who came to pay homage to the town's seventh-century Saint Chad. The church is small as cathedrals go, but it is one of England's most beautiful, and the only cathedral in the country to still have three spires—called the "Ladies of the Vale." Lichfield Cathedral would be minus at least one spire if Cromwell's Civil War troops had had their way. They shot down the central one, pillaged the church for lead and other materials, and in other ways wreaked as much havoc as they could. Rebuilding the cathedral lasted for the next two centuries. Much of the effort went into the splendid **west façade,* decorated with 113 statues—only five of which are original. The whims of the soldiers have worked in the cathedral's favor, too. The *Lady Chapel* is lit by superb 16th-century stained glass, removed from a Cistercian abbey in Herkenrode,

Belgium, after Napoleon disestablished it. In the *south transept*, notice Richard Westmacott's busts of Dr. Johnson and David Garrick, the famous actor who was Johnson's pupil at Lichfield's grammar school (they are both buried at Westminster Abbey). One of the cathedral's most famous monuments is *The Sleeping Children*, by Sir Francis Chantrey, in the choir. Bostonians might recognize the sculptor's work; he fashioned the bust of George Washington for the State House.

You may want to make an excursion about 11 km. (7 miles) east of Lichfield on Route A 5 to *Tamworth*, an ancient town where Alfred the Great's daughter Aethelflaed probably had a palace 1,000 years ago. A later, Norman *castle* still stands, built over the remains of Aethelflaed's fortress and enlarged with a banquet hall in the days of Henry VIII. While you are in Tamworth, take a look at the 14th-century *church* dedicated to Saint Editha, the daughter of another Saxon king, Edgar. An extraordinary double spiral staircase leads to the top of the tower.

TRAVEL ROUTE 20: ***London–*St. Albans– Aylesbury–*Warwick–**Stratford-upon-Avon– *Coventry (–*Birmingham) (174 km.; 108 miles)

See map on page 217.

This Travel Route will take you from the extremes of England's past to its present—from St. Albans, one of Rome's most important settlements in Britain, to Coventry, a striking modern city. Between these two points, you will cross a green English countryside that is said to be full of squires and spires—a reference to its many country estates and village churches—to Britain's Middle Ages treasure, Warwick.

Leave London to the north on either Highway M 1 or A 5 and drive 32 km. (20 miles) toward *St. Albans,* an old town with a history that is always referred to in superlatives. The town was one of the most important Roman settlements in Britain; it is named after England's first martyr; its ancient cathedral has the longest nave in Europe and is built on higher ground than any other cathedral in England; its inn, The Fighting Cocks, is said to be the oldest in England, and one of the country's first licensed pubs.

The first thing you should do when you arrive in this town on the River Ver is to walk along some of its old streets—*Fishpool Street, George Street,* and *Romeland Hill* are especially picturesque—and take a look at the Medieval and Georgian houses.

The Fighting Cocks is at the end of Abbey Mill Lane, across from St. Albans' 18th-century *silk mill.* The clock tower on High Street was erected in 1411. So-called *French Row,* just beyond, is a group of 14th-century houses. One of them, the *Fleur de Lys Inn,* housed King John for a time after he was taken prisoner at Poitiers in 1356. St. Albans has two *almshouses*—Pemberton's Almshouses, from 1624, on St. Peter's Street, and another group, founded by Sarah, Duchess of Marlborough, on Hatfield Road.

The town's namesake, Saint Alban, was a Roman soldier garrisoned here, in what was then known as Verulamium. He was beheaded in 303 for attempting to hide Saint Amphibalus, the priest who had converted him. Around 790, King Offa of Mercia founded an abbey to honor the martyr, and a new church—using Roman bricks, which no doubt must have pleased the sainted Alban—went up on the site at the end of the 11th century. It still forms the core of the **cathedral*—much enlarged and restored over the years, though not always for the better. The 13th-century *Lady Chapel* was converted to a grammar school during the reign of Henry VIII; the Puritans whitewashed the cathedral's interior, covering the magnificent wall paintings from the 13th and 14th centuries. The chapel was restored in 1870, and the murals on the Norman pillars in the *nave* are visible once again.

There is a shrine to Saint Alban in *St. Albans Chapel,* and next to it is the oak *Watching Loft,* from which the monks once kept an around-the-clock vigil over the saint's relics.

What is left of the walls of Verulamium runs through a park just west of the cathedral. The Roman *theater*—with a stage and auditorium, as opposed to an amphitheater—and scant remains of the *forum* are next to the church of St. Michael. The adjacent *museum* displays a remarkable collection of mosaic floors, pottery, coffins, and other Roman artifacts. Take a look inside the *church of St. Michael,* too. It was founded in 948 and is the final resting place of Sir Francis Bacon (1561–1626), the great English philosopher.

There are several historic estates just outside of St. Albans. The most famous of them, **Hatfield House,* is just 8 km. (5 miles) to the east (see page 233). **Gorhambury,** 4 km. (2.5 miles) to the west past St. Albans, is the 18th-century home of the Earl of Verulam, a descendant of Sir Francis Bacon. Sir Francis's house, now in ruin, is in the park.

Route A 414 leads west from St. Albans and, in about 11 km. (7 miles), comes to *Hemel Hempstead,* where you take Route A 41 going west. After 8 km. (5 miles) you will come to *Northchurch,* where a side road, Route B 4506, leads to **Ashridge Park,** a 13th-century estate, originally a monastery, where the children of Henry VIII were raised. Only a barn and a crypt from those days remain. The newer Gothic style house that the Earl of Bridgewater commissioned James Wyatt to build here in 1808 is now a management-training center. Just a mile beyond Ashridge you will come to another mansion, this one Elizabethan, called *Manor House.* In its rooms you will find an outstanding collection of musical instruments.

Route A 41 continues 7 km. (4 miles) to *Tring,* at the foot of the Chiltern Hills (see below). Railroad buffs come to Tring to admire the cutting that the great 19th-century railway engineer Robert Stephenson made across the summits of one of the hills just west of town. Tring is also a favorite among animal lovers. In 1892, Baron Ferdinand de Rothschild turned over the family seat and his amazing collection of mammals, reptiles, birds, and fish—most of them stuffed—to the British public. The British Museum now administers Tring as a *zoological museum.* In another 11 km. (7 miles), A 41 comes to **Aylesbury,** a market town that is a good place to begin an excursion into the *Chiltern Hills.* (Travel Route 16, see page 197, also takes you into these beech-forested rises. The Chilterns are especially good for walking, and the tourist information bureau in Aylesbury's County Hall can give you information on the best trails.) Aylesbury, however, is not a rural backwater. Much of the town is new,

and you may have to turn your back on some of the more modern expanses of concrete if you want to indulge in what's left of the Medieval spirit of the place. By all means walk down *Temple* and *Church streets* to take in the houses from the 17th and 18th centuries, and stop at the *County Museum* on Church Street for a look at the history of Buckinghamshire. *Market Square* is still lined with some of Aylesbury's oldest buildings. The 18th-century *County Hall* stands there, as does the *Kings Inn,* a 14th-century inn that is now in the hands of the National Trust. Sir Gilbert Scott, the Victorian architect who built the Albert Memorial in London, took his hand, rather heavy at times, to the *church of St. Mary,* but he left some of the original building intact and filled the windows with magnificent Victorian stained glass.

Aylesbury is surrounded by the pleasant pastoral farmland that is typical of Buckinghamshire. You may want to make a foray outside of town to its historic estates. King Louis XVIII of France lived 3 km. (about 2 miles) southwest of town at *Hartwell House* from 1808–1814. (Hartwell House was the last of many places he lived outside of France during Napoleon's regime.) The Jacobean mansion now houses a college, but it is open to the public.

As you leave Aylesbury, continue west on Route A 41 about 5

km. (3 miles) and you will come to a turnoff to the south for **Nether Winchenden House,** a remarkable Tudor mansion that was the home of Sir Francis Bernard, who was governor of New Jersey in 1758 and of the Massachusetts Bay Colony from 1760–1768. Some 9 km. (6 miles) beyond Aylesbury, Route A 41 comes to ***Waddesdon.** The Baron Rothschild built a French Renaissance mansion, **Waddesdon Manor,* here after he gave his estate in Tring (see page 226) to the public. His love of animals is evident throughout, particularly in the ornate aviary. It is also clear that the Baron had a taste for such worldly possessions as fine porcelain, tapestries, and paintings by the Old Masters.

Route A 41 soon crosses into Oxfordshire, another agricultural county, and 18 km. (11 miles) beyond Waddesdon comes to **Bicester.** Stop long enough for a

Waddesdon Manor

look at its 12th-century *church of St. Edburg.* The ruins next to it were once an Augustinian priory. Soon after Bicester, A 41 crosses another county line and enters Northamptonshire, said to have more country estates than any other county in England. This seems to be true, if the next few towns you come to are typical of the region. Just outside the stone village of *Aynho* is *Aynhoe Park,* a 17th-century mansion built next to the ruins of a Norman castle. In another 9 km. (5.5 miles), A 41 comes to **Banbury,** a pretty old market town with special significance for Americans. In 1560, Henry VIII sold an old estate, **Sulgrave Manor,* to one Lawrence Washington. A century later, Colonel John Washington, great-grandfather of America's first President, sailed to the colonies, and the rest is history. The Washington family's coat of arms—three stars above two stripes—may have inspired the American flag. You can make the comparison for yourself: the design is carved into the porch of the stone manor, and the estate always flies the stars and stripes. The interior may remind you of Mount Vernon—it is hung with portraits of George Washington and furnished with many of his belongings. There is nothing American about nearby **Broughton Castle,** an 800-year-old manor house surrounded by a moat. The castle once belonged to William of Wykeham, a 14th-century bishop of Winchester.

Over the years Broughton's gracious rooms have amassed an outstanding collection of china and Chinese wallpapers. *Chacombe Priory*, another neighborhood estate, is an abbey founded in 1066 and converted to a mansion in the 16th century.

From Banbury, Route A 41 continues across rolling countryside for 32 km. (19 miles) to ***Warwick**, an amazingly unspoiled town dominated by what most aficionados of the Middle Ages consider to be England's best castle. What makes **Warwick Castle* special is the way in which it blends all of the elements of a Medieval fortress—its 14th-century towers and walls are perfectly intact—with the grandeur of a stately mansion. Much of the sumptuous interior dates from 1871, the result of rebuilding after a fire. Even so, you will discover it contains all the elements you would expect to find in a castle—above ground, a Great Hall filled with armor and staterooms hung with paintings and tapestries; below ground, dungeons and torture chambers. The luxurious gardens along the River Avon were laid out in the 18th century by the greatest of all British landscape architects, Capability Brown. The castle has been owned by Madame Tussaud's since 1978 and also features wax figures.

The town below the castle has its charm, too, as you'll no doubt notice as you start down *Mill Street*, lined with old houses, from the castle. The *church of St.*

Mary is Norman, though it was rebuilt after a fire in 1694. The **Beauchamp Chapel* survived the blaze, however, and with its Gothic vaults, stained glass, and the tomb of its benefactor, an early Earl of Warwick, it is now the pride of the church. Many of Warwick's best old buildings are museums: *Oken's House Doll's Museum* occupies the house of a 16th-century merchant; the *Warwickshire Museum*, which provides a good look at area history—social, natural, and otherwise—is in the Market Hall, from 1670; and the 14th-century **Lord Leycester Hospital* houses two museums, one of the Queen's Own Hussars and one with items of local interest—including a chair in which King James is said to have sat. The real attractions at the hospital, though, are the retired soldiers who occupy its timbered buildings, just as they have since the Earl of Leycester established the foundation in 1571.

From Warwick you can take Route A 46 south just 13 km. (8 miles) to *Stratford-upon-Avon* (see page 93) and connect with Travel Route 19. To continue on Travel Route 20, leave Warwick to the east and follow Route A 425 just 3 km. (2 miles) to ***Royal Leamington Spa.** The American man of letters Nathaniel Hawthorne was but one of the well-heeled patrons of this spa, whose saline springs and peaceful gardens have attracted health seekers since the 19th century. Follow Route A 46 another 9 km. (5.5 miles) north to the village that Sir Walter Scott made famous, **Kenilworth.** Scott, the master of the romantic novel, lived in Kenilworth for a while, and it was here, in 1815, that he wrote the novel that he named after the town. Another famous past resident of this peaceful little town was Robert Dudley, Earl of Leicester. The Earl was a favorite of Elizabeth I, and she presented him with *Kenilworth Castle.* The place wasn't a shack to begin with, and Dudley enlarged it. Most of the castle is now in splendid ruin, though its Norman tower and 14th-century Great Hall are well preserved. Kenilworth's other architectural landmark is a *monastery* from the 12th-century, also in ruin but impressive nonetheless.

Just off Route A 46 you'll discover **Stoneleigh Abbey** amid a magnificent forest of oaks. The palatial abbey was built from 1714–1726 on the ruins of a 12th-century Cistercian monastery. The religious occupants obviously kept one eye on heaven and the other on such worldly trappings as the lovely oak paneling and perfect Norman doorways.

Continue 8 km. (5 miles) on A 46 to Coventry (174 km.; 108 miles from London).

*Coventry

See map on page 230.

It is hard to tell if the 385,000 residents of this modern industrial city in the Midlands are more proud of their famous ancestor, Lady Godiva, or of their futuristic shopping malls and parking lots. It doesn't really matter, as there is enough history and modern city planning in Coventry for a pleasant day's worth of sightseeing. Coventry is not a vacation center and most visitors come to do business with the town's numerous transportation, engineering, and chemical firms.

Schoolchildren around the world seem to know the story of Coventry's own Lady Godiva, who in the 11th century struck a deal with her husband, Count Leofric of Mercia. The stern Count told his wife he would lower the burdensome taxes he levied on townspeople if she would ride through the town naked, "dressed only in her own hair." The civic-minded lady agreed, but she bid the citizenry to remain indoors behind shuttered windows. Allegedly, the only one to sneak a peek was Peeping Tom. What many people don't know is that Count Leofric and Lady Godiva also founded a Benedictine monastery in Coventry in 1043, and it became the town's first cathedral.

Oddly enough for a town whose claim to fame is nudity, Coventry was famous for its woolen fabrics (which it sold at huge outdoor markets) as early as the 14th century, and until the end of the 17th century it was the center of the English clothing industry. The factories of Coventry have also produced many British

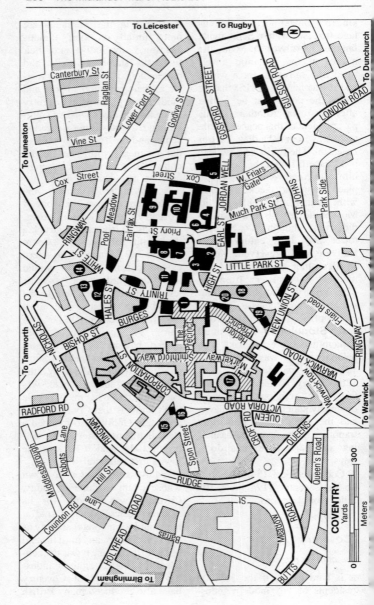

cars and bicycles, and during World War II they were the major supplier of Britain's armaments. Because of this, the town was virtually leveled by German bombs on the night of November 14, 1940.

A naked Lady Godiva on horseback, in the form of a bronze statue put up in 1949, still dominates **Broadgate** (1), Coventry's postwar central square. West of here stretches The Precinct, a modern pedestrian zone characterized by many shops, a plentitude of glass and steel, and very little charm. The streets east of Broadgate tend to be more interesting. On *High Street,* just in front of the *Council House* (2) is **St. Mary's Hall** (3), built in 1342 as the seat of the Merchant's Guild. Flemish tapestries in the *Great Hall* commemorate Henry VII and Elizabeth of York, who visited Coventry in 1500 and no doubt feasted lavishly in this room on food prepared in the kitchen downstairs. Coventry wasn't nearly as gracious to Mary Stuart, who was imprisoned in 1569 in the adjoining Caesar's Tower, built in the 13th century. The tower is now all that remains of the castle of the Earl of Chester.

Just to the east (left) on Jordan Well is the **Herbert Art Gallery and Museum** (4), a pleasantly eclectic collection of Coventry's past—Anglo-Saxon crossbows, an Alvis motor car, and the like—with some works of modern art. Nearby are several other cultural institutions of modern Coventry, including the *College of Art* (5) on Gosford Street and, behind the Herbert Gallery, the new buildings of the *Central Library* (6). Without question the most striking sight in Coventry is the charred skeleton of the **Old Cathedral** (7), burned in the air raid of 1940 and known simply as "The Ruins." Only the bell tower and an old Norman door dating to around 1300 survive intact. The Ruins are linked, physically and symbolically, by a porch to the **New Cathedral** (8), designed by Sir Basil Spence and dedicated in 1962. It has sharp concrete angles, dramatic lighting that symbolizes the glory of the Baptism (the light represents God illuminating man's existence), a wall hanging behind the altar by Graham Sutherland, a baptismal font hollowed out of a boulder from Bethlehem, all of which produce a highly charged, almost theatrical atmosphere. Even skeptics, however, are moved by the spirit of the place, and that of the adjacent *Chapel of Unity,* used by all denominations to pray for world peace.

As befits this city of old and new, swimmers in the nearby, glass-enclosed *municipal pools* (9) can see The Ruins as they do their laps. The modern tower of the *Lancaster College of Technology* (10) rises over the pools to the south.

One of Coventry's finest old buildings, *Holy Trinity Church* (11), was built just to the west of

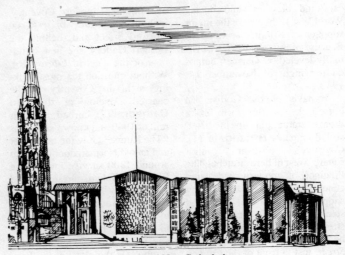

Old and New Cathedral

the Cathedral between the 13th–17th centuries. It, too, was all but leveled in the War, but it has been painstakingly rebuilt. Sarah Kemble and William Siddons, two of the most celebrated actors of their day, were married here in 1773. No doubt they felt at home in the church, as this neighborhood has long been Coventry's theater district. Two of Britain's most famous stages, the *Coventry Theatre* (12) on Hales Street and the *Belgrade Theatre,* (opened on Corporation Street in 1958), are nearby. Also nearby, the *Museum of British Road Transport* (13) is a must for transportation buffs. A display of over 400 pieces covers the history of transportation from the bicycle to the Royal Daimler, built in Coventry. The Coventry Theatre abuts a lovely park,

Lady Herbert's Garden (14). The only reminders of the surrounding city in this oasis of greenery are pleasant ones, the remains of a 14th-century city wall and two old city gates, the *Swanswell Gate* and the *Cook Street Gate.*

Two other gems of old Coventry are to the south of the Garden,

Pedestrian zone

off Corporation Street. ***Bond's Hospital** (15), a lattice-work building put up as a poorhouse in 1506, is still providing food and shelter to the city's poor and aged. *St. John's Church* (16), next door, was built in 1344, restored in 1875, and restored again after the War. Just down Queen Victoria Road is one of Coventry's most modern creations, the **Circular Market** (17), an enormous indoor shopping center. Still farther south, on Greenfriar's Road, is another old almshouse that still functions as such: ***Ford's Hospital** (18), built in 1529 and very nicely preserved. From here you can see an octagonal tower, all that remains of *Christ Church*

Ford's Hospital

(19), built in the 14th century and destroyed in the war. Hertford Precinct leads back toward Broadgate, passing the modern *main post office* (20).

TRAVEL ROUTE 21: ***London–**Peterborough– **Lincoln–Grimsby (301 km.; 187 miles)

See map on page 235.

The sights along this Travel Route read like a checklist of English history—it passes the homes of Elizabeth I, Oliver Cromwell, Isaac Newton, and Samuel Pepys; three of England's finest cathedrals, the ones at Peterborough, Southwell, and Lincoln; and one of the nation's most outstanding recent architectural accomplishments, the Humber suspension bridge.

From London, take Route A 1 north for 29 km. (18 miles) to *Hatfield*. One of this town's many claims to fame is that from a window of the timbered *Eight Bells Inn*, on Park Street, Dick Turpin, the famous 18th-century robber and highwayman, jumped onto the back of a horse and made a dramatic escape. (Turpin was later caught and hanged for his escapades along the Great North

Road, once the major route to Scotland and northern England; Route A 1 more or less follows its path.) A beautiful row of Georgian houses climbs steep Fore Street just beyond the inn. Hatfield's major attraction, though, is ****Hatfield House,** where Mary Tudor kept her half sister, Elizabeth, a virtual prisoner in what is now called the old palace. It was in the garden at Hatfield that

Hatfield House

Elizabeth learned the throne was hers. Elizabeth's successor, James I, traded Hatfield for the estate of the Earl of Salisbury, and Salisbury built the present Hatfield House (1607–1611). The most remarkable room of the new palace at Hatfield is the enormous marble *Hall,* hung with Flemish tapestries depicting the four seasons.

Continue north from Hatfield on Route A 1 to another architectural accomplishment, this one from the 20th century, **Welwyn Garden City,** a model city built as a satellite to London in the 1920s. With its well-planned housing blocks and gardens, Welwyn is a good example of urban planning. There are many fine old houses in the neighborhood around Welwyn, among them *Lockey's,* a brick mansion from 1771. A good way to see the countryside and more houses is to take Route B 656 north for about 5 km. (3 miles) to the village of *Ayot St. Lawrence.* Here, in a

house called *Shaw's Corner,* the playwright George Bernard Shaw lived from 1906 until his death in 1950. His furnishings and personal effects still fill the house. Route B 656 continues for 2 km. (1.5 miles) to ***Knebworth House,** another estate with a literary past. The house was built in 1491 for the Lytton family, and from 1803–1873 was the home of novelist Bulwer Lytton, who wrote *The Last Days of Pompeii* and several other 19th-century classics. You now travel north on Route A 1 through *Stevenage,* and 11 km. (7 miles) beyond the town of Knebworth, you will come to *Baldock.* A short side trip of 1.5 km. (1 mile) west on Route A 505 brings you to **Letchworth,** another planned garden city, this one from 1903. Like Welwyn, it too is a fairly good example of urban planning. Even so, many visitors find the most interesting building in town to be the old Jacobean mansion *Letchworth Hall,* which is now a hotel.

Continue north on Route A 1. About 30 km. (18 miles) beyond Baldock you will come to Route A 45, which will take you east for 13 km. (8 miles) to *Cambridge* (see page 60). In another 8 km. (5 miles), A 1 comes to **Buckden,** where the considerable remains of *Buckden Palace* still stand. Buckden was a residence of the bishops of Lincoln from the 12th century until 1838, and is still in the hands of an order of missionaries. The palace's most famous resident, though, was Catherine of Aragon, the first wife of Henry VIII. She lived here from 1534–1535, immediately after her divorce from Henry. The town of Buckden has several old *coaching inns,* a reminder that busy A 1 follows the route of the Great North Road. The large lake just to the west of Buckden is *Grafham Water,* a reservoir and popular recreation spot. (Route B 661 leads to its shores.)

Leave Buckden on Route A 141 for a side trip of about 14 km. (9 miles) to ***Huntingdon,** a town on the River Ouse that already had a long and illustrious past before Oliver Cromwell was born here in 1599. Huntingdon and its sister city across the Ouse, *Godmancester,* lie at the intersection of three Roman roads, which made the settlements a prime target for Danish and Norman conquerors. Cromwell, who commanded the antiroyalist troops during England's Civil War in the 1640s, was born at *Hinchingbrooke House,* a 13th-century monastery that the crown presented to the Cromwells in the 16th century. Generations of loyalist Cromwells entertained Queen Elizabeth I and King James I at Hinchingbrooke. The antiroyalist Oliver (whom the town records now refer to as "England's gloss for five years") attended the grammar school on Market Street, which is now a *Cromwell museum.* Another student there was the great diarist Samuel Pepys (1633–1703), who was raised nearby in *Brampton,*

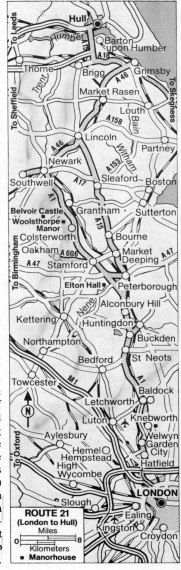

just 3 km. (1.8 miles) west of Huntingdon off A 604. Pepys once said that although he spent much of his time in London, he was happy to have this farmhouse in the Ouse Valley, "a pretty place to retire to." With its rolling fields and orchards, this landscape was a favorite place of painter John Constable.

Just beyond Brampton you will rejoin Route A 1, which in another 30 km. (18 miles) comes to **Peterborough** (137 km.; 85 miles from London), an expanding industrial city with steelworks. Don't let this keep you from stopping, because from the foundations of the church that the Saxon King Peada built here in 656, England's greatest Norman building rose at the end of the 12th century. There are two elements that make this **cathedral** one of the supreme achievements of Medieval architecture. To see the first, you need look no farther than the *west front* of the Gothic façade, with its three recessed arches. To see the second, walk the length of the *nave,* built from 1194–1197, and regard the painted wooden *ceiling.*

To view the rest of old Peterborough, walk the streets around its marketplace. The *Guildhall* is from the 17th century; the *church of St. John the Baptist* was built from 1401–1407. Peterborough's *City Museum and Art Gallery,* in Priestgate Street, displays a good cross section of Peterborough history: fossilized prehistoric reptiles, Roman artifacts, and carvings made by the French pris-

Westfront of Peterborough Cathedral

oners from the Napoleonic wars who were held at the nearby Norman Cross barracks. About 10 km. (6 miles) west of Peterborough on Route A 605 is **Elton Hall,** a 17th-century mansion built around the *gatehouse* and other remains of a 14th-century house. The house is distinguished for its magnificent *library*. Among its many rare volumes are early English Bibles and prayer books, including the one that Henry VIII used.

From Peterborough you may take either of two routes north to *Lincoln.* You may continue on Route A 1, with a detour at Newark, or you may drive directly on Route A 15 (see page 239). If you opt to go through Newark, about 23 km. (14 miles) north of Peterborough on Route A 1 you will come to **Stamford,** a town with a turbulent past, enough of which is etched into the stone of its buildings to give it the ranking of one of Europe's finest Medieval cities. Stamford flourished under the Saxons, was destroyed by the Danes in 870, reconquered by the Saxons in 972, conquered by the Normans a century later, and destroyed again by the troops of Henry VI during the War of the Roses. Medieval Stamford flourished, though, and by the time Sir Walter Scott visited in the late 18th century, he said its *High Street*—which curves up from the River Welland and may have been the main street of the Saxon town—was the most beautiful street between Edinburgh and London. It's easy to see how that may be true, and Stamford has many other fine streets as well. Those around *St. George's Square* are lined with houses from the 17th–19th centuries. So is the street known as *Barn Hill,* and so are St. Peter's Street and Broad Street, where there is also one of England's best surviving alms-houses, *Browne's Hospital,* from 1474. Founders John and William Browne are commemorated in the town's finest Medieval church, *All Saints',* one of 14 churches built in Stamford during the Middle Ages. Other notable churches include *St. John's,* fronted by magnificent arcades, *St. Martin's,* and *St. George's,* both with remarkable Medieval stained glass. Another almshouse, the *Burghley Hospital,* was built in the late 16th century on the site of a 12th-century hospital. The *bastion* is all that remains of the town's towers, and the castle hasn't fared much better—about all that remains is a 13th-century wall. Many examples of Stam-fordware, the famous pottery made here from 900–1250, have survived intact and are on display in the *town museum* on Broad Street. The museum also has a very popular, sideshow-type display—the clothes of one Daniel Lambert (1770–1809), England's most famous fat man of all time. Stamford has a palace just outside of town, ****Burghley House.** What is probably England's finest Elizabethan house was finished for Sir William Cecil, Queen Elizabeth's Lord High Treasurer, in 1587. A grand *staircase* modeled after the one at the Louvre, an enormous *obelisk* in the courtyard, mural-filled salons called the *Heaven Room* and the *Hell Room,* carvings by Grinling Gibbons (the great English woodcarver who also did the choir at St. Paul's in London), a gallery of paintings by the likes of Titian and Michelangelo—these are all touches that Lord Cecil added to make this palatial house a home. You may also want to make the excursion to *Oakham,* 16 km. (10 miles) west on Route A 606. The Norman banqueting hall of its castle has a collection of odd mementos—180 horseshoes that royalty has donated to the castle over the centuries.

Route A 1 continues north from Stamford and in another 22 km. (13 miles) comes to **Colsterworth,** where Isaac Newton was born in 1642 at *Woolsthorpe Manor.* Legend has it that an apple falling from a tree in the orchard inspired Newton's theory of gravity. A descendant of the tree still grows. Newton was educated about 11 km. (7 miles) to the north in **Grantham.** (You will pass through lovely orchard and farm country on your way here up A 1.) Grantham is still an important market town, and it has several old inns from the days when it was a major coach stop on the route north to London. Bees alight on the beehive that is the sign for the *Beehive Inn* on Castlegate; Princess Margaret stayed at the *Grantham House* in 1503 on her trip north to marry King James IV of Scotland; the *Angel and Royal Hotel* opened its doors for business in the 14th century. Grantham still pays tribute to Isaac Newton, who attended the town's grammar school. A statue of the physicist stands in front of the *Guildhall,* and many of his belongings are on display next to Bronze Age and Roman artifacts in the town library and museum. Grantham's most notable structure is the **church of St. Wulfram's,* built in the 14th century; its tower, 90 meters (295 feet) high, is visible for miles around.

From Grantham you can make a side trip of 10 km. (6 miles) southwest on Route A 607 to ****Belvoir Castle,** a perfect Medieval castle that is for the most part a 19th-century recreation. The castle was indeed built as a fortress, then rebuilt in the 17th century, and rebuilt again, around 1800, by James Wyatt. The architect took advantage of the manor's incredible view over the wooded Vale of Belvoir and devised a turreted extravaganza that is a romantic composite of what a castle should look like and is furnished in opulent rococo fashion. There is, however, nothing artificial about its amazing **art collection:* Goebelin tapestries, miniatures, paintings by Rubens and Rembrandt.

Continuing north on Route A 1, 22 km. (13 miles) beyond Grantham, you will come to ***Newark-on-Trent,** which over the centuries has witnessed the Roman legions that marched by on the old Roman road between Lincoln and Exeter; the death of King John in 1216; and several sieges during the Civil War. Newark's most famous occupant, though, is no doubt Robin Hood, the well-intentioned bandit who roamed nearby *Sherwood Forest,* now a popular vacation area. Newark's 12th-century *castle* is in ruin, but much of its history is captured in displays at the *Museum and Art Gallery* in the Old Grammar School, founded in 1549. The *church of St. Mary Magdalene,* nearby, is a striking structure that rises above a Norman crypt and is topped by a dramatic spire.

From Newark, you may make a side trip of about 11 km. (7 miles) southwest on Route A 616 for *Southwell,* a small town with a large 12th-century ****cathedral** that is one of England's undiscovered treasures. The church is largely Norman but incorporates later styles as well. It is at its best in the *Chapter House,* decorated with incredibly realistic carvings of foliage. The *choir,* too, is noted for its carvings, especially those on the rood screen, said to contain 220 images of human heads. The *Airmen's Altar* is a 20th-century addition, made from fragments of planes shot down over France during World War I. The ruins just to the south of the minster were once a palace of the Archbishops of York.

From Newark it is just 26 km. (16 miles) to **Lincoln* (see page 75) on Route A 46.

If you choose to take the route through Bourne, leave Peterborough on Route A 15 and continue north for 11 km. (7 miles) to *Glinton.* You may want to make a short side trip of 1.5 km. east on

Southwell Cathedral

Route B 1166 to *Peakirk,* where more than 500 species of birds from all over the world inhabit *Waterfowl Gardens.* Some 14 km. (8.5 miles) beyond Glinton, Route A 15 comes to **Bourne,** a pleasant market town whose most famous son is Hereward the Wake, said to be the last Saxon nobleman to resist William the Conqueror. Hereward's valor is legendary, though possibly fictional. Even so, a great Norman *castle* rose on the site of his manor; little remains but some mounds and part of a moat. Bourne's numerous Georgian houses have fared better and still line the town's pretty streets. Lord Burghley, the Lord High Treasurer under Elizabeth I, was born in the house on Market Square that is now the *Burghley Arms Hotel.* The Lord did well in this world, as you can see by his palace, *Burghley House,* just outside of Stamford (see page 237). From Bourne it is only 27 km. (16 miles) north on Route A 15 to *Lincoln* (218 km.; 135 miles; see page 75).

From Lincoln, continue your drive north on Route A 46. Just north of Lincoln you will find yourself in a beautiful countryside of rolling chalk hills. Cross this landscape for about 50 km. (30 miles) to *Market Rasen* and for another 13 km. (8 miles) to **Caistor,** site of a Roman camp. The town's *church of Sts. Peter and Paul* dates to the 12th century. Its most beloved monument is proof that longevity is not a modern phenomenon—it commemorates Sir Edward Maddison, who died in 1553 at the age of 100. In another 21 km. (13 miles) Route A 46 comes to **Grimsby,** a thriving fishing port—the most important one in Britain—on the North Sea at the mouth of the River Humber. The chief attraction here is fish which the town's 3,000 fishermen bring in by the ton every day. Needless to say, the most lively spot in town is the fish market. Quite in keeping with the spirit of the town, the *Welholme Gallery* displays an extensive collection of model ships. Grimsby has other attractions, too, most notably the 13th-century *church of St. James* and the many seaside resorts that lie to the south of town. The closest is *Cleethorpes,* with a good zoo and aquarium. To continue north from Grimsby, follow Routes A 180 and A 15 about 40 km. (25 miles) to *Barton-upon-Humber,* where the Humber Bridge—at 1,400 meters (4,600 feet) the longest suspension bridge in the world—crosses the Humber.

TRAVEL ROUTE 22: ***London–*Leicester–Sheffield–Leeds on Superhighway M 1 (304 km.; 188 miles)

See map on page 242.

Since this Travel Route provides the fastest way to drive from London to Leeds and, from there, north into Scotland, you may be more interested in reaching your destination than in sightseeing. However, the Travel Route describes some of the major sights on and just off the highway; Travel Routes 16–21 explore this area in much greater depth.

Luton (52 km.; 32 miles from London) is an important manufacturing town—automobiles, hats, and engines, among other goods—that is of interest to tourists because of its airport (European flights, primarily) and its incredible mansion just 3 km. (2 miles) southeast of town, ****Luton Hoo.** In itself this 18th-century French-style house by architect Robert Adam is a masterpiece, as is its magnificent, 1,500-acre park. The real treasures, though, are inside: the ****Wernher Collection,** with paintings by Filippino Lippi, Titian, and other masters; Fabergé jewelry, fine porcelain, and other items once in the possession of the czars. As you leave Luton, drive west 3 km. (2 miles) to the adjoining town of *Dunstable* and from there 5 km. (3 miles) south on B 4541 to **Whipsnade,** where the Zoological Society of London maintains a large cageless *zoo.* Wild animals roam huge enclosures that stretch across the slopes of the Chiltern Hills. You can walk or drive through the zoo, or tour it on a miniature railroad or on camel back. Route A 5 leads 11 km. (7 miles) north from Dunstable to the village of *Hockcliffe* and ****Woburn Abbey,** a 17th-century mansion built over the ruins of an old monastery and now the seat of the Duke of Bedford. Inside is his magnificent collection of paintings, by Rembrandt, Van Dyck, Gainsborough, and many, many other masters. The Duke has made the grounds into an enormous ****Safari Park,** where deer, bison, wild cattle, and other animals roam. Another excursion from Luton is a trip of 15 km. (9 miles) north on Route A 6 to *Silsoe,* where there is a French château, ***Wrest Park,** surrounded by a large garden that may remind you of Versailles—rose beds, two lakes and a canal, a *garden pavilion* built in 1735, and an *orangery.* The entrance to the M 1 is just west, near *Toddington.*

Northampton (106 km.; 66 miles from London) is an old shoe-manufacturing town, and you can see shoes worn through the ages—from those worn by

Wrest Park

Romans to Dame Margot Fonteyn's ballet slippers—at its *Central Museum and Art Gallery.* The *Abington Park Museum* is a reconstruction of an 18th-century street, with domestic and agricultural tools from years past. Northampton has several fine churches, including one of England's few surviving Norman round churches, the **church of the Holy Sepulchre.* The *town hall* merits a look, not only because of its Gothic grandeur, but also because Northampton has had more mayors than any other city in Britain.

Castle Ashby has been the home of the Compton family since the house was built in 1574. Inside, there are stunning Belgian tapestries and a fine collection of paintings by Dutch, Italian, and British artists; Capability Brown designed the *gardens. Althorp* has in recent years become quite popular—it is the home of the family of the Princess of Wales. *Delapre Abbey,* a former nunnery, now houses county offices, but its fine park is open to the public.

Rugby (131 km.; 81 miles from London) is famous above all for the game that was first played here, at the elite Rugby School, in 1823. The school was also the setting of *Tom Brown's School Days,* written by alumnus Thomas Hughes. Nearby **Stanford Hall* is a gracious mansion filled with fine furnishings. Its stables now house a collection of vintage automobiles and motorcycles and a replica of one of the first flying machines. The

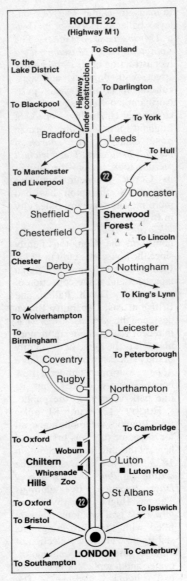

ROUTE 22
(Highway M1)

To Scotland

Highway under construction

To the Lake District

To Darlington

To Blackpool

To York

Bradford

Leeds

To Hull

22

To Manchester and Liverpool

Doncaster

Sheffield

Sherwood Forest

Chesterfield

To Lincoln

To Chester

Derby

Nottingham

To King's Lynn

To Wolverhampton

To Birmingham

Leicester

To Peterborough

Coventry

Rugby

Northampton

To Oxford

To Cambridge

Woburn

Chiltern

Whipsnade Zoo

Hills

Luton

Luton Hoo

St Albans

22

To Oxford

To Ipswich

To Bristol

LONDON

To Canterbury

To Southampton

grounds are lovely, all the more so because the River Avon runs through them.

*Leicester (157 km.; 97 miles) is an important industrial center, but it has quite a bit more to offer by way of museums, churches, and its university. The town's history dates from the Romans, who built the fortified camp known as *Ratae Coritanorum* here. The Romans also built *High Street*—rather, they paved the Foss Way, England's old road laid by ancient Britons in 483 B.C., and that in turn has become High Street. You can see much of this past at the *Jewry Wall Archaeology Museum*, which takes its name from the so-called Jewry Wall, the ornate façade of the Roman baths and exercise hall. The nearby **church of St. Nicholas* was built with Roman bricks. Only a Norman hall remains of Leicester's *castle*, which played an important role in British history—here, in the 13th century, Simon de Montfort, Earl of Leicester, summoned the people's representatives, a body that later became the British Parliament. King Henry IV was knighted at the nearby **church of St. Mary de Castro*, built in 1150. Another religious treasure is the *Codex Leicestrensis,* a 15th-century Greek translation of the New Testament, on display in the timbered **Guildhall.*

A good place to see Leicester's history is the **Newark Houses Museum.* The *Leicestershire Museum and Art Gallery* has a large collection of British paintings. In **Loughborough,** 17 km. (11 miles) to the north on Route A 6, is the bell foundry that cast the 15-ton "Great Paul." This, the biggest bell in England, hangs at St. Paul's in London. Loughborough also sets the record for chimes; those in its *Memorial Tower,* erected in 1923, are said to be the largest in the world.

From *Newtown Linford,* 9 km. (5.5 miles) northwest of Leicester on Route B 5327, you can make excursions into *Charnwood Forest.* In nearby *Bardgate Park* are the ruins of the mansion where Lady Jane Grey once lived. Route B 582 leads 17 km. (11 miles) west from Leicester to *Market Bosworth,* where in 1485 Henry VII killed Richard III on a field just outside of town.

Nottingham (197 km.; 122 miles from London), which climbs up a slope from the banks

Leicester Guildhall

of the River Trent, has long been associated with lace and with the sheriff who pursued Robin Hood in nearby Sherwood Forest. Robin Hood and his men are represented in bronze in front of the sheriff's headquarters, Nottingham's 17th-century *castle.* The castle is a museum now, filled with prehistoric finds, Medieval treasures, and a fine collection of paintings by the likes of Holbein and Gainsborough. Nottingham is a good place to have a drink—in the *Trip to Jerusalem,* said to be England's oldest inn, founded in 1189 and taking its name from Crusaders, who used to stop in for a spot. If someone asks you to step downstairs, don't be alarmed—it's just to show you one of the ancient subterranean passageways that run beneath Nottingham.

*Newstead Abbey, 14 km. (8 miles) north of Nottingham on Route A 60, was founded by Henry II in the 12th century. In 1540, the monastery came into the hands of Sir John Byron, ancestor of the famous Romantic poet whose mementos fill the house's rooms. **Eastwood,** 10 km. (6 miles) northwest of Nottingham on Route A 610, was the birthplace, in 1885, of D. H. Lawrence, who used the surroundings for many of his novels and short stories. **Derby** (205 km.; 127 miles from London), the home of Rolls-Royce Motors and Royal Crown Derby porcelain, is an unabashedly industrial town, but it has many old and interesting buildings. (A good place to see its industrial history is the *Old Silk Mill Industrial Museum*, as well as the town's *Library, Museum,* and *Art Gallery.*) Derby also served as the setting for George Eliot's novel *Adam Bede,* and it was the birthplace of several famous Britons, including the 19th-century philosopher Herbert Spencer. Its best church is the **cathedral of All Saints,* built from 1509–1527 but remodeled in 1725 by architect James Gibbs, who retained its Gothic grandeur. The most unusual place of worship is *Our Lady of the Brigg,* a 15th-century chapel on St. Mary's Bridge over the River Derwent.

Ashbourne, 20 km. (12 miles) northwest on Route A 52, is a small stone-built town with a 13th-century church and a 16th-century grammar school. The real attraction here, though, is *Dovedale Ravine,* a glorious landscape of forests, limestone hills, and trout streams. ****Kedleston Hall,** 5 km. (3 miles) northwest of Derby, has been the home of the Curzon family for the past 850 years. The present, 18th-century mansion is a masterwork by architects James Paine and Robert Adam—mostly Adam, who created the **Hall,* surrounded by columns, and the even more dramatic *rotunda.* The family's 12th-century *chapel* still stands in the park, where there is also a small *museum* housing items that the Marquess Curzon collected when he was Viceroy of India from 1898–1905.

Chesterfield (239 km.; 148 miles from London) is an important mining town on the edge of the Derbyshire coal fields. Chesterfield has its own version of the Leaning Tower of Pisa—the tower of its 14th-century *parish church* leans by more than 2 meters (6.5 feet). Chesterfield also has many historic timbered houses, though its most famous residence is ****Chatsworth,** 11 km. (7 miles) to the east off Route A 619. The First Duke of Devonshire commissioned this Palladian mansion in 1687, though the house you see today is the result of many alterations made over the years. With each improvement, the house (called the "Palace of the Peaks" because of its proximity to the mountainous landscape known as The Peaks, which run from Derby to Scotland) seems to have grown

Chesterfield's "Leaning Tower"

more awesome. The interior has ceilings by Verrio, paintings by Van Dyck and Rembrandt, and other exquisite furnishings. The **gardens*, fronting the River Derwent, reflect the best landscape designs of the 17th–19th centuries. They still contain such wonders as a fountain that spews water 90 meters (300 feet) into the air, but the conservatories that Sir Joseph Paxton built in 1826— and which he used as prototypes for the Crystal Palace in London—are, alas, gone.

Another mansion, **Haddon Hall**, lies just south of Chatsworth on the River Wye. (To reach Haddon Hall from Chatsworth, follow Route B 6012 south.) This house, built from the 12th–15th centuries and surrounded by a wall that dates from the Crusades, is one of England's best-preserved Medieval palaces. Treasure that it is, it fell into disrepair and was painstakingly restored in the early 20th century. Its most notable rooms are the *chapel, the *dining room, and the *Banquet Hall. The house has a bit of romantic history: Dorothy Vernon, a 16th-century resident, eloped with Sir John Manners down the long flight of steps leading to the garden. The two lovers' families are buried in the yard of the parish church in **Bakewell**, a quiet little town on the River Wye just 3 km. (2 miles) north on Route A 6. *Matlock Bath*, 14 km. (8 miles) southwest of Chesterfield on Route A 632, is a historic spa located in a ravine forged by the River Derwent. Expect to encounter crowds in the summer, because the forested gorge is a popular excursion spot, and the town is quite near the moors and valleys of the *Peak District National Park*. A little farther south in *Cromford* are remains of the first cotton mill in Derbyshire to use hydraulic power to spin cotton. **Hardwick Hall,* 10 km. (6 miles) southeast of Chesterfield, is one of the most elegant Elizabethan mansions in England—and certainly the one with the largest expanse of windows. The house was built between 1590–1597 by Bess of Hardwick, one of the most colorful figures of the Elizabethan age. She accrued her vast wealth through her many marriages, the first one at the age of 12. **Bolsover Castle,* 9 km. (6 miles) east of Chesterfield on Route A 632, is an 11th-century Norman castle, parts of which were restored for use in a new mansion in the 17th century. The place is in ruins now, but is nonetheless intriguing. **Barlborough Hall**, 10 km. (6 miles) east of Chesterfield on Route A 619, is another Elizabethan mansion, this one dating from 1585. **Worksop**, 21 km. (13 miles) farther east on A 619, is an industrial town that has an *Augustinian priory* from 1103. Most of the abbey is in ruins, though the transept, and some of the towers survive. In **Whittington**, 3 km. (2 miles) north of Chesterfield on Route A 619, a small group of nobles met in 1688 to conspire against King James II and put his daughter, later Queen Mary II, and her husband, Prince William of Orange, on the throne. The coup succeeded, and one of the conspirators, the Earl of Devonshire, received the entire county of Devonshire in return for his part in the plot.

Sheffield (256 km.; 159 miles from London) is the center of Great Britain's steel industry. Situated at the confluence of the rivers Don and Sheaf, it is a good starting point for excursions into the moors and forested valleys of the *Peak District National Park.* Sheffield is also the place to shop for cutlery, which has been a source of the city's fame since the beginning of the Middle Ages. The town was bombed heavily during World War II and has since been blessed—or cursed, depending on your taste—with some very modern buildings. But much of the old remains, including the *cathedral,* built from the 14th–15th centuries and enlarged during the 20th century, and across from it, the *Cutlers' Hall,* built in 1832 and a good example of Victorian "Greek" architecture.

The core of Sheffield's modern city office complex is the *Town Hall,* built in pseudo-Renaissance style in 1897 and topped by a tower, 70 meters (230 feet) high, which in turn is topped by a statue of the Roman god Vulcan. The nearby *City Hall* is a classical style building from 1932. The **Graves Art Gallery* is also here. The gallery owns more than 1,500 paintings—by Rubens, Turner, Constable, and the like—

Sheffield Cathedral

and rotates them every six to eight weeks. As a result, a return visit often rewards you with a museum full of new paintings.

Just north of Sheffield M 1 veers northeast and M 18 veers northwest. M 18 leads to **Doncaster** (260 km.; 161 miles from London), another important industrial city, and an agricultural center as well. The town's claim to fame is horse racing, and none of its races is more famous than the *St. Leger,* run since 1778 (nowadays in the second week of September). The *parish church* in **Adwick-le-Street,** 7 km. (4 miles) northwest on Route A 638, is the final resting place of James and Margaret Washington, ancestors of America's first President. *Conisbrough,* 3 km. (2 miles) southwest of Doncaster on Route A 630, has a 12th-century Norman castle with a remarkably well-preserved keep—considered to be the most beautiful Norman round keep in England.

If you continue on M 1 past Sheffield you will soon come to **Leeds,** (304 km.; 188 miles from London), which has been important to the British clothing industry since Edward III settled Flemish clothmakers here. The *Abbey House Museum* shows how people lived in the 18th–19th centuries in its displays of household furnishings and crafts, and has gone so far as to re-create a street lined with inns and shops of the period. The *Leeds Industrial Museum* occupies an old woolen mill—once the world's largest—and praises the city's industrious past with its collection of old machinery and equipment. Roman antiquities are on display at the *Philosophical Hall Museum,* and the *City Art Gallery* exhibits a good collection of works by Constable, Gainsborough, and, in its new Moore Sculpture Gallery, the works of 20th-century sculptors, including those of its namesake, Henry Moore.

Leeds's most historic building is *Kirkstall Abbey,* built in the 12th century. Part of the abbey is now in ruins, but much of it remains intact, including the nave of the church, the Chapter House, and the abbot's residence. ***Harewood House,** 12 km. (7 miles) northwest off Route A 61, is an exquisite country estate that is more or less a composite of everything that was outstanding

about domestic design of the 18th century. It has ceilings by architect Robert Adam, Chippendale furniture, and a garden by Capability Brown. Leeds's other famous estate is ***Temple Newsam,** whose most famous resident was Lord Darnley, born here in 1545 and later the second husband of Mary, Queen of Scots. The new house, built in the 17th century, is now a museum that displays old furniture, silver, paintings, and other items you would expect to find in one of England's great country houses.

Highway M 1 ends in Leeds and resumes between Darlington and Newcastle (see Travel Route 26, page 263). **Bradford** (322 km.; 192 miles from London), an important industrial center well known for wool, adjoins Leeds to the west. It is nicely situated on the edge of the Yorkshire moors and Yorkshire Dales National Park (see page 249). There is a good display of the textile machinery with which the town built its fame over the years in **Bolling Hall,** a 14th-century mansion on the southern edge of town. You can see the interior of one of Bradford's fine Victorian buildings at *Millford House,* the furnished home of a 19th-century mill owner. Bradford is also the location of the *National Museum of Photography, Film, and Television,* which possesses the largest movie screen in Great Britain. *Cartwright Hall,* the city art gallery, has an impressive collection of paintings by British and foreign artists.

The North of England

It is rather hard to think about the northern stretches of England without conjuring up images of the Brontë sisters walking across the moors toward Wuthering Heights or the poet William Wordsworth musing over the Lake District's Windermere. These images aren't really so farfetched, for this northern landscape of glens and dales has inspired Englishmen for centuries, and in many parts it has changed little. The north is not all pastoral, though. Some of England's greatest industrial cities, Leeds and Sheffield among them, are in the north, as is one of the most Medieval English cities, York.

TRAVEL ROUTE 23: Leeds–Skipton–*Kendal–***Lake District

See map on page 250.

This Travel Route is a must for travellers who are literary, for it passes through two of the favorite terrains of English literature—the Yorkshire moors that inspired the Brontë sisters and the Lake District, the haunt of William Wordsworth and other Romantics. Even if literary pilgrimages are not to your taste, you couldn't find a more scenic corner of England.

There are two routes between Leeds and Skipton. The first takes you through the moors made famous by the Brontës. Leave Leeds on Route A 647 and follow it through adjoining *Bradford*. From there, Route A 650 will take you 16 km. (10 miles) north to **Keighley,** an industrial town that specializes in textiles and electrical equipment. There's not much about Keighley that will encourage you to linger—with the possible exception of *Cliffe Castle*, a Victorian mansion that houses a good collection of antiques and art, and, just east of town off Route A 650, *East Riddlesden Hall*, a finely furnished manor house built in 1640. The real attraction of Keighley is its position on the edge of the Yorkshire moors, a dramatic landscape of green fields and woods that open onto the barren heath. If you are tempted to put "cliffe" on the end of "heath," that is probably because this is exactly the terrain that Heathcliff and Cathy inhabited in Emily Brontë's Gothic novel, *Wuthering Heights*. Emily and her sisters Charlotte (who wrote *Jane Eyre*) and Anne (who wrote *The Tenant of Wildfell Hall*) lived just 7 km. (4 miles) south of Keighley in the village of *Haworth*. Their father's parsonage is now the *Brontë Parsonage Museum*, filled with mementos of the women and their manuscripts.

Charlotte and Emily are buried in the village churchyard, and you can walk out of town across their beloved bleak moors to *Far Withens,* 5 km. (3 miles) away, the estate that may be the model for the one in *Wuthering Heights.*

You will encounter more of this landscape as you drive north from Keighley about 14 km. (8.5 miles) on Route A 629 into **Skipton,** which lies on the edge of *Yorkshire Dales National Park.* The Park encompasses a terrain of dales and steep hills, of limestone crags and cascading rivers, of ruined abbeys and desolate moors. Travel Route 26 also leads through some of the park's most beautiful dales.

You will also see some of the park if you travel from Leeds to Skipton directly on Routes A 660 and A 65. Leaving Leeds on A 60, you can travel 17 km. (11 miles) to *Otley,* an industrial town where Thomas Chippendale, England's great furniture maker, was born in 1711. Just 11 km. (7 miles) up Route A 660 is the far more interesting town of **Ilkley.** Prehistoric man and then the Romans saw the advantages of this spot above the River Wharfe, overlooking the moors. The Romans built a fort at Ilkley, the foundations of which now lie beneath a beautiful 16th-century *manor house* (with a good museum of local history) and the parish *church of All Saints.* The moors around the town are still studded with ancient man-made rock formations, some of them inscribed with Bronze Age markings. Before you continue the 14 km. (9 miles) into Skipton on Route A 59, you may want to make a short side trip of 7 km. (4 miles) up Route B 6160 to ***Bolton Priory,** a 12th-century abbey that is now in delightful ruins. From the priory you can make a pleasant drive—better yet, walk—into the surrounding *Bolton Woods.* One of the most popular excursion spots is *The Strid,* where the River Wharfe broils through a narrow gorge (follow signs). The river gives this section of the Yorkshire Dales its name—*Wharfedale.*

From the abbey a narrow road leads about 5 km. (3 miles) to *Barden Tower,* a Medieval lodge built for gamekeepers of the Forest of Barden. The place has been restored several times over the centuries, but has once again fallen into disrepair. Whatever route you have taken to Skipton, by now you will no doubt be enchanted by the Yorkshire Dales. You may want to stop at Skipton's *tourist information bureau* on High Street for brochures, maps, and other information on the region, including walking maps—those who know the region well say the only way to appreciate its full beauty is to hike across the top of the ridges. The best places to get information on the park are the outlets of the *National Park Information Centre* (the closest one is in *Grassington;* see below).

Before leaving Skipton for the alluring hills, take time to tour **Skipton Castle,* a 12th-century

Norman structure—with many later additions, including its 14th-century towers—that from 1307–1955 was the home of the earls of Cumberland. Even if you are just passing through the region on

ROUTE 23
(Leeds to Lake District)

your way north, you may want to take time out for a short excursion from Skipton north for 13 km. (8 miles) on Route B 6265 to **Grassington,** a scenic little place above the River Wharfe. Even if you go no farther than its pleasant *folk museum* in the town square, you will get an idea of the quiet beauty of these wooded dales. If you are up to a walk, by all means take a hike about 5 km. (3 miles) outside of town to *Kilnsey Crag,* one of the dramatic limestone cliffs that punctuate the hillsides. The *National Park Information Centre* in town is a good source of material on the park.

From Skipton, Route A 65 continues north through lovely landscape for 23 km. (14 miles) to **Settle,** an old town from which you can explore the surrounding wild country. The heart of this area is *Malham,* about 10 km. (6 miles) from Settle on narrow back roads (follow signs). There is another *National Parks Information Centre* in Malham, so you can get maps and advice about the must-sees. They will probably include the large lake of *Malham Tarn* and **Gordale Scar,* a geological formation that is often compared to the Grand Canyon. (The Scar is lovely, but no match.)

Route A 62 now continues north another 12 km. (7.5 miles) to **Clapham,** a small town (with another *information center*) that is overwhelmed by the **Ingleborough,* which at about 700 meters (2,400 feet) is one of the tallest of the Yorkshire hills and one of three peaks known as the "Alps Pennina." A trail, 40 km. (24 miles) long, connects the Ingleborough with the other two, *Pen-y-Ghent* and *Whernside*. Even if you are not up to a trek of that length, it is a fairly easy climb to the top of the Ingleborough from Clapham, and the views are worth the exertion. Clapham has its underground wonder, too: the *Ingleborough Cave*, filled with stalactites and stalagmites.

In another 7 km. (4 miles) Route A 65 comes to **Ingleton**. There's an easy walk to be had here along the *Glens*, a ravine in which two streams converge in a series of waterfalls. Charlotte Brontë attended the *Clergy Daughters' School* another 6 km. (3.5 miles) up the road in *Cowan Bridge*. (She described her school life here in *Jane Eyre*.) In 9 km. (6 miles) you come to **Kirby Lonsdale**. The town is picturesque, but its views over the River Lune and the surrounding countryside are even more so. The great landscape artist Joseph Turner painted the view from the *churchyard of St. Mary the Virgin* (a Norman masterpiece that is worth a good look itself), and the essayist John Ruskin praised it. Route A 65 continues north another 21 km. (13 miles) to *Kendal* (113 km.; 70 miles). Kendal, an old wool-making town, has plenty to recommend it—Catherine Parr, the sixth and last wife of Henry VIII, was born in its ruined castle; the *clock tower* atop the town hall chimes the hour in English, Welsh, Scottish, and Irish songs; and there is good fishing on the River Kent. The town's greatest lure, however, is its position at the foot of the Lake District.

***The Lake District

See color map.

The Lake District is not particularly large (only 90 square km.; 35 square miles). The longest of its famous lakes stretches for only 17 km. (10.5 miles), and the tallest of its acclaimed peaks, *Scafield Pike*, is only 950 meters (3,200 feet) high. What makes the Lake District so beautiful is the way this landscape comes together—the way its green slopes plummet into icy lake waters, the way its green meadows are dotted with limestone cottages. There you can, as William Wordsworth did, walk "through bare grey dell, high wood, and pastoral cove." There is also something about the compactness in combination with the variety of the Lake District that makes it a special haven for travellers. We outline two drives that more or less make a circuit of the lakes. If you have the time—a week or two, preferably—enjoy the lakes the way that Jane Austen and generations of other travellers (many of them literary types) have, by walking the trails and ferrying across on steamers.

You might begin your tour in

the *tourist information office* in *Kendal,* where you can stock up on brochures and maps. To begin a drive of the district, leave Kendal on Route A 591, which in about 14 km. (9 miles) comes to **Windermere,** a tourist town on the lake of the same name. With the adjacent town of *Bowness,* Windermere is sort of the center of operations for the Lake District. For example, there is no better place to learn about the region than at the nearby *Brockhole Lake District National Park Visitor Centre.* Especially in the summer, when the town tends to be crowded, Windermere is not the best place to take in the serenity for which the region is so famous. But if you want quiet, it is as close as a short row into the waters of the lovely lake. You can also steam across the lake on one of the boats at the *Windermere Steamboat Museum* (steamers leave from several other docks in town, too) or take a train along the River Leven on the *Lakeside and Haverthwaite Railway.*

From Windermere follow Route A 592 through the steep *Kirkstone Pass* to what is considered to be the most beautiful of the lakes, *Ullswater.* Follow the road along the steep shores for 24 km. (15 miles)—an incredibly beautiful drive—to the little town of **Pooley Bridge.** If you want to leave the car behind, you can also take a steamer the length of Ullswater from the village of *Glenridding* to Pooley Bridge. Pooley plays a part in the region's

ancient history—just outside the town, at the site of 13th-century *Dacre Castle* (a private home), the kings of England, Scotland, and Cumberland met in 927. As you drive on Route B 5320 from Pooley Bridge to *Penrith,* you will pass two ancient earthwork mounds, one of them called *"King Arthur's Round Table,"* the other one *"Mayburgh."* From Penrith you can follow Route A 6 along the eastern edge of the Lake District back to *Kendal,* a drive of about 44 km. (27 miles).

From Kendal you may choose to explore other regions of the Lake District by following Route A 591 through *Windermere* and along the eastern shore of the lake to its northern tip and **Ambleside,** a town that is prettier than Windermere (even though it lies just out of sight of the lake) and is more accessible to beautiful, less crowded terrain. It is hard to imagine visiting the town without paying a visit to the *church of St. Mary* with its chapel in memory of the man who sang the praises of the Lake District, William Wordsworth. The town's other man-made attraction is the tiny stone *bridge house,* now an information center, that once housed a basket weaver, his wife and six children—a reminder that the simple life is not always a picnic. The real attractions of Ambleside, though, are the mountains that surround it, and you may indeed amble into them. One of the most pleasant climbs—quite easy—is up

Ambleside: Old Bridge House

Loughrigg Fell, from the heights of which you will enjoy unforgettable views toward **Grasmere.** You may descend into this town, or make the short drive there of about 2 km. (3 miles) on Route 591. For many visitors, Grasmere is the Lake District. Wordsworth lived here, and he called it the "loveliest spot man hath ever known." You may think otherwise on a summer's day when the village is crowded with tourists. But looking at the surrounding peaks, including *Helvellyn,* the region's tallest, and the still waters of its pretty lake, the Grasmere, it is easy to see what the poet meant. Wordsworth, his wife, and his sister Dorothy lie in the yard of the *church of St. Oswald.* You can pay homage to him at *Dove Cottage,* where he lived from 1799–1808, then see his manuscripts and other memorabilia in the adjacent *Wordsworth Museum.* Wordsworth's last home, *Rydal Mount*

(no simple cottage) is also nearby and open to the public. (You can make a pleasant walk to the house from Grasmere along the shores of Rydal Water.) Actually, there's no better way to enjoy the scenery than to walk the many trails from Grasmere into the surrounding fells. One of the most popular short walks is the one to *Tongue Gill Force,* a waterfall about one km. (half a mile) outside the village. From Grasmere, you can follow Route A 591 about 26 km. (16 miles) north to **Keswick,** on the shores of the dramatic *Derwentwater,* a lake rimmed by the wooded slopes of some of the tallest mountains in England. Derwentwater is all the more beautiful because it is dotted with little islands, and if you are tempted to rent a boat and row out to one, do so; most of them are now owned by the National Trust. A popular ascent—a day's outing—from

Derwentwater

Keswick is the climb up *Skiddaw,* one of the region's highest.

Keswick has several notable man-made attractions, too. The *Castlerigg Stone Circle* 3 km. (2 miles) east, is the work of Bronze Age man, who used this magnificent plateau with its incredible views for rituals. The *Cumberland Pencil Factory* on Main Street is a reminder that the area's graphite deposits made Keswick the world's first manufacturer of pencils, in 1558. The *Fitz Park Museum and Art Gallery* has relics of Wordsworth, Hugh Walpole, Samuel Coleridge, and other literary lions who frequented the lakes. From Keswick you may take Route A 66 east for 27 km. (17 miles) to *Penrith* (see page 252), where you can get onto Superhighway M 6 for the drive north to *Carlisle* (see page 257) and Scotland. You may also drive to Carlisle on a much more scenic route through the northern extremes of the Lake District by taking Route A 591 to *Bothel* and then taking Route A 595 west. On either route, the trip to Carlisle is about 50 km. (30 miles).

From Keswick you may also cross the *Whinlatter Pass* and drop into **Buttermere,** a pleasant village near the lake of the same name. (You can also walk to Buttermere from Keswick across the meadows and ridges.) This western section of the Lake District is a little wilder and less visited than the section around Windermere. You may also want to explore the southern section, around *Conistonwater*. The main village here, **Coniston,** was to John Ruskin as Ambleside was to Wordsworth. The essayist is buried in the churchyard, and his manuscripts and personal effects—including his rock collection—are on display at the *Ruskin Museum. Brantwood,* his estate on the east side of the lake, is open to the public. The most popular walk from Coniston is the one to *Coniston Old Man,* a rock-faced summit to the west of town.

TRAVEL ROUTE 24: Manchester (–Liverpool)–Preston (–*Blackpool)–Lancaster–*Kendal–*Carlisle (–Glasgow) (191 km.; 118 miles)

See map on page 256.

Since the mid-19th century the factory workers in industrial Britain have spent their leisure time at resorts on the northwest coast. This Travel Route visits both seats of industry, such as Lancaster, and seats of pleasure, such as Blackpool. It ends in the Lake District, one of the most beautiful regions in the world.

There are two routes from Manchester (see page 206) to Preston. The first and shortest follows M 61, then A 49 north through *Chorley*.

The second, more interesting, route runs north via **Bolton,** an industrial town known for its cotton spinning plants. It is surrounded by many large mansions. ***Smithill's Hall,** northwest of Bolton, was built in the 14th century and incorporates some later additions. The timbered buildings and paneled *Great Hall* are particularly well-preserved. ***Hall i' th' Wood,** to the north, is a fine half-timbered house built in 1493. Samuel Crompton, who invented the spinning mule, a machine that revolutionized the textile industry, lived here for many years. It now houses a folk museum. **Turton Tower,** also to the north, is a 12th-century Norman mansion. Remodeled in the 16th century, it is now a museum.

Leave Bolton from the north on A 666 and continue to **Blackburn,** a center of the cotton industry since the 14th century, when Flemish weavers settled here. The *Lewis Textile Museum* on Exchange Street traces the history of this important industry. *Hoghton Tower* is a fine 16th-century fortified mansion just outside of Blackburn. Its banqueting hall is striking, and it is here that James I is supposed to have dubbed a loin of beef Sir Loin. The town provides a good base for excursions into the valley of the River Ribble. Continue west to **Preston** (52 km.; 32 miles from Manchester), an important commercial port that owes its prosperity to the cotton industry.

Take A 583 west to ***Blackpool,** one of the biggest and busiest seaside resorts in Europe. Some seven million people vacation here each year. As a result, the town has been called the most beautiful amusement park in the world. Blackpool's beach is flanked by an 11-km.- (7-mile-) long shore *promenade*. (Its fine beach is called the "Magnificent Seven.") The annual, autumnal *Illumination of Blackpool,* in which the promenade becomes a riot of light, draws people from all over the area. The 160-meter- (525-foot-) high **Blackpool Tower,* built in 1894, is a sort of Tower of Babylon, with a roof garden (from which a panoramic view of the Pennine Mountains, the Lake District, and the Isle of Man can be had), an aquarium, a zoo, a circus, and a ballroom that can accommodate 2,500 people.

Other sights in Blackpool include an *ice palace;* three *amusement piers;* several *amusement parks;* the largest indoor *swimming pool* in Great Britain; and *Stanley Park,* a garden containing over 30,000 roses. A single track railway runs along the beach, and horse-drawn carriages carry passengers through the town.

Lytham St. Anne's, a beach resort south of Blackpool, has four championship golf courses. North of Blackpool are the resorts

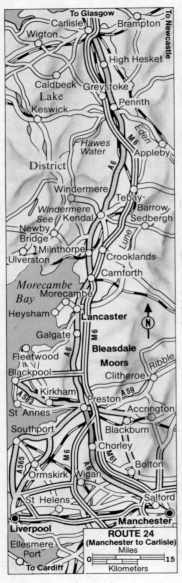

ROUTE 24
(Manchester to Carlisle)

of *Thorton-Cleveleys* and *Fleetwood*.

Return to Preston, and continue north on A 6 through the lovely *Bleasdale Moors*. Side roads lead off the highway to the many picturesque villages that dot the heather-covered hills. (Alternatively, you can follow M 6 directly to Lancaster.)

Situated at the mouth of the River Lune, **Lancaster** (84 km.; 52 miles from Manchester) is dominated by a Norman *castle* built by William the Conqueror and later expanded by John of Gaunt, Duke of Lancaster. George Fox, who founded the Quakers, was imprisoned behind its thick walls from 1663–1665. The city's 15th-century *church of St. Mary* contains beautiful oak pews that were hewn in 1340. Lancaster's *city museum* also has an interesting collection of archaeological and historic exhibits, as well as works by local artists.

Lancaster is a good center for excursions to *Morecambe* and *Heysham,* two ancient villages that grew until they merged into one lively seaside resort. Both afford beautiful views over Morecambe Bay to the mountains of the Lake District.

Continue north on A 6 through *Carnforth* to *Milnthorpe*. Just past Milnthorpe, A 590 branches west into the Lake District (see page 251).

Follow A 6 north to ***Leven's Hall,** one of the largest Eliz-

Leven's Hall

abethan mansions in south Cumbria, surrounded by a 100-acre park. Its rooms are paneled and decorated with splendid stucco.

Continue north to ***Sizergh Castle,** a 14th-century mansion that has been the seat of the Strickland family for 700 years. It has a marvelous *tower* and a beautiful Tudor *hall.* Continue north to **Kendal* (see page 252).

A 6 now begins to climb the 400-meter- (1,312-foot-) hill of *Shap Fells.* From the summit, there is a wonderful panoramic view.

Descend through Shap to ***Penrith,** a market town of red sandstone that presents a deceptively peaceful appearance to visitors today; in fact, it has seen more battles (against Scottish invaders) than any other city in England. Many of the old houses are built in fortified fashion around quadrangles, accessible only by a single low archway, making them easy to defend. The ruins of the massive **Penrith Castle* date from the 15th century. King Richard III lived for a time in the **Gloucester Arms Inn,* and there are contemporary portraits of the King and his predecessor Richard II in Penrith's *parish church.* In the church cemetery there is a monument called **Giant's Grave,* which is more than 1,000 years old.

Penrith is a good base for excursions into the Lake District (see page 251). *Ullswater Lake* is just to the southwest. To the west of Penrith lie the wild *Cumberland Hills,* scene of many fierce border battles between the Scots and the English.

From Penrith, continue north on A 6 through *High Hesket* to ***Carlisle** (191 km.; 118 miles from Manchester).

For 300 years, Carlisle marked the northern outpost of the Roman Empire, and it is quite close to Hadrian's Wall (see Travel Route 31, page 274).When the Romans abandoned the frontier in the fourth century, the Scots conquered Carlisle. They, in turn, were driven out by King Arthur and his army. In 1092, King William Rufus built a large Norman **castle* in Carlisle. Mary Stuart, Queen of Scots, was imprisoned in the castle's *Queen Mary's Tower* in 1568. Carlisle was the site of constant frontier warfare between England and Scotland until 1745, when the city surrendered to Bonnie Prince Charlie and his army of Scottish highlanders.

The city's **cathedral,* built between 1093–1133, was the site of novelist Sir Walter Scott's marriage in 1797. The old *town granary* and the **city museum,* which has a good exhibit of Roman antiquities, are both worth visiting. Carlisle is a good center for excursions into the Lake District and the border area between England and Scotland.

North of Carlisle, A 74 crosses the Scottish border, passes the mouth of the River Liddel, traverses the Solway Firth, and proceeds directly to *Glasgow* (149 km.; 92 miles from Manchester).

Carlisle Cathedral

TRAVEL ROUTE 25: ****Lincoln–***York (118 km.; 73 miles)

See map on page 260.

The Yorkshire Wolds, between the cities of Lincoln and York, are a chain of hills flanked by flat, fertile plains. This Travel Route traverses the Wolds to connect these two fascinating cities.

From Lincoln (see page 75), there are two routes to York: through Hull or through Selby (see page 259).

To go through Hull, leave Lincoln on Newport Street and follow A 15 north through *Caenby Corner* and *Brigg* to *Barton-upon-Humber*. Cross the new Humber Bridge and proceed to **Hull**, formally called Kingston-upon-Hull.

The third largest port in England (after London and Liverpool), and one of the largest fishing ports in the world, Hull sits on the wide mouth of the River Humber. It has a modern ferry port, with connections to the Continent. Among Hull's attractions are: the 14th- and 15th-century *Holy Trinity Church,* one of the largest parish churches in England; the 16th-century *Grammar School;* the *archaeology museum;* the *transportation museum* featuring vintage cars; the *Ferens Art Gallery,* known particularly for its collection of landscape paintings by Old Masters; and the 17th-century **Wilberforce House,* where abolitionist William Wilberforce was born in 1759. The house is now a museum. The town's most recent attraction is the *Humber Bridge,* which crosses the River Humber and is the world's longest single-span suspension bridge.

From Hull, follow A 1079 northwest to ***Beverley,** a town of many 18th-century houses. ****Beverley Minster,** at the south end of main street, was built between the 13th–14th centuries on the site of an eighth-century church. The original church was one of the best-known pilgrimage sites in northern England, as well as a haven for fugitives. Anyone who managed to reach the *frith stool* (chair of peace) in the church's minster came under the protection of the church. This stone chair can still be seen; sadly, it no longer provides protection from the law. The *choir* and *transept* are in Early English style; the *nave* is in Decorated and English Gothic style, as is the beautiful **West Front,* with its two towers. The church's most precious treasure is the elaborately carved Percy Tomb, built in the 14th century. There are fanciful carvings of angels, symbolic beasts, and other subjects throughout the church.

*St. Mary's Church, at the north end of main street, was built in the 14th–15th centuries. Of particular interest are its central *tower;* the **west façade,* built in a transitional style between Decorated and English Gothic; and the large **southern portal,* with an inner Norman arch and an outer Early English arch. The church's interior is rich in 15th- and 16th-century sculptures. Behind St. Mary's is the *North Bar Gate,* dating from

1409, and the last remaining of the city's five Medieval gates.

Continue northwest on A 1079 through the Yorkshire Wolds, a chain of grass-covered limestone hills curving toward the sea. The flat, fertile plains that stretch away from the Wolds provide Northern England with a rich wheat-producing region.

Follow A 1079 past small quiet villages, many of which have lovely parish churches and markets that spring to life on market days. Shortly past the town of *Hayton,* a worthwhile side trip on A 1247 leads east to the market town of ***Pocklington,** where you will find several Medieval churches and the magnificent **Burnby Hall Gardens,* built around lily ponds.

Return to A 1079 and continue to ****York* (122 km.; 76 miles; see page 104).

The second route from Lincoln to York passes through Selby. From Lincoln, you have your choice of two routes to Selby.

The first leaves Lincoln from the north on A 15. Just before *Brigg,* turn west onto A 18. **Scunthorpe,** on A 18, is a seat of the region's busy iron and steel industry. In the town *museum* are some interesting prehistoric artifacts. Continue west on A 18 across the River Trent and through the *Levels,* flat plains that were drained in the 17th century. Today, peat is collected from the bogs in this area. Near *Thorne,* a small town on the River Don, turn north onto A 614 to **Selby.*

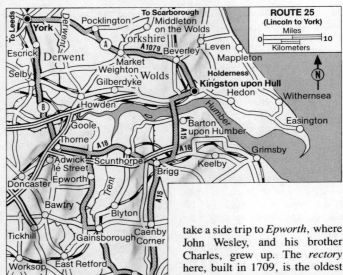

take a side trip to *Epworth*, where John Wesley, and his brother Charles, grew up. The *rectory* here, built in 1709, is the oldest Methodist pilgrimage site in the world. Return to Gainsborough, and continue to ***Selby**, an industrial town situated on the River Ouse. Despite its riverfront location, it can accommodate only small ocean-going vessels at high tide. It is famous for its **Abbey Church*, part of a Benedictine abbey built in 1097. Although the church was partially destroyed by fire in 1906, it is one of the best preserved Medieval monastery churches in England, still lit by beautiful stained-glass windows. Its 100-meter- (328-foot-) long Norman *nave* dates from the 12th century. The *Triforium* is Early English, and the *choir* is Decorated style.

The second route from Lincoln to Selby proceeds northwest, to **Gainsborough,** situated on the River Trent. The town's *Old Hall,* a 15th-century mansion, has an interesting history. It hosted King Richard III in 1484 and in 1540 it was the meeting place of King Henry VIII and Catherine Parr, who later became his sixth wife. The mansion was also the first meeting place of the English Pilgrims (who later went to America). John Wesley, a founder of the Methodists, often preached here. The Old Hall is now a museum.

From Gainsborough you can

From Selby, travel north on A 19 to *****York** (118 km.; 73 miles; see page 104).

TRAVEL ROUTE 26: Leeds–*Harrogate–Darlington–Newcastle-upon-Tyne–Carter Bar (–Edinburgh) (234 km.; 145 miles)

See map on page 262.

The romantic Yorkshire Moors have captured the imagination of people all over the world. They are the background for one of literature's most romantic love stories, Emily Brontë's *Wuthering Heights*. This Travel Route traverses the moors and visits many interesting towns, from the spa and resort of Harrogate to the industrial centers of Darlington and Durham.

From *Leeds* (see page 247) drive north past *Harewood,* and the famous *Harewood House* (see page 247) to ***Harrogate.** This spa's 88 *mineral springs* claim to heal gout, inflammation, rheumatism, skin problems, and other ailments, and Harrogate's opera house, theaters, concert halls, and ballrooms make it an entertaining place in which to take a cure. Among the city's many parks and gardens, the largest is the *Valley Gardens.* The *Harlow Car Gardens,* just outside of town, are home to the Northern Horticultural Society. Harrogate's resort season starts in July, with the *Hallé Music Festival,* and continues through October. The town is a good base for excursions into the Yorkshire Moors.

From Harrogate continue north on A 61 to ***Ripley,** where the 14th-century Ripley **castle,* home to the Ingilby family since 1350, stands in a huge garden. It has an interesting tower, constructed in 1550, and a gatehouse built in 1450.

North of Ripley, and west of A 61, is ****Fountains Abbey,** a beautiful and beautifully preserved abbey founded in 1132 by a group of Benedictine monks who adopted Cistercian rules and became prosperous in the local wool trade. Despite the abbey's remote location—one observer said it was "fit more for the dens of wild beasts than for uses of man"—its intricately designed *nave* and the *Chapel of the Nine Altars* are considered to be architectural masterpieces, and even its drainage system is remarkable.

Return to A 61 and continue north. An access road leads to *Markenfield Hall,* a mansion built between the 14th–16th centuries.

*Ripon, on A 61, is set in the Yorkshire Moors. Its small, beautiful **cathedral* stands on the remains of a seventh-century Saxon church. The cathedral, which was begun in 1154 and completed in the 16th century, incorporates several building styles. The *west façade,* with its two Early English towers, is the only one of its kind in England; the choir is in English Gothic, as

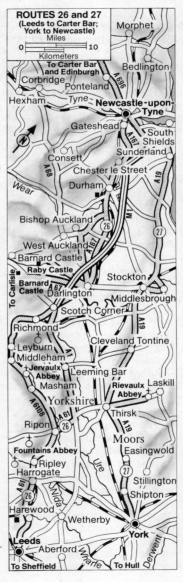

ROUTES 26 and 27
(Leeds to Carter Bar;
York to Newcastle)

Miles
0   10
Kilometers

To Carter Bar
and Edinburgh
Corbridge
Ponteland
Hexham   Tyne   **Newcastle-upon-Tyne**
Gateshead
South Shields
Consett   Sunderland
Chester le Street
Durham
Wear
Bishop Auckland
West Auckland
Barnard Castle
Raby Castle
Barnard Castle   Stockton
Darlington
Middlesbrough
Scotch Corner
Richmond
Cleveland   Tontine
Leyburn
Middleham
Jervaulx Abbey   Leeming Bar
Masham   **Rievaulx Abbey**   Laskill
Yorkshire
Thirsk
Ripon
Moors
Easingwold
Fountains Abbey
Ripley
Harrogate
Stillington
Shipton
Harewood
Wetherby   **York**
Leeds
Aberford
To Sheffield   Wharfe   To Hull
Morphet
Bedlington
To Carlisle
Nidd
Ure
Derwent

are the transepts and towers. In the Saxon crypt is a narrow opening called *St. Wilford's Needle*. According to tradition, anyone who can pass through the opening is chaste.

At the center of Ripon lies the *marketplace,* marked by a 30-meter- (98-foot-) obelisk bearing a carving of the town's coat of arms. The 13th-century **Wakeman's House,* now a museum, is also on the marketplace. In the town hall are Ripon's coat of arms, and *Wakeman's Horn,* which was presented to Ripon in 866. Following a centuries-old tradition, an official horn blower sounds the horn every evening at nine.

A worthwhile side trip can be made east from Ripon on B 6265 to ***Newby Hall**, which the architect Robert Adam designed in the 18th century. Inside you'll find one of the largest collections of classical statues in England, as well as some valuable tapestries. The mansion's **garden* is especially beautiful.

Shortly past Ripon, A 61 intersects A 1, the Great North Road. If you wish, you can go directly on to Scotch Corner on A 1. However, a longer and more interesting route begins in Ripon and follows A 6108 northwest through some of the most beautiful parts of Yorkshire.

Just past the large, picturesque market town of *Masham,* on the banks of the River Ure, is **Jervaulx Abbey,* founded by Cistercians in 1156 and now in ruins.

From Land's End, Cornwall's westernmost point, you can see as far as the Isles of Scilly.

South of Rugby, in central England, the Oxford Canal meanders through a picturesque landscape.

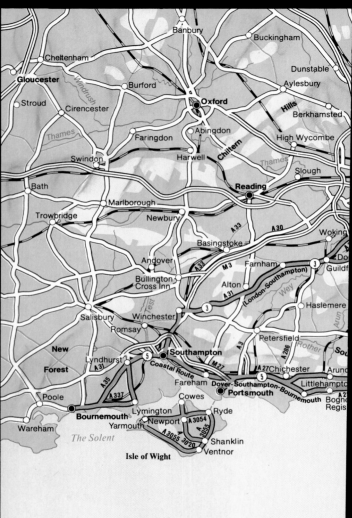

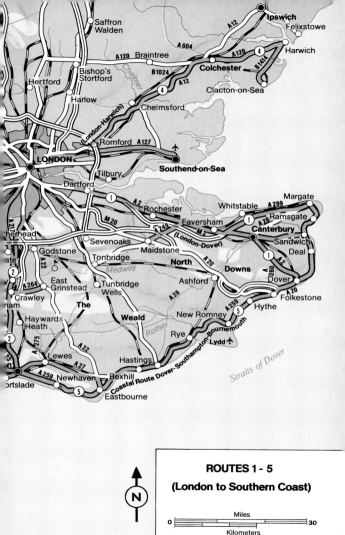

ROUTES 1 - 5

(London to Southern Coast)

Miles

0   30

Kilometers

N

Old manor houses visibly express one facet of the British way of life. This house stands near Bredon, to the northeast of Tewkesbury.

Cliveden House, a majestic mansion surrounded by expansive gardens, lies to the northeast of Maidenhead.

Lake District National Park, situated in the heart of Cumbria County, offers one of the most beautiful landscapes in England.

A magnificent view of Durham's massive Norman cathedral can be enjoyed from Prebend's Bridge, across the River Wear.

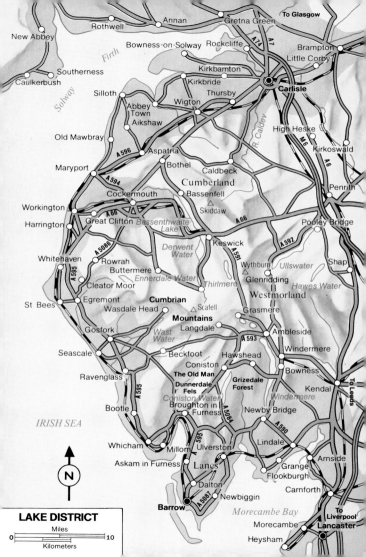

Perched atop a steep rock, Harlech Castle overlooks the Welsh town of the same name.

Mount Snowdon, the highest mountain in Wales, lends its name to Snowdonia National Park.

Even so, its Chapter House is a fine example of Early English style. *Middleham,* on A 6108, is the location of *Middleham Castle,* built in 1170. This castle, now mostly in ruins, was a favorite residence of King Richard III. His son, Edward, died there in 1484. Both the Norman *keep* and the 13th-century outer *walls* are well preserved. Beyond the castle is a moor where race horses from local stables take their exercise every morning. You can make a side trip south from Middleham to the ruins of *Coverham Abbey,* built in 1212.

Return to A 6108 and continue northwest across the River Ure to the town of *Leyburn.* From this vantage point, you'll receive a magnificent view of *Wensleydale,* the broadest of Yorkshire's valleys. It is watered by the Ure and has three spectacular waterfalls. Its marvelous landscape was celebrated in many of William Wordsworth's poems. Excellent hiking paths lead into the valley from Leyburn.

Continue north on A 6108 through the lonely moors of *Bellerby* and *Barden.* On Barden moor, a side road leads west to the ruins of *Ellerton Abbey,* and then farther west to the 12th-century *Marrick Priory.*

A 6108 continues north through the wild *valley* of the River Swale to **Richmond,** an attractive town rich in historic buildings. Its massive Norman *castle,* now in ruins, was built in 1071 by Alan Rufus, the Earl of

Richmond. The castle's magnificent *keep* towers over the Norman gatehouse. Other interesting buildings in Richmond include an English Gothic *tower,* once part of a Medieval monastery, and the *Theatre Royal,* a Georgian theater built in 1788 that is the second oldest theater in operation in England. From Richmond, A 6108 leads northeast to *Scotch Corner.*

From Scotch Corner, follow A 1 northeast to **Darlington** (96 km.; 59 miles from Leeds), an historically important industrial center. England's first railway line was opened here in 1825 by George Stephenson and Edward Pease. The train achieved a speed of 14 km. (8 miles) per hour, an incredible feat at the time. Stephenson's steam engine, *Locomotion,* is on view in *Bank Top Station.* Also in Darlington is *St. Cuthbert,* a church built between 1180–1200, with a lovely 14th-century belltower.

Two interesting side trips can be made from Darlington. **Raby Castle,** west on Route 6279 was built between the 11th–14th centuries. The former residence of the Nevilles and the Vanes, it is one of the largest inhabited Medieval castles in England (open to the public during spring and summer). Of particular interest are its *picture gallery* and its lovely garden. **Barnard Castle** is west of Darlington on A 67. It is the location of the *Bowes Museum,* housed in an impressive mansion built between 1869–1875 after

Bowes Museum

the style of a French château. The museum's fine collection includes paintings by El Greco, Goya, Primaticcio, Tiepolo, Boucher, Courbet, and other artists; Sèvres and Meissen porcelain; valuable tapestries, portraits, and historic artifacts; old manuscripts; and many other works of art. The museum also contains a display depicting the life-style of a 19th-century lead-mine worker.

From Darlington, there are two routes to Durham. The most direct is via A 167 north through *Aycliffe,* with its 13th-century church and two Saxon market crosses. The longer and more interesting route leads northwest on A 68 to **Bishop Auckland.**

Placed at the confluence of the rivers Wear and Gaunless, spanned by a 14th-century *bridge,* Bishop Auckland has been the country seat of the bishops of Durham since the 12th century. The 16th-century *castle,* with a 13th-century chapel, stands in a 150-acre *park. Escombe,* just west of Bishop Auckland, has a beautifully preserved, gemlike *parish church* built in the seventh century with stones from an earlier Roman castle called Vinovium.

From Bishop Auckland, take A 688 east and rejoin A 167; continue north to ****Durham,** situated on a forested peninsula on the River Wear. Although the city is surrounded by factories and coal mines, it is one of the loveliest in England. Its massive ***cathedral,* founded in 1092, has some beautifully preserved Norman sections. It is thought to be the first church where ribbed vaulting was used on a large scale. The *vault* in its *nave* may be the oldest Gothic vault in Europe. The cathedral's interior is richly ornamented: note especially the **choir,* the **throne of the archbishop,* the *bishops' graves,* and 12th- and 13th-century *wall paintings.* The bones of Saint Cuthbert, who died in 687, are interred behind the high altar. A beautiful view of the cathedral can be had from *Prebend's Bridge* across the Wear.

**Durham Castle,* founded in 1072 by William the Conqueror, stands on a narrow neck of land and once guarded the approach to Durham. Its *doorway is one of the most beautiful examples of Norman Romanesque art in Great Britain. The Norman *chapel* is well-preserved, as are the *state rooms* containing 16th-century Flemish tapestries; a Renaissance *stairway;* and a 14th-century

Durham Cathedral

keep, which was restored in 1840. The *University of Durham* surrounds the cathedral and the castle, and parts of the university have been housed in the castle since 1836. The 13th-century *Great Hall* is now a students' dining room.

Also of interest in Durham are the 12th-century *Elvert Bridge* and the 14th-century *Guildhall.* Just north of Durham are the ruins of the Augustinian **Finchale Priory,* built in the 12th–13th centuries on the banks of the River Wear.

From Durham, continue on A 167 north to the mining center of *Chester-le-Street,* which has an interesting parish church. Just to the east is the 14th-century *Lumley Castle.* Continue north on A 1 to **Newcastle-upon-Tyne** (185 km.; 115 miles from Leeds). This commercial center is situated on the River Tyne, one of the only rivers that flows from the

North Sea. Its important industries include coal, railway manufacture, and shipyards. The city is named after a *castle* built in 1083 by Robert Curthose, a son of William the Conqueror. The castle's **keep* is well-preserved; its 13th-century *gatehouse* is now a museum of Roman antiquities. Newcastle's *university* also houses an **antiquities museum,* which displays Great Britain's most valuable collection of Roman and Roman-British artifacts.

The city's most notable structures are products of the Industrial Age. The *High Level Bridge* is a street and railroad crossing constructed between 1846–1849 by Robert Stephenson, a son of George Stephenson, Britain's railroad pioneer. When it was built, it was considered to be one of England's premier technological wonders. The **Tyne Bridge* is a steel-arch structure built in 1928. The Tyne tunnel, connecting Jarrow and Howdon streets, cuts under the mouth of the river for almost 1.5 km. (1 mile).

There are many old churches in town, including the 15th-century *cathedral,* with its remarkable tower. The *Laing Art Gallery* has an interesting collection of paintings and craftwork.

From Newcastle, the quickest route to Scotland is via A 696 northwest through *Ponteland.* Placed at the edge of the wild moor landscape of Northumbria, Ponteland's church dates from the 12th century. Continue north-west through *Otterburn* and *Redesdale,* and then on A 68. Past *Catcleugh Reservoir,* you'll reach the Scottish border in the *Cheviot Hills* near *Carter Bar.* Highway 68 continues northwest to *Edinburgh.*

TRAVEL ROUTE 27: ***York–Thirsk–Middlesbrough–Sunderland–Newcastle-upon-Tyne (140 km.; 87 miles)

See map on page 262.

This travel route runs parallel to Travel Route 26, and takes in much of the same romantic scenery of the Yorkshire Moors.

Leave *York* (see page 104) through Bootham Bar Gate, and pick up A 19 north. At *Shipton* you can take a side trip west to the 18th-century *Beningbrough Hall,* which has lovely friezes, a re-markable staircase, and a number of richly paneled rooms.

Continue north on A 19 through *Easingwold* to **Thirsk** (37 km.; 23 miles from York), a charming old town with an inter-esting English Gothic *parish church.* About 20 km. (12 miles) east of town is ***Rievaulx Abbey,** founded by the Cister-cians in 1131. The Early English *choir* and the *chapter house* still stand. An excellent panoramic view of the moors can be had from a small hill east of the abbey. Farther east is *Helmsley,* site of the ruins of a Norman *castle.* Interesting 18th-century country houses are scattered through the area.

Continue north on A 19 to ***Cleveland Tontine** and the **Mount Grace Priory.* Built in 1397, this Carthusian monastery is quite well preserved. Drive through *Egglescliffe* to *Stockton-on-Tees,* an important industrial town on the River Tees. Shipyards and iron and steel mills are the chief industries here. The neigh-boring town to the east is **Middlesbrough,** an important in-dustrial center and commercial port at the mouth of the River Tees. The town of *Marton,* to the south, is the birthplace of Captain James Cook, the famous 18th-century explorer, in 1728.

Cross the Tees and continue north on A 19 to **Sunderland** (120 km.; 74 miles from York). The town, situated at the mouth of the River Wear, is still depen-dent for its livelihood on ship-building, an industry that began here in 1346. Coal is also an important source of revenue. The windows of many of England's most famous cathedrals, includ-ing those in St. Paul's Cathedral in London and the cathedral in Coventry, were made in the town's glassworks.

About 7 km. (4 miles) west of Sunderland lies *Washington Old Hall,* the residence from 1183–1630 of the Washington family, forebears of George Washington. Parts of the original 12th-century mansion are incorporated into the newer structure, which was erected in 1610. Restored with U.S. funding, it is now an historical museum.

From Sunderland, continue west on A 1844 to *Gateshead* and *Newcastle-upon-Tyne* (140 km.; 87 miles; see page 265).

TRAVEL ROUTE 28: Hull–Scarborough–*Whitby–Middlesbrough (165 km.; 102 miles)

See map on page 268.

Several world famous resorts are located on England's northeastern coast, set between the rugged scenery of the Yorkshire Moors and the turbulent waters of the North Sea. Travel Route 28 traverses this coastline from south to north.

Leave *Hull* (see page 258) on Clarence Street, which runs into A 165. Continue north to Route 1238, then follow it east through *Sproatley* to ***Burton Constable.** This palatial mansion, built in 1570, boasts rooms that were furnished in the 18th century by such famous architects as Robert Adam, and James Wyatt. Its **garden* is threaded with paths leading past ponds, playgrounds, a small zoo, a model railroad, antique stores, and a riding academy.

Return to A 165 and continue through the towns of Leven and *Lissett* to **Bridlington,** an interesting old resort town facing a lovely sandy beach. The **Priory Church* dates from the 12th century, and the city gate, *Bayle Gate,* was built in 1388.

Two side trips can be made from Bridlington. Just east of town is **Flamborough Head,* a seabird sanctuary with caves, a lighthouse, and cliffs rising 130 meters (426 feet) from the sea and providing wide views of the coast. To the west of Bridlington is the 16th-century ***Burton Agnes Hall.** It not only contains a rich collection of period furniture and Chinese porcelain but also one of the country's most valuable assemblages of French Impressionist paintings, including works by Renoir, Cézanne, Corot, Utrillo, and Gauguin.

From Bridlington continue on A 165 through *Filey,* a seaside resort with sandy and rocky beaches, to ***Scarborough** (83 km.; 51 miles from Hull). Part fishing village, spa, and historic site, all of its different characteristics have merged to make Scarborough one of England's most popular seaside resorts. The town lies between two large, lovely bays, and is surrounded by miles of sandy beach and splendid cliffside scenery. In the *harbor,*

traditional fishing boats (called mules and cobles) deliver their catch to a large covered *fish market*. On the headland over the harbor stand the ruins of a 12th-century *castle*. South of the headland, Scarborough's old streets wend down to a seaside *fair* lined with cockle stalls, bingo halls, and amusement arcades. Behind Scarborough stretch the Yorkshire Wolds, a broad landscape of forest and flowers, and moor and heath.

From Scarborough, follow A 171 north along the coast. Smaller roads branch east off the highway to such beach resorts as *Ravenscar* and *Robin Hood's Bay*.

Continue on to ***Whitby,** a pretty, colorful harbor town with 5 kms. (3 miles) of sandy beach. Captain James Cook, who discovered many Pacific Islands and charted Australia and New Zealand, lived at *16 Grape Lane* for many years, and learned his trade in Whitby Harbour. Whitby was also the seat of the Greenland Whaling fleet.

*St. Mary's Church, on Church Street, is situated at the top of 199 steps. Founded under the Normans, it has been remodeled several times over the centuries. Parts of the *choir* and the *south portal* remain from the original structure. *Caedmon Cross,* in the churchyard, commemorates Caedmon, the first English Christian poet, who lived in Whitby abbey in the seventh century. The ruins of **Whitby Abbey* are nearby. Although founded in

657 by Saint Hilda, most of what remains dates from the 12th–13th centuries.

From Whitby, you can take either of two routes to Middlesbrough. Route A 174 hugs the rocky coast, passing by *Staithes* and *Boulby Cliff* which, at 220 meters (721 feet), is the highest cliff on the English coast. Or you can take A 171 which traverses inland moors via *Guisborough,* with its remarkable ruins of a 12th-century *abbey.* Both roads meet in **Middlesbrough** (see page 266, 165 km.; 102 miles from Hull).

From Middlesbrough, it is possible to continue north to *Newcas-*

Whitby Abbey

tle and *Scotland* on the route described in Travel Route 27.

TRAVEL ROUTE 29: ***York–*Scarborough (66 km.; 41 miles)

See map on page 270.

York is northwestern England's premier city and Scarborough its best resort. This travel route connects the two, with a stop on the way at the magnificent Castle Howard.

Leave *York* (see page 104) from the northeast on Monkgate Street, cross the River Foss, and continue along Heworth Green Street to A 64. In **Whitwell-on-Hill,** on the banks of the River Derwent, you'll see the ruins of *Kirkham Priory,* which was founded in 1122. Its 13th-century *gatehouse,* adorned with sculptures, and its 14th-century *cloister* are both well preserved.

Just northeast of Whitwell-on-Hill, a side road leads northwest

to ****Castle Howard,** one of the grandest of England's grand houses and one of its best-known, as the popular series *Brideshead Revisited* was filmed there. Designed by Sir John Vanbrugh for the third Earl of Carlisle, it was built between 1664–1726. In the 18th century, Nicholas Hawksmoor, a student of Sir Christopher Wren, designed an addition to the house and a circular *mausoleum* for the grounds.

The most remarkable of the

Castle Howard

castle's rooms are its *Great Hall,* with ceilings 25 meters (82 feet) high; the *Grand Staircase;* the *Music Room;* the 50-meter- (164-foot-) long *Long Gallery;* and the *Tapestry Room.* The priceless artworks on view include a unique collection of 17th–20th century costumes, 18th-century tapestries, statues, the altar of the ancient temple of Delphi, Meissen porcelain, an exquisite cast iron railing, and paintings by Gainsborough, Reynolds, Romney, Tintoretto, Veronese, Rubens, and Van Dyck. The cas-

tle *gardens* are vast and in them stands the marble **Temple of the Four Winds,* built by Vanbrugh between 1724–1726, as well as the mausoleum designed by Hawksmoor. The palace *chapel ceiling* is a copy of the one Holbein designed for the Chapel Royal in St. James's Palace in London.

Continue northeast on A 64 to **Malton,** a market town on the River Derwent. Malton is built on the site of a fortified Roman camp that was called Dervenio. Just northeast of Malton is *Old Marton,* location of the ruins of a *monastery church* founded in 1150.

From Malton, A 64 traces the western slopes of the *Yorkshire Wolds* (see page 258) to **East Heslerton.** The town's parish church houses lovely statues of Saint Ambrose, Saint Augustine, Saint Gregory, and Saint Jerome, the church fathers. The statues were brought from Bristol in 1876. Continue through *Staxton,* where A 64 turns north to **Scarborough** (see page 267).

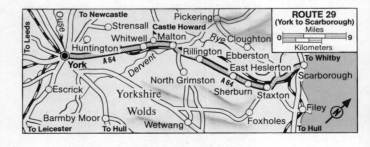

TRAVEL ROUTE 30: Newcastle-upon-Tyne–*Berwick-upon-Tweed (–Edinburgh) (131 km.; 81 miles)

See map on page 272.

England's northeastern coast is so rich in history and scenery that parts of it have been officially designated as regions of outstanding natural beauty. This Travel Route traverses the lonely, rugged landscape of this breathtaking region, from Newcastle-upon-Tyne to Berwick-upon-Tweed.

From *Newcastle* (see page 265), you may follow either of two routes to Berwick-upon-Tweed. The most direct route follows A 1 north to *Morpeth*, where you'll find the ruins of a 14th-century *castle* and *parish church*. A 1 continues through *Alnwick* (see page 272) and *Belford* to Berwick-upon-Tweed.

However, you may prefer to take the longer coastal route between the two cities, which is far prettier than A 1. Leave Newcastle on either Jesmond or Sandyford roads, and follow A 1058 east to **Tynemouth,** a lovely resort of wide streets and 18th-century houses. It is also the site of the remains of a *priory* that was founded in the 11th–12th centuries by the Benedictines on the ruins of a seventh-century Anglo-Saxon church. However, most of the surviving structure dates from the 11th century, and the fortified *Gatehouse* was built in the 14th century. *Whitley Bay,* Tynemouth's neighbor to the north, is an equally popular resort.

North of Whitley Bay stands ****Seaton Delaval Hall,** which was designed for the Delaval family in 1728 by Sir John Vanbrugh, the architect for Blenheim Palace (see page 215) and Castle Howard (see page 269). The original structure, part of which burned in 1822, was built in the style of an Italian palazzo. The house is said to be haunted by ghosts of Delaval family members, the most famous of whom is known as the "White Lady." The mansion, currently the home of Lord Hastings, opens only some of its many rooms and its lovely *gardens* to the public. Visitors may see the *dining* and *living rooms,* the *Great Hall,* the *Long Gallery* with its Chinese art, the *Minstrels' Gallery,* the *Mahogany Parlour,* and the *White Lady Room.* All are decorated with period furniture and porcelain and paintings by Lawrence, Lely, Reynolds, and others. The Norman *chapel,* built in 1102, is one of the most beautiful small churches in England, and has two magnificent 13th-century *tombstones.*

Continue north along the coast on A 1068 past *Bedlington*, home of the breed of terrier of that name, and across the River Wansbeck. Small offshore islands and castle ruins are visible from the road, and a series of tiny fishing villages dot the sandy beaches. *Warkworth,* on the River Coquet, is built around the ruins of

a 13th-century **castle,* and its well-preserved 15th-century *keep.* From here north, to Berwick-upon-Tweed, the coast is outstanding; it is part of a *national park,* and has been designated an area of outstanding natural beauty.

Alnmouth is a beautifully located beach resort and the site of one of the oldest golf courses in England, laid out in 1869. From here, A 1068 runs inland along the River Aln for about 6 km. (4 miles) to *Alnwick.* A 1068 enters town through the *Hotspur Gate,* all that remains of the Medieval city wall. ***Alnwick Castle,* residence of the dukes of Northumberland, was built in the 12th–13th centuries. At the time, the River Aln marked Britain's northern frontier and the castle's thick walls are a measure of the strategic importance it once had. Its rooms are elegantly furnished. Of particular interest are the collection of *Medieval weapons,* a *library* of hand-written prayer books and early prints, and the Roman and pre-Roman antiquities.

Only the 14th-century *gatehouse* remains of *Alnwick Abbey,* founded in 1147. A stroll through *Hulne Park* brings you to *Hulne Priory,* which was the first Carmelite convent in England. Built in 1240, much of the priory's original structure remains. The town's *St. Michael's Church* dates from the 15th century.

Return to the coastal road and continue north to *Craster,* and the nearby *Dunstanburgh Castle*, a 14th-century border fortification built atop a rock. In *Seahouses*, a coastal town north of *Embledon* and *Beadnell*, you may cross by boat to the *Farne Islands*, which are preserves for seabirds and seals. On one of the islands, a 14th-century *chapel* marks the spot where Saint Cuthbert lived as a hermit from 676–684.

On A 1068, you'll pass **Bamburgh**, a small village that was the Saxon capital of Bernicia and Northumbria many centuries ago. *Bamburgh Castle*, one of the largest sea fortifications in Great Britain, dominates the town. It was once the seat of the kings of Northumbria. In the village, a *museum* is devoted to a local heroine called Grace Darling. She was the lighthouse keeper's daughter, who, in 1838, helped her father rescue five passengers from a foundered steamboat.

Continue north along the coast through *Belford* and *Beal*, to the island called ***Holy Island**, or Lindesfarne. Because the island is connected to the mainland by a low-lying causeway, you must pay careful attention to the tide table before crossing. One of the earliest Christian centers in Great Britain, the island is a mystical place full of richly evocative religious ruins. Missionaries from Iona settled here in the seventh century and left stone crosses and inscribed stones. In 684, Saint Cuthbert was anointed bishop on Lindesfarne. He was also buried on the island, but when the Christians fled invading Vikings in 875, they brought his remains to Durham (see page 264). The island's *Benedictine abbey* was founded in 1083; the 16th-century *castle* has been beautifully restored.

Return to the mainland, and follow A 1 north over the River Tweed to ***Berwick-upon-Tweed** (131 km.; 81 miles from Newcastle), the northernmost town in England. Once a Scottish port, the town changed hands 13 times before becoming part of England. It is surrounded by Elizabethan *walls,* and a *walk* leads round the top of them, providing magnificent views along the way. Little remains of the town's *Norman castle*. Three lovely old *bridges* span the salmon-laden River Tweed. One, with 15 arches and built of stone, was built by order of James I in 1611.

The Scottish border lies along the northern edge of Berwick and from here, A 1 continues directly to Edinburgh.

TRAVEL ROUTE 31: Newcastle-upon-Tyne–*Hexham–*Carlisle (93 km.; 57 miles)

See map below.

This Travel Route crosses northern England from east to west, following **Hadrian's Wall**, the most spectacular Roman relic in Britain. Built between A.D. 120–126, the wall snakes through the craggy northern landscape for 120 km. (75 miles). Some surviving sections are nearly five meters (16 feet) high and three meters (10 feet) thick. Along its course, the wall is punctuated with turrets and forts, and lined by the Vallum, a ditch six to eight meters (19–26 feet) wide that was designed to protect the builders as they worked. The wall marked the northern frontier of the Roman Empire and protected the south from invasions by the Scottish Picts. It was abandoned in 383.

Leave *Newcastle-upon-Tyne* (see page 265) from the west on A 69. Just outside the city, note traces of the *Vallum* at the side of the road. The remains of one of the wall's *watchtowers* can be seen a bit farther along. Near *Heddon-on-the-Wall*, Route B 6318 angles north, along a moat, to *Greenhead* (see page 275), where it rejoins A 69.

Continue west to **Corbridge,** a picturesque town on the River Tyne that was once the capital of Northumberland. The town's *parish church,* built in Early English style, has a Saxon *portal* and a seventh-century *window*. In the churchyard you'll see a well-preserved *pele (peal) tower* that provided refuge from bands of marauding Scots during the 14th century. Corbridge is close to the Roman camp *Corstopitum,* of which considerable ruins remain. It is also a short walk away from *Hadrian's Wall*. The nearby *Aydon Castle* was built in 1305 (not open to the public).

Hexham, on the River Tyne, is both a center for visitors exploring the northern *dales* and Had-

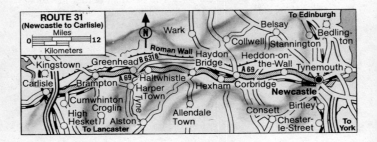

rian's Wall, and a busy sheep- and cattle-market town. The magnificent 13th-century *St. Andrew's Church* dominates the marketplace. Many art historians consider it to be a definitive example of Early English architecture. Built on the site of a seventh-century church, only a **crypt, apse,* and *nave* remain from the original structure. Also of interest are the 15th-century *chancel,* the Saxon *bishop's seat,* the *choir pews,* the *portraits* of 15th-century bishops, the *monument* to the Roman standard bearer Flavinus, and the Saxon **Acca Cross,* which was fashioned in 740. A Saxon *frith stool* in the chancel marks the center of a Medieval circle of sanctuary. Any fugitive from justice could enter the circle, which extended for a mile from the frith, and claim the protection of the Church.

*Moot Hall, on the marketplace, was the 15th-century council chamber. Just east of the Hall is *Manor Office,* a prison that was built in 1330.

Continue west to **Warden,** where the North Tyne and South Tyne rivers meet. The town has a Saxon *church tower* dating from the seventh and eighth centuries, with an even older Roman *doorway.*

Near *Haydon Bridge,* a lovely path leads southwest to the 14th-century *Langley Castle.* At Bardon Mill you can visit the remains of *Vindolanda,* an excavated Roman camp from the fourth century that billeted 500 auxiliary troops. Continue on A 69 through the towns of *Haltwhistle* and *Greenhead,* to Brampton. Along the way, small side roads branch north to well-preserved portions of the *Wall,* and to various spots of isolated beauty in the moors. At *Carvoran,* near Greenhead, you'll find a very well preserved portion of the *Roman town wall.* At the *Roman Army Museum,* lifesize figures in uniform and carrying weapons help to recreate the life of the Roman troops.

Brampton, a sandstone town near the River Irthing, provides another good base for excursions into the surrounding moors. Just northeast of town you'll find the ruins of **Lanercost Priory,* built in 1165 with a nave in Early English style. Services are still held weekly in the priory. Nearby is **Naworth Castle,* a 14th-century mansion set in a lovely park.

Continue west on A 69 across the River Eden to ***Carlisle** (93 km.; 57 miles from Newcastle; see page 257).

TRAVEL ROUTE 32: The Isle of Man

See map below.

This island of 614 square km. (237 square miles) and 56,000 inhabitants lies in the middle of the Irish Sea, halfway between England and Northern Ireland. Even so, the island is Scandinavian historically, ruled by the Norse from the ninth century until 1265, when it went to Scotland. Since 1333 it has been under English overlordship. The island has its own Parliament, the longest-standing one in the world, and is, in fact, the smallest independent state in the Western Hemisphere. The government issues its own currency, though British currency is accepted, and its own stamps are the only usable postal tender. English is the common language, and only a few residents still speak Manx.

The *Manx Information Centre* in London at 14 Dover Street can provide you with information on the island. There is air service from London, Manchester, Liverpool, and several other British airports (the island's airport is just outside Castletown). Many visitors arrive by ferry (most of the boats take cars) from Liverpool and Fleetwood. The crossing takes about 30 minutes.

If you come to the Isle of Man by boat, you will probably dock in its capital, **Douglas.** If you have come to the island looking for desolate beaches and wild countryside, you will no doubt think that you have come to the wrong place—especially if you arrive in June, when the *Tourist Trophy Motor Cycle Races,* known simply as "T. T.," are run on the island. Even in quieter times, Douglas has a busy beachfront promenade, dance halls, even casinos. However, Douglas is no Las Vegas, and it has many quiet streets lined with trim houses. It also has the *Manx Museum,* where you can bone up on local history and lore (the tailless Manx cat comes from the island).

Much of the rest of the Isle of Man is the quiet retreat you may imagine it to be. In addition to Douglas and its pleasant bayside suburb of *Onchan,* there are six other oceanside towns on the island.

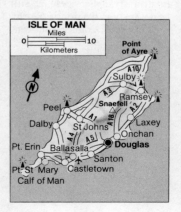

ISLE OF MAN

"Lady Isabella"

Laxey is a small fishing village and resort with a harbor protected by cliffs. The *Lady Isabella,* the town's tremendous waterwheel, is billed as the world's largest. It used to provide power for Laxey's now defunct lead mines. Laxey lies at the foot of the island's tallest mountain, *Snaefell,* and you can make the ascent to the top on the *Snaefell Electric Railway.* From the peak's heights of 600 meters (2,000 feet) you can see all the way to England, Scotland, Wales, and Ireland.

Ramsey is the island's other "big town," second to Douglas and much quieter. The big attraction in Ramsey is its setting—the beautiful bay on one side, mountains on the other. Its palm grove is a testament to the island's mild year-round climate.

Port Erin is the oldest town on the island, and its most attractive. Its bay, protected by an old breakwater, is ideal for swimmers.

Seabirds are protected in the sanctuary on *The Calf of Man,* an island just offshore.

Port St. Mary is a fishing port with links that make it a favorite of golfers. There is a nice walk from the village of about 1.5 km. (1 mile) to the **Manx Village Folk Museum,* a collection of old Manx cottages.

Castletown was the capital of the island until 1869, and its picturesque port is still dominated by the important-looking tenth-century *Rushen Castle,* one of Britain's best-preserved fortresses. There is a good nautical museum on Bridge Street.

Peel has a *castle,* too, largely in ruins. The castle *cathedral,* built in the 13th century, lost its roof in 1727 to workmen building stables for the island's governor. Peel is the home port of the island's fishing fleet, and its smoked kippers are one of the island's main exports. If you visit on Midsummer's Day, you can witness a nice piece of local history: Just 2 miles inland from Peel is *Tynwald Hill,* where new laws are proclaimed every year on July 5, a tradition that dates back 1,000 years.

There isn't much in the inland portion of the island—much in the way of civilization, that is. There are, however, forested glens, rushing brooks teeming with trout, lonely moors, and deserted mountaintops. You can enter these wild places from the shore roads around the island.

Wales

Magic, music, and legend are never far away in Wales. It borders England, yet it is apart. Travel Routes 33, 34, and 35 explore this familiar yet foreign country, and offer both a general and a detailed tour of Wales.

TRAVEL ROUTE 33: *Gloucester–*Cardiff–*Swansea–**Pembroke–**St. David's–*Aberystwyth (473 km.; 293 miles)

See map on page 281.

Industry has found a pastoral setting on the southern coast of Wales, where factories are overshadowed by swimming bays, and smokestacks are dwarfed by mountains. This Travel Route explores both natural and man-made aspects of the country, with a stop in Cardiff, Wales's capital city.

Leave *Gloucester* (see page 200) from the west on Lower Westgate Street, and pick up A 40. At the first fork, A 48 branches south through *Newnham* and the *Forest of Dean* to the mouth of the River Severn. Continue through the towns of *Blakeney* and *Lydney* to the bordertown of **Chepstow,** an historic fortress town set on limestone cliffs on the River Wye. Its 13th-century *castle* (with a Norman tower) built on a bluff overlooks the river and the steep streets of the town. Chepstow's *city gate* dates from the 16th century, and remains of the original 16th-century *city walls* still stand. (From Chepstow, M 4 leads east, over the River Severn, to Bristol (see page 159).

Continue west on A 48 to **Caerwent,** called Venta Silurum by the Romans. Part of the original *city walls* are still standing. **Caerleon,** on the banks of the River Usk, is an ancient Roman town whose name means "Camp of the Legion." The modern town encompasses 50 acres of Roman ruins, including the foundation of an *amphitheater* and the *barracks of Isca,* where 6,000 Roman troops camped in A.D. 80 to subdue the local inhabitants.

*Newport, just west of Caerleon, is the third largest city in Wales, and a busy industrial center. It has a Medieval *castle,* parts of which are well-preserved. The **cathedral of St. Woolos* was built between the 12th–15th centuries, and has Norman *arches* and a Medieval *tower*. The interior is a beautiful example of Norman architecture.

You may go directly to Cardiff on A 48. However, the inland route on A 468 is prettier. Drive to **Caerphilly,** an old market town with a beautiful 13th-century ****castle** that, with its moat and walls, covers 30 acres. Caerphilly is also known for the crumbly cheese of the same name, which is now made elsewhere. Continue south on A 470 to ***Cardiff** (106 km.; 66 miles from Gloucester).

This thriving seaport has been the capital of Wales since 1955. Its *Civic Centre* is located in *Cathays Park.* The modern, spacious buildings house the *City Hall,* which contains a marble hall lined with monuments to Welsh heroes. ****The National Museum of Wales** has a varied collection of native Welsh objects from such fields as geology, architecture, botany, and history.

*Cardiff Castle sits in the center of town. Built in 1090 on the ruins of a Roman fort, extensive additions were made in the last century by the family of the Third Marquess of Bute. The castle's Norman *keep* and *state rooms* are splendidly furnished with 18th- and 19th-century pieces. Cardiff's *church of St. John the Baptist* has one of the most beautiful *towers* of any church in Wales.

From Cardiff, take A 4119 northeast to **Llandaff,** a western suburb of the city. **Llandaff Cathedral* dates from the 13th–14th centuries but has been restored twice: once in 1882, and again after World War II, when it

was badly damaged by bombs. The interior of the cathedral is dominated by a huge modern Christ figure cast in aluminum by Jacob Epstein.

Continue to **St. Fagans** on the western outskirts of Cardiff. This village of thatched roof houses is home to the 13th-century *St. Fagans Castle,* of which only a wall survives to surround the ***Welsh Folk Museum,* a fascinating collection of traditional Welsh buildings, among them a *woolenmill,* a *chapel,* and a *cooper's shop.* Demonstrations of Welsh crafts are held regularly.

Leave the environs of Cardiff on A 48 and drive south on A 4050 to the coast and **Barry,** a popular seaside resort. You'll find the best beaches in the area on *Barry Island,* which is connected to the mainland by a causeway. Continue along the coastal highway (B 4265) through *Rhoose* (and Glamorgan Airport) to **Llantwit Major,** a charming village, whose narrow, winding streets give it a 15th-century air. Llantwit Major has a 12th-century Celtic *parish church,* which was redone in the 15th century in English Gothic style. In its eastern section are the remains of 13th- and 14th-century *wall paintings.*

B 4265 proceeds west to *Ewenny,* location of the ruins of an early Norman fortified *priory,* as well as the town's many *pottery workshops.* At **Brigend,** an old market town with a 12th-century *castle,* rejoin A 48 and continue northwest to **Margam,** with its ruins of 12th-century *Margam Abbey.* The abbey's **chapter house* is particularly noteworthy. The *museum* in the abbey churchyard displays a number of interesting Celtic stones bearing inscriptions.

Follow A 48 north through the industrial region around *Port Talbot* and on to *Briton Ferry.* At this point, you may cross the River Neath via A 483 and continue directly to Swansea. If time allows, however, make a short side trip northeast on A 465 to **Neath.** This ancient village is set in the *Vale of Neath,* a lovely valley that threads through this largely industrial region. Neath's 13th-century *castle* is now in ruins.

Return to A 48 and continue to ***Swansea** (201 km.; 125 miles from Gloucester).

This important industrial city and seaport (the second largest city in Wales) enjoys an exceptionally beautiful setting. Situated at the mouth of the River Tawe on the curve of Swansea Bay, the city was a seaside resort center until the 18th century, when its industrial development began. Today, the *University College of Swansea* is one of the best in Wales. The city's *museum* contains Welsh antiquities and a good collection of china. In the *Glynn Vivian Art Gallery,* you'll find works by Welsh painters. The paintings of Sir Frank Brangwyn (1867–1956), the noted British

artist and decorator are exhibited in the modern *Guildhall.*

Swansea still provides vacationers with a beautiful swimming bay and an ideal base from which to explore the ***Gower peninsula,** a region of sandy beaches, heather-covered hills, marshes, trout streams, cliffs, and caves. The peninsula, rich in prehistoric sites, was designated a national park in 1957. The pretty fishing villages and resorts tucked into bays and on the coastal cliffs of the peninsula include *Mumbles, Caswell Bay, Langland Bay, Port Enyon,* and *Rhossili.*

Leave Swansea from the northwest on A 484 and drive through *Loughor* and *Llanelli* to *Kidwelly.* This port city's 14th-century *parish church* and 13th-century *Cydweli Castle* are both of interest.

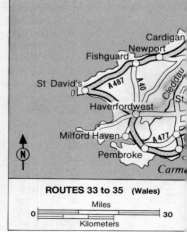

ROUTES 33 to 35 (Wales)

Miles

0 ⊨════════════════⊨ 30

Kilometers

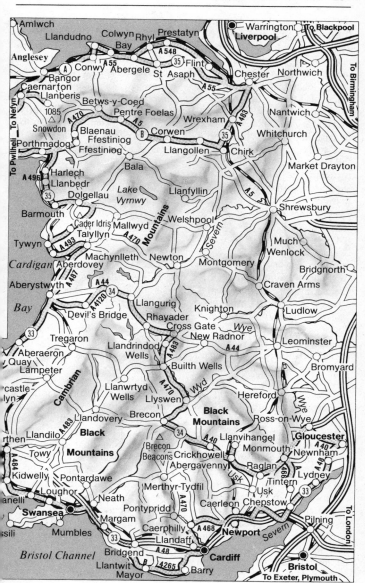

Continue north to ***Carmarthen,** set on a bluff over the River Tywi. The Welsh name for Carmarthen is Caerfyrddin which means "Merlin's City." According to legend, this is the birthplace of Merlin, the Arthurian sorcerer. In *Priory Street* you'll find a *tree trunk* upon which Merlin cast the spell, "When Merlin's oak shall tumble down, then shall fall Carmarthen town." So as not to tempt fate, the tree has been supported with iron bands. Carmarthen also has an impressive 14th-century *church*, an interesting *anthropological museum*, and massive ruins of a Norman *castle*.

Leave Carmarthen from the west on A 40 and continue to *St. Clear's*. From here, you can make a side trip south to **Laugharne.** The poet *Dylan Thomas* lived in a house behind the castle in Laugharne for many years and is buried in the local churchyard. Both sites are open to visitors. Thomas based the characters in his play "Under Milkwood" on his neighbors in this village. Also of interest are the 12th-century *castle,* which was restored in the 16th century, and the *Town Hall,* where members of the council meet every other Monday.

From St. Clear's continue southwest on A 477 to ***Tenby,** one of the most beautiful beach resorts in Wales. Inside its old *city gates* are remarkable Tudor and Georgian houses. Of particular interest are the 15th-century **Tudor Merchant's House* and the **parish church,* dating from the 13th–15th centuries. From Tenby, you may take a boat to *Caldey Island,* site of a Medieval church and monastery, and to the impressive *Pembrokeshire Coast National Park.*

Follow the coast to **Penally,** site of a 13th-century *church,* to ***Manorbier.** Set in a lonely valley near a bay almost surrounded by red sandstone cliffs, this town is built around the ruins of a 12th-century *castle* and moat. From Manorbier, A 4139 turns west and continues through *Lamphey,* where there are ruins of a Medieval *Bishop's Palace,* to ****Pembroke** (312 km.; 193 miles from Gloucester).

This small town, which consists of a single main street, boasts one of the largest and most impressive Norman castles in Britain, ****Pembroke Castle,** birthplace of Henry VII, the first Tudor King of England, in 1457. The castle, occupying a striking position, surrounded on three sides by water, was begun in 1090 and completed in the 13th century. The round **keep* dates from 1210 and is encircled by defensive outer walls that are punctuated by seven bastion towers. Under the castle is a huge natural cave called *Wogan* that can be entered through the castle's northern hall. Pembroke's sister city to the west is *Pembroke Dock;* both offer fine sailing, boating, and beaches.

Continue north on A 477 over **Milford Bay,* and through the port city of *Milford Haven* to *Neyland* and **Haverfordwest.** This town is an important agricultural center and a good base for exploring the *National Coast Park*. Its parish church, *St. Mary's,* dates from the 13th–15th centuries. The *Castle Museum* is also worth visiting. From Neyland, you can make a worthwhile excursion southeast to the 12th-century *Picton Castle,* on whose grounds the *Graham Sutherland Gallery* is situated, with works by the 20th-century British painter and other artists.

A 487 runs northwest through *Roch, Newgate,* and *Solva* to **St. David's** (355 km.; 220 miles from Gloucester), the smallest cathedral city in Great Britain and the oldest bishop's see. *St. David's Cathedral* was built between the 12th–14th centuries on the site of a Celtic church founded by Saint David, the patron saint of Wales, and enlarged in

the 15th–16th centuries. Its **shrine of St. David* was an important pilgrimage site in the Middle Ages. Notice also the round, richly decorated *arches,* the *nave roof* carved of Irish oak, the magnificent fan *vault* of *Trinity Chapel,* and the carved *choir pews.* Next to the cathedral are the massive ruins of the impressive 14th-century *Bishop's Palace.*

The nearby village of *St. Non's Bay* was the birthplace of Saint David (Saint Non was his mother). The village is the site of a very old *chapel* and *St. Non's Well.*

From St. David's, continue northeast on A 487 to *Fishguard,* a picturesque town with a beautiful beach. An inscribed stone commemorates the last invasion in 1797 of foreign troops on British soil when a French fleet, sent to seize Bristol, was driven north to Fishguard. The French apparently saw a number of Welsh women wearing red cloaks on the beach, mistook them for soldiers, and surrendered. The railway station in *Fishguard Harbor* provides train connections to Ireland.

Continue northeast on A 487 to **Cardigan,** a market town at the mouth of the River Teifi. You may want to rent a rowboat to explore the lovely beaches, cliffs, and peninsulas surrounding the town. Cardigan also has impressive ruins of a 12th-century *castle.* From Cardigan, a worthwhile side trip leads east along the *val-

St. David's Cathedral

ley of the River Teifi to the ruins of the 13th-century *Cilgerran Castle.* The castle stands on a promontory of the Teifi and Plysgog rivers and has been a favorite subject of several painters, Turner among them.

Follow A 487 north from Cardigan. Along the way, you'll see many side roads that branch off to small fishing villages. Near *Post-Mawr,* A 486 heads north to **New Quay,** a small beach resort at the southern end of Cardigan Bay. The steep hills behind the town protect the port and also contribute to its mild climate. The fishing village of **Abaraeron** occupies a particularly lovely stretch of the coast and has a fine sandy beach. Continue on A 487 through *Lla-*

non and *Llanrhystyd* to ***Aberystwyth** (448 km.; 278 miles from Gloucester), situated at the mouth of the River Rheidor. The Prince of Wales was a student at Aberystwyth's *University College* in 1969. The town is also the site of the ruins of the 13th-century *Aberystwyth Castle.* The town's **National Library of Wales* houses a large collection of books, maps, and other Welsh documents, and the *Aberystwyth Arts Centre* at the university displays Welsh art and hosts travelling exhibitions. A cable car runs up *Constitution Hill,* which provides a wonderful panoramic view of the area. A narrow gauge railway threads through the lovely **Rheidol Valley.*

TRAVEL ROUTE 34: *Gloucester–*Monmouth–*Brecon–*Rhayader–*Aberystwyth (226 km.; 140 miles)

See map on page 281.

The mountains of central Wales possess a haunting beauty. This Travel Route skirts the bare, black peaks of the region and traverses Brecon Beacons National Park, and its lakes, waterfalls, and dense forests.

Leave *Gloucester* (see page 200) on Lower Westgate Street and take A 40 west towards *Ross-on-Wye* (see page 208). A 40 crosses the River Wye, then turns south. Just south of *Whitchurch* is **Symond's Yat Rock,* a hill between two reaches of the river that provides a striking panorama of the wide valley. Continue on A 40 to

*Monmouth (44 km.; 27 miles from Gloucester).

This historic town lies at the confluence of three rivers, the Trothy, the Monnow, and the Wye. King Henry V was born in Monmouth in 1387 in an 11th-century *castle* now in ruins, and is commemorated by a statue outside *Shire Hall,* in Agincourt

Monnow Bridge

Square. Next to him stands a statue of another famous local son, C. S. Rolls, the Rolls of Rolls-Royce, whose father, Lord Llangattock, lived near Monmouth. In the middle of Monnow bridge stands a 13th-century *fortified gate. Monmouth Museum* contains many mementos from the lives of Lord Nelson and Lady Hamilton.

If you have time, take an excursion south on A 466 to the magnificent *Tintern Abbey,* a romantic ruin that inspired William Wordsworth to write a poem about its sylvan beauty. Built between 1131–1287, the abbey is splendidly situated in a meadow near the River Wye. The east end and the rose window of the abbey church are almost intact.

Leave Monmouth from the southwest on A 40 and continue to **Raglan.** *Raglan Castle,* built in 1431 and now a hotel, served as a fortress during the War of the Roses and later became the home of the earls of Worcester. A few miles to the south is a remarkable mansion called *Cefntilla Court,* built in 1616 as the home of Lord Raglan.

Continue to **Abergavenny,** a pretty old town on the River Usk surrounded by mountains more than 500 meters (1,500 feet) high. The town's Medieval *castle* is in ruins. The *Abergavenny and District Museum,* housed in a 19th-century stone hunting lodge, exhibits local farm and domestic equipment. In *Blaenavon,* a few miles to the south, is the *Big Pit Mining Museum.*

A worthwhile side trip to **Llanvihangel Crucorney** can be made from Abergavenny. *Llanvihangel Court* was built in 1559, and its gardens are graciously designed. The *Skirrid Mountain Inn* in town was built in 1110. It is the oldest inn in Wales.

Continue northwest on A 40 along the lovely valley of the River Usk, which skirts the southern edge of the bare *Black Mountains,* and cuts through **Brecon Beacons National Park.** The countryside abounds with fish-laden brooks, lakes, waterfalls, and dense forests and is dotted with castle ruins, small Welsh villages, and promontories that afford marvelous views. Pony trekking is a popular way to see the area.

Continue to **Brecon** (103 km.; 64 miles from Gloucester), an excellent center for exploring the surrounding *national park.* A worthwhile destination in itself, Brecon's location at the confluence of the rivers Usk and Honddu, enhances the lovely natural setting of this pretty town. Its red sandstone *cathedral dates from the 13th–14th centuries. On the grounds of the *Castle Hotel* are the remains of a *Medieval castle* and the *city walls.* The *county museum exhibits a good collection of archaeological finds, pottery, and local art.

From Brecon, continue east, then north, on A 470 through the valley of the River Wye. The important agricultural center of **Builth Wells** is also a popular base for sports fishermen and pony trekkers. From here, follow A 483 north to ***Llandrindod Wells,** one of Wales's largest and most popular spas. The town offers wonderful parks, a boating lake, and several good walking paths.

Continue north on A 483 to the town of *Cross Gates,* where A 44 leads west to **Rhayader** (167 km.; 103 miles from Gloucester).

This quiet town deserves its excellent reputation for fishing and hiking, and as a center for pony trekking through the *Elan valley* into the *Lake District of Wales.* From the town, you'll enjoy remarkable views of the Cambrian mountains, lakes, and reservoirs.

From Rhayader, A 470 traverses a particularly beautiful stretch of the Wye valley to ***Llangurig.** Situated on a ravine at the edge of the River Wye, it is the highest town in Wales. Its *monastery church* dates from the 14th century. Hiking trails lead in every direction into the surrounding mountains, and fishing on this section of the Wye is excellent.

From Llangurig, drive west on A 44 across the wild, romantic, lonely mountains of *Plynlimon Fawr* where the rivers Wye and Severn have their source. Some of the mountains soar to 800 meters (2,624 feet).

The village of *Ponterwyd* is located at the confluence of the rivers Rheidol and Costell, near the reservoirs of Nant-y-Moch. Turn south onto A 4120, and continue to ****Devil's Bridge,** one of the most popular tourist attractions in Wales. Three bridges span the narrow gorge of the River Rheidol, where it empties into the River Mynach. Built in the 12th century, Devil's Bridge itself is the lowest of the three. A series of spectacular *waterfalls cascade down the gorge. One is almost 100 meters (320 feet) high.

Continue west on A 4120, past many scenic vantage points, to *Aberstwyth* (226 km.; 140 miles from Gloucester; see page 284).

TRAVEL ROUTE 35: *Aberystwyth–**Caernarfon– *Bangor (–*Betws-y-Coed–**Llangollen)–**Chester (262 km.; 162 miles)

See map on page 281.

For simple natural beauty, northern Wales cannot be surpassed. From the rugged coastline, to the majestic mountains of Snowdonia National Park, to the Llewelyn peninsula, this Travel Route samples all that the region has to offer.

From Aberystwyth (see page 284), follow A 47 through *Talybont,* set in the lovely Dovey valley, to ***Machynlleth,** a beautiful town on the River Dovey. This was the home of Owen Glendower, the Welsh national hero who drove the English out of Wales in 1404 and set up a Welsh parliament here. Of interest are the modern **Parliament House,* built in the same style as the original parliament building, and **Royal House,* Glendower's home.

Continue on A 47 to the *Centre for Alternative Technology,* established in 1974. Volunteers from all over the world assemble here to work toward developing alternative energy production and agricultural technologies. The products they develop are for sale.

At this point, you may choose between two routes to Dolgellau. A 487 north provides the most direct route; however, a more interesting route follows A 493 west along the wide mouth of the River Dovey to **Aberdovey,** a charming fishing port with a lovely sandy beach, sailing and golf facilities.

Continue along the coast on A

493 to ***Tywyn,** a seaside resort at the base of the *Cader Idris mountain range.* In the town's *parish church* is the rectangular **St. Cadfan's Stone.* Over 2 meters (6 feet) high and covered with ancient Celtic symbols, the stone is said to be the oldest evidence of the Welsh written language. The *Narrow Gauge Railway Museum,* exhibits trains and equipment including the original (more than 100 years old) cars of the *Talyllyn Railway* that, pulled by steam engines, took passengers to **Abergynolwyn.* From here, hiking trails thread their way to *Lake Talyllyn* and other destinations in the surrounding countryside.

Just past Tywyn, A 4405, one of the most beautiful mountain roads in Wales, branches east. Follow it to **Craig-yr-Aderyn Rock,* which is a nesting area for seabirds, particularly cormorants. Continue to ***Talyllyn,** a small village at the foot of Cader Idris, the so-called "chair of Arthur" and one of the most famous mountains in the area. According to legend, anyone who sleeps the night on the mountain will wake up either blind, mad, or a poet. The nearby *Talyllyn Lake* provides a paradise for anglers.

Continue along the south shore of the lake back to A 487, and ***Dolgellau.** The local dark slate used in many of its buildings give this town a brooding but picturesque appearance. Dolgellau is a popular base for climbers, fishermen, and hikers.

In *Llanelltyd* you'll see the remarkable 13th-century ruins of *Cummer Abbey.* From here, turn west onto A 496 and follow the north shore of **Afon Mawddach* (afon is the Welsh word for river) to ***Barmouth.** This modern resort has several miles of beaches and a 3-km.- (1.8-mile-) long **seashore promenade.*

*Llanbedr, just to the north of Barmouth on A 496, is situated at the entrance to **Afon Artro.* Nearby, 2,000 **Roman steps* lead to the summit of *Llyn Cwm Bychan Mountain.* Many ancient stone circles also can be found in this area. A side road leads west off A 496 to the small village of *Llandanwg,* which boasts a wide, sandy beach carpeted with seashells.

Continue north to the well-situated town of ****Harlech,** where you can enjoy magnificent views of the rugged mountains of *Snowdonia National Park,* and the shores of the *Lleyn peninsula.* Owen Glendower's wife and family were captured in Harlech by Henry V. ****Harlech Castle** dominates the town from atop a steep rock. The castle was built by

Edward I between 1283–1289 on the site of an earlier Celtic fortress. The Welsh national song, "Men of Harlech," celebrates the heroic 1468 defense of the castle against attacking troops during the War of the Roses (see page 13).

From Harlech, you can opt for either of two routes to Chester (see page 211). One skirts the coast, passing through *Caernarfon, Bangor,* and *Conwy.* The other goes inland through *Betws-y-Coed, Llangollen,* and *Wrexham* (see page 291).

To take the coastal route, leave Harlech from the north on A 496, and drive through *Talsarnaw* to *Penrhyndeudraeth* where you turn west onto A 497 and cross the River Traeth Mawr. To the north, there is a marvelous view of Snowdon, the highest peak in Wales. **Porthmadog,** set at the end of the Lleyn peninsula, offers wonderful sailing. It is also an excellent base for excursions into ****Snowdonia National Park.** This park is one of the largest in Great Britain, extending north from here to Conwy. It is a region of steep, bare mountains, romantic lakes, rocky passes, rushing streams, and densely forested valleys. The Welsh call Snowdonia the eagles' nesting place. Although eagles no longer live here, the name accurately conveys the grandeur of this region.

Snowdon rises to 1,088 meters (3,568 feet). Many hiking trails lead to its summit, although the *Snowdon Mountain Railway* from

Snowdon

Llanberis provides a somewhat easier means of ascent. The town of *Llanberis* is located between Padarn and Peris lakes, at the famous *Pass of Llanberis*. The *Ffestinio Railway* line originating in Porthmadog, also traverses the park.

Follow A 497 west to ***Criccieth,** a small, sheltered seaside town with two excellent beaches. David Lloyd George (1863–1945), who was British Prime Minister from 1914–1918, was raised near here and lived in the village for a time. *Criccieth Castle,* which stands on a headland above the village, was built in 1286 by Edward I.

Lloyd George was born in nearby ***Llanystumdwy,** a good base for pony trekking. The local *museum* contains many mementos of his life; he is buried here on the banks of the River Dwyfor. Continue on A 497 to the old market town of **Pwllheli,** set on a popular yacht harbor. It provides a good starting point for excursions to the Lleyn peninsula. From Pwllheli, take A 499 north across the neck of the peninsula. Drive through *Llanaelhaearn,* which is beautifully placed at the foot of three peaks called The Rivals, and continue through Clynnog Fawr and Llandwrog to ****Caernarfon** (188 km.; 116 miles from Aberystwyth).

This ancient town, the ceremonial capital of Wales, is surrounded by 13th-century **walls* and dominated by the Medieval ***Caernarfon Castle.* On July 1, 1969, Prince Charles was proclaimed Prince of Wales at the historic castle. He is not the only monarch associated with this city—Caernarfon was also the birthplace of Edward II. Just east of the city is **Segontium,* an excellently preserved Roman camp. Finds from the area are on display in the nearby **museum.* Caernarfon is also known for its excellent fishing and as an impor-

Caernarfon Castle

tant shopping center for the region.

A worthwhile side trip from Caernarfon leads east via A 4086 to *Llanberis,* at the foot of Snowdon (see page 288).

Continue northeast on A 487 to ***Bangor** (203 km.; 126 miles from Aberystwyth). The name means "protective fence" and was derived from the walls surrounding a monastic settlement founded here in 548. Bangor's present *cathedral,* designed by the 19th-century architect Sir George Gilbert Scott, stands on the site of this earlier church. The city's *municipal buildings* are housed in the former Bishop's Palace, dating from the 16th–17th centuries. The *Museum of Welsh Antiquities* is part of Bangor's university.

You can take two side trips from Bangor. The first leads east on A 5 to the island of *Anglesey,* where *Holyhead,* an important port on the island, provides connections to Ireland. On the eastern side of the island you'll discover a little town with the longest name in the world, *Llanfairpwllgwyngyllgogerychwyrndrobwllllantysyliogogogoch*— known as *Llanfair* for short. The second side trip is to **Penrhyn Castle,* just east of Bangor. Built between 1827–1840 on the site of a Tudor mansion, the castle is now the property of the National Trust. It houses a *museum* with an array of dolls from all over the world and a collection of old locomotives.

From Bangor, follow A 55 northeast past the lovely beach resorts of *Llanfairfechan* and *Penmaein-mawr* to ***Conwy.** This fortified town at the mouth of the River Conwy has well-preserved *city walls* and a massive 13th-century **fortress.* The thick fortress walls are laid out in the shape of a Welsh harp. Other interesting sights in town include **St. Mary's Church,* dating from the 13th–14th centuries, with a remarkable *altar wall;* **Plas Mawr,* a picturesque Elizabethan house exhibiting the art collection of the Royal Academy of Wales; the 15th-century timbered house, *Aberconway,* now an antiques store; and many other Medieval houses. *Bodnant Gardens,* just a short distance outside Conwy, are among the most beautiful in Great Britain.

Cross the River Conwy and follow A 496 north to ***Llandudno,** a popular resort with sandy beaches and a long *promenade.* Atop the 200-meter- (656-foot-)

Conwy

high *Great Orme's Head,* accessible by cable car, you'll find two very large gardens: **Happy Valley Rock Gardens* and the *Haulfre Gardens.*

From Llandudno, follow A 546 east to the popular beach resort ***Colwyn Bay.** The remarkable *Welsh Mountain Zoo,* is located nearby on a forested hill.

From *Abergele,* you can choose between two routes to Chester. You can continue along the coast on A 548 through the seaside towns of *Rhyl; Greenfield,* site of some interesting abbey ruins; *Flint,* with its 13th-century castle; and *Connah's Quay* to *Chester* (see page 211). Or you can take the inland route, via A 55, which passes through *St. Asaph,* which has a very small cathedral built in the 13th–15th centuries; *Holywell; Northop,* with an interesting 16th-century parish church; *Ewloe,* with a 13th-century castle; and *Hawarden,* to ***Chester* (see page 211).

The inland route from Harlech to Chester begins on A 496 north out of Harlech to *Maentwrog.* From here, A 496 ascends steeply to **Ffestiniog,* a marvelous base for excursions into nearby moors. South of town are the magnificent *Cynfal Falls.*

Blaenau Ffestiniog was the center of Welsh slate mining for two centuries. Two *mines* are open to visitors. The narrow gauge *Ffestiniog Railway,* pulled by steam locomotives, runs between here and Porthmadog (see page 288). The town provides a good base for excursions into ***Snowdonia National Park* (see page 288).

From Blaenau Ffestiniog, follow A 470 north across the 400-meter- (1,312-foot-) high *Crimea Pass* to **Dolwyddelan,** in the picturesque **Lledr Valley,* at the foot of Moel Siabod. Of interest is the 13th-century **Dolwyddelan Castle,* with its well-preserved Norman *tower.*

Continue on A 470 through scenic **Fairy Glen,* on the River Conwy, to ***Betws-y-Coed** (162 km.; 100 miles from Aberystwyth), a name meaning chapel in the woods. Located at the confluence of the Conwy Llugwy and the Lledr, the town is surrounded by the green and densely wooded Gwydir Forest. The 15th-century *bridge* over the Conwy offers a magnificent panoramic view of the lovely area. You may take a side trip north from town to the *Tudor Gwydir Castle.*

Now follow A 5 east past the *Conwy Falls* and through the towns of *Pentre Foelas, Cerrig-y-Drudion,* and *Corwen,* and into the lovely **Dee valley* to ****Llangollen** (214 km.; 133 miles from Aberystwyth).

Since 1947, the town has hosted the well-known *International Musical Eisteddfod,* a folk dancing and singing contest, every summer. Contestants from more than 30 countries participate, turning the town into a colorful amalgam of national costumes and flags. **Plas Newydd* is a black-and-white timbered house where Lady Eleanor Butler and Sarah Ponsonby, the famous "Ladies of Llangollen," lived between 1778–1831. The two Irish aristocrats, known for their wit, entertained guests that included the Duke of Wellington, Sir Walter Scott, and William Wordsworth among other notables.

Across the *Llangollen Canal*—on which you can take a pleasant boat trip—stand the ruins of the eighth-century castle, *Dinas Bran*. West of town lies **Valle Crucis Abbey,* a Cistercian abbey founded in 1202. Its well-preserved *western façade* is in Early English style. It has 14th-century *windows* and the remains of some lovely *pointed arches.*

Continue west of A 5 through the *Vale of Llangollen* to ****Chirk,** a Welsh border town. The magnificent *Chirk Castle* was built in 1310 and has been inhabited since then. Admiral Sir Thomas Seymour lived here with his wife Catherine Parr, Henry VIII's widow. In 1645, Charles I stayed here. The castle's original 17th- and 18th-century furnishings still adorn its rooms. Another interesting building in Chirk is the 15th-century *parish church.*

Proceed north on A 483 through *Ruabon* to the small industrial town of **Wrexham,** an important commercial center located in this rich coal mining area of northern Wales. The town's 15th-century *parish church* has a particularly lovely **tower.* **Gresford,** on A 483, has a remarkable 15th-century *church.* Continue through *Marford,* location of some lovely 18th-century houses, and *Rossett,* where there is a 17th-century *mill,* to ****Chester** (262 km.; 162 miles from Aberystwyth; see page 211).

The Channel Islands

See map on page 295.

The Channel Islands of Jersey, Guernsey, Alderney, Sark, and Hern have been ruled by the British crown since the 11th century. Yet, in many ways they constitute a foreign country. Jersey and Guernsey issue their own postage stamps and elect their own parliaments. Sark is organized under a feudal lord—a system of government that a transplanted Medieval knight would find completely familiar.

One reason for these differences is the distance between the islands and Great Britain. The islands lie 160 km. (99 miles) off England's southern coast. In fact, Jersey lies much closer to France than to England. The combination of an exceptionally mild climate and fertile soil have allowed island residents to produce some of the most famous breeds of cattle in the world. The islands' coastlines possess such great natural beauty that Victor Hugo, who lived on Guernsey, called them "charming gardens of the sea."

Ferry service to the islands is excellent.

Jersey

At 72 sq. km. (27 sq. miles), Jersey is the largest of the Channel Islands. Situated only 21 km. (13 miles) from the coast of France, its atmosphere is unmistakably French. Most towns on the island have French names, and in rural areas the local dialect is an amalgam of English and French. Jersey's varied *coastline* is famous for its contrasts: wild, rugged stretches are interspersed with peaceful, sandy bays.

Jersey

St. Helier, Jersey's capital, is on St. Auban's Bay. The town is dominated by the 16th-century *Elizabeth Castle,* built under Elizabeth I, which stands on an offshore island and is connected to the mainland by a causeway passable only at low tide. In the center of town lies *Royal Square,* consisting of the *Parliament* building, the *Court House,* and the *Old Inn.* French products, such as perfumes and brandys, are sold duty-free in the town.

Every summer the town hosts the famous *Battle of Flowers.*

293

From St. Helier, a short walk leads to the *ocean port*, which is surrounded by flat, sandy beaches. St. Helier also provides a good base for excursions to Jersey's many old castles and prehistoric memorial stones.

Leave St. Helier on the coastal road going west and skirt the sandy St. Auban's Bay to the small town of *St. Auban*, whose old houses and narrow streets rise steeply from the shore. Beyond St. Auban, the road traces a rugged section of the coast. *Portelet Bay* is surrounded by steep granite cliffs. Further on is *St. Brelade Bay*, one of the island's most beautiful swimming bays. The road continues along the coast through *Beau Port* and *Petit Port*, two quiet bays, and past the rugged cliffs of *Corbiere Point*. A bit farther along is the 8-km.-(5-mile-) long *St. Ouen Bay*, popular with surfers. Car races are also held at the beach in the summer.

Along the island's north shore, small bays nestle between high cliffs. The coastal road descends steep heather-covered hills to wide, sandy beaches. It passes through the towns of *Plemont, Greve de Lecq, Bonne Nuit Bay, Bouley Bay,* and *Rozel Harbour*.

Gorey is a lively fishing village on Jersey's east coast. The town is set at the foot of *Mont Orgeuil Castle*, whose Medieval walls are illuminated at night. The stretch of coast between Gorey and St. Helier is flat and sandy. The bay of *St. Clement*, with its many crevices and rocks, is a beautiful place to explore at low tide.

Guernsey

The second largest of the Channel Islands, Guernsey is 15 km. (9 miles) long and 8 km. (5 miles) wide. Despite its rugged coast, it has many secluded sandy beaches tucked between its granite rocks.

St. Peter Port, Guernsey's capital, is characterized by old granite houses, narrow streets, stone stairways, picturesque squares, and a bustling harbor. Don't miss the picturesque *open market* where island products are sold from colorful booths that stand on sawdust-covered floors. The local produce includes huge crabs, lobsters, tomatoes, greenhouse grapes, flowers, heavy cream, and butter. After 10:00

Guernsey

A.M. no cars are permitted on St. Peter Port's Medieval streets. Near town stands the Medieval *Castle Cornet.*

Between St. Peter Port and the wild cliffs on the southern coast, steep valleys run down to many beautiful bays, such as *Fermain Bay, Moulin Huet Bay,* and *Portelet Bay.* On the island's west coast you'll find larger bays with fine sandy beaches. They include *Cobo Bay; Vazon Bay,* where there is good surfing; and *Rocquaine Bay,* connected by a causeway to the ruins of a *monastery* on *Lihou Island.*

Guernsey's flat, sandy northern coast is dotted with fishing harbors such as *St. Sampson* and *Grand Havre.* Nearby is the popular beach on *L'Ancresse Bay.*

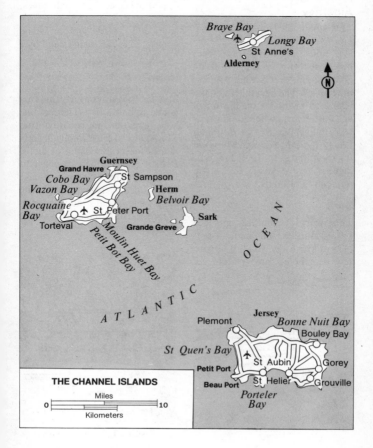

THE CHANNEL ISLANDS

Miles

0 — 10

Kilometers

Interesting sights on Guernsey include a *neolithic grave* in *La Houque de Dehus; Hauteville House,* Victor Hugo's home, which now serves as a museum; and the *shell-covered chapel* in *Les Vauxbelets.* The chapel's interior, which can accommodate only one minister and two worshippers, may be the smallest church in the world.

Alderney

This small, charming island is 6 km. (3.7 miles) long and 2.5 km. (1.5 miles) wide. The only town here is the tiny St. Anne, with its cobblestone streets and colorful old houses. The best places on the island to swim lie on the north and east coasts, where dunes protect the bays. *Braye Bay* and *Longy Bay* are particularly good for swimming. In the fishing village of *Braye* you'll find some interesting old inns.

Sark

This peaceful island is only 5.6 km. (3.4 miles) long and 2.4 km. (1.5 miles) wide. You'll find very few cars here; most people get around on horse-drawn carriages and bicycles. Island society is predominantly feudal; Sark's Seigneur (feudal lord) enjoys privileges that exist nowhere else in Britain. *La Seigneurie,* the traditional 17th-century residence of the Lords of Sark, is not open to visitors but the gardens may be toured on certain days.

The island's rugged shore is dotted with caves, small lakes, and natural stone arches. At the south end is *Little Sark,* an island connected to the main island by a natural causeway, *La Coupee.*

Herm

You easily walk through this tiny island in half a day. There is one hotel here, one inn, and no traffic. The beautiful *Shell Beach* is aptly named for its abundance of shells. *Belvoir Bay,* on the east coast, is known as painter's corner. A cave lies hidden between its granite cliffs. The island's interior is full of forested hills and meadows that abound in flowers.

Alderney

Sark: La Seigneurie

Practical Information

The following chapter is divided into two sections. The first, **General Trip Planning,** offers information you'll need for planning and researching your trip as well as tips on transportation to and around England and other items of interest. (See listing in Contents for the full range of subjects covered.)

The second section, **Town-by-Town,** is organized alphabetically by town and provides information that will be helpful on site, such as local tourist offices, hotels and transportation.

General Trip Planning

Choosing When To Go. Spring is a particularly good time to see the beauty of the countryside. The wonderful English gardens are in full bloom, the fresh green competing everywhere with luxuriant flowers. The Lake District is filled with wild daffodils, the orchards in Kent are in full blossom, and the forests abound with bellflowers and primroses. This profusion of beauty is a reason Great Britain is often described as one large garden.

The fall months are also a wonderful time to travel because you can avoid the July–August high season, when the English are on vacation—and all the resort hotels are booked. During the fall, prices for lodging and excursions go down by 25 percent. This is also the best time to travel by car because the roads are much less crowded.

London's profusion of cultural activity makes it enthralling almost all year round. The "London Season," lasting from the end of May until the end of July, is a particularly high point. It includes a wide variety of art exhibits, theater performances, festivals, and various sporting events, including the Derby (the world-famous horse race) and tennis championships at Wimbledon. The Trooping of the Color, the military pageant that marks the Queen's birthday, is one of the most exciting events in June.

Average Temperature and Climate. Britain's climate is usually distinguished by temperate weather, but it can be rather unpredictable. Spring, when the weather is very mild, is probably the most seasonable climate in which to travel. Summers are not particularly hot, but the humidity can be uncomfortable because many buildings are not air-conditioned. The late fall and winter are generally characterized by rain and dense fog. Although temperatures rarely fall below freezing, the dampness can be penetrating. Be sure to pack your rain gear and plenty of warm clothes.

The temperature in Britain is measured in degrees centigrade and Fahrenheit. Below is a listing of average daily temperatures by month in Britain:

Average Daily Temperature

	C°	F°		C°	F°
January	3.9	39	July	17.2	63
February	4.1	39.4	August	16.7	62
March	6.1	43	September	13.9	57
April	8.9	48	October	10.0	50
May	12.2	54	November	6.7	44
June	15.6	60	December	5.0	41

Metric/U.S. Weight, Measure, Temperature Equivalents.

Throughout the text, metric weights and measures are followed by U.S. equivalents in parentheses; likewise, Fahrenheit degrees are provided for centigrade temperatures. The following table is a quick reference for U.S. and metric equivalents.

Metric Unit	U.S. Equivalent	U.S. Unit	Metric Equivalent
Length		**Length**	
1 kilometer	0.6 miles	1 mile	1.6 kilometers
1 meter	1.09 yards	1 yard	0.9 meters
1 decimeter	0.3 feet	1 foot	3.04 decimeters
1 centimeter	0.39 inches	1 inch	2.5 centimeters
Weight		**Weight**	
1 kilogram	2.2 pounds	1 pound	0.45 kilograms
1 gram	0.03 ounces	1 ounce	28.3 grams
Liquid Capacity		**Liquid Capacity**	
1 dekaliter	2.38 gallons	1 gallon	0.37 dekaliters
1 liter	1.05 quarts	1 quart	0.9 liters
1 liter	2.1 pints	1 pint	0.47 liters

(Note: there are 5 British Imperial gallons to 6 U.S. gallons.)

Dry Measure		Dry Measure	
1 liter	0.9 quarts	1 quart	1.1 liters
1 liter	1.8 pints	1 pint	0.55 liters

To convert centigrade (C°) to Fahrenheit (F°):
$C° \times 9 \div 5 + 32 = F°$.

To convert Fahrenheit to centigrade:
$F° - 32 \times 5 \div 9 = C°$.

National Holidays. Listed below are the national holidays in Britain. Specific dates for some holidays vary from year to year.

New Year's Day (January 1)
Good Friday
Easter Sunday
May Day
Spring Bank Holiday (end of May)
Summer Bank Holiday (end of August)
Christmas (December 25)
Boxing Day (December 26)

In addition, a myriad of cultural events animate Britain during the year. Among these are spectacular equestrian shows, impressive flower exhibitions, and superb theater, opera, and dance.

Time Zones. London is five hours ahead of Eastern Standard Time. Therefore, if it is noon in New York and Toronto, it is 5:00 P.M. in London. There is a 13-hour time difference between Sydney, Australia, and London. When it is noon in Sydney, it is 1:00 A.M. the following day in London.

Central European Time (CET) is standard in Great Britain from the third Sunday in March until the fourth Sunday in October. In winter, Greenwich Mean Time (GMT) applies (CET less one hour). Consequently, watches and clocks must be set back one hour.

Passport and Visa Requirements. To enter England, United States citizens must have a valid passport. No visa is required for any stay shorter than three months.

Canadian and Australian citizens also must have a valid passport. No visa is required, and length of stay is individually determined when entering Britain.

Customs Entering Britain. Items used personally for private or professional purposes (e.g., fur coats, watches, cameras, portable type-writers, etc.) do not have to be declared upon arrival in England. There are no currency restrictions.

To simplify passage through customs, travellers who have nothing to declare are now commonly given a green card. Travellers with goods that have to be declared must follow the red signs.

Customs Returning Home From Britain. United States residents may return with $400 worth of foreign purchases without paying duty. For those over 21 these purchases may include 1 liter of alcohol, 100 cigars (non-Cuban), 200 cigarettes, and 1 bottle of perfume.

If you travel with original articles from home that were manufactured abroad, carry all receipts with you so that you will not have to pay duty.

Canadian residents may return with $300 worth of duty-free foreign purchases, 40 ounces of alcohol, 50 cigars, 200 cigarettes, and 2 pounds of manufactured tobacco.

Australians over the age of 18 may return with $400 worth of duty-free foreign articles, 1 liter of alcohol, and 250 grams of tobacco products.

Embassies and Consulates in England and Wales. Help and information can be obtained at the following offices:

> American Embassy
> Grosvenor Square
> London W1A1AE
> Tel: 01-499-9000

> Canadian High Commission
> Macdonald House
> Grosvenor Square
> London W1X0AB
> Tel: 01-629-9492

> Australian High Commission
> Australia House
> Strand
> London WC2B4LA
> Tel: 01-379-4334

In addition to the above, there are consular offices throughout the country in many major cities and touring areas.

British Embassies and Consulates.

In the U.S.: British Embassy
3100 Massachusetts Avenue
Washington, D.C. 20008
Tel: (202)-462-1340

British consulates are also located in Miami, New Orleans, New York, Philadelphia, Anchorage, Portland, Seattle, and Dallas.

In Canada: British High Commission
80 Elfin Street
Ottawa K1P5K7
Tel: (613)-237-1530

British consulates are also located in Halifax and St. John's.

In Australia: British High Commission
Commonwealth Avenue
Canberra
Tel: 706-666

British consulates are also located in Brisbane, Melbourne, Pestle, and Sydney.

Getting to Britain by Air. *From the U.S.:* The major air carriers flying from the United States to Britain are British Airways, Pan Am Airways, Trans World Airlines, Air India, Kuwait Airlines, Virgin Atlantic, El Al, Continental, Delta, Northwest Airlines, and Air New Zealand.

From Australia: Among the airlines that fly from Australia to London are British Airways and Qantas.

From Canada: Among the carriers that fly to Great Britain are Air Canada and British Airways.

There is a bewildering variety of ever-changing special fares, hotel packages, fly/drive, and other deals that depend upon the travel season, the amount of time you can spend, the number of places you wish to visit, etc. Keep an eye on the advertisements in your newspaper's travel section and make your travel arrangements through a reliable travel agent or tour operator to get the best fares and packages.

Getting to Britain by Boat. The only transatlantic passenger ship that sails from North America to England is Cunard Lines' *Queen Elizabeth II*. It sails from April to October between New York, France, and England. Although expensive, an ocean cruise is a sumptuous, relaxing way to travel. More detailed information can be obtained from travel agencies, or you can contact:

Cunard Lines
555 Fifth Avenue
New York, N.Y. 10017
Tel: (212) 880-7500
Nationwide reservation 1-(800)-5-Cunard

Hotels and Other Accommodations. Every year, the British Tourist Authority (BTA) publishes new hotel listings with information on amenities and prices. You can purchase these listings from information offices in Great Britain. Details about regional accommodations can be obtained free of charge from a catalog issued by the BTA. The British Automobile Association (AA) also publishes lists of hotels and restaurants.

For a small fee, tourist bureaus in Great Britain will gladly arrange for hotel rooms or accommodations in bed and breakfast places via

Book-A-Bed Ahead (BABA). For approximately £1.75 one can make use of the "BABA" service all over the country. Many tourist agencies require a deposit, which is later deducted from the hotel bill.

It is always advisable to book rooms in advance, especially during the summer months. While most hotel and guesthouse accommodations include a private bath, you should double check when you make your reservation.

Based on the British Tourist Authority's rankings, we have rated hotels according to four categories: Luxury (🏠🏠🏠); First Class (🏠🏠🏠); Good (🏠🏠); and Less Expensive (🏠). (Both Luxury and First Class are delineated by three houses, a designation that indicates the quality of service and accommodations. The higher prices for luxury hotels are reflected in the amenities they offer.) Prices usually include an overnight stay and a generous breakfast. Hotels often offer lower rates for children. For stays of one week (in many hotels even three days), package deals are available, but often you must eat all your meals at the hotel. In addition, each year the BTA publishes a brochure on "Good Value Hotels" that includes many modest hotels with cooking facilities. These private hotels start at £30 per person per week, and are especially suitable for families with children.

Average hotel prices (per person) can fluctuate greatly, depending on the quality of the hotel and its location. Expect prices in London to be anywhere from 20–50 percent higher than in the suburbs or the countryside. The chart below gives a general range of hotel prices:

Hotel Rating	London	Elsewhere in England
🏠🏠🏠 Luxury	£60 and up	£51 and up
🏠🏠🏠 First Class	£50 and up	£44–46 and up
🏠🏠 Good	£28–43 and up	£35 and up
🏠 Less Expensive	up to £27	£20 and up

To obtain advance booking in London, you can write to:

> London Visitor and Convention Bureau
> 26 Grosvenor Gardens
> London SW1

For a reservation upon arrival, contact the tourist information center at Victoria Station or at the airport.

Many hotels automatically add a service charge of 10–15 percent to their bill. If a service charge is not included in the bill, it is customary to divide a tip of 10–15 percent of the bill among the staff who have provided good service. Small tips are also customary for special services, such as carrying suitcases or pressing clothes.

Most hotels accept credit cards; however many smaller inns—especially those in the countryside—do not. Be sure to find out ahead of time.

Other Accommodations. *Pensions* (*Boardinghouses and Guest-houses*): If you plan to stay in one city for some time and care about economy, or if you enjoy simplicity and contact with local people, consider staying at a pension. Rooms in pensions are usually rented by the week with full or half pension (half pension = overnight stay, breakfast, and dinner; full pension = overnight stay, breakfast, lunch, and dinner). The weekly rate for half pension ranges from about £40–50 in cities and from £35–45 in the countryside.

Bed and Breakfast Establishments: Bed and Breakfasts provide guests with a room for the night and a hearty breakfast the following morning. Rates range from £15–35 in London to £9–30 elsewhere in the country. Most rooms do not have private bathrooms, radios, televisions, or telephones. These establishments are usually run by families who want to make some extra money and enjoy company. Generally, hosts and guests share the same roof. Bed and Breakfasts are clearly indicated by signposts that can be spotted in towns, villages, and throughout the countryside. In many places, rooms can be booked through the local tourist information centers scattered all around Britain, or from out of town via Book-A-Bed-Ahead (BABA), for a fee of £1.60.

Guest Inns: Many of the traditional English inns have been centers of hospitality for centuries, and represent a colorful aspect of British life in general and the British countryside in particular. They offer accommodations and food at moderate prices. Most of these inns can be found in the brochure *Some Inns of Britain*, which is available from the British Tourist Authority.

Farm Accommodations: Many English farms accept guests. Count on simple but clean accommodations, abundant, tasty food from the fields and barnyards, and a hearty welcome. In the summer season, average prices for rooms with breakfast and dinner vary between £70–100 per week.

Motels: Numerous modern motels offer accommodations to drivers along the highways and expressways. Prices for double rooms with breakfast vary between £15–20 per person. Many motels allow guests to make free telephone reservations to other motels. Brochures, maps with motel locations, and price lists are supplied by the British Motels Federation, 10 Bolton Street, London W1.

Currency Regulations. British currency is based on the pound sterling, which is divided into 100 pence. Bank bills are divided into £50, £20, £10, £5, and £1 denominations. British coins are £1, 50p, 20p, 10p, 5p, 2p, and 1p. The half penny is now obsolete.

There are no limits on the amount of money that can be brought into or taken out of the country. Other currency regulations are subject to sudden change, and we recommend that you check with your bank before leaving. Your national currency may be exchanged at most banks or at the airport. To obtain the most favorable exchange rate, first track currency fluctuations in the newspaper, then change your money at a bank to avoid a surcharge.

Business Hours and Closings. In England and Wales, banks are open Monday through Friday from 9:30 A.M. to 3:30 P.M. Exchange bureaus (open until 9:00 or 10:00 P.M.) are located in airports, air terminals, London's Victoria Station, and other railroad stations. Traveler's checks may be cashed at banks.

Most museums, galleries, etc., open their doors on Saturdays and Sundays; however, many historic homes and museums are not open to the public on a daily basis—particularly those outside major cities. To avoid disappointment, be sure to ask about visiting hours at the local tourism office.

Postage. From Great Britain, letters to the United States and Canada that are not over 10 grams cost 31p to mail. For each additional 10 grams, the cost is 14p. Small packages and printed papers are 23p, and each additional 10 grams is 7p. Newspapers and periodicals (weight limit: 2,000 grams) are 18p, and each additional 10 grams is 4p.

To Australia, letters not over 10 grams are 34p, and each additional 10 grams is 15p. For small packages and printed papers, the cost is 24p, and each additional 10 grams is 8p. Newspapers and periodicals are 19p, and each additional 10 grams is 5p.

Postcards are 26p to all destinations.

Automatic stamp dispensers can be found outside post offices so that stamps may be purchased at any time.

Telephones. There are five different kinds of public telephones. The two push-button varieties require money to be inserted *before* dialing (2p, 10p, and 50p coins only for one type; the second type takes all coins from 2p to £1). A third type of telephone works only with credit cards; a fourth type, with a so-called phone-card. Phone-cards may be purchased at all post offices and at many shops. After the card is inserted in the telephone, the price of the call is debited to the card. The fifth, less modern type of telephone, works only with 10p coins that are inserted after the connection is made.

Dialing codes in London:

General Information	191
London Directory Inquiries	142
Inland Long Distance Calls	100
Continental Calls	104 or 105
Overseas Calls	107 or 108
Emergencies	999 for fire, police, or ambulance

For assistance with overseas calls, try the Westminster International Telephone Bureau (1 Broadway), close to the St. James underground station and the new buildings of Scotland Yard. It is open from 9:00 A.M. to 7:00 P.M. seven days a week.

Travelling in Britain. The English transportation system is one of the world's best. Trains link the major cities, and even in remote or sparsely populated areas the nearest station is only a few miles away. Local bus systems are well organized throughout the country, and express bus lines run between towns. Larger cities are linked by regular air service.

Taxis. Available taxis are indicated by the "For Hire" sign. Fares start at 80p, and after about ³/₄ mile, the meter clicks at a cost of 20p per ¹/₄ mile. There is a surcharge of 20p for each additional passenger. In small towns this charge is sometimes less. In London there is a 40–60p surcharge on evenings and weekends. You should tip at least 10–15 percent of the fare—and never under 20p.

Getting to London from the Airport. It is approximately 15 miles from Heathrow Airport to central London. The taxi fare should run about £17–20 plus tip.

You can also take the Underground, London's convenient subway system, from Heathrow Central to the city for £1.50, if you don't mind carrying your bags a distance to the station.

Gatwick Airport is about 29 miles from central London—roughly an hour's drive. The taxi fare should cost approximately £27 plus tip.

Rail is still the fastest and least expensive way to get from Gatwick to Victoria Station. The train commutes every 15 minutes during the day and hourly at night. The 30-minute ride costs about £4.20.

A taxi from Stansted Airport to central London will cost about £25. A train service from Bishop's Stortford to Liverpool Street Station takes between 35 and 50 minutes. Taxis and buses also run between the station and the airport. In addition, London Transport's Airbus can take you close to Victoria Station and to Paddington Station for about £2.50.

Buses. It is possible to traverse the entire country by bus. All the large cities of Great Britain are linked by regular coach service, and leisurely double-deck buses connect country towns and villages. If you are travelling by bus, note that a "Stop" sign means that the bus will always stop to pick up passengers, but a "Request" sign means that the driver will stop only if requested to do so.

Visitors to London may use all red buses and subway lines with a Visitor Travelcard for one, three, four, or seven days. Prices are about $15 for three days, $18 for four days, and $24 for seven days. Detailed information can be obtained from all British tourism offices and many travel agencies.

If you plan to travel extensively, purchase the *Express Coach Guide,* issued twice a year by the National Bus Company, 25 New Street Square, London, E.C. 4. Coaches differ from buses because they are larger and more comfortable for lengthy excursions. The National Express coach service offers the greatest number of travel routes, and its reasonable prices make it as convenient as train travel.

Driving in Britain. Be sure to review British traffic regulations before setting off on an extended tour, especially if you are unaccustomed to driving on the left side of the road.

Car Rental. Car rental agencies can be found throughout the country's major cities and at the airports. From the British Tourist Authority you can get up-to-date listings of reliable rental agencies free of charge. Major companies such as Avis, Budget, Godfrey Davis, Hertz, Mitchells, Swan National, and others have local branches almost everywhere in Britain.

Ask about special discounts; for example, if you rent a car for a period of three to four weeks, the discount is usually 10 percent. In spring, fall, and winter, you may save as much as 20–30 percent. Normally, you must pay the rental fee in advance.

Further information about prices, special rates, and regulations can be obtained from the rental firms or automobile clubs at home, or from travel agencies. It is advisable to buy a collision damage waiver, which will cover all costs in case of damage.

Roads. The main roads that crisscross the country are as follows: A 1 (Great North Road), A 2 (Dover Road), A 3 (Portsmouth Road), A 4 (Bath Road), A 5 (Watling Street; Holyhead Road; also North Wales Road), A 6 (Carlisle Road via Derby), A 7 (Edinburgh–Carlisle Road). Expressways are indicated by the letter A before a number; the letter M delineates highways.

Driving Regulations. Remember that the English drive on the left side of the road. Familiarize yourself with the relevant traffic rules and regulations of the *Highway Code* (official driver's guide). It is given free of charge upon arrival in Britain.

Speed limits are indicated in miles per hour. At present, the speed limit on highways and roads with double lanes is 113 kmh (70 mph); 97 kmh (60 mph) on urban roads, including rural areas; 64 kmh (40 mph) on local roads; and 48 kmh (30 mph) in cities.

A word of advice: when driving on winding country roads, you will need to exercise special caution when passing the numerous bicycles. Above all, when in doubt, don't pass.

Parking in cities is often regulated. A single or double yellow line along the road near the curb means no parking. There are also signs indicating parking regulations. Parking meters differ according to the

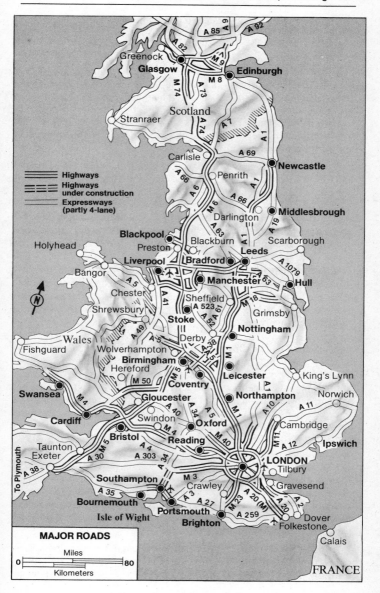

MAJOR ROADS

Highways
Highways under construction
Expressways (partly 4-lane)

part of town and vary between two and five hours. The fees and time allotted are marked on the meters. In general, parking is free in the evening, on Saturday afternoon, and all day on Sunday.

The quality of gasoline (usually referred to as "petrol") is indicated by stars: two stars (90 octane), three stars (94 octane), four stars (97 octane). The price of gasoline may differ greatly according to gas station and region. Gasoline is pumped by the liter or gallon. Motor oil generally comes in liters.

Drivers and front seat passengers must wear safety belts. It's the law.

The minimum age for driving vehicles in Britain is 16 for mopeds and 17 for cars and motorcycles.

Traffic Information. Information concerning the state of the roads and traffic conditions can be obtained from the Motoring Information Service in London: Tel: 01-246-8021.

The Automobile Association, Fanum House, Leicester Square, London, W.C. 2, and the Automobile Club, 85 Pall Mall, London, S.W. 1, will gladly provide any further information. Both organizations also provide breakdown and towing assistance. Tel.: 01-954-7373.

The Tunnel Under the Channel. In the early sixties, the governments of both England and France agreed to construct a car tunnel under the English Channel, linking the two countries. After much ado over the costs of the tunnel as well as other logistical problems, construction finally began in late 1987.

Ferry Service. The surest way to get from Britain to the Continent is by ferry. There are a multitude of ferry, hovercraft, and jetfoil services linking over a dozen British ports to the British Isles and continental Europe. With the exception of the jetfoil, these services offer space for passengers with cars in addition to carrying foot passengers.

Reservations can be made through travel agencies or directly with representatives of the ferry services.

Contact the British Tourist Authority (see page 315) for information on ferry connections, fares, and addresses.

Trains. Day trains are equipped with restaurant or lounge coaches, and night trains generally provide sleeping accommodations. Different kinds of discounts for travelling within Great Britain are available. There are various types of network passes, regional passes, and holiday passes; the most important are listed below:

Britrail Pass. The Britrail Pass, an equivalent of the Eurailpass, is a rail network pass that can be procured year-round and allows unlimited travel by train. The pass is also valid for ferry services of the British

Railways (e.g., on Windermere Lake, to the Isle of Wight). You must get a Britrail Pass *before* travelling in Great Britain from a travel bureau or at agencies of the British Rail. The cost of a ticket, which is bought for a period of 7, 14, 21, or 30 days, is, respectively about $115, $175, $220, and $260.

Circular Tour Tickets. A circular tour includes an itinerary consisting of at least three destinations that eventually return to the original point of departure. These circular tour passes are valid for three months and should be ordered in advance from travel agents outside Great Britain. In many cases, the passes are also valid for bus and steamer service.

Runabout Tickets. These holiday passes are valid for six or seven days during the summer season, for a specific region (e.g., northern England, the Lake District, etc.).

Day Return Tickets. Day return tickets are up to 40 percent cheaper than regular tickets. Weekend and monthly return tickets are also available.

Restaurants and Pubs. Unlike the predominating myths that surround English cuisine, the food in most English restaurants is not all that bad (see page 6). Lunch costs from £3.50–7; dinner, about double that amount. Elegant restaurants in tourist resorts and in London are expensive. The British Tourist Authority's guide *Hotels and Restaurants in Britain* offers a list of excellent yet reasonable restaurants in England and Wales. Mealtimes are generally fixed in hotels and restaurants. They are similar to ours, and should be observed because there is no service after hours.

Specialty restaurants and restaurants with international cuisines are numerous, especially in London and in other large cities and tourist resorts. A selection of these restaurants can be found in the brochure *Your Guide Through London,* available for a small fee from the British Tourist Authority.

"Grill Rooms," often attached to hotels and restaurants, are very popular, especially at lunchtime. Low-priced meals can be enjoyed in the restaurants of department stores, in self-service restaurants, and in fast-food places such as Lyons, The Golden Egg, Wimpy, Fuller's, Motor Chefs, Fortes, etc.

Pubs. Pubs, or Public Houses, are an English institution. On weekdays, they are usually open from 11:00 A.M. to 10:30 or 11:30 P.M., but are closed for two and a half to three hours in the afternoon. Closing time is earlier on Sundays. No children under 14 are allowed, and teenagers under 18 are served only non-alcoholic beverages. The entrance to most pubs is marked by a big "L" for "licensed"—i.e., licensed to serve alcoholic drinks. Pubs marked with a "U," "unlicensed," are subject to certain restrictions on the sale of alcoholic beverages.

Pubs are famous for their hearty English food and "atmosphere." Often they occupy three different rooms: a public room, or bar, mainly for drinking beer while standing; a saloon, or lounge, for meeting friends and enjoying small meals; and a cocktail room. People 16 years or older may order alcoholic beverages with meals in the cocktail room, where prices on the menu run about £2.50. Many pubs, in London as well as in the countryside, are rightfully admired for their historic and original designs.

Tea Rooms, Cafés, and Snackbars. These are encountered practically everywhere. Besides tea and coffee, these establishments serve refreshments, small meals, and snacks at moderate prices. Alcohol is never served in these establishments.

Shopping. Most shops are open from 9:00 A.M. to 5:30 P.M. Monday through Saturday, except for one afternoon during the week, usually on Wednesday or Thursday. Shopping hours on the Channel Islands (with the exception of Thursday) are from 9:00 A.M. until late in the evening.

Oxford Street in London is considered the most famous shopping street in the area, best known for its enormous department store, Selfridge's. Bond Street is extremely well known for its stores which offer goods for more luxurious tastes. This area's best example is Savile Row, where you can find superbly crafted suits for rather astonishingly high prices. Don't forget Knightsbridge, where the world-famous Harrod's is located.

Visit the Design Centre at 28 Haymarket, S.W. 1, for reference information on various goods available in London ("Made in Great Britain"), and for catalogs of stores where they are sold at reasonable prices. It is open Monday, Tuesday, Friday, and Saturday from 9:30 A.M. to 5:30 P.M., and on Wednesday and Thursday from 9:30 A.M. to 8:00 P.M. A similar organization is the Craft Centre of Great Britain, at 43 Earlham Street, W.C. 2, which is open Monday to Friday from 10:00 A.M. until 5:00 P.M. (Thursday, until 6:00 P.M.) Tourist bureaus in other cities can provide information about comparable centers.

In London, tourist attractions change quickly. Young visitors from all over the world are probably still drawn to Carnaby Street because it represents a slice of history from the sixties, and most tourists will also pay a visit to King's Road in the artistic Chelsea quarter. However, in

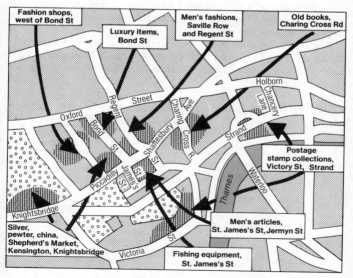

Specialty shopping in London

the last few years, many people have been frequenting Covent Garden (a 15-minute walk from Piccadilly Circus). Covent Garden was for 300 years London's principal flower and vegetable market, made famous in the musical *My Fair Lady*. A few years ago, the shutters were drawn for the last time in these large Victorian halls, and recent renovations have been turning this area into a vibrant new world. An outstanding antique market is held every Monday from 9:00 A.M. to 3:00 P.M. in Jubilee Hall, and on Sunday night one can see fine craftsmen at work. The Central Hall houses a special shopping center open six days a week until 8:00 P.M.; besides first class stores, it boasts no less than six restaurants. In the area around the halls, in the former shops and pubs surrounding the Covent Garden Opera House, new boutiques, galleries, and fine crafts stores have opened. Another significant attraction is the ascetic St. Paul's church, built in the 17th century by the architect Inigo Jones.

Buying goods on the Channel Islands is truly a delight, because no duty is levied. Among favorite, reasonably priced, quality articles "Made in England" we find: tweed fabrics, lamb's-wool jackets, men and women's clothing of top quality, including cashmere, fashionable goods for young people, costume jewelry, sports items, and toys. Ladies' toiletries and other cosmetics are also of fine quality and are worth buying.

To avoid paying the 15 percent VAT ("value added tax"), have your purchases shipped by mail to your home address, or to the port or airport from which you will leave.

Many department stores hand items bought without the VAT directly to the client. A form must be filled out and handed to customs upon leaving. No payment will be required, but the seller will be reimbursed for the value added tax.

Clothing Sizes. Listed below are men's and women's standard clothing sizes equivalents for the U.S., England, and Europe.

		U.S.	U.K.	Europe
Chest	Small	34	34	87
	Medium	36	36	91
		38	38	97
	Large	40	40	102
		42	42	107
	Extra Large	44	44	112
		46	46	117
Collar		14	14	36
		14½	14½	37
		15	15	38
		15½	15½	39

	U.S.	**U.K.**	**Europe**
	16	16	41
	16½	16½	42
	17	17	43
Waist	24	24	61
	26	26	66
	28	28	71
	30	30	76
	32	32	80
	34	34	87
	36	36	91
	38	38	97
Men's Suits	34	34	44
	35	35	46
	36	36	48
	37	37	49½
	38	38	51
	39	39	52½
	40	40	54
	41	41	55½
	42	42	57
Men's Shoes	7	6	39½
	8	7	41
	9	8	42
	10	9	43
	11	10	44½
	12	11	46
	13	12	47
Men's Hats	6¾	6⅝	54
	6⅞	6¾	55
	7	6⅞	56
	7⅛	7	57
	7¼	7⅛	58
	7½	7⅜	60
Women's Dresses	6	8	36
	8	10	38
	10	12	40
	12	14	42
	14	16	44
	16	18	46
	18	20	48
Women's Blouses and Sweaters	8	10	38
	10	12	40
	12	14	42
	14	16	44
	16	18	46
	18	20	48

	U.S.	U.K.	Europe
Women's Shoes	4½	3	35½
	5	3½	36
	5½	4	36½
	6	4½	37
	6½	5	37½
	7	5½	38
	7½	6	38½
	8	6½	39
	8½	7	39½
	9	7½	40
Children's Clothing	2	16	92
(*One size larger for knitwear*)	3	18	98
	4	20	104
	5	22	110
	6	24	116
	6X	26	122
Children's Shoes	8	7	24
	9	8	25
	10	9	27
	11	10	28
	12	11	29
	13	12	30
	1	13	32
	2	1	33
	3	2	34
	4½	3	36
	5½	4	37
	6½	5½	38½

Sports. Great Britain is definitely a country for sports enthusiasts. Golfers, sailors, bicyclists, and those who love fishing will find a real vacation paradise in England and Wales. Those enamored of soccer, horse races, dog races, and rowing competitions will always get their money's worth.

Cricket matches are held daily in the summer, and the best matches are played at the Oval Ground and at Lord's (the Middlesex ground at St. John's Wood). Soccer—or football, as it is called in Britain—is voraciously enjoyed in the winter, and the best matches may be seen at Chelsea, West Ham, Tottenham, and Highbury. The Cup Final, played at Wembley Stadium at the end of May, is the climactic game and is covered by the British television networks.

You will find a list of some of the country's main participant sports and sporting centers below:

Fishing: Blagdon (West Somerset), Exmoor, Dartmoor, Norfolk Broads, in Wales.

Golf: Harlech (Wales), Westward-Ho (Devon), Sandwich and Deal (Kent), and Liverpool.

Shark Fishing: The coasts of South Cornwall.

Horse Racing: Lincoln, Newmarket, Epsom, Ascot, Kempton Park, Sandown Park, and Windsor.

Pony Trekking: Black Mountains (Wales), West Wales, Lake District, and the northern English border country.

Bicycling: Everywhere in England and Wales. Information can be obtained from the Cyclists Touring Club and the British Cycling Federation.

Rowing: You can row on the Serpentine, in Regent's Park, and on the Thames. Rowing competitions are held in Henley-on-Thames and between Putney and Mortlake (the famous University Boat Race, Oxford versus Cambridge, which takes place on the last Sunday in March or the first Sunday in April).

Swimming and water sports: Brighton, Eastbourne, Hastings (all of southeast England), Southsea, Bournemouth, Isle of Wight (all of southern England), Torquay, Weston-super-Mare (both in the southwest of England), Scarborough (Yorkshire), Southport, Blackpool, Morecambe and Heysham (western England), Llandudno (northern Wales), Jersey and Guernsey (Channel Islands), and the Isle of Man.

Sailing: Torquay, Cowes (Isle of Wight), and Norfolk Broads.

Hiking: Cotswolds, Yorkshire valleys, Lake District, and many other areas.

Surfing: Newquay, Bude, St. Ives (all in Cornwall), Jersey, and Guernsey (the Channel Islands).

Aside from the abundance of outdoor sports you can observe or participate in, you'll find that darts, a game of skill, is another national passion played in almost every pub throughout the country.

General Sources of Information. Addresses of the British Tourist Authority in the United States, Canada, and Australia:

In the U.S.:   British Tourist Authority
                   40 West 57th Street
                   New York, N.Y. 10019
                   Tel: (212) 581-4700

                   British Tourist Authority
                   John Hancock Center, Suite 3320
                   875 North Michigan Avenue
                   Chicago, Ill. 60611
                   Tel: (312) 787-0490

In the U.S.:   British Tourist Authority
Cedar Maple Plaza, Suite 210
2305 Cedar Spring Road
Dallas, Texas 75201-1814
Tel: (214) 720-4040

British Tourist Authority
World Trade Center, Suite 450
350 South Figueroa
Los Angeles, Calif. 90071
Tel: (213) 628-3525

In Canada: British Tourist Authority
94 Cumberland Street
Suite 600
Toronto, Ontario
M5R 3N3
Tel: (416) 925-6326

In Australia: British Tourist Authority
Midland House
171 Clarence Street
Sydney N.S.W.
2000
Tel: 29-8627

General Addresses of the British Railways Offices:

Britrail Travel International
630 Third Avenue
New York, N.Y. 10017
Tel: (212) 599-5400

Britrail Travel International
800 South Hope Street, Suite 603
Los Angeles, Calif. 90017
Tel: (213) 624-8787

Britrail Travel International
Cedar Maple Plaza
2305 Cedar Springs Road
Dallas, Texas 75219
Tel: (214) 748-0860

General Addresses of the British Railways Offices:

Britrail Travel International
333 Michigan Avenue
Chicago, Ill. 60601
Tel: (312) 263-1910

Britrail
409 Granville Street
Vancouver BCV6C1T2
Canada
Tel: (604) 683-6896

Britrail
94 Cumberland Street
Toronto M5R1A3
Canada
Tel: (416) 929-3333

Tourist Information Centers in England and Wales:

British Tourist Authority
Thames Tower
Black's Road
Hammersmith
London W69EL (for written inquiries only)

Wales Tourist Board
34 Piccadilly
London W 1
Tel: 01-409-0969

Isle of Man Tourist Board
13 Victoria Street
Douglas
Tel: (8624) 74323

There is also a general information desk at Gatwick Airport: General inquiries: Tel: (0293) 28822 or 6684211. Information booths of the London Visitor and Convention Bureau are located at Harrod's and at Selfridge's.

Town-by-Town

Included under each town listing are population and county as well as information on local tourist offices, hotels, and airports (when applicable). Hotels are classified according to our rating system (see page 302). Those hotels marked with an asterisk (*) are of historic or architectural interest. The number of rooms is indicated in parentheses ( ). Note also that we have indicated which tourism offices are open only during the high tourist season (July–August) and which offer the Book-a-Bed-Ahead (BABA) service (see page 302).

Aberaeron (Population 1300; Dyfed)
   Information: Harbour Car Park, Market Street (seasonal)—BABA.
Accommodations: 🛈 Feathers Royal* (16).

Aberdovey/Aberdyfi (Population 1200; Gwynedd)
   Information: The Wharf—BABA. **Accommodations:** 🛈🛈🛈 Plas Penhelig* (12). 🛈🛈 Penhelig Arms (11); Trefeddian (46).

Abergavenny (Population 10,000; Gwent)
   Information: 2 Lower Monk Street (seasonal)—BABA. **Accommodations:** 🛈🛈🛈 (*Luxury*) Angel* (29).

Aberystwyth (Dyfed)
   Information: Eastgate—BABA. **Accommodations:** 🛈🛈🛈 Conrah Country* (22). 🛈🛈 Belle Vue Royal* (50); Cambrian* (12); Sea Bank (22). 🛈 Four Seasons (17).

Aldeburgh (Population 2800; Suffolk)
   Information: The Cinema, High Street (seasonal)—BABA.
Accommodations: 🛈🛈🛈 (*Luxury*) Brudenell (47); White Lion (34). 🛈🛈 Uplands* (20).

Alderney (Population 1700; Channel Islands)
   Information: States Office, St. Anne. Transportation: Airport in Alderney. **Accommodations:** 🛈🛈 Belle Vue (20); Inchalla (12).

Alfriston (Population 800; Sussex)
   Accommodations: 🛈🛈🛈 (*Luxury*) Star Inn* (32). 🛈🛈🛈 Deans Place* (43). 🛈🛈 George Inn* (8).

Alnmouth (Population 1200; Northumberland)
   Accommodations: 🛈🛈 Schooner* (21).

Alnwick (Population 7500; Northumberland)
Information: The Shambles, Northumberland Hall (seasonal)—BABA. **Accommodations:** 🏨🏨🏨 White Swan* (41). 🏨🏨 Hotspur* (28).

Alton (Population 14,700; Hampshire)
Information: Council Offices, High Street. **Accommodations:** 🏨🏨🏨 Grange (9); Swan* (28).

Amesbury (Population 5500; Wiltshire)
Information: Redworth House, Flower Lane—BABA. **Accommodations:** 🏨🏨 Antrobus Arms* (20).

Andover (Population 30,600; Hampshire)
Information: Town Mill Car Park, Bridge Street (seasonal)—BABA. **Accommodations:** 🏨🏨🏨 Bere Hill House (20); Danebury (24). 🏨🏨 White Hart* (21).

Arundel (Population 2700; Sussex)
Information: 61 High Street—BABA. **Accommodations:** 🏨🏨🏨 Avisford Park* (82). 🏨🏨 Burpham Country (7); Howards* (9); Norfolk Arms* (34).

Ascot (Population 7500; Berkshire)
Accommodations: 🏨🏨🏨 (*Luxury*) Berystede (88). 🏨🏨 Royal Berkshire (52).

Ashbourne (Population 5700; Derbyshire)
Information: 13 Market Place. **Accommodations:** 🏨🏨 Green Man & Blacks Head* (17).

Ashburton (Population 3600; Devon)
Accommodations: 🏨🏨 Dartmoor Motel (22); Holne Chase* (15); Tugella House* (6).

Ashby-de-la-Zouch (Population 10,600; Leicestershire)
Information: Lower Church Street (seasonal). **Accommodations:** 🏨🏨🏨 Royal Crest* (31).

Ashford (Population 35,600; Kent)
Information: Information Kiosk, High Street. **Accommodations:** 🏨🏨🏨 (*Luxury*) Eastwell Manor* (24). 🏨🏨🏨 Spearpoint (27). 🏨🏨 Croft (28); Downsview (16).

Aylesbury (Population 46,100; Buckinghamshire)
   Information: County Hall, Walton St. **Accommodations:** 🏚🏚🏚 (*Luxury*) Bell (17). 🏚🏚 King's Head* (22).

Bakewell (Population 4200; Derbyshire)
   Information: Old Market Hall, Bridge Street. **Accommodations:** 🏚🏚 Croft Country House* (8).

Bamburgh (Population 700; Northumberland)
   Accommodations: 🏚🏚 Lord Crewe Arms* (27). 🏚 Sunningdale (18).

Banbury (Population 36,600; Oxfordshire)
   Information: Banbury Museum, 8 Horsefair—BABA. **Accommodations:** 🏚🏚🏚 (*Luxury*) Whately Hall* (74). 🏚🏚 Banbury Moat House (32); Cromwell Lodge (32).

Bangor (Population 17,000; Gwynedd)
   Information: Theatre Gwynedd, Beach Road (seasonal)—BABA. **Accommodations:** 🏚🏚 British (50); Telford (9).

Barmouth (Population 2300; Gwynedd)
   Information: Station Road (seasonal)—BABA. **Accommodations:** 🏚🏚🏚 Plas Mynach Castle Country House* (12). 🏚🏚 Bryn Melyn (10); Ty'r Craig* (12).

Barnstaple (Population 21,000; Devon)
   Information: 20 Holland Street—BABA. **Accommodations:** 🏚🏚🏚 Imperial (56). 🏚🏚 Barnstaple Motel (57); North Devon Motel (26); Royal & Fortescue* (61).

Barry (Population 42,500; South Glamorgan)
   Information: Barry Island (seasonal)—BABA. **Accommodations:** 🏚🏚 Mount Sorrell (37).

Basingstoke (Population 75,000; Hampshire)
   Accommodations: 🏚🏚🏚 (*Luxury*) Crest (86); Ladbroke (108); Tylney Hall* (37). 🏚🏚🏚 Red Lion* (63). 🏚🏚 Wessex House (8).

Bath (Population 83,900; Avon)
   Information: Abbey Church Yard—BABA. **Accommodations:** 🏚🏚🏚 (*Luxury*) Apsley House* (7); Francis* (90); Redcar* (29). 🏚🏚🏚 Bath (96); Berni Royal* (30); Duke's* (22); Fernley* (48); Ladbroke Beaufort (123); Lansdown Grove* (41); Pratt's* (46). 🏚🏚 Brompton House (10); Gainsborough (16); St. Clair (10); Somerset House* (9); Wentworth House (20).

Berwick-upon-Tweed (Population 12,000; Northumberland)
   Information: Castlegate Car Park (seasonal)—BABA. **Accommodations:** 🏨🏨🏨 King's Arms* (37). 🏨🏨 Queens Head (6).

Betws-y-Coed (Population 800; Gwynedd)
   Information: Royal Oak Stables (seasonal)—BABA. **Accommodations:** 🏨🏨🏨 Royal Oak (21). 🏨🏨 Fairy Glen (10); Park Hill (11).

Beverley (Population 17,200; Humberside)
   Information: 30 Saturday Market. **Accommodations:** 🏨🏨🏨 (*Luxury*) Beverley Arms* (61); Tickton Grange* (16). 🏨🏨 Lairgate* (24). 🏨 Kings Head* (9).

Bexhill-on-Sea (Population 34,700; Sussex)
   Information: De la Warr Pavilion, Marina—BABA. **Accommodations:** 🏨🏨 Southlands Court (28).

Bibury (Population 700; Gloucestershire)
   Accommodations: 🏨🏨🏨 Bibury Court* (16); Swan* (24).

Bideford (Population 13,000; Devon)
   Information: The Quay (seasonal)—BABA. **Accommodations:** 🏨🏨 Durrant House* (58); Riversford (17); Royal (33); Yeoldon House (10). 🏨 Rosskerry (10).

Birmingham (Population 1,041,000; West Midlands)
   Information: 2 City Arcade—BABA. The Piazza, National Exhibition Centre—BABA; Birmingham Airport. **Transportation:** International Airport Elmdon 8 km. (5 miles) from center of town (buses leave every 20 minutes from Dudley Street). **Accommodations:** 🏨🏨🏨 (*Luxury*) Albany (254); Holiday Inn (304); Plough & Harrow* (44). 🏨🏨🏨 Grand* (184); Meadow Court (12); Post House (204). 🏨🏨 Asquith House* (14); Gables (17); Hagley Court (25); Ladbroke International (197); Sheridan House (9). 🏨 Lyndhurst (14); Middleton House (11); Wentsbury (12); Woodlands (18).

Bishop Auckland (Population 34,800; Durham)
   Accommodations: 🏨🏨 Park Head (12). 🏨 Binchester Hall (21); Queens Head* (10).

Bishop's Stortford (Population 21,500; Hertfordshire)
   Information: Council Offices, 2 The Causeway. **Accommodations:** 🏨 Brook House* (24).

Blackpool (Population 145,400; Lancashire)
Information: 87a Coronation Street; 1 Clifton Street; Blackpool Airport. **Transportation:** Suire's Gate Airport 5 km. (3 miles) from center of town. **Accommodations:** 🏨 (*Luxury*) Imperial (159); Pembroke (201). 🏨 New Clifton (78). 🏨 Boston (55); Brabyns (25); Carlton (58); Checquers (46); Claremont (143); Cliffs (168); Lansdowne (72); Savoy (130); Warwick (52).

Blaenau Ffestiniog (Population 6500; Gwynedd)
Information: Isallt, High Street (seasonal)—BABA.

Bognor Regis (Population 35,000; West Sussex)
Information: Place St. Maur des Fosses, Belmont Street—BABA. **Accommodations:** 🏨 Clarehaven* (28); Royal Norfolk* (52). 🏨 Black Mill House (26), Royal* (29).

Bolton (Population 148,200; Greater Manchester)
Information: Town Hall—BABA. **Accommodations:** 🏨 (*Luxury*) Crest (100). 🏨 Egerton House (25); Last Drop* (80).

Boston (Population 27,100; Lincolnshire)
Information: Market Place—BABA. **Accommodations:** 🏨 White Hart (31). 🏨 Burton House (6); New England (25).

Bourne (Population 7000; Lincolnshire)
Accommodations: 🏨 Angel* (11).

Bournemouth (Population 144,600; Dorset)
Information: Westover Road—BABA. **Accommodations:** 🏨 (*Luxury*) Crest (102); Highcliff (110); Palace Court (106); Royal Bath (131). 🏨 Anglo-Swiss (63); Bournemouth Moat House (152); Chine (108); Cliff End* (40); Cecil (27); Courtlands (46); Durley Dean (112); East Cliff Court (70); Ladbroke (69); Langtry Manor* (18); White Hermitage (84). 🏨 Albany (19); Burley Court (41); Cadogan (50); Chesterwood (44); Cliffside (64); Durley Hall (81); Durlston Court (59); East Anglia (71); Fircroft (49); Manor House* (27); Norfolk* (65); Pavilion (47); Royal Exeter* (38); St. George (21); Whitehall (48).

Bourton-on-the-Water (Population 3000; Gloucestershire)
Accommodations: 🏨 Chester House (22); Old Manse* (10); Old New Inn* (17).

Bradford (Population 464,000; West Yorkshire)
Information: City Hall—BABA; Central Library, Princes Way—BABA. **Transportation:** Leeds/Bradford Airport; Air Terminal: Chester Bus Station. **Accommodations:** 🏨🏨🏨 (*Luxury*) Stakis Norfolk Gardens (126); Victoria (60). 🏨🏨🏨 Novotel Bradford (136). 🏨🏨 Dubrovnik* (14).

Brampton (Population 4700; Cumbria)
Information: Moot Hall (seasonal). **Accommodations:** 🏨🏨 Sands House* (13); Tarn End* (6).

Brecon (Population 6500; Powys)
Information: Market Car Park (seasonal)—BABA. **Accommodations:** 🏨🏨🏨 (*Luxury*) Castle of Brecon* (53). 🏨🏨 Bishops Meadow Motel (22); Nant Ddu Lodge Country House* (8); Nythfa House (16); Wellington (21). 🏨 Lansdowne (12).

Bridgwater (Population 26,400; Somerset)
Information: Town Hall, High Street (seasonal)—BABA.

Bridlington (Population 26,900; Humberside)
Information: 25 Prince Street—BABA. **Accommodations:** 🏨🏨 Expanse (49); Monarch (43). 🏨 Marine (14).

Bridport (Population 6600; Dorset)
Information: 32 South Street (seasonal)—BABA. **Accommodations:** 🏨🏨 Bull* (17); Haddon House* (13); Eype's Mouth (20); Little Wych Country House* (6); West Mead (26). 🏨 Bridport Arms (8).

Brighton and Hove (Population 152,700; East Sussex)
Information: Marlborough House, 54 Old Steine, Brighton; Sea Front, King's Road, Brighton (seasonal); Town Hall, Norton Road, Hove. **Accommodations:** 🏨🏨🏨 (*Luxury*) Dudley (80); Royal Albion* (115). 🏨🏨🏨 Alexandra* (60); Courtlands (60); Curzon* (45); Norfolk Resort* (115); Old Ship* (153); Sackville (47); St. Catherine's Lodge (55); Whitehaven (17). 🏨🏨 Apollo (87); Lawns (45); Prince Regent* (18); Seafield (14); Sutherland* (13). 🏨 Cosmopolitan* (25); Imperial (71); Marina House (10); Seafield House (16).

Bristol (Population 394,000; Avon)
Information: Colston House, Colston Street—BABA. **Transportation:** Luesgate Airport, 12 km. (7.5 miles) from center of town (bus from platform 2, Coach Station, Marlborough Street). **Accommoda-**

tions: 🏨🏨🏨 (*Luxury*) Avon Gorge (76); Crest (151); Grand* (179); Holiday Inn (285); Ladbroke Dragonara* (201). 🏨🏨🏨 Redwood Lodge (72); St. Vincent Rocks (46); Unicorn* (192). 🏨🏨 Clifton (63); Oakfield (27).

Broadstairs (Population 20,000; Kent)
Information: Pierremont Hall, 67 High Street. **Transportation:** Manston Airport, 8 km. (5 miles). **Accommodations:** 🏨🏨🏨 Royal Albion* (21). 🏨🏨 Castle Keep (29).

Broadway (Population 3000; Worcestershire)
Information: Cotswold Court (seasonal). **Accommodations:** 🏨🏨🏨 (*Luxury*) Dormy House* (50); 🏨🏨🏨 Broadway* (23); Collin House* (7).

Bude (Population 6000; Cornwall)
Information: The Crescent Car Park (seasonal); A 39, Stamford Hill, Stratton (seasonal). **Accommodations:** 🏨🏨🏨 Grenville (71); Hartland (30); Strand (40). 🏨🏨 Burn Court (34). 🏨 Bude Haven (11); Camelot (13); Edgcumbe (15); Grosvenor (13); St. Margaret's (10).

Builth Wells (Population 1500; Powys)
Information: Groe Car Park (seasonal)—BABA. **Accommodations:** 🏨🏨 Lion* (19). 🏨 Pencerrig Country House* (28).

Burford (Population 1700; Oxfordshire)
Information: The Brewery, Sheep Street—BABA. **Accommodations:** 🏨🏨🏨 Bary Tree* (24). 🏨🏨 Corner House* (9); Golden Pheasant (12); Highway* (10); Lamb Inn* (14); The Winters Tale (9).

Bury St. Edmunds (Population 32,900; Suffolk)
Information: Abbey Gardens, Angle Hill (seasonal)—BABA. **Accommodations:** 🏨🏨🏨 (*Luxury*) Angel* (43); Suffolk (41). 🏨🏨🏨 Priory* (17). 🏨🏨 Everards* (16). 🏨 Dunston Guest House (11).

Caerleon (Population 7000; Gwent)
Accommodations: 🏨🏨 Priory* (23).

Caernarfon (Population 10,500; Gwynedd)
Information: The Slate Quay (seasonal)—BABA. **Accommodations:** 🏨🏨 Royal* (58). 🏨 Menai Bank (16); Plas Bowman* (7); Prince of Wales (22).

Cambridge (Population 103,000; Cambridgeshire)
Information: Wheeler Street—BABA. **Accommodations:** 🏨🏨🏨

(*Luxury*) Blue Boar (48); Garden House (117); Post House (120). 🏨🏨🏨
Gonville (62); University Arms (115). 🏨🏨 Arundel House* (72); Royal
Cambridge (74); Sorrento (20). 🏨 All Seasons Guest House (10);
Ashley (10).

Canterbury (Population 36,300; Kent)
Information: 13 Longmarket—BABA. **Accommodations:** 🏨🏨🏨
(*Luxury*) Chaucer (47); County* (74). 🏨🏨🏨 Falstaff* (25). 🏨🏨 Canter-
bury (30); Ebury* (17); Ersham Lodge* (25); Slatters (30). 🏨 House of
Agnes* (9).

Cardiff (Population 279,400; Glamorgan)
Information: 3-6 Bridge Street—BABA. **Transportation:** Gla-
morgan Airport, 19 km. (12 miles) from center of town (bus from
Central Bus Station). **Accommodations:** 🏨🏨🏨 (*Luxury*) Post House
(150); Royal (63); Stakis Inn on the Avenue (145). 🏨🏨🏨 Ladbroke
Wentloog Castle (54); St. Mellons (11). 🏨🏨 Angel* (80); Central (78);
Phoenix (50). 🏨 Wynford (22).

Cardigan (Population 3900; Dyfed)
Information: Prince Charles Quay (seasonal)—BABA.

Carlisle (Population 76,100; Cumbria)
Information: Old Town Hall, Greenmarket. **Accommodations:** 🏨🏨🏨
Crest (100); Cumbrian Thistle* (70); Ladbroke Crown and Mitre*
(96). 🏨🏨 Central (83); Cumbria Park (44); Swallow Hilltop (110);
Pinegrove (20); Vallum House (10).

Carmarthen (Population 13,200; Dyfed)
Information: Lammas Street (seasonal)—BABA. **Accommodations:** 🏨🏨🏨 Ivy Bush Royal* (80).

Chelmsford (Population 59,000; Essex)
Information: AA Office, 205 Moulsham Street. **Accommodations:**
🏨🏨🏨 Pontlands Park Country* (8); South Lodge (42). 🏨🏨 Boswell
House* (13); County (54); Miami (49).

Cheltenham Spa (Population 85,000; Gloucestershire)
Information: Municipal Offices, Promenade—BABA. **Accommodations:** 🏨🏨🏨 (*Luxury*) Golden Valley Thistle (99); The Greenway*
(12); Queen's* (77). 🏨🏨🏨 Carlton* (49); De La Bere* (35); Wyastone
(13). 🏨🏨 Askham Court* (19); Cotswold Grange* (27); Malvern View
(6); Wellesley* (23). 🏨 Beaumont House* (8); Cleeve Hill (14).

Chepstow (Population 8900; Gwent)

Information: Gate House, High Street (seasonal)—BABA. **Accommodations:** 🏠🏠🏠 Castle View* (10); George* (15). 🏠 Ferry Marine (16).

Chester (Population 116,600; Cheshire)

Information: Town Hall, Northgate Street—BABA; Chester Visitor Centre, Vicar's Lane—BABA. **Transportation:** Hawarden Airport, 12 km. (5 miles) from center of town. **Accommodations:** 🏠🏠🏠 (*Luxury*) Abbots Well (127); Blossoms* (71); Chester Grosvenor* (108); Post House (64); Queen (91). 🏠🏠🏠 Ladbroke (121); Plantation Inn (93); Rowton Hall (42). 🏠🏠 Brookside (23); Cavendish* (21); City Walls* (17); Dene (44); Westminster (57); Weston (22). 🏠 Green Bough (11); Maison Romano* (11).

Chesterfield (Population 96,400; Derbyshire)

Information: Peacock TIC and Heritage Centre, Low Pavement—BABA. **Accommodations:** 🏠🏠🏠 Chesterfield (60). 🏠🏠 Portland* (24).

Chichester (Population 21,000; West Sussex)

Information: St. Peter's Market, West Street—BABA. **Accommodations:** 🏠🏠🏠 (*Luxury*) Dolphin and Anchor* (54). 🏠🏠🏠 Chichester Lodge (43). 🏠🏠 Ship* (36).

Chippenham (Population 20,500; Wiltshire)

Information: The Neeld Hall, High Street—BABA. **Accommodations:** 🏠🏠 Angel* (53); Bear* (8).

Chipping Campden (Population 2000; Gloucestershire)

Information: Woolstaplers Hall Museum, High Street (seasonal). **Accommodations:** 🏠🏠🏠 The Malt House (5); Three Ways (37). 🏠🏠 Cotswold House* (25); King's Arms* (15); Noel Arms* (19).

Chipping Norton (Population 5200; Oxfordshire)

Information: 22 New Street. **Accommodations:** 🏠🏠🏠 White Hart* (22). 🏠 Fox* (6).

Chirk (Population 3700; Clwyd)

Accommodations: 🏠🏠 Hand* (11).

Christchurch (Population 37,600; Dorset)

Information: 30 Saxon Square—BABA. **Accommodations:** 🏠🏠🏠 (*Luxury*) Avonmouth (41). 🏠🏠 Fisherman's Haunt* (18); Waterford Lodge (14).

Church Stretton (Population 3400; Salop)
   Information: The Library, Church Street (seasonal). **Accommodations:** 🏨 Sandford* (24); Stretton Hall* (12).

Cirencester (Population 16,100; Gloucestershire)
   Information: Corn Hall, Market Place—BABA. **Accommodations:** 🏨 King's Head* (70). 🏨 Corinium Court* (9); Stratton House* (26). 🏠 La Ronde (10); Raydon (16).

Clacton-on-Sea (Population 36,500; Essex)
   Information: 23 Pier Avenue; Central Seafront, Marine Parade (seasonal). **Accommodations:** 🏨 King's Cliff (15); Waverley Hall (57).

Cleethorpes (Population 38,000; Humberside)
   Information: 43 Alexandra Road—BABA. **Accommodations:** 🏨 Kingsway (55). 🏨 Wellow (10). 🏠 Lifeboat (28).

Clevedon (Population 15,000; Avon)
   Accommodations: 🏨 Walton Park (35).

Colchester (Population 85,500; Essex)
   Information: 1 Queen Street—BABA. **Accommodations:** 🏨 George* (47). 🏨 King's Ford Park* (15); Red Lion* (20); Rose and Crown* (28). 🏠 Peveril (17).

Colwyn Bay (Population 25,500; Clwyd)
   Information: 77 Conway Road; Station Road (seasonal)—BABA. **Accommodations:** 🏨 Seventy Degrees (41). 🏨 Ashmount (20); Lyndale (14); Colwyn Bay (19); Norfolk House (27).

Conwy (Population 14,000; Gwynedd)
   Information: Castle Street (seasonal)—BABA. **Accommodations:** 🏨 (*Luxury*) Castle (25). 🏨 Castle Bank* (9). 🏠 Llys Llewlyn* (9); Park Hall* (10); Sychnant Pass Country Park (11).

Corbridge-on-Tyne (Population 2200; Northumberland)
   Information: Vicar's Pele, Market Place (seasonal)—BABA. **Accommodations:** 🏨 Angel Inn* (6); Riverside (11).

Coventry (Population 392,000; West Midlands)
   Information: Central Library, Smithford Way. **Transportation:** Coventry Airport, 6 km. (4 miles) south of town. **Accommodations:** 🏨 (*Luxury*) Crest (160); Leofric (90). 🏨 De Vere (190); Hylands (56); Novotel (56); Post House (196). 🏨 Beechwood (28).

Criccieth (Population 1600; Gwynedd)
  Information: The Square (seasonal). **Accommodations:** 🏨 Lion (41); Parciau Mawr* (7); Plas Gwyn* (16). 🏨 Abereistedd* (12); Bron Eifion* (19); Caerwylan* (31); George IV* (34); Gwydny* (10).

Cromer (Population 5400; Norfolk)
  Information: Town Hall, Prince of Wales Road (seasonal). **Accommodations:** 🏨 Colne House (38). 🏨 Cliff House (27); Cliftonville* (46); Gloucester (10).

Darlington (Population 96,000; Durham)
  Information: District Library, Crown Street—BABA. **Accommodations:** 🏨 Stakis White Horse (40). 🏨 Blackwell Grange Moat House* (98); Coachman* (25); Grange* (11); Kings Head* (86).

Dartmouth (Population 6000; Devon)
  Information: Royal Avenue Gardens (seasonal)—BABA. **Accommodations:** 🏨 (*Luxury*) Dart Marina (34). 🏨 Royal Castle* (20); Royle* (10).

Deal (Population 26,100; Kent)
  Information: 5–11 King Street—BABA. **Accommodations:** 🏨 Clarendon (12); Royal* (30).

Derby (Population 216,000; Derbyshire)
  Information: Central Library, The Wardwick. **Transportation:** East Midlands Airport, Castle Donington, 15 km. (9 miles) from center of town. **Accommodations:** 🏨 (*Luxury*) Crest (66). 🏨 Breadsail Priory* (17); International (44). 🏨 Gables (66); Midland* (62); Pennine (100). 🏨 Georgian House* (19); Howard* (20); Kedleston (13).

Devil's Bridge (Population 100; Dyfed)
  Accommodations: 🏨 Hafod Arms* (20).

Dolgellau (Population 2400; Gwynedd)
  Information: The Bridge (seasonal)—BABA. **Accommodations:** 🏨 Royal Ship (23).

Doncaster (Population 80,100; South Yorkshire)
  Information: Central Library, Waterdale—BABA. **Accommodations:** 🏨 Punch's* (25). 🏨 Danum Swallow (66); Earl of Doncaster (53). 🏨 Regent* (34).

Dorchester (Population 13,700; Dorset)
Information: Acland Road—BABA. **Accommodations:** 🏠 Antelope* (20); Casterbridge* (15); King's Arms* (27).

Dover (Population 34,500; Kent)
Information: Townwall Street—BABA. **Accommodations:** 🏠🏠🏠 (*Luxury*) Dover Moat House (80). 🏠🏠🏠 Dover Motel (67); White Cliffs* (62). 🏠 Cliffe Court* (30); Granham Webb (32); Mildmay (22); St. James* (18). 🏠 Ardmore Guest House* (4); St. Martins Guest House* (8).

Droitwich Spa (Population 14,000; Hereford and Worcester)
Information: Heritage Centre, Heritage Way. **Accommodations:** 🏠🏠🏠 (*Luxury*) Château Impney* (67); Raven (55). 🏠 St. Andrew's House (28).

Dunster (Population 1000; Somerset)
Accommodations: 🏠🏠🏠 (*Luxury*) Luttrell Arms* (21). 🏠🏠🏠 Exmoor House* (6).

Durham (Population 24,800; Durham)
Information: Market Place—BABA. **Accommodations:** 🏠🏠🏠 Royal County* (120); Three Tuns* (54). 🏠 Bowburn Hall (20); Bridge (46); Kylesku (10); Ramside Hall (11); Redhills (6).

Eastbourne (Population 73,900; East Sussex)
Information: 3 Cornfield Terrace—BABA; Terminus Road Precinct; Lower Promenade, Seafront (seasonal). **Accommodations:** 🏠🏠🏠 (*Luxury*) Grand* (178); Cavendish (114); Queens (108). 🏠🏠🏠 Chatsworth (45); Cumberland (70); Lansdowne (136); Wish Tower (75). 🏠 Congress (44); Croft (10); Downland (16); Langham (83); Lathom (40); 1–3; Sandhurst* (51). 🏠 Wynstay Private (7).

East Grinstead (Population 19,700; West Sussex)
Accommodations: 🏠🏠🏠 (*Luxury*) Gravetye Manor* (14). 🏠🏠🏠 Felbridge (48); Roebuck* (31).

Exeter (Population 98,800; Devon)
Information: Civic Centre, Paris Street—BABA. Exeter Service Area (M5), Sandygate (seasonal)—BABA. **Transportation:** Clyst Honiton Airport; 7 km. (4 miles) from center of town. **Accommodations:** 🏠🏠🏠 Buckerell Lodge Crest (54); Edgerton Park (17); Ladbroke Motor Inn (61); Rougemont (63); Royal Clarence* (61). 🏠 Berribridge House* (6); Exeter Moat House (44); Gipsy Hill Country House (20);

Great Western (42); Imperial* (28); Lord Haldon* (15); St. Olaves Court* (12).

Exmouth (Population 28,800; Devon)
Information: Alexandra Terrace (seasonal)—BABA. **Accommodations:** 🏨 (*Luxury*) Imperial (63). 🏨 Devoncourt (68); Grand (85). 🏨 Aliston House (10); Barn (11). 🏨 Cavendish (70); Royal Beacon* (35).

Falmouth (Population 17,500; Cornwall)
Information: Town Hall, The Moor. **Accommodations:** 🏨 Falmouth (73); Penmere Manor* (33); St. Michaels (75). 🏨 Broadmead (12); Carthion (18); Melville (22); Royal Duchy (44); Somerdale (18). 🏨 Croft (29); Grove (15); Park Grove (17).

Farnham (Population 32,200; Surrey)
Information: Locality Office, South Street. **Accommodations:** 🏨 (*Luxury*) Frensham Pond (19). 🏨 Bush* (65); Eldon (14); The Bishops Table* (16). 🏨 Trevena House (19).

Faversham (Population 15,100; Kent)
Information: Fleurs de Lis Heritage Centre, 13 Preston Street. **Accommodations:** 🏨 Ship* (13).

Felixstowe (Population 19,900; Suffolk)
Information: 91 Undercliff Road West. **Accommodations:** 🏨 Waverley (12). 🏨 Marlborough (46); Ordnance (11). 🏨 Princes Terrace Guest House (7).

Ffestiniog (Population 6500; Gwynedd)
Accommodations: 🏨-Abbey Arms (13).

Fishguard (Population 5000; Dyfed)
Information: Town Hall (seasonal)—BABA. **Accommodations:** 🏨 Cartref (14); Fishguard Bay* (62).

Folkestone (Population 46,500; Kent)
Information: Harbour Street—BABA; Pedestrian Precinct, Sandgate Road (seasonal). **Accommodations:** 🏨 Burlington (59). 🏨 Garden House (45); Langhorne Garden (30); White House (32). 🏨 Abbey House (21).

Gainsborough (Population 17,400; Lincolnshire)
Information: Trinity Centre, Trinity Street. **Accommodations:** 🏨 Hickmann-Hill* (8).

Glastonbury (Population 9200; Somerset)
Information: 1 Marchant's Building, Northload Street (seasonal).
Accommodations: ⌂⌂⌂ George & Pilgrims* (14).

Gloucester (Population 92,000; Gloucestershire)
Information: St. Michael's Tower, The Cross—BABA. **Accommodations:** ⌂⌂⌂ (*Luxury*) Crest (100). ⌂⌂⌂ Bowden Hall* (24); Gloucester Hotel and Country Club* (77); Tara (24). ⌂⌂ New Inn* (32); Twigworth Lodge* (12). ⌂ Fleece* (40).

Grange-over-Sands (Population 3500; Cumbria)
Information: Victoria Hall, Main Street (seasonal)—BABA. **Accommodations:** ⌂⌂⌂ Cumbria Sand (124); Graythwaite Manor* (24). ⌂⌂ Berners Close (51); Grange* (40); Netherwood* (23). ⌂ Kents Bank (8); Methven (12).

Grantham (Population 29,600; Lincolnshire)
Information: The Guildhall Yard, St. Peters Hill (seasonal)— BABA. **Accommodations:** ⌂⌂⌂ Angle & Royal* (32); George* (46). ⌂⌂ Kings (17).

Great Malvern (Population 31,000; Hereford and Worcester)
Information: Grange Road—BABA. **Accommodations:** ⌂⌂⌂ Abbey* (107); Colwall Park (14); Cottage in the Wood (20); Foley Arms (26); Mount Pleasant* (14). ⌂⌂ Beauchamp (13); Broomhill* (10); Cotford (14); Essington (10); Holdfast Cottage* (9); Malvern Hills; Montrose (14); Thornbury (16); Walmer Lodge (9).

Great Yarmouth (Population 52,000; Norfolk)
Information: 1 South Quay; Marine Parade (seasonal). **Accommodations:** ⌂⌂⌂ Imperial (41); Star* (42). ⌂⌂ Ambassador (35). ⌂ Palm Court* (47).

Grimsby (Population 93,600; South Humberside)
Information: Central Library, Town Hall Square. **Accommodations:** ⌂⌂⌂ (*Luxury*) Crest (132); Humber Royal Crest (52).

Guernsey (Population 54,000; Channel Islands)
Information: Crown Pier, St. Peter Port; The Airport, La Villiaze, Forest. **Transportation:** Guernsey Airport; 5 km. (3 miles) from St. Peter Port (bus available). **Accommodations:** ⌂⌂⌂ (*Luxury*) *St. Peter Port:* St. Pierre Park (135). ⌂⌂⌂ *St. Martin:* Ronnie Ronalde's (57). *St. Peter Port:* Duke of Richmond (75); La Frégate* (13); Old Government House (73); Royal (79). ⌂⌂ *St. Martin:* Bella Luce* (31); Green Acres (48); St. Margaret's Lodge (43). *St. Peter Port:* Havelet* (32); The

Mallard Country Club (47); Moore's (40). *St. Saviour:* L'Atlantique (21). ⌂ *Catel:* Hougue du Pommier* (40). *St. Martin:* La Trelade (45). *St. Peter Port:* Moore's Central (40). *St. Saviour:* La Girouette Country House (14).

Guilford (Population 58,000; Surrey)
　　Information: The Civic Hall, London Road. **Accommodations:** ▩▩▩ (*Luxury*) Angel* (27); Hogs Back (50). ▩▩▩ Boughton Hall Country House* (12).

Harlech (Population 1200; Gwynedd)
　　Information: High Street (seasonal)—BABA. **Accommodations:** ▩▩ Noddfa House (7).

Harrogate (Population 65,000; North Yorkshire)
　　Information: Royal Baths Assembly Rooms, Crescent Road—BABA. **Accommodations:** ▩▩▩ (*Luxury*) Cairn (136); Crown (122); Harrogate International (214); Majestic (157). ▩▩▩ Granby* (93); Grants (17); Green Park (44). ▩▩ Caesars (10); Cavendish (11); Dirlton (41); Italia (25). ⌂ Alexa House* (12); Gillmore (20).

Harwich/Dovercourt (Population 15,300; Essex)
　　Information: Parkeston Quay (seasonal)—BABA. **Accommodations:** ▩▩▩ Tower* (16). ▩▩ Cliff (34). ⌂ Continental (14); Garland (6).

Hastings/St. Leonards (Population 73,200; East Sussex)
　　Information: 4 Robertson Terrace—BABA; The Fishmarket (seasonal). **Accommodations:** ▩▩▩ Beauport Park* (23). ▩▩ Queens (115). ⌂ Burlington (17); Gainsborough (12).

Hatfield (Population 29,000; Hertfordshire)
　　Accommodations: ▩▩▩ Comet (57).

Haverfordwest (Population: 9600; Dyfed)
　　Information: 40 High Street (seasonal)—BABA. **Accommodations:** ▩▩ Mariners* (28). ⌂ Pembroke House* (23).

Hawworth (Population 3500; Yorkshire)
　　Information: 2–4 West Lane—BABA. **Accommodations:** ▩▩ Ferncliff (6); Old White Lion* (12).

Hereford (Population 47,000; Hereford and Worcester)
　　Information: Shirehall Forecourt, 1 a St. Owen's Street—BABA. **Accommodations:** ▩▩▩ (*Luxury*) Green Dragon (88). ▩▩▩ Hereford

Moat House (32). 🏨 Castle Pool* (27); Litchfield Lodge (12); Merton (14); Somerville (10). 🛏 Graftonbury (41).

Herm (Population 600; Channel Islands)
   Information: Administrative Office. **Accommodations:** 🏨 White House (30).

Herstmonceux (Population 2200; East Sussex)
   Accommodations: 🛏 Cleavers Lyng (8).

Hexham (Population 10,000; Northumberland)
   Information: Manor Office, Hallgate—BABA. **Accommodations:** 🏨 Beaumont (22); County (10); Royal* (25).

High Wycombe (Population 60,000; Buckinghamshire)
   Information: Council Offices, Queen Victoria Road—BABA. **Accommodations:** 🏨 (*Luxury*) Crest (108). 🛏 Drake Court (21).

Holyhead (Population 11,000; Gwynedd)
   Information: Marine Square, Salt Island Approach (seasonal)— BABA.

Hove (Sussex) *See Brighton and Hove.*

Hull (Population 271,000; North Humberside)
   Information: Central Library, Albion Street—BABA; Corporation Road, King George Dock, Hedon Road. **Transportation:** Airport Brough, 18 km. (11 miles) from center of town. **Accommodations:** 🏨 (*Luxury*) Crest Humber Bridge (102). 🏨 Pearson Park* (39); White House (52).

Huntingdon (Population 18,200; Cambridgeshire)
   Information: The Library, Princes Street—BABA. **Accommodations:** 🏨 George* (25).

Hythe (Population 12,200; Kent)
   Information: Scanlons Bridge Road (seasonal)—BABA.

Ilfracombe (Population 9500; Devon)
   Information: The Promenade—BABA. **Accommodations:** 🏨 Cliffe Hydro (38); Langleigh Country* (6); Torrs (17); Tracy House (11). 🛏 Carlton (50); Imperial (100); St. Helier (25).

Ilkley (Population 13,600; West Yorkshire)
Information: Station Road—BABA. **Accommodations:** 🏨🏨🏨 (*Luxury*) Craiglands (73). 🏨🏨🏨 Overdale Health (7); Rombald's* (22). 🏨🏨 Cow and Calf (17); Greystones (10); Grove* (6). 🏨 Craigend Lodge Vegetarian Guest House* (9).

Ipswich (Population 123,000; Suffolk)
Information: Town Hall, Princes Street—BABA. **Accommodations:** 🏨🏨🏨 (*Luxury*) Belstead Brook* (33); Ipswich Moat House (46); Post House (118). 🏨🏨🏨 Crown and Anchor (55); Golden Lion* (23); The Marlborough at Ipswich (22).

Isle of Man (Population 30,000)
Information: Commissioner's General Office, Parliament Square, Castletown; 13 Victoria Street, Douglas; Village Commissioner's Public Library, 10 Elm Tree Road, Onchan; Town Hall, Derby Road, Peel; Commissioner's Office, Station Road, Port Erin; Commissioner's Office, Town Hall, Promenade, Port St. Mary; Town Hall, Ramsey. **Transportation:** Ronaldsway Airport. **Accommodations:** 🏨🏨🏨 *Castletown:* Golf Links (75). *Douglas:* Palace (135). 🏨🏨 *Douglas:* Sefton* (80).

Isle of Wight (Population 91,000)
Information: 1 Bath Road, Cowes (seasonal); 21 High Street, Newport; Western Esplanade, Ryde (seasonal); The Esplanade, Sandown; 67 High Street, Shanklin; 34 High Street, Ventnor (seasonal); Quay Road, Yarmouth (seasonal). **Accommodations:** 🏨🏨🏨 (*Luxury*) *Ventnor:* Royal (55); Winterbourne (19). 🏨🏨🏨 *Lowes:* Fountain (20); Holmwood (19). *Newport:* Bugle (26). *Ryde:* Yelf's (21). *Shanklin:* Cliff Tops (102). *Totland Bay:* Country Garden (16). *Ventnor:* Bonchurch Manor (11). 🏨🏨 *Bembridge:* Elm Country (12); Highbury (9). *Cowes:* Cowes* (13). *Freshwater Bay:* Albion (43). *Shanklin:* Belmont (16); Fernbank (20); Luccombe Hall (31). *Totland Bay:* Sentry Mead (13). *Ventnor:* Madeira Hall (18). *Whippingham:* Padmore House (11). *Yarmouth:* George (20). 🏨 *Bembridge:* Birdham (14). *Shanklin:* Melbourne Ardenlea (46).

Isles of Scilly (Population 2000)
Information: Town Hall, St. Mary's—BABA. **Transportation:** Helicopter service to and from Penzance (see also page 00). **Accommodations:** 🏨🏨🏨 *Tresco:* Island (34), Old Grimsby. 🏨🏨 *St. Mary's:* Bell Rock (17), Hughtown; Godolphin (31), Hughtown.

Jersey (Population 76,000; Channel Islands)
Information: Weighbridge, St. Helier. **Transportation:** Jersey Airport, 8 km. (5 miles) from St. Helier. **Accommodations:** 🏰🏰🏰 (*Luxury*) *St. Brelade:* L'Horizon (105). *St. Helier:* Grand* (115). *St. Saviour:* Longueville Manor* (33). 🏰🏰🏰 *Portelet Bay:* Portelet (86). *Rozel Bay:* Chateau La Chaire (15). *St. Brelade:* Atlantic (46); Chateau Valeuse (26). *St. Helier:* Beaufort (54); Pomme d'Or (151). *St. Lawrence:* Little Grove (14). 🏰🏰 *Archireondel:* Les Arches (54). *Gorey:* Dolphin* (17); Old Court House* (58). *St. Helier:* Apollo (53); De la Plage (98); Savoy* (61); Mountainview (36); Royal Yacht (45). 🏰 *Beaumont:* L'Hermitage (109). *St. Brelade:* Beau Rivage (27).

Kendal (Population 21,600; Cumbria)
Information: Town Hall, Highgate—BABA. **Accommodations:** 🏰🏰🏰 The Country Thistle (31); Woolpack* (57). 🏰🏰 Heaves* (16).

Kenilworth (Population 19,400; Warwickshire)
Information: The Library, 11 Smalley Place. **Accommodations:** 🏰🏰🏰 (*Luxury*) De Montfort (95). 🏰🏰🏰 Clarendon House (24). 🏰🏰 Chesford Grange (106); Kenilworth Moat House (48).

Keswick (Population 4900; Cumbria)
Information: Moot Hall, Market Square—BABA. **Accommodations:** 🏰🏰🏰 (*Luxury*) Keswick (64); Underscar* (19). 🏰🏰🏰 Red House* (23). 🏰🏰 George* (17); Grange Country House* (10); King's Arms* (20); Ladstock Country House* (20); Lairbeck (12); Latrigg Lodge (7); Lyzzick Hall* (21); Priorholm (9); Royal Oak* (48); Skiddaw (52). 🏰 Acorn House* (10); Allerdale (6); Chaucer (32); Crow Park (26); Linnett Hill (7); Richmond House (12).

Kingsbridge (Population 3600; Devon)
Information: The Quay (seasonal)—BABA. **Accommodations:** 🏰🏰🏰 (*Luxury*) Buckland-Tout-Saints* (13). 🏰🏰 Crabshell Motor Lodge (24); Kings Arms* (12); Rockwood (6); Vineyard* (11).

King's Lynn (Population 33,000; Norfolk)
Information: Saturday Market Place. **Accommodations:** 🏰🏰🏰 (*Luxury*) Duke's Head (72). 🏰🏰 Mildenhall (54); Stuart House (19); Tudor Rose* (13).

Kingston-upon-Hull (North Humberside) *See Hull.*

Kingston-upon-Thames (Population 140,200; Surrey)
Information: Heritage Centre, Fairfield West. **Accommodations:** 🏰🏰 Antoinette of Kingston (100).

Lacock (Population 1400; Wiltshire)
Accommodations: 🏨 (*Luxury*) Beechfield House* (16). 🏨 Sign of the Angel* (6).

Lancaster (Population 45,100; Lancashire)
Information: 7 Dalton Square—BABA. **Accommodations:** 🏨 (*Luxury*) Post House (117).

Launceston (Population 5300; Cornwall)
Information: Market House Arcade, Market Street—BABA. **Accommodations:** 🏠 Eagle House* (18).

Lavenham (Population 1500; Suffolk)
Accommodations: 🏨 (*Luxury*) Swan* (48).

Leamington Spa (Population 44,300; Warwickshire)
Information: Jephson Lodge, The Parade—BABA. **Accommodations:** 🏨 Manor House* (53); Blackdown* (11); Regent* (80). 🏨 Abbacourt (21); Angel* (18); Beech Lodge* (12); Berni Inn (30); Falstaff* (54); Lansdowne (10).

Leeds (Population 711,000; West Yorkshire)
Information: Library Buildings, Calverley Street—BABA. **Transportation:** Leeds/Bradford Airport (bus connection from Air Terminal, Bishopsgate Street). **Accommodations:** 🏨 (*Luxury*) Crest (40); Ladbroke Dragonara (234); Merrion (120); Metropole (113); Queen's* (198). 🏨 Ladbroke (143); Stakis Windmill (40); Wellesley (54); 🏨 Golden Lion (88).

Leicester (Population 289,000; Leicestershire)
Information: 12 Bishop Street—BABA. **Transportation:** East Midlands Airport, Castle Donington, 32 km. (20 miles) from center of town. **Accommodations:** 🏨 (*Luxury*) Post House (172). 🏨 Grand* (93); Holiday Inn (188); Ladbroke International (220); Leicester Forest Moat House (31); Leicestershire Moat House (29). 🏨 Belmont* (61); Johnscliffe (10). 🏠 Eaton Bray (73); Rowans* (15).

Leominster (Population 5000; Hereford and Worcester)
Information: 6 School Lane—BABA. **Accommodations:** 🏨 Royal Oak* (16); Talbot* (30).

Lewes (Population 14,400; East Sussex)
Information: Lewes House, 32 High Street. **Accommodations:** 🏨 (*Luxury*) Shelleys* (21). 🏨 White Hart* (33).

Lichfield (Population 29,000; Staffordshire)
Information: Donegal House, Bore Street—BABA. **Accommodations:** 🏨 George* (39); Little Barrow (26); Swan* (31).

Lincoln (Population 74,800; Lincolnshire)
Information: 9 Castle Hill—BABA; 21 The Cornhill—BABA. **Accommodations:** 🏨 (*Luxury*) Eastgate Post House (71); White Hart* (51). 🏨 Castle* (21); Grand (50); Moor Lodge (25). 🏨 Barbican (17); Duke William* (11); Europa (26); Washingborough Hall* (12). 🏨 Hillcrest (15).

Littlehampton (Population 21,000; West Sussex)
Information: Windmill Complex, The Green (seasonal)—BABA.

Liverpool (Population 492,000; Lancashire)
Information: 29 Lime Street—BABA; Atlantic Pavilion, Albert Dock—BABA. **Transportation:** Liverpool Airport, 8 km. (5 miles) from center of town (buses from Lime Street Station and South John Street). **Accommodations:** 🏨 (*Luxury*) Atlantic, Tower Thistle (226); Crest Liverpool-City (160); Holiday Inn; 🏨 Crest (50). 🏨 Gateacre Hall* (36); Grange (25); Green Park (24); Lord Nelson (58); 🏨 Feathers (80); Shaftesbury (69).

Lizard (Population 800; Cornwall)
Accommodations: 🏨 Housel Bay (27); Lizard* (9); Polbrean (11).

Llanbedrog (Population 900; Gwynedd)
Accommodations: 🏨 Bryn Derwen (10).

Llandrindod Wells (Population 4100; Powys)
Information: Rock Park Spa—BABA. **Accommodations:** 🏨 Commodore (55); Glen Usk (68); Metropole (121).

Llandudno (Population 20,000; Gwynedd)
Information: Chapel Street—BABA. Kiosk, North Promenade (seasonal); Arcadia Theatre (seasonal). **Accommodations:** 🏨 (*Luxury*) Bodysgallen Hall* (28). 🏨 Empire (56); Gogarth Abbey (41); Imperial* (134); Marine (76); St. George's (90); St. Tudno (21). 🏨 Belle Vue (15); Bromwell Court (11); Chatsworth House (56); Headlands (17); Royal (35); Tan Lan (18). 🏨 Bedford (28); Branksome (48); Bron Orme (9); Clontarf (10); Cornerways (9); Cranleigh (13); Dunoon (59); Gwesty Leamore (12); North Western (52); Sandringham (18).

Llanfairfechan (Population 3800; Gwynedd)
Accommodations: 🏠 Llanfairfechan (11).

Llangollen (Population 4000; Clwyd)
Information: Town Hall (seasonal)—BABA. **Accommodations:**
🏠🏠🏠 Hand (58); Royal* (33). 🏠🏠 Bryn Howel* (38); Chain Bridge (37).
🏠 Tyn y Wern (10).

London (Population 6.8 million)
Information: *See page 317.* **Transportation:** *Heathrow Airport:* 24
km. (15 miles) from city center; Underground (subway) service on
Piccadilly line every 5 minutes (travel time approx. 40 minutes). Air-
buses to Victoria Station every 20 minutes, Euston Station every 30
minutes, making stops in between (see also p. 305). *Gatwick Airport:*
43 km. (26 miles) from city center. Trains every 15 minutes to Victoria
Station during the day, every hour at night (see also p. 305). **Accom-
modations:** *Central London:* 🏠🏠🏠 (*Luxury*) Athenaeum, 116 Piccadilly,
W1 (112); Berkeley, Wilton Place, Knightsbridge, SW1 (160);
Berners, Berners Street, W1 (234); Blakes, 33 Roland Gardens, SW7
(50); Brown's, Albermarle Street, W1 (125); Cavendish, Jermyn
Street, SW1 (253); Claridge's, Brook Street, W1 (205); Dorchester*,
Park Lane, W1 (275); Dukes, 35 St. James' Place, SW1 (51);
Grosvenor House, Park Lane, W1 (472); Howard, Temple Place, WC2
(141); Hyatt Carlton Tower, 2 Cadogan Place, SW1 (228); Hyde Park*,
Knightsbridge, SW1 (179); London Hilton, 22 Park Lane, W1 (445);
Londonderry, 19 Old Park Lane, W1 (150); Portman Inter-Continental,
22 Portman Square, W1 (276); Savoy*, The Strand, WC2 (200). 🏠🏠🏠
Barbican City, Central Street, EC1 (444); Bayswater Fair Inn, 8–16
Princes Square, W2 (111); Bonnington, 92 Southampton Row, WC1
(242); Commodore, 50–52 Lancaster Gate, W2 (86); Eros, 67 Shaftes-
bury Avenue, W1 (67); Forum, 97 Cromwell Road, SW7 (907);
Ladbroke Charles Dickens, 66 Lancaster Gate, W2 (191); Plaza*, 42
Princes Square, W2 (334); Westland, 154 Bayswater Road, W2 (30);
Westminster, 16 Leinster Square, W2 (106). 🏠🏠 Acton Park, 116 The
Vale Acton, W3 (18); Ashburn, 111 Cromwell Road, SW7 (40); Bick-
enhall House, 119 Gloucester Place, W1 (21); Chester House, 134
Ebury Street, Belgravia, SW1 (12); Elizabeth, 37 Eccleston Square,
SW1 (25); Granada, 73 Belgrave Road, SW1 (17); Knightsbridge, 10
Beaufort Gardens, SW3 (20); Lincoln Court, 15 Lancaster Gate, W2
(34); New Ambassadors*, 12 Upper Woburn Place, WC1 (101);
Regent Palace, Piccadilly Circus, W1 (989); Royal Norfolk, 25 London
Street, W2 (60). 🏠 Albatross, 13 Talbot Square, W2 (19); Beaver, 57
Philbeach Gardens, SW7 (50); Belvic*, 105 Belgrave Road, SW1 (14);
Concord, 155 Cromwell Road, SW5 (40); Crescent 49–50 Cartwright

Gardens, WC1 (29); Gresham, 36 Bloomsbury Street, WC1 (44); Kensington International, 2–4 Templeton Place, SW5 (51); Mac-Donald & Devon, 43–46 Argyle Square, WC1 (61); Strutton Park*, 45 Palace Court, W2 (27).

Outside London: 🏨🏨🏨 (*Luxury*) Holiday Inn Swiss Cottage, 128 King Henry's Road, NW3 (291); Ladbroke Hampstead, Primrose Hill Road, NW3 (84). 🏨🏨🏨 Carnarvon, Ealing Common, E5 (145); Hendon Hall*, Ashley Lane, NW4 (52); Swiss Cottage, 4 Adamson Road, NW3 (64); Travelodge, Autobahn M1, Scratchwood Service Area, NW7 (100). 🏨🏨 Bardon Lodge, 15 Stratheden Road, SE3 (23); Buckland, 6 Buckland Crescent, Swiss Cottage, NW3 (15); Central, 35 Hoop Lane, Golders Green, NW11 (36); Clarendon*, 8–16 Montpellier Road, SE3 (215); Eltham, 31 West Mount Road, Eltham, SE9 (10); Kenton House, 5 Hillcrest Road, W5 (51); Royal Park, 350–356 Seven Sisters Road, Finsbury Park, N4 (53). 🏨 Croft Court, 44 Ravenscroft Avenue, NW11 (20); Langorf, 18–20 Frognal, Hampstead, NW3 (32); Parkside, 384 Seven Sisters Road, Finsbury Park, N4 (83); Royal Crimea, 354 Uxbridge Road, W3 (9).

Heathrow Airport: 🏨🏨🏨 (*Luxury*) Penta, Bath Road, Hounslow (670); Post House, Sipson Road, West Drayton (597); Sheraton Heathrow, Bath Road, West Drayton (405); Sheraton Skyline, Bath Road, Hayes (354). 🏨🏨🏨 Ibis, 112–114 Bath Road, Hayes (244); Master Robert Motel, 336 Great West Road, Hounslow (64).

Gatwick Airport: 🏨🏨🏨 (*Luxury*) Hilton, Gatwick Airport (333); Penta, Povey Cross Road, Horley (260). 🏨🏨🏨 The Chequers Thistle*, Brighton Road, Horley (78). 🏨🏨 Skylane, Brighton Road, Horley (59).

Lostwithiel (Population 2100; Cornwall)
Information: Community Centre, Liddicoat Road.

Lowestoft (Population 58,500; Suffolk)
Information: The Esplanade—BABA. **Accommodations:** 🏨🏨🏨 Victoria (45). 🏨🏨 Denes (10); Wherry (23). 🏨 Clarendon Prince (9).

Ludlow (Population 7500; Salop)
Information: Castle Street (seasonal). **Accommodations:** 🏨🏨🏨 (*Luxury*) The Feathers at Ludlow* (37). 🏨🏨🏨 Angel* (17). 🏨🏨 Cliffe* (10); Overton Grange* (17).

Luton (Population 16,100; Bedfordshire)
Information: Central Library, St. Georges Square. **Accommodations:** 🏨🏨🏨 (*Luxury*) Chiltern (99); Crest (139); Strathmore Thistle (151). 🏨🏨 Leeside* (12).

Lymington (Population 11,900; Hampshire)
Accommodations: 🏨🏨🏨 (*Luxury*) Passford House* (53). 🏨🏨 Stanwell House* (33).

Lyndhurst (Population 2900; Hampshire)
Information: Main Car Park (seasonal).

Lynton–Lynmouth (Population 2000; Devon)
Information: Town Hall, Lee Road, Lynton—BABA. **Accommodations:** *Lynton:* 🏨🏨🏨 Valley of Rocks* (73). 🏨🏨 Combe Park (9); Crown (16); Lynton Cottage* (21); Neubia House (12); North Cliff (18); Rockvale* (9). 🏨 Castle Hill House* (9); Chough's Nest (12); Sandrock (10). *Lynmouth:* 🏨🏨 Bath (24); Rising Sun* (18); Tors (39). 🏨 Beacon (7).

Maidenhead (Population 50,000; Berkshire)
Information: Central Library, St. Ives Road—BABA. **Accommodations:** 🏨🏨🏨 (*Luxury*) Crest* (190); Fredrick's (35). 🏨🏨🏨 Kingswood* (11); Taplow House* (27).

Maidstone (Population 74,200; Kent)
Information: The Gatehouse, Old Palace Gardens, Mill Street— BABA. **Accommodations:** 🏨🏨🏨 (*Luxury*) Great Danes (128); Post House (119). 🏨🏨 Boxley House* (15); Emma (43); Grangemore (35). 🏨 Carval (7).

Malton (Population 4000; North Yorkshire)
Information: Market Place (seasonal)—BABA.

Manchester (Population 451,000; Greater Manchester)
Information: Manchester International Airport; Town Hall Extension, Lloyd Street—BABA. **Transportation:** Manchester International Airport (bus from Chorlton Street Bus Station). **Accommodations:** *Downtown:* 🏨🏨🏨 (*Luxury*) Britannia* (362); Grand (140); Piccadilly (255); Portland Thistle* (219). 🏨🏨🏨 Britannia Ringway (125); Post House (200); Willow Bank (123). 🏨🏨 Montana (25); Simpsons (40); Trafalgar International (22); Victoria Park* (19). 🏨 Landsdowne (51); Wilmslow (52).
Manchester International Airport: 🏨🏨🏨 (*Luxury*) Excelsior (308). 🏨🏨🏨 Valley Lodge (105). 🏨🏨 Bowdon (41).

Margate/Cliftonville (Population 50,300; Kent)
Information: Marine Terrace. **Transportation:** Manston Airport, 8 km. (5 miles) from town. **Accommodations:** 🏨🏨🏨 Grosvenor Court (84); Walpole Bay (44).

Marlborough (Population 6500; Wiltshire)
   Information: St. Peter's Church, High Street (seasonal)—BABA.
Accommodations: 🏨 (*Luxury*) Castle & Ball* (38).

Masham (Population 1700; North Yorkshire)
   Accommodations: 🏨 Jervaulx Hall* (8).

Matlock (Population 3600; Derbyshire)
   Information: The Pavilion. **Accommodations:** 🏨 (*Luxury*) New
Bath (56); Riber Hall* (11). 🏨 Temple* (13).

Middlesbrough (Population 152,000; Cleveland)
   Information: 125 Albert Road. **Accommodations:** 🏨 Blue Bell
Motor Inn (60); Highfield (26); Ladbroke Dragonara (144). 🏨 Bal-
timore (31); Marlton Hotel & Country Club (52); Marton Way (52).

Minehead (Population 8300; Somerset)
   Information: Market House, The Parade. **Accommodations:** 🏨
(*Luxury*) Northfield (28). 🏨 Beach (34). 🏨 Beaconwood (16);
Benares (21).

Monmouth (Population 6800; Gwent)
   Information: Church Street—BABA. **Accommodations:** 🏨
Kings Head (28). 🏨 Talocher Farmhouse (9).

Morecambe (Population 42,300; Lancashire)
   Information: Marine Road Central—BABA. **Accommodations:**
🏨 Headway (51). 🏨 Claredon (31); Elms (39); Rimington (6); Strath-
more (55).

Newark-on-Trent (Population 24,300; Nottinghamshire)
   Information: The Ossington, Beast Market Hill. **Accommodations:** 🏨 Robin Hood* (20). 🏨 Grange (6).

Newbury (Population 23,200; Berkshire)
   Information: Newbury District Museum, The Wharf—BABA.
Accommodations: 🏨 (*Luxury*) Chequers* (59). 🏨 Elcot Park*
(31).

Newcastle-upon-Tyne (Population 291,600; Tyne and Wear)
   Information: Central Library, Princess Square—BABA; Black-
friars Tourist Centre, Monk Street; Newcastle Airport—BABA. **Transportation:** Newcastle Airport, 8 km. (5 miles) from center of town.
Accommodations: 🏨 (*Luxury*) Gosforth Park Thistle (178); Holiday

Inn (150); 🏨 Avon (87); County Thistle* (115); Northumbria (68); Royal Station* (131); Stakis Airport (100). 🏨 White's (22). 🏚 Dene (17); Eldon (20); West Parade (65).

Newmarket (Population 14,400; Suffolk)
   Accommodations: 🏨 Bedford Lodge (12); Newmarket Moat House (49); Rosery Country House (11). 🏨 Rutland Arms* (49); White Hart (21).

New Milton (Population 4400; Hampshire)
   Accommodations: 🏨 (*Luxury*) Chewton Glen* (44).

Newport (Population 133,000; Gwent)
   Information: Newport Museum & Art Gallery, John Frost Square—BABA. **Accommodations:** 🏨 (*Luxury*) Celtic Manor* (17); Ladbroke Mercury (119). 🏨 Priory (21); Queen's* (43); Westgate (75).

Newquay (Population 15,400; Cornwall)
   Information: Cliff Road—BABA. **Accommodations:** 🏨 (*Luxury*) Barrowfield (76). 🏨 Bristol (95); Riviera (50); St. Rumons (77); Trebarwith (46). 🏨 Bewdley (31); Cedars (36); Corisane Manor (19); Edgcumbe (86); Minto House (31); Philema (32); 🏚 Kontiki (70); Sandy Lodge (46); Trevone (35).

New Quay (Population 800; Dyfed)
   Information: Church Street (seasonal)—BABA. **Accommodations:** 🏨 Black Lion (7).

Newton Abbot (Population 19,700; Devon)
   Information: 8 Sherborne Road—BABA. **Accommodations:** 🏨 Globe (18); Queens (26); 🏚 Hazelwood House (6).

Northampton (Population 157,000; Northamptonshire)
   Information: 21 St. Giles Street. **Accommodations:** 🏨 (*Luxury*) Northampton Moat House (134), 🏨 Weston Moat House (64). 🏨 Coach House (30); Grand (63); Lime Trees (22).

Norwich (Population 122,000; Norfolk)
   Information: Guildhall, Goal Street—BABA. **Transportation:** Airport, 6 km. (3.5 miles) northwest of town. **Accommodations:** 🏨 (*Luxury*) Post House (120). 🏨 Arlington (41); Landsdowne (45); Nelson (94). 🏨 Beeches* (24); Caistor Hall* (21); Georgian House (13); Oaklands (42). 🏚 Arrow (13).

Nottingham (Population 278,600; Nottinghamshire)
Information: 18 Milton Street; County Hall, Loughborough Road, West Bridgford; Castle Gatehouse, Castle Road (seasonal). **Transportation:** East Midlands Airport, Castle Donington, 21 km. (13 miles) from center of town. **Accommodations:** 🏰🏰🏰 (*Luxury*) Albany (152); Strathdon Thistle (69). 🏰🏰🏰 Stakis Victoria (167). 🏰🏰 Balmoral (26); Brackley House (14); Portland (49). 🏰 St. Andrews Guest House (10).

Okehampton (Population 4000; Devon)
Information: 3 West Street (seasonal)—BABA. **Accommodations:** 🏰 The Old Mill Guest House* (3).

Oxford (Population 116,600; Oxfordshire)
Information: St. Aldates—BABA. **Accommodations:** 🏰🏰🏰 (*Luxury*) Eastgate (42); Randolph* (109). 🏰🏰🏰 Cotswold Lodge (52); Ladbroke Linton Lodge (72); Royal Oxford (27); Travelodge (102). 🏰🏰 Old Parsonage* (34); Parklands (32); River* (17); Victoria (15); Westwood Country (18). 🏰 Willow Reaches Private (8).

Padstow (Population 2800; Cornwall)
Accommodations: 🏰🏰🏰 (*Luxury*) Metropole (43). 🏰🏰 Old Custom House* (14).

Paignton (Population 35,100; Devon)
Information: Festival Hall, Esplanade Road. **Accommodations:** 🏰🏰🏰 (*Luxury*) Palace (54). 🏰🏰🏰 Redcliffe* (63). 🏰🏰 Alta Vista (28); St. Ann's (28); Seaford (24). 🏰 Lyndhurst (30); Oldway Links* (20); Torbay Holiday Motel (66).

Pembroke (Population 5500; Dyfed)
Information: Pembroke National Park, Drill Hall, Main Street. **Accommodations:** 🏰🏰 Coach House Inn (14); Holyland* (8); Old Kings Arms (21); Underdown Country House (6).

Penrith (Population 11,600; Cumbria)
Information: Robinson's School, Middlegate (seasonal). **Accommodations:** 🏰🏰 Abbotsford* (11); George (31). 🏰 Strickland* (17); Station (20).

Penzance (Population 19,400; Cornwall)
Information: Alverton Street—BABA. **Transportation:** Regular helicopter service to the Isles of Scilly. **Accommodations:** Mount Prospect (26); Queen's* (71). 🏰🏰 Marine (35); Penmorvah* (10); Union* (29). 🏰 Warwick House* (7); Alexandra* (21); Dunedin (9); Keigwin (9); Richmond Lodge (7); Sea and Horses (11); Tarbert* (14).

Peterborough (Population 110,000; Cambridgeshire)
Information: Town Hall, Bridge Street—BABA; Central Library, Broadway. **Accommodations:** 🏨🏨🏨 (*Luxury*) Crest (99). 🏨🏨🏨 Bull* (112); Peterborough Moat House (98).

Plymouth (Population 255,500; Devon)
Information: Civic Centre, Royal Parade—BABA; 12 The Barbican (seasonal)—BABA. **Transportation:** Plymouth Airport, 8 km. (5 miles) north of town. **Accommodations:** 🏨🏨🏨 (*Luxury*) Mayflower Post House (106). 🏨🏨🏨 Astor (56); New Continental* (76); Novotel (100). 🏨🏨 Invicta (23); Merchantman (14); Merlin* (24); Mooreton (8); Strathmore (59). 🏨 Ashgrove (11); Transatlantic (8).

Poole (Population 114,000; Dorset)
Information: Poole Quay—BABA; Arndale Centre. **Accommodations:** (*Luxury*) Hospitality Inn (68). 🏨🏨🏨 Antelope* (13); Haven* (96). 🏨🏨 Dolphin (71). 🏨 Harmony (11).

Porlock (Population 1300; Somerset)
Accommodations: 🏨🏨🏨 Oaks (11). 🏨🏨 Anchor and Ship* (24); Ship Inn* (11).

Porthmadog (Population 3000; Gwynedd)
Information: High Street (seasonal)—BABA. **Accommodations:** 🏨🏨🏨 Royal Sportsman (16). 🏨🏨 Tyddyn Llwyn (8).

Portsmouth (Population 191,000; Hampshire)
Information: Castle Buildings, Clarence Esplanade, Southsea—BABA; Continental Ferry Terminal, Mile End (seasonal)—BABA. **Accommodations:** 🏨🏨🏨 (*Luxury*) Crest (169); Holiday Inn (170). 🏨🏨🏨 Pendragon (58). 🏨🏨 Chequers (13); Salisbury (24).

Preston (Population 95,000; Lancashire)
Information: Town Hall, Lancaster Road. **Accommodations:** 🏨🏨🏨 (*Luxury*) Crest (132). 🏨🏨🏨 Vineyard (14). 🏨🏨 Tickled Trout (66).

Pwllheli (Population 4100; Gwynedd)
Information: Y Maes (seasonal)—BABA. **Accommodations:** 🏨🏨 Rhyllech (15).

Ramsgate (Population 39,600; Kent)
Information: Argyle Centre, Queen Street. **Transportation:** Airport in Manston, 4 km. (2.5 miles) from town. **Accommodations:** 🏨🏨 San Clu (52); Savoy (25). 🏨 Spencer Court* (9).

Reading (Population 142,000; Berkshire)
    Information: Civic Offices, Civic Centre. **Accommodations:** 🏨
(*Luxury*) Post House (143); Ramada (200). 🏨 George* (68); Ship
(32). 🏨 Aeron Private (19); Roebuck* (12) 🏠 Crossways Guest House
(16).

Rhyl (Population 22,600; Clwyd)
    Information: Town Hall; Promenade (seasonal)—BABA. **Accom-
modations:** 🏨 Westminster (56).

Richmond (Population 7200; North Yorkshire)
    Information: Friary Gardens, Queens Road (seasonal)—BABA.
Accommodations: 🏨 King's Head* (27); Terrace House* (8). 🏨
Frenchgate* (12).

Ripon (Population 12,500; North Yorkshire)
    Information: Wakemans House, Market Place (seasonal)—BABA.
Accommodations: 🏨 Unicorn* (27). 🏨 Ripon Spa* (41); Crescent
Lodge* (12).

Rochester (Population 31,300; Kent)
    Information: Eastgate Cottage, High Street—BABA. **Accom-
modations:** 🏨 (*Luxury*) Crest (105). 🏨 Gordon* (17); Royal Victoria & Bull* (31).

Ross-on-Wye (Population 4600; Herefordshire)
    Information: 20 Broad Street—BABA. **Accommodations:** 🏨
(*Luxury*) Chase* (40). 🏨 Glewstone Court* (6); Walford House* (13).

Rugby (Population 60,400; Warwickshire)
    Information: Rugby Library, St. Matthews Street. **Accommoda-
tions:** 🏨 Clifton Court* (14). 🏨 Mound (18).

Rye (Population 4500; East Sussex)
    Information: 48 Cinque Ports Street—BABA. **Accommodations:**
Flackley Ash* (19). 🏨 Mermaid Inn* (29).

St. Albans (Population 127,500; Hertfordshire)
    Information: 37 Chequer Street—BABA. **Accommodations:** 🏨
(*Luxury*) The Noke Thistle (57). 🏨 Sopwell House* (29). 🏨 Haven
(48).

St. David's (Population 1600; Dyfed)
    Information: City Hall (seasonal)—BABA. **Accommodations:**
🏨 Warpool Court* (25).

St. Ives (Population 6000; Cornwall)
Information: The Guildhall, Street-an-Pol—BABA. **Accommodations:** 🏠🏠🏠 Porthminster* (50). 🏠🏠 Boskerris (20); Tregenna Castle (83). 🏠 Bella Vista (7).

Salisbury (Population 36,000; Wiltshire)
Information: Fish Row—BABA; City Hall, Malthouse Lane—BABA. **Accommodations:** 🏠🏠🏠 (*Luxury*) White Hart (70). 🏠🏠 County* (35); King's Arms* (18).

Sark (Population 600; Channel Islands)
Information: Tourist Information Office. **Accommodations:** 🏠🏠 Petit Champ* (16).

Scarborough (Population 43,500; North Yorkshire)
Information: St. Nicholas Cliff—BABA. **Accommodations:** 🏠🏠🏠 Royal* (137). 🏠🏠 Brooklands (52); Central* (40). 🏠 Avoncroft* (30).

Seaford (Population 18,200; East Sussex)
Information: Station Approach. **Accommodations:** 🏠 Clearview (12).

Selby (Population 11,100; North Yorkshire)
Information: Bus Station, Park Street. **Accommodations:** 🏠🏠 Londesborough Arms* (37).

Sheffield (Population 539,000; South Yorkshire)
Information: Town Hall Extension, Union Street—BABA. **Accommodations:** 🏠🏠🏠 (*Luxury*) Grosvenor House (103). 🏠🏠🏠 Charmwood* (21). 🏠🏠 The Pace (32). 🏠 Alpha (29).

Shrewsbury (Population 87,300; Salop)
Information: The Square—BABA. **Accommodations:** 🏠🏠🏠 (*Luxury*) Lion* (59). 🏠🏠🏠 Prince Rupert* (70). 🏠🏠 Shelton Hall* (11).

Skegness (Population 13,600; Lincolnshire)
Information: Embassy Centre, Grand Parade. **Accommodations:** 🏠🏠🏠 County (44). 🏠🏠 North Shore (30).

Skipton (Population 12,400; North Yorkshire)
Information: 8 Victoria Square—BABA. **Accommodations:** 🏠 Highfield (10).

Southampton (Population 214,000; Hampshire)

Information: Above Bar Precinct. **Transportation:** Eastleigh Airport 7 km. (4 miles) from center of town. **Accommodations:** (*Luxury*) Polygon (109); Post House (132). ᵐᵐᵐ Dolphin* (73); Southampton Park (75). ᵐᵐ Moat House (74).

Southend-on-Sea (Population 154,700; Essex)

Information: Civic Centre, Victoria Avenue—BABA; High Street Precinct—BABA. **Transportation:** Rochford Airport, 3 km. (2 miles) from town; buses from High Street. **Accommodations:** ᵐᵐ Balmoral (19); Roslin (44); Tower* (15).

Southport (Population 86,900; Merseyside)

Information: Cambridge Arcade. **Accommodations:** ᵐᵐᵐ (*Luxury*) Prince of Wales* (98). ᵐᵐᵐ Royal Clifton (115). ᵐᵐ Bold* (23). ᵐ Ambassador Private (8).

Stockport (Population 143,000; Greater Manchester)

Information: 9 Princes Street. **Accommodations:** ᵐᵐ Acton Court (24); Alma Lodge* (70); Wycliffe Villa (12).

Stoke-on-Trent (Population 257,200; Staffordshire)

Information: 1 Glebe Street—BABA. **Accommodations:** ᵐᵐᵐ (*Luxury*) North Stafford (69). ᵐᵐᵐ Haydon House* (17); Stakis Grand (93). ᵐᵐ Central (39).

Stow-on-the-Wold (Population 1900; Gloucestershire)

Information: The Library, St. Edwards Hall (seasonal). **Accommodations:** ᵐᵐᵐ (*Luxury*) Unicorn Crest* (20); Wyck Hill House* (15). ᵐᵐᵐ Fosse Manor (21). ᵐᵐ Old Stocks (19). ᵐ Grapevine* (19).

Stratford-upon-Avon (Population 20,800; Warwickshire)

Information: Judith Shakespeare's House, 1 High Street—BABA. **Accommodations:** ᵐᵐᵐ (*Luxury*) Alveston Manor* (110). Shakespeare* (66). ᵐᵐᵐ Arden* (63); Falcon* (73). ᵐᵐ Dukes* (20); Grosvenor House* (57); Haytor (15). ᵐ The Coach House Private* (12); Hardwick* (12); Hylands (17); Moonraker (15).

Sunderland (Population 210,000; Tyne and Wear)

Information: Crowtree Leisure Centre, Crowtree Road—BABA. **Accommodations:** ᵐᵐ Gelt House (23); Roker (45); Seaburn (82).

Swansea (Population 173,200; West Glamorgan)
Information: Singleton Street—BABA; Ty Croeso, Gloucester Place—BABA; Oystermouth Square, The Mumbles (seasonal)—BABA. **Transportation:** Fairwood Common Airport (bus from Coach Station, Singleton Street). **Accommodations:** 🏨🏨🏨 Dolphin (66). 🏨🏨 Windsor Lodge* (20).

Taunton (Population 37,400; Somerset)
Information: The Library, Corporation Street—BABA. **Accommodations:** 🏨🏨🏨 (*Luxury*) Castle* (35). 🏨🏨🏨 Falcon (10). 🏨🏨 St. Quintin (10); Corner House (22).

Tavistock (Population 7600; Devon)
Information: Bedford Square (seasonal)—BABA. **Accommodations:** 🏨🏨🏨 (*Luxury*) Bedford (31).

Teignmouth (Population 13,200; Devon)
Information: The Den, Sea Front—BABA. **Accommodations:** 🏨🏨 Bay (20); Glendaragh* (10); London* (26). 🏨 Drakes (6); Glenside (10).

Tenby (Population 4900; Dyfed)
Information: Guildhall, The Norton. **Accommodations:** 🏨🏨🏨 Imperial (46). 🏨🏨 Atlantic (33); Buckingham (22); Croft (20). 🏨 Red House* (29).

Tewkesbury (Population 9700; Gloucestershire)
Information: The Museum, 64 Barton Street (seasonal)—BABA. **Accommodations:** 🏨🏨🏨 (*Luxury*) Bell* (25); Royal Hop Pole Crest* (29). 🏨🏨🏨 Tewkesbury Park* (52). 🏨🏨 Tudor House* (16).

Tintagel (Population 1500; Cornwall)
Accommodations: 🏨🏨 Bossiney House (20); Atlantic View (10).

Torquay (Population 108,500; Devon)
Information: Vaughan Parade. **Accommodations:** 🏨🏨🏨 (*Luxury*) Imperial (167); Palace* (141). 🏨🏨🏨 Belgrave (54). 🏨🏨 Ansteys Lea (27); Bowden Close (20); Bute Court* (46); Cavendish (62); Palm Court (72); Viscount (20). 🏨 Albaston (12); Balmoral (23); Glen (18); Nordcliffe (20); Sydore (13); Templestowe (90); Vernon Court (19); Windsurfer (10).

Totnes (Population 5600; Devon)
Information: The Plains (seasonal)—BABA. **Accommodations:** 🏨🏨 Royal Seven Stars* (18).

Towyn *See Tywyn.*

Truro (Population 15,000; Cornwall)
Information: Municipal Building, Boscawen Street. **Accommodations:** 🏨 Brookdale (39); Carlton (23); The Royal* (34).

Tunbridge Wells (Population 45,300; Kent)
Information: Town Hall, Mt. Pleasant. **Accommodations:** 🏨🏨🏨 (*Luxury*) Spa* (70). 🏨🏨🏨 Russell (21). 🏨🏨 Firwood (5); Hand & Sceptre (25); Royal Wells Inn* (38); Wellington (64).

Tynemouth (Population 72,000; Tyne and Wear)
Accommodations: 🏨🏨 Park (27).

Tywyn/Towyn (Population 4200; Gwynedd)
Information: Publicity Office, High Street (seasonal)—BABA.
Accommodations: 🏨 Corbett Arms (25); Greenfield (14).

Warwick (Population 20,700; Warwickshire)
Information: The Court House, Jury Street. **Accommodations:** 🏨🏨🏨 (*Luxury*) Ladbroke (127). 🏨🏨🏨 Glebe* (13); Warwick Arms* (29).

Wells (Population 8200; Somerset)
Information: Town Hall, Market Square—BABA. **Accommodations:** 🏨🏨🏨 Crown* (18); Swan* (32). 🏨🏨 Ancient Gate House* (11); White Hart* (15); Worth House* (8).

Weston-super-Mare (Population 57,600; Avon)
Information: Beach Lawns—BABA. **Accommodations:** 🏨🏨🏨 (*Luxury*) Grand Atlantic (79). 🏨🏨🏨 Royal Pier (41). 🏨🏨 Batch Farm Country* (10); The Berni Royal (37).

Weymouth (Population 45,000; Dorset)
Information: Pavilion Theatre Complex, The Esplanade; King's Statue, The Esplanade (seasonal)—BABA. **Accommodations:** 🏨🏨 Crown (79); Glenburn (13); Old York (10); Prince Regent* (40).

Whitby (Population 13,700; North Yorkshire)
Information: New Quay Road—BABA. **Accommodations:** 🏨🏨 Royal (134); Saxonville (21); Sneaton Hall* (9). 🏨 White House* (11).

Winchester (Population 33,200; Hampshire)
Information: The Guildhall, The Broadway—BABA. **Accommodations:** 🏨🏨🏨 (*Luxury*) Lainston House* (32); The Royal* (59). 🏨🏨 Winton Court* (28). 🏨 Harestock Lodge* (17); Stratton House* (6).

Windermere (Population 8000; Cumbria)
   Information: Victoria Street—BABA. **Accommodations:** 🏨🏨🏨 (*Luxury*) Beech Hill* (46); Belsfield* (71). 🏨🏨🏨 Burn How (26); Burnside (46); Cedar Manor* (6); Wild Boar* (38). 🏨🏨 Bordriggs Country (14); Oakthorpe* (20); Ravensworth (13). 🏨 Brendon Chase (9); Fairfield Country House* (11); Knoll* (12).

Windsor (Population 31,200; Berkshire)
   Information: Central Station, Thames Street—BABA. **Accommodations:** 🏨🏨🏨 (*Luxury*) Castle* (85). 🏨🏨🏨 Christopher (24); Harte & Garter* (51). 🏨🏨 Aurora Garden (13); Royal Adelaide (37). 🏨 Clarence (20).

Wolverhampton (Population 256,000; West Midlands)
   Information: Mander Centre, 16 Queen's Arcade. **Accommodations:** 🏨🏨🏨 Mount* (58). 🏨🏨 Fox (29); Goldthorn (86); Park Hall* (57). 🏨 Glenville (22).

Woodstock (Population 3000; Oxfordshire)
   Information: The Library, Hensington Road—BABA.

Worcester (Population 75,000; Hereford and Worcester)
   Information: Guildhall, High Street—BABA. **Accommodations:** 🏨🏨🏨 (*Luxury*) Giffard (104). 🏨🏨🏨 Ye Olde Talbot (17). 🏨🏨 Star (45).

Worksop (Population 36,500; Nottinghamshire)
   Information: Queen's Buildings, Potter Street.

Worthing (Population 90,600; West Sussex)
   Information: Town Hall, Chapel Road—BABA; Marine Parade (seasonal)—BABA. **Accommodations:** 🏨🏨🏨 Chatsworth* (17). 🏨🏨 Ardington (55); Beechwood Hall* (14); Eardley* (83).

York (Population 100,900; North Yorkshire)
   Information: De Grey Rooms, Exhibition Square—BABA; York Railway Station. **Accommodations:** 🏨🏨🏨 (*Luxury*) Dean Court* (36); Ladbroke Abbey Park (84). 🏨🏨🏨 Disraeli's* (14); Kilima (15); Mount Royale* (19). 🏨🏨 Abbots Mews* (42); Ambassador* (19); Blue Bridge (15); Heworth Court* (13); Knavesmire Manor* (10). 🏨 Annjoa (9); Blakeney (20); Farthings (6); Manor Country Guest House (15); Orchard Court (10).

Index

If more than one page number appears next to the name of a town or an attraction, the bold face number indicates the page where the detailed description appears in the text.